Blythe Spirit

Also by Ian Collins

Blythe Spirit

The Remarkable Life of Ronald Blythe

IAN COLLINS

JOHN MURRAY

First published in Great Britain in 2024 by John Murray (Publishers)

2

Copyright © Ian Collins 2024

A CIP catalogue record for this title is available from the British Library

Hardback ISBN 9781399819060
ebook ISBN 9781399819077

Typeset in Bembo 11.5/14pt by
Palimpsest Book Production Limited, Falkirk, Stirlingshire

Printed and bound in Great Britain by Clays Ltd, Elcograf S.p.A.

John Murray policy is to use papers that are natural,
renewable and recyclable products and made from wood grown
in sustainable forests. The logging and manufacturing processes are expected to
conform to the environmental regulations of the country of origin.

Carmelite House
50 Victoria Embankment
London EC4Y 0DZ

www.johnmurraypress.co.uk

John Murray Press, part of Hodder & Stoughton Limited
An Hachette UK company

The authorised representative in the EEA is Hachette Ireland, 8 Castlecourt Centre,
Dublin 15, D15 XTP3, Ireland (email: info@hbgi.ie)

For Elsie and Joyce and all the dear ones.

He who binds to himself a joy
Does the winged life destroy
He who kisses the joy as it flies
Lives in eternity's sunrise.
William Blake, 'Eternity'

But true Love is a durable fire
In the mind ever burning;
Never sick, never old, never dead,
From itself never turning.
Sir Walter Raleigh, 'Walsingham'

Contents

PART FIVE: The Clay Meadow

Prologue

ONE HOT AUGUST day in 1988 I took in a sweeping view on the Suffolk–Essex border and then dropped into a green tunnel – like Alice tumbling down the rabbit hole.

A deep track fell and rose and wound towards the River Stour and first to a Tudor longhouse almost engulfed by a wildly magical garden. Within this sheltered hollow there was a murmuring of birds and a tapping of typewriter keys. The sounds were oddly in unison.

The door stood open. A robin hopped among stacked plant pots in a room which appeared to be outside the house and outside time as I had previously known it. Then, bounding down the stairs, at the age of sixty-five, came Ronald Blythe. A purposeful man of letters momentarily resembled the White Rabbit.

I was chasing a foreword for my first book, on art in East Anglia. But the pace slowed instantly, and my horizon started to broaden infinitely, as we began our introduction mid-conversation.

My grandmother had been postmistress in Charsfield, the village near Woodbridge recast in a classic Blythe text as *Akenfield*. Meeting with shared centuries of Suffolk ancestry, we parted with the promise of a short essay and the launch of a 35-year friendship.

Elsie Hearn, my grandmother, had joined the General Post Office at the onset of old-age pensions. Family legend has it that decrepit farmworkers, or more likely their widows, who received 5 shillings (25p) a week from seventy, would come for payment from winsome Elsie, and if she was off duty would wait for her return. Going without was normal for them even in the shadow of the workhouse.

With few marital options following the male slaughter of the First World War, Elsie wed a minor rogue, then lived with a second misfortune. The last photo we have of her, gaunt in a summer dress

Elsie Hearn, Charsfield, 1914.

and hat as she paddles in the sea at Southwold with her infant daughter, Joyce, is dated September 1933. After that, only a postcard. An X has been inked on a window of a forbidding building, explained overleaf with the words 'My Room'. This parody of a holiday hotel was the Ipswich tuberculosis sanatorium, where Elsie died in 1934 aged thirty-nine. An aunt rescued Joyce – my mother – from an orphanage.

Later I would live in the former harbour master's cottage in Southwold and already thought Suffolk a place of bliss – but with a beauty hiding a darker history. The books of Ronald Blythe, so evocative, so far from nostalgia, seemed to have been written in my bones.

While I worked as a journalist in London, Ronnie – as he wanted everyone to call him – was midway on my weekend journey. I often stopped off and then stayed on with my partner Joachim. Bottengoms, the house bequeathed to our host by the artists John and Christine Nash, became our home from home. We joined the circle of 'dear ones' partly inherited from the painters. We looked after cats and plants when Ronnie stayed with friends in Wales or Scotland, or travelled on speaking engagements by complex arrangements of buses, trains and taxis. We came for twenty Christmases.

I drove Ronnie on many of the adventures which found their way into his weekly 'Word from Wormingford' column in the *Church Times*. 'Ian says he *must* swim, strips and throws himself into the North Sea, which soon throws him out. Dry dogs and small children stare at him pityingly, so big, so unwise.'[1] When we talked late into the night over whisky, I asked the man who had always lived alone what sort of partner he might have chosen. 'Someone like you,' he said. But our loving bond was wholly platonic: he was my mentor and faithful friend.

An old charmer aged into youthfulness, with his liveliest writing in his seventies and eighties. He was alert to the past while absolutely alive in the present. The future held no fear for him due to the indelible, though somehow indefinable, nature of his faith. It was rooted in the seasonal cycle of growth, death and rebirth – the East Anglian earth itself.

Joachim and I were among friends given powers of attorney when Ronnie was ninety. Gently and gradually over the next decade we applied them to keep him happily at home with support from a renewed circle of dear ones.

As it was, to the end on 14 January 2023, two months after his hundredth birthday and publication of the bestselling selection of his essays *Next to Nature: A Lifetime in the English Countryside*, helpers gained more than they gave. Glad to wake each morning, and ready to die, Ronnie had the gift of appreciation and the protection of philosophy. He had attained the writer's life he always wanted and now was savouring the company of a last cat and final friends, the current glass of sherry and the view from the window – beaming out with benevolence, curiosity, amusement and acceptance. After a wrongful diagnosis of dementia, a place of contentment akin to a state of grace.

A skin of disarming diffidence covering a core of steel, Ronnie could never ask for anything. At some point, as I worked for years and years on a life of the painter John Craxton, it was understood that I would write his biography too. He respected the genre without wishing to hurry it along in his case. I felt that the man himself, for whom writing was as natural and vital as breathing, should have the last word in his lifetime. Talking openly became the oxygen of our friendship. But, all the while, I kept notes and scoured the Blythe canon for biographical clues; he made me his literary executor so I could unlock remaining secrets and then publish freely.

Where uncredited, Blythe words in this intimate study come from our talks. And indeed, the conversation is extended as we recount the story together. With no guilt or regret, Ronnie wanted his tale told. Everything I learned, however strange and surprising, underlined his literary achievement. His unabashed physicality was a remarkable feat given his background. Kissing the joy as it flies, as William Blake put it, he was perfectly free in body, mind and spirit.

Craxton and Blythe had been born in the autumn of 1922, and each would have five siblings. But the artist was supremely fortunate in a bohemian, cultured and well-connected London clan; the author

Ian and Ronnie on Ronnie's ninety-ninth birthday.

was the outsider's outsider – obscured in a picture of dirt-poor rural poverty: dismissed from formal education at fourteen, he taught himself by looking, listening and wondering. For this 'chronic' reader, a library became a university.

Craxton the untrammelled nomad secured a dream of Greece; Blythe travelled essentially in his imagination: two gay sensualists and uplifting creative spirits triumphed in the art of life. Seriously playful, they shared a genius for puncturing solemnity.

In a career covering seven decades – and more than forty volumes of elegant, wise and witty stories, novels, poems, essays and memoirs, as well as anthologies, literary criticism, reportage and social history – Ronald Blythe would be widely praised as a confessional writer. But there was a more profound silence in which the boy who found himself in a library always held something back.

This book sets out to celebrate the writing and complete the portrait.

Ian Collins
Southwold, September 2024

PART ONE

The Nightingale's Nest

How curious is the nest. No other Bird
Uses such loose materials or weaves
Their dwellings in such spots.
    John Clare, 'The Nightingale's Nest'

I

Suffolk Stock

Ronald Blythe's family had been named through ancient origins in the sandy valley of the River Blyth — rising near Laxfield in north-east Suffolk and flowing barely a dozen miles to reach the North Sea between Southwold and Walberswick. 'Blyth' came from the old English word *blithe*, meaning gentle or pleasant and fitting Ronnie to a tee.

His forebears were wandering shepherds — makers of the wool wealth of medieval East Anglia which built and decorated over five hundred majestic Suffolk churches. Then came centuries of decline and forced migration. Even the 'Blythe' surname was unfixed. Ronnie wrote of parish registers with 'generations of Blythe-Blyth-Bly-Bligh ancestors (parsons' spelling)'.[1] Vague indifference, or ignorance, carried into recorded occupations, with many working skills dismissed in the word 'labourer'.

The biblical language of sheep and shepherds resonated in churches where farming congregations were detained on the day of rest. 'My Georgian ancestors in Suffolk put straw in their box pews, and fastened themselves in for long sermons. The parson in his lofty pulpit stared down. There they were, his flock. There he stood, their shepherd.'[2]

David Blyth, Ronnie's great-great-great-grandfather, baptised in 1781, came from Barking near Needham Market in central 'High Suffolk'. He married Sarah Smith, and they had nine children during the Napoleonic Wars and the aftermath of rural recession. The slump hit poor families doubly hard, ending the home-spinning by which women augmented the pay of men and children from land work. From the 1830s there were dispersals to the factories of London and Lancashire, and to America and Australasia, as well as movement within Suffolk. Many left behind subsisted in cottages whose squalor was notorious.

David's fourth son, Taylor Smith Blyth, was born at Combs near Stowmarket and recorded as another agricultural worker, though his name suggests a family link to the cloth trade. He migrated five miles to Creeting St Peter, where he and his wife Mary Ann had seven children destined for farm or domestic labour. Taylor weathered hard times and lived into his eighty-fourth year – a tremendous feat for a man raised in poverty and remaining there.

His third son Charles was a shepherd. He married Harriet Moore and they had eight children between 1863 and 1882. The census at the start of each decade found them in a different parish, moving to survive as bad economic conditions worsened.

For all the hardships of farmworkers, agriculture in mid-nineteenth-century Suffolk was steadily evolving. Following the Enclosure Acts, which turned areas of common land into privately owned or rented fields, the county became largely arable. Crop yields were raised by a rotational system – a year of resting the land with clean fallow or tares, then a cycle of mangold or turnips, barley, clover or pulses, and wheat. Livestock standards improved with careful breeding of chesnut Suffolk Punch heavy horses for global export and prized Red Poll cattle. The black-faced Suffolk sheep tended by Charles Blyth came from crossing Norfolk, Southdown, Hampshire and Sussex varieties until the sturdy breed was the most fertile in Britain.

Rewards for Suffolk shepherds depended on results – with a penalty for lost ewes and a premium for reared lambs exceeding the number of ewes. The men and their families had to guard against sheep being 'casted': left on its back, and unable to right itself, a valuable animal might die in a day. Orphaned lambs were either hand-reared or the lamb of a dead ewe was tied into the fleece of a dead lamb so the surviving mother smelled its offspring and continued feeding.

Like gamekeepers, shepherds were set apart from other farm labourers, by skill as well as solitude, and liable to be mocked behind their backs. Keepers were licensed killers (and farmers' spies); flock tenders were shearers, tail loppers, midwives and castraters. Shepherds cut the male lamb's purse then bit through the spermatic cord to remove the testicles. Teeth were cleaner than knives.

But it was a meditative and mystical life for men governed by movement of the sun and sleeping under the stars. They became astronomers, naturalists and guardians of folklore. With his own family history in mind, Ronnie wrote: 'After the pastoral people stopped wandering, their shepherds still had to lead their flocks from feeding-ground to feeding-ground on the hills, making pens, fires, and, inevitably, poems. For when you lie dreaming on your back under the stars, you think of the strangest, most beautiful things. Which is how we got the Psalms. And the names of the stars. And mystics and writers such as Thomas Traherne and Richard Rolle.'[3]

Shepherds teamed with dogs or small sons; ideally one in front of the flock and one at the rear. With pieces of turnip or linseed cake in their pockets, they trained older ewes to trail them – the others following to folds, fresh pasture or market.

The lead sheep, with a bell around its neck, was the 'bellwether'. In *Far from the Madding Crowd*, Ronnie's favourite Hardy novel, which he would edit and introduce, Farmer Oak's flock falls off the cliff having followed the leader's bell. In a box of oddments Ronnie kept an old sheep's bell as a talisman and warning – shaking it for 'a sound from a lost countryside, earthly, archaic, and not unlike some old bell for the Elevation. Its tongue hung out and its sides were still par-polished by fleece. Thomas Hardy said that the note of a sheep-bell was like the ticking of a clock to country people, and reminded us that its ring changes were caused by the animal's feeding or running. Gabriel Oak heard it like a firebell heralding total disaster. No longer his own man, he descended into a common labourer.'[4]

Born into rural servitude, Ronnie's great-grandfather Charles attended only the most rudimentary charity school in winter. Otherwise, by the age of eight, poor children like him were working on the land. On hard-pressed farms it was the natural order: 'The 1870 Education Act astounded the farmers. Since when did boys and girls not pick up stones on their fields to mend the lanes, scare rooks, or work? Not to labour until they were 12 years old! There was rural war.'[5]

There was complicity in truancy among parents who depended on working children to keep them all out of the poorhouse – the workhouse where families were divided at the door as they all entered into the economy of slavery. Suspicion of schooling was the stronger since free elementary education was not standard in Suffolk until 1891. This in a county where earlier nineteenth-century children had plaited straw in workshops from the age of four.

In 1881 Charles and his family were based in Little Waldingfield, near the historic wool town of Lavenham. A decade later he was recorded as Charles Blythe, a widower living five miles southward at Great Cornard. He was still a shepherd and his nineteen-year-old daughter Martha was housekeeper and carer to four younger children. He died in 1899, four years after his long-lived father.

The 1891 census recorded that Charles's third child, David, was living with his wife Martha near the village of Acton. He was listed as a farm labourer; she as a weaver of horsehair upholstery fabric on a home loom: they were Ronnie's grandparents. The couple were raising the first of seven children, William, who, like many an eldest child at that time, was born before their wedding. A recent technical innovation, as well as an education act, had dispensed with the need for a small child to sit in the loom with the horse tail, serving hair to the weaver.

Native to south Suffolk and north Essex, *tyes* and *teys* began as remote pasture from which a farmhouse or stranded cottages grew. Through sheer grit and shared industry in such a rural outpost, as Ronnie recalled, David and Martha rose above their inherent status as labourers and dared to take on a tenancy at Cuckoo's Tye – 'a small moated farm at the end of a wide green land. The once common pasture close by was a hamlet named Newman's Green, a place full of relations once or twice removed, so that we never did quite know the connection. It was the heyday of honorary aunts and uncles, rather as all cooks were called Mrs. Concealing bastardy became an art-form, the truth only coming out when some liaison threatened to come uncomfortably near the list of whom one may not marry which hung in the church porch. The list was so long that most rural populations would have died out had it been obeyed to the letter. However, obedience has never been East Anglia's strong point.'[6]

Martha gave birth to her sixth child – Albert George, Ronnie's father – in 1898. The first name paid respect to the late prince consort, dead for thirty-seven years. It was a formality only. The boy was always known as George. Gentle George. But, being left-handed, he had a painful schooling – with beatings until he learned to write with his right hand, though he never did it well. Left-handed children, deemed weak, dirty or cursed, also had unfortunate hands tied behind chairs to prevent temptation. George was saved from further sin by conscription into the church choir.

Glad to leave school at twelve, he hated toiling on his parents' farm – where he had already helped for almost half of his short life. Now his father expected him to drive a flock of sheep fifteen miles to market in Bury St Edmunds with only a dog for company and comfort. Boy and mutt broke the homeward walk by bedding down in a hedge. Unable to extricate himself from such bondage, he caused a rumpus when freeing the family's pet linnet. And he bolted an outhouse door on a fleeing fox – releasing the captive when pursuing hunters and hounds had passed on. Casual cruelties of the countryside were not for him.

George could at least enjoy ploughing contests between farm lads for fastest and straightest lines. He cared deeply for working horses – the placid heavyweights steering and powering every farm. Their wellbeing vital, they all had names. Boxer, Bowler, Blossom, Captain, Duke, Diamond, Major, Kitty, Ginger and Gypsy were Suffolk favourites. East Anglian ploughmen were called horsemen – showing the priority of teamwork and the order of importance within it. Lithe lads with pairs of heavy horses could look masterful or romantic, but by early manhood they had an uneven gait 'as one foot will be in the rut and the other above it. They will walk like land sailors.'[7] Any limp could worsen with arthritis from wet and cold conditions.

Novice horsemen learned to give simple words of command, so that a Suffolk Punch pairing harnessed to a plough was taught to turn or step forward or back. The degree of movement was signalled by a change of emphasis and inflexion. Some men sang to their horses, and in the privacy of an open field – where plough teams walked eleven miles to work an acre of soil – shy George, the choir boy, did too.

Sadly, the struggle for betterment ran against the grain of the times, as an agricultural recession begun in the 1870s dug ever deeper. The rot had set in with harvest-destroying rain and a flood of cheap grain from the New World. Tenant farmers were driven into debt

A Stiff Pull by Peter Henry Emerson, 1890.

and their workers towards destitution. Lucky to get any rent at all, landowners tended to press less than tithe holders, usually clerical figures, who had claimed a tenth of agricultural produce in a parish since the Middle Ages. As more and more tenancies were given up, some landlords gave the right to farm practically for free to save buildings from collapse and land from creeping wilderness.

New opportunities in a crisis were seized by doughty migrants from Scotland, who found stricken East Anglia less unyielding than Ayrshire and Fifeshire. The incomers worked even harder and for even less than the natives. The women pitched in – mucking out byres and sties with no thought to what neighbours might think. Outsiders had no social standing to worry about and were too busy to pause for Victorian propriety, save perhaps on Sundays.

But David and Martha were as worn out as the land. Cutting their losses, they rented Vicarage Cottage in Acton. With Martha engaged as cook to the vicar, they were still better off than so many others – including, as it turned out in ever-worsening times, their children. George became a hired hand like most of the boys and men around him, with all the fear servitude entailed. Low pay for long hours could dwindle to nothing in wet weather. 'We dreaded the rain,' an old farmworker recalls in Ronald Blythe's seminal book *Akenfield*. 'It washed our few shillings away.'[8]

Although relieved to be rid of cruel schooling, George was among former pupils returning every Saturday evening – after horses were tended (unharnessed, fed, watered, groomed) and tea eaten – to hear Mr Spurgeon, the now elderly schoolmaster, read from *The Times*. The tutor told them of crimes, inventions and political speeches. Eventually he would quaver his way through Great War victories and casualty lists. By then George could no longer hear him for the roar of the slaughter.

2

Pack Up Your Troubles

U NTIL HE WAS sixteen, the world for George Blythe was the sum
of a day's walk – out in the morning and back in the evening,
unless sleeping in a hedge. He was further fettered by farm labour.
Then, swept up less by patriotic fervour than a longing to escape, he
joined a singing column and marched away to war.

In August 1914 the minimum age for full army enlistment was
nineteen, but blind eyes were turned in the clamour to fight for
King and Country (and at 5 feet 6 inches tall, George was an inch
above the British Army average). A casual attitude was also adopted
in the matter of names, with the underage recruit from Acton
wrongly listed in the Suffolk Regiment record as Alfred G. Blythe.
He had the number 2720 until a national surge of conscripts and
casualties saw a reordering to 240715. Part of what became known
as the 'Lucky Suffolks', with no hint of irony, George was overseas
for the entire conflict and lucky to return at all.

A first posting was across the Irish Sea, to the Curragh camp near
Dublin and an army of requisitioned horses. George had enlisted to
be shot of farm work, but this behind-the-lines tending to animals
was due to his youth, and over ensuing years of warfare it probably
saved him. He then served briefly on the Western Front at Ypres,
which he called 'Wipers' – as did all the servicemen who knew it.
Perhaps because he was still below the legal age for front-line service,
this is omitted from official records.

On 30 July 1915 the formerly land-locked teenager, now a captain's groom, left Liverpool on the converted liner *Aquitania*, one of 978 'other ranks' plus twenty-nine officers in the Suffolk Regiment's 5th Battalion. George would remain a lowly private, keeping his head down in every sense. They were bound for the Turkish peninsula of Gallipoli, which an Allied force – British, French, New Zealander and Australian – aimed to storm en route to controlling the Dardanelles Strait and taking Constantinople. Part of a grand plan to relieve Russia and break deadlock on the Western Front, this new attack was meant to end the war quickly. But conflict only widened. Huge losses brought thoughts of abandonment even before the Suffolks joined the fray.

Zigzagging to avoid submarines, the liner rolled appallingly in the Bay of Biscay. Many on board thought they might die of seasickness before Gibraltar was passed on 4 August and Malta two days later. And then they glided in crystal Aegean waters in a travesty of a holiday cruise, luckier than the poet Rupert Brooke who had died here in April from an infected mosquito bite. A three-day respite on Lemnos was enlivened by messaging between vessels. Someone on a ship of seasoned Australian troops yelled 'Are we downhearted?' 'No!' cried the Suffolk men. 'You bloody soon will be!' came the reply.

Steaming into Suvla Bay on 10 August, they landed from lighters for an assault across scorching rocks. Private F. Clarke from Sudbury wrote home: 'None of us thought we would come out of it alive. Our brigade captured about a thousand yards but with a temperature of about 110 degrees and very little water, and with shells bursting all around within inches of us, you may imagine we had a very hot time.'[1] A first freezing night summed up the climatic torture to come. From 14 August a 72-hour offensive left 195 killed, wounded or missing: the dead included the commanding officer, Lieutenant Colonel Morriss Armes from Sudbury. He led from the front with a revolver until hit for a second and third time.

Small advances at vast cost gave way to retrenchment or retreat. Unburied bodies fed teeming maggots. Dysentery ravaged, thirst raged. A diet of hard biscuits was broken with stale bread. By 24 September 392 of the 5th Suffolks were killed, injured, sick or missing. In tough terrain motor transport and vehicles drawn by heavy horses were replaced by mule carts and donkeys. They carried water, food, ammunition and medical supplies from coast to trench, returning with the wounded, and the dead for shorter distances. George Blythe saw to the loading and unloading, grooming and grazing if there was any greenery around.

Between the shelling and sniping, Turkish troops could be heard tunnelling to lay mines beneath them. On 24 October Suffolk casualties hit 659. Now the weather turned killingly cold. Baggage was on the beach, ready for a break on Lemnos, when a three-day blizzard brought hypothermia and frostbite. Monsoon rain turned trenches into rivers. When finally reaching Lemnos, the battalion was down to 268 still standing, with only 62 men (19 officers and 43 other ranks) in 'Class A' condition. With some augmenting of numbers, 818 soldiers had been killed or wounded in four months. In the Suffolk Regiment's official history, this was the Great War at its worst.

Ronald Blythe would long consider novelising his parents' stories, but in the end he gave his father the opening voice in *Akenfield*, the saga of a Suffolk village from the 1880s to the 1960s. What passes for factual reporting with statistical underpinning is in fact a more personal and poetic account, with a deeper and more universal truth drawn from a lifetime of listening. The author took names for his witnesses from tombstones – Leonard Thompson, the old farmworker who recalls Gallipoli, is on the war memorial in Walberswick parish church. But the memories are chiefly those of George Blythe:

'The first things we saw were big wrecked Turkish guns, and the second a big marquee. It didn't make me think of the military but of the village fetes. Other people must have thought like this because I remember how we all rushed up to it, like boys getting into a circus, and then found it all laced up. We unlaced it and rushed in. It was full of corpses. Dead Englishmen, lines and lines of them, with their eyes wide open. We all stopped talking. I'd never seen a dead man before and here I was looking at two or three hundred of them. It was our first fear. Nobody had mentioned this. I was very shocked. I thought of Suffolk and it seemed a happy place for the first time.'[2]

On marching close to the front line, and meeting up with old acquaintances, he and his companions asked after friends who had arrived a month before. '"How is Ernie Taylor?" – "Ernie? – he's gone." "Have you seen Albert Paternoster?" – "Albert? – he's gone."

We learned that if 300 had "gone" but 700 were left, then this wasn't too bad. We then knew how unimportant our names were.'[3]

George would end his days in Suffolk as a gravedigger, after plenty of practice at Gallipoli. He helped clear the battlefields of corpses. Some of the dead were buried where they fell, in rocky terrain and trenches, as best as could be managed by survivors still under fire. 'We pushed them into the sides of the trench but bits of them kept getting uncovered and sticking out, like people in a badly made bed,' the veteran remembers in *Akenfield*. 'Hands were the worst; they would escape from the sand, pointing, begging – even waving! There was one which we all shook when we passed, saying, "Good morning", in a posh voice. Everybody did it. The bottom of the trench was springy like a mattress because of all the bodies underneath . . .

'You got very frightened of the murdering and you did sometimes think, "What is all this about? What is it for?" But mostly you were thinking of how to stay alive. The more the killing, the more you thought about living. You felt brave and honoured that you should be fighting for England. You knew that all the people at home were for it. We believed we were fighting for a good cause and so, I expect, did the Turks.'[4] The former choirboy, who had walked into war amid massed singing, added: 'Our parents and all the cottage people were very religious and very patriotic. The patriotic songs and church hymns seemed equally holy. They took our breath away.'[5]

On 15 December, the Gallipoli misadventure finally given up, 327 Suffolk survivors plus horses, mules and donkeys sailed to Alexandria and a camp on a peaceful Mediterranean shore. George Blythe recognised a biblical landscape. Crossing the green Nile Delta by rail in February 1916, he saw buffalo turning waterwheels and wooden ploughs drawn by a comically paired camel and donkey. Camping below the pyramids, the Suffolk soldiers took trams into Cairo to visit the bazaar and zoo. For a green English country lad, barely glimpsing London, it all seemed like a mirage.

Two months later men and beasts went in cattle trucks to defend the Suez Canal. Sandstorms and sandfly fever were bitter foes, testing farm ditchers to the limit digging trenches in the Saharan sand. In February 1917 the 5th Suffolks crossed the Sinai Desert on wire netting for the invasion of Palestine. They joined the attack on Gaza, which fell, in ruins, after a third battle in November. The Suffolk men put victory down to General Edmund Allenby

The Lucky Suffolks crossing the
Sinai Desert, 1917.

taking command of the Egyptian Expeditionary Force. He hailed
from Felixstowe.

Jaffa was taken later in November, and George was in the guard
of honour when General Allenby entered Jerusalem on 11 December.
Ronnie wrote the story his father told him: 'He rode ahead of his
troops on a white horse with flags flying and bands playing. It was
to be very grand. He had helped to destroy the ancient and enormous Ottoman Empire. There were plans afoot to bring the Jews
back to Palestine. The military procession marched to the gates of
Jerusalem . . . when, quite suddenly, there was a ragged halt and
confusion. Something unrehearsed. Because, as he reached the gates,
General Allenby remembered something, how Christ had entered
Jerusalem on a colt, not a horse, on his way to bring *his* kingdom
into human hearts. Allenby came to a stop and dismounted, and
walked into Jerusalem. The trumpets and drums were silenced, the
flags lowered, as he entered the Holy City.'[6]

By Christmas 1917 the battalion had marched 250 miles, joined four
battles and endured strafing from snipers and planes, to end camped

in the rain on basic rations bar tots of rum. But New Year's Eve saw a move to an occupied German religious settlement, and for the first time since leaving England, George slept in a house.

Through 1918 the Suffolks pursued Turkish forces in a sweep through Palestine and Lebanon taking in the ancient cities of Acre, Tyre and Sidon. In September they fought at the decisive Battle of Megiddo, devastating Ottoman armies. News of the final armistice, signed with Germany on 11 November, brought false hopes of being home for Christmas. And the word 'armistice', as Ronnie pointed out, means only a temporary truce.

After advancing through lovely countryside to a warm welcome in Beirut, the Lucky Suffolks were shipped back to Cairo and landed in the global influenza pandemic which would kill more people than the Great War. Planned demobilisation from January 1919 was delayed by Egyptian riots. While detained in case they were needed – a call which never came – the Suffolks were put up in the finest barracks in Egypt. Lucky at last.

It is hard to find out what happened to ordinary soldiers in the First World War and Suffolk regimental archives were further depleted by fire. To have served from start to finish without physical or mental injury is almost inconceivable. Casualty lists are woefully incomplete. Many lived, in habitual silence, not to tell the tale.

George Blythe was a captain's groom before tending to pack animals on a Middle Eastern marathon – and there is scant record of the horses and ponies, let alone donkeys and mules. Until now, when equine survivors which could not be sold locally were ordered to be shot. For a veteran horseman, it was the last straw.

George returned in spring 1919 to an Acton where the old order seemed unchanging though so many familiar faces had been erased. Lord Howe – nearly as remote a figure as George V – had sold his ancestral Acton Hall estate during the Gallipoli campaign, but the feudal system ground on. Soon a scroll in the parish church honoured 142 Great War veterans: 29 had died; more yet would succumb to injury. A calamitous tally for a village whose population reached a record low of 447 in the census of 1921.

Officer Siegfried Sassoon wrote his most famous poem, 'Everyone Sang', after Armistice Day revelry. Ronnie, seeing the first draft in a Cambridge exhibition, was moved by writing 'tiny beyond expectation'. The enormity of the verses made more sense to him as a depiction of poor young men who, packing up their troubles from 1914, had sang their way out of terrible times – marching towards death:

> Everyone suddenly burst out singing;
> And I was filled with such delight
> As prisoned birds must find in freedom
> Winging wildly across the white
> Orchards and dark-green fields; on – and on – and out of sight.

George knew the bitter irony in Suffolk clay being termed 'loving land'. It clung to working feet like the shackles of serfdom. In May 1919 he tried to join the 18th Royal Hussars (Queen Mary's Own) – the former captain's groom choosing a cavalry regiment where they might be expected to take better care of the horses. But, aged only twenty-one, he was ruled unfit for further military service. He tried making cutlery in Sheffield and bricks back in Acton, before being forced to return to farm work in sad disillusionment. So George became a stockman – tending a dairy herd, with the long hours that entailed – since he no longer had the heart for horses.

George Blythe.

George Blythe, among 800 veterans at a 5th Suffolks reunion dinner in Bury Corn Exchange in February 1920, was not present when the battalion was disbanded at a St Mary's church service in December 1921. Here the regimental cenotaph records the names of 360 officers and 6,513 other ranks killed in the Great War.

George took no part in later Remembrance Day proceedings. The man who stayed stumm for most of his life never observed two-minute silences. Ronnie wrote: 'My father, a teenager at Gallipoli, refused to attend these rites, the band playing, the mayor in his robes, the snowy war memorial in the little Suffolk town. Once central, it has long been put at the side of the road so as not to delay a flood of cars. Otherwise you would have taken your life in your hands.'[7]

3
Tilly Elkin

WHILE GENERATIONS OF Blythes toiled as agricultural workers, Ronnie's maternal family were swept into the great smoking and stinking cauldron of London by the Industrial Revolution. By the end of the nineteenth century, in the world's greatest city, their poverty was more overwhelming than if they had stayed in the sticks.

Ronnie's mother Matilda Elizabeth Elkin – Tilly – always told her children she was born 'above the tea gardens on The Strand', a hint of gentility hiding the shame of destitution. Her birthplace, nearby and on another social planet, was 2 Harford Place. In a fetid close opposite Drury Lane's Theatre Royal, the Elkin family shared a small room in one of the worst slums in London. In 1895 The Strand medical officer reported: 'Harford Place is 18 feet wide, but is obstructed at its entrance by a house in Drury Lane and reduced to 9 feet. All the eight houses are similar, all are let in tenements, and there is no business establishment in the court. Each house has a small back yard, in which the water supply and closet are situated. The houses on the north side are somewhat better than those on the south, but both sets are in an area too overbuilt to afford sufficient air.'[1]

Tilly's parents, Joseph Elkin and Emily Boggis, married in August 1892 – in the year Emily gave birth to another man's daughter who also bore her name. By 1901 the couple had five children together; three daughters and two sons. By 1902 five-year-old Tilly was the sole survivor. Amid the dire conditions of Harford Place, none of her full siblings, Emma, Harriet, Joseph and Edward, lived beyond twenty-one months. She grew up thinking half-sister Emily Boggis, raised by other relatives, an aunt.

When Tilly was taking her first steps the social reformer Charles Booth and a team of inspectors were walking every London street, knocking on all doors to compile *Maps Descriptive of London Poverty 1898–1899*. A seven-colour code ranged from black ('Lowest class. Vicious, semi-criminal'), dark blue ('Very poor, casual. Chronic want') and light blue ('Poor. 18 to 21 shillings a week for a moderate family') to well-to-do red and golden yellow for the wealthy. The vicinity of Drury Lane – the name synonymous with vice and dereliction – was bruised black and dark blue, a cue for demolition.

Around Drury Lane, the Booth investigators listed a smithy, foundry, carpenter's shop, stone yard, donkey stable, dairy with cattle sheds, and all manner of flailing humanity – labourers, street traders, porters, artisan makers and menders, printers, cab touts, sandwich men (walking adverts), rat-catchers, prostitutes, pimps, beggars, thieves – most of them failing to make a decent living and many seeking oblivion in alcohol before removal to the workhouse or nearby mortuary.

But from an early age Tilly went to Drury Lane to buy milk from the small grocery store of a superbly enterprising Mr Sainsbury. Amid the stewed eel and cats' meat shops marking an impoverished neighbourhood, he was founding a supermarket empire.

Like a lot of men in the neighbourhod, Joseph Elkin worked as a porter. Many served Clare Market, which teemed with the poor on gaslit Saturday evenings. Fish and vegetables were sold from two lines of barrows flanked by filthy butchers' stalls where scrawny animals were butchered on the spot, the carcases set about with saws and cleavers and sold in rough hunks. Heads, feet and offal were boiled in an adjoining tripe-house.

Clare Market was levelled in the slum clearance plan for Kingsway and the Aldwych in Tilly's infancy. Most local porters then worked in the fruit and vegetable market halls of Covent Garden, within an Italianate arcaded square designed by Inigo Jones and owned by the Duke of Bedford. From 4 a.m. 800 licensed porters charged tuppence a turn to carry from cart to stall a load of baskets heaped one above the other on their heads. Weekly earnings could reach 2 guineas (£2.10) in summer but fall away in winter. This when Charles Booth thought a 'moderate' family of five needed 21 shillings – a guinea – a week to escape poverty. The Elkins were one such family usually falling short. Joseph's address suggests he was a market porter before joining Rippingille's Albion Lamp Company, whose High Holborn outlet, for its Birmingham-made oil lamps and stoves, offered more stable wages. Emily still had to work as a charwoman.

To get through the year the poor of Covent Garden catered to multifarious theatre demands for artists and artisans. Each mid-winter the Theatre Royal pantomime starring Dan Leno fed a cast of children. The Elkins braved an investment in scissors, needles, thread and leather to make ballet shoes. Ronnie could proudly say, a century later, that his grandparents, whom he never met, had made shoes for Anna Pavlova. Tilly delivered them to the stage door. Once, in the supreme pleasure of her life, she watched the Russian prima ballerina dance.

Drury Lane became more drunk and disorderly when the Duke of Bedford called last orders on Covent Garden's pubs in a vain bid to keep porters sober. A Booth inspector noted on 26 July 1898: 'A hot, thundery day. Sleepy, weedy men in the courts & streets & stout burly women. A few drawn-faced children. Many small public houses, full today of women and children.'[2] The worst fact of Tilly's childhood was that alcoholism came into her own family, engulfing her mother and terrorising them all.

The Wren church of St Clement Danes – whose bells ring out 'oranges and lemons' in the nursery rhyme – shone as a lodestar. Rector Septimus Pennington and his daughter Georgina Louisa, aka Louie, were restoring the building islanded in The Strand and leading a community mission. Septimus baptised Tilly; Louie taught her in Sunday school and became her heroine. The rector's daughter married her father's successor and protégé, William Pennington-Bickford, and together they ran a 'Louie Home' on the Sussex coast as a hostel for inner-city children. It gave hundreds of youngsters like Tilly a thrilling introduction to the seaside.

Tilly attended St Clement Danes School as it shifted with slum clearance before reopening in Drury Lane premises in 1908. The Elkins now had two rooms in a new tenement at 7 Betterton Street. Tilly walked daily along Drury Lane to school or Mr Sainsbury, twice to church on Sunday and again on weekday evenings for study classes and magic-lantern slide shows with the Band of Hope, youth wing of the temperance movement.

Emily Elkin.

She adored reading, especially the King James Bible, and wrote in a copperplate script — signing an ornate certificate at twelve in a promise to abstain from alcohol: the pledge would be absolute and lifelong. Seeing the dissolution of her mother, and suffering from its consequences, had made port another word for poison. A glass might be raised at later family weddings, but the contents remained untasted; the grimace on Tilly's clenched lips never lifted.

Diminutive Tilly Elkin developed an hour-glass figure, the ample feminine outline admired in her youth. Fashion conscious, she was skilled in making the most of herself when cutting and sewing her own clothes. Hard work had yet to give her a forlorn look. Sewing was difficult given eyesight damaged by gazing at a solar eclipse. And her looks were marred by a nose broken in childhood. She said she fractured it 'falling upstairs'. Perhaps she did. It was a time when children suffered terribly from accidents and violence.

Escaping into Bible stories, Tilly walked on a regular pilgrimage to St Paul's Cathedral — seeking out the third and largest version of William Holman Hunt's Pre-Raphaelite picture *The Light of the World*, the treasure Charles Booth had gifted. Knocking on an overgrown door, bearing a dawn-bringing lantern, Jesus is portrayed as the ultimate inspector of spiritual poverty. The widely reproduced painting lit in Tilly more than a missionary zeal. Creeping weeds might have been meant to signify sin, but a stifled city child saw heavenly greenery. At a time of mass exodus from the land, she longed for the countryside.

In the 1911 census Joseph and Emily, porter and cleaner, were listed in Betterton Street with Matilda 14, Louisa 6 and Florence 5 months. Conditions, if still squeezed, and clouded by Emily's perilous health, were improved enough for all three girls to survive childhood.

Tilly Elkin left school with a Shakespeare Prize 'for industry and general intelligence' before the drudgery of domestic service. A love of singing, which saw her perform with her school choir at the Royal Albert Hall, continued in church. She longed to teach, ideally as a missionary, but the next best thing was Voluntary Aid Detachment (VAD) training as a nursing assistant, which she duly did from the start of the First World War, in August 1914, when she was seventeen. Tilly was a nurse for her mother, who died, aged forty-nine, in 1917.

The task of supporting the war effort became so colossal that the voluntary aspect of VAD work was superseded by relatively high wages for women with no private income. Knitting and sewing teams sang as they worked for £1 a week. Tilly made army tents – the heavy, tar-coated canvas fed into industrial sewing machines by boys too young for military service. She also met injured soldiers at London's railway stations and escorted them to care centres.

Tilly and her friend Emily Jones were working in one of the thousands of makeshift hospitals and convalescent homes treating maimed men when Emily fell in love with Frederick Blythe from Suffolk. He was among the first British soldiers on the Western Front to suffer chlorine gassing. They wed in 1915 but she never ceased nursing him.

Fred had a younger brother, George, who did not return from army service in the Middle East until 1919. Introduced to his sister-in-law's friend, he proposed to Tilly on their second meeting. They were married in his home village of Acton on Lammas Day: 1 August 1920. George's brothers William and Arthur acted as witnesses having barely met the bride.

In a foreword to the J. L. Carr novella *A Month in the Country*, set in this summer, Ronnie wrote: 'It was a strange time to be

Tilly Elkin.

young, a time full of corroded myths.'[3] But Tilly was deeply in love
– with the countryside. At her wedding, London friends sang the
comic song 'How Ya Gonna Keep 'Em Down on the Farm (Now
That They've Seen Paree)?' Addressed to returning soldiers faced
with the tedium and toil of rural peace, the lyrics applied to George
alone. Tilly was in a bucolic dream.

   She always remembered pink ranks of rosebay willowherb waving
as the beribboned vicarage brougham bore her from the Blythe
family cottage, down tree-arched avenues to the church where she
would worship every Sunday. The bridegroom, a choirboy here,
came only for harvest festivals: he had returned to a hard homeland
too horrified for faith. The dead metal of three medals wound up
usefully in their children's toy box.

4

The Murder House

GEORGE AND TILLY began married life in a typical thatched and pink-washed Suffolk longhouse dating from around 1600 and divided into three narrow dwellings. George walked to work at Bear's Farm, with a large labour force scraping the landscape towards Lavenham. He also set up a sideline as a thatcher, patching the roof of his home himself.

Tilly toiled as hard as her husband: fetching water from a garden well, washing and cleaning without appliances, preparing and preserving food, cooking on a cast-iron range and feeding its fire, fixing oil-lamps, making and mending clothes, tending domestic animals, stretching the household budget as far as the last farthing, helping with the harvest for an annual cash bonus. The difference between them was that she was happy to have escaped her past while his history made for a permanent haunting.

They lived in what was known as the Murder House since a killing had taken place in a part now occupied by widowed Mrs Pleasance. In November 1846 Catherine Foster had added arsenic to suet dumplings served to her farm labourer husband, John, three weeks after their wedding. The dying man had vomited in the garden, suggesting the cholera rampant at the time until peckish chickens also died. Catherine was the last woman hanged in Suffolk and 10,000 people in party mood saw her execution in Bury St Edmunds. All this before her eighteenth birthday.

Tilly continued to work during her first pregnancy as most women

The Murder House.

did back then (farm labourers even giving birth in fields). Possibly
fainting through exhaustion, she went into premature labour one night
after falling down the stairs. A young husband and stockman stood in
for a midwife. Their firstborn son, to be called Gordon, was delivered
dead. George cut the cord, washed and wrapped the body in a sheet,
and buried him secretly at the churchyard edge under cover of darkness.

Soon, Tilly was pregnant again. Ronald George Blythe was born
in the Murder House on 6 November 1922. The birth fell on the
feast day of St Leonard, patron saint of women in labour and of
those in captivity and confinement. Such patronage would prove
appropriate for both mother and child. White christening robes were
sent from a mission school in Ceylon run by Sister Joan, Tilly's
beloved correspondent. The exquisitely embroidered fabric was then
stored away like a holy relic for future offspring.

There would be six live babies within ten years, each in turn
briefly immaculate in the precious christening robes. With three
miscarriages and one stillbirth, Tilly was to draw the line after ten
pregnancies. She concluded that the best form of birth control was
to go to bed when George was sleeping.

At eighteen months, Ronnie had a brother, Harold, and they
shared a bed until leaving home. Then came Bernard, Constance
(Connie), Eileen and Gerald. Baby Gerry was not expected to survive
infancy due to a heart defect. Tended by Tilly with loving vigilance,
he would live to seventy-five, a grandfather and an Australian.

Compact and sturdy, Ronnie was blessed with robust health which would last a century. Especially to Harold, but to the younger siblings also, something tender and unworldly in his nature was thought to need protection. They did not see the steely quality he noted in himself.

Almost from the start, he seemed a changeling – set apart by watchful behaviour. His first word was neither 'Mama' nor 'Dada', but 'dark'. This reported utterance was conflated with the most vivid memory from his infancy for an early story:

'The first word I ever spoke, they said, was "dark". They were retiring, it seems, and were sunk into those repetitive banalities which close the day. "How dark it is," they murmured to each other, as they strolled the long low rooms in the travelling lamplight . . . the sad, quiet word must have faltered about me for, to their astonishment, I echoed "dark".

'Could this have been the night the huge white bird crashed down the chimney and beat against the looking-glasses in terror? It is possible.'[1]

An author gladly doing without many possessions during a long and enlightening lifetime never needed a torch. His eyes alert to gradations and revelations of darkness, nocturnal walks remained a passion. 'Everything changes at night,' he told nature writer Patrick Barkham. 'The trees change. Even places you know backwards take on another life at night. They become mysterious. I don't find it fearful.'[2]

But Tilly Blythe did. Her nerves jangled further in the Murder House; she was scared if alone with glancing and fluttering shadows. When George went to the pub, as he did from the start, she could be driven by a panic attack into waiting in the street until turning-out time. No wonder her hatred of alcohol never wavered.

In any event, Ronnie retained a first memory of the flailing bird – terrified and terrifying as it emerged from the chimney shrouded in soot, a spectral symbol of doom like a soiled albatross hurtling around the room until finally escaping through an opened window. The fact that it escaped was the thought which lingered.

In a revelatory essay entitled 'An Inherited Perspective' he described 'the indigenous eye' and how a native writer's feeling for nature and landscape deepens when it remains 'hedged about' by familiar considerations. 'From childhood on, what he sees he is. Flesh becomes place.'[3]

He came to perceive a human duty to hoard small and precious memories burned through all our senses 'for it is these which re-shape art and philosophy as Proust so dazzlingly taught us'. Thus: 'as well as my frightened bird in the dark bedroom, when I was still less than three, I remember the smell of rotting plums in the dank grass and the nice stink of our pigsty, and the hard couch in Mrs Pleasance's cottage . . . and the clank of pails at the pump, and being scared by geese'.[4] A more insidious aroma was summed up as 'stagnation'. Stagnant water was known to be a killer, but stagnant lives could be lethal too.

Mrs Pleasance owned a pony and trap, and on occassion Ronnie was allowed a bouncing and rocking ride. The novelty of rapid movement was ruined by the nausea of motion sickness, which became a lifelong misery and may prompt a psychological explanation. Whatever the cause, the man who reached his nineties without ever taking aspirin or paracetamol always travelled with a pack of Quells.

While buses and trains were thought worth the risk of queasiness, he never learned to drive nor cared to travel by car at all. Subscribing to the problem-clearing creed of St Augustine, 'It is solved by walking,' he declared at ninety: 'There's nothing better than walking; there's nothing worse than jogging.'[5] The point was to move slowly – observantly, reflectively and preferably in a familiar landscape. 'Going over the same ground, if only once or twice a year, claims it for oneself.'[6]

Never choosing to live as many as fifty miles from his birthplace, Ronnie remained mostly within a ten-mile radius. Work or family visits would take him briefly to America and Australia; his longest spell in London lasted four days. Although he often wondered whether it marked a weakness of character, staying close to home gave him his distinction – a far-sighted familiarity – as a writer.

It was a childhood without privacy: doors were unlocked; a paling was lifted so Ronnie and then Harold could crawl into the back garden of Mrs Pleasance as well as their own; in an outhouse at the end of the Blythe plot a three-seat lavatory rose above a cesspit emptied on the vegetable patch by Father in what was known in Suffolk as 'bucket and chuck it'. The communal privy beyond the covered well and horse pond stood next to the sty whose pig was key to the cottage economy. A fattening sow, petted by the children, turned leftovers into home-grown, home-cured meat. But the butchering – rendering the garden and kitchen red – was a horror never repeated. George could not abide any more killing.

With scant word from the wider world, neighbours expected to know each other's business. Respectability lay in conformity. A strict social code was brutally enforceable in cottages tied to farm labour: low rent, winter fuel and other small perks boosted poor pay, but 'trouble-makers' (union members or known Liberal or Labour voters) could be summarily dismissed and evicted. Families and all they owned were often seen dumped by the roadside.

'Much suffering was caused by everyone knowing everything about you,' Ronnie was to reflect. 'The news of the world which runs across the screens every night is often spoken of as the destroyer of the provincialism which gave stay-at-home life its rich flavour, but we are apt to forget its benefits. Among these is a hitherto unknown tolerance of what is going on next door. Or just an indifference to it.'[7]

For all the prying and spying, rural Suffolk between the wars was a place of secrets. About the most important things in life – emotions and motivations; the damage and dreams we all carry – little could be said. Amid the daily hubbub of children and animals, there was a profound and oppressive silence. A year older than George, Tilly bore mortification in private. Social shame was an easily caught affliction.

But the Blythe domestic realm was never hushed. A bare cottage was filled and governed by the ticking of an elaborate clock hiding a gimcrack mechanism – a wedding present from George's parents. Ronnie recalled the insistent sound of passing seconds and a whir-ring wheeze as the timepiece struggled to measure out the quarter-hours. Its efforts summed up a life sentence of hard labour. Something in the striking seemed to denote the triumph of the human spirit and the holiness of a hovel.

There were further nocturnal sounds in a building permeated with damp, rot and beastly lodgers (bat roosts in the eaves; bird and rat nests in the thatch): 'I would lie in bed and listen to a spider on a route-march on wallpaper which had come adrift, tap-tap-tapping in the dark. And the beams would give a little groan, worn out with having to hold up tons of house.'[8]

For much of the year the Blythe siblings moved briskly under thick jerseys knitted by Mother. Extreme cold would always be known as 'three pullovers weather'. Shared beds made the most of bodily heat; Father's army greatcoat became a blanket, his enamel army water bottle a bed-warmer.

Domestic warmth came from a kitchen range fire sustained in embers overnight: 'As children we heard the house being warmed up from scratch every morning, the tinkle of the kindling, the lighting of oil-stoves, the stamping of feet as logs and coals were fetched, and then miraculously porridge steaming in a hot kitchen. Keeping the fire in overnight was an expert business . . . the finding the flame, the puffing it into a blaze, the laying of the wood in a kind of wigwam above it and the knowing when to stop.'[9]

A late devotee of central heating looked back on a boyhood in which 'we baked at the front and froze at the back'.[10] Vigorous play had a vital purpose in the struggle to keep warm and stay alive. Each Christmas they sang the Gustav Holst and Christina Rossetti carol 'In the Bleak Midwinter' with special feeling. A Bethlehem where frosty wind made moan, earth stood hard as iron and water like a stone was viscerally real for a Suffolk child chilled to the bone in an inter-war midwinter. Ronnie recalled 'frozen milk being carried across from the farm by mittened hands with numb fingertips'.[11] Pails of water from the garden well turned solid overnight on a brick floor in the larder; thatch dripped icicles.

One form of wintry weather brought jubilation. '"It has been snowing!" we yelled, even before we drew the curtains, its sound-lessness speaking so loudly. Oh, if it would only last forever. We rolled our snowball along the lane until it was as high as ourselves and as heavy as lead, and surely must roll on into April. We saw it turning into a trickling sorbet, then into nothing.'[12]

The Murder House would also vanish, burning down soon after the Second World War. On the bus Ronnie passed blackened chimney stacks in a bed of nettles, until the site was cleared for bungalows and the ornamental village sign of a very altered Acton.

5

The Satan Tree

ACTON AND ITS environs were awash with Blythes in the 1920s. The focal point was Vicarage Cottage, where Ronnie's grandparents presided. He loved staying in the detached, double-fronted refuge with a large garden during the births of siblings.

Grandfather David, who died when Ronnie was seven, was 'a quizzical authoritarian whose sky-blue eyes and brown face under a weathered hat created uncertainty. He petted and mussed children much as he did sheep-dogs or, similarly, bade them to be quiet and sit. "Do what he says," advised Grandmother.'[1]

Born Martha Allen at Newman's Green in 1866, Ronnie's grandmother was a kindly figure ultimately to outlive three domineering husbands. She was ruled more by superstition than religion – shrieking when Ronnie came with a gift of lilac or snowdrops. After a death in the house, she knew she must hurry down the garden to tell the bees, and hang black crepe on the hive, or they would die too. Normally so sweet-natured, Grandma had a dreadful warning which caused the children to take a longer walk home:

'When I was a child in Suffolk many pastures contained isolated may-trees, huge hawthorns, sumptuous and heady in late spring, and creaking and dark in mid-winter. That in the meadow leading to my grandmother's house was called the Satan Tree and we made a cautious half-detour when we walked in its direction. It was the first tree I can remember, possibly because of its name. In retrospect, nothing could be less satanic, indeed the reverse, for I see it full of flowers and birds, and slightly billowing, as may-trees do, a rich, grand plant which will bloom inside me for as long as I live . . . It was never allowed in our house.'[2]

Martha Blythe knew that harebells, being witches' flowers, were not to be touched. An elderflower bush in her garden warded off visitations of evil; blackberries hung unpicked in October because the devil had spat on them (spumes of froghopper foam taken for demonic spittle). A character from a Thomas Hardy story, born before the author had published a word, she lived into the age of television. In a neighbourly gathering to watch the coronation of Elizabeth II on a screen in fitful black and white, the elderly Victorian piped up: 'I have to ask a question: *can they see us?*'

But some remained hidden from view. One Blythe kinsman had been lodged in Sudbury Union Workhouse, described in the register as 'farm labourer' and 'imbecile': poverty could send you mad, through sickness, malnutrition, dread or despair, if not actually killing you. The mentally infirm of Sudbury and its surrounding parishes could also be removed to Essex Hall – an Italianate mansion and failed railway hotel in Colchester notorious as the Eastern Counties Asylum for Idiots, Imbeciles and the Feeble-Minded. Ronnie knew

David and Martha Blythe.

it as the Royal Eastern Counties Institution for Mental Defectives where treatment was said to be more progressive than the name.

On a constant round of family visits, a watchful, listening child committed significant things, and deceptively trivial comments, to a memory as clear and sharp as broken glass. An aunt was recalled ruefully reflecting on marital parsimony: 'A woman should never marry a man who undid string.' The closest relations were Uncle Fred and Aunt Emily, Tilly's old friend. They had four children – the last, christened Frederick, just weeks old when his father died from the effects of gassing on the Western Front compounded by tuberculosis. This youthful demise in 1924 came too late for listing on the church war memorial.

All Saints church claimed sole dominion over the spiritual life of the village; nonconformists – most of the labouring families hereabouts – walked three miles each Sunday to and from the chapel in Great Waldingfield. Anglicanism between the wars stood for the established order; until 1936 its conservative-preaching clerics were still paid from tithes. All Saints was set amid similar medieval marvels. Holy Trinity Long Melford, St Peter and St Paul Lavenham and St Peter's church on Market Hill in Sudbury were all within four miles: a triangle drawn between these three great wool churches would find Acton roughly in the middle. That invisible border marked the real boundaries of most local people's lives.

Acton further revolved around the Crown public house, a spacious Georgian inn with scrubbed floors and furniture, where Ronnie's father George and friends eked out thruppenny half-pints of beer of an evening while playing darts, dominoes or cribbage and smoking hand-rolled cigarettes. Sometimes they sang.

There was also a general store run by a Mr Jacobs. Ronnie remembered a crammed and pungent emporium with 'silvery cake-tins, sides of bacon, boiled sweets in tall glass jars, cigarettes, ham on the bone, fish from Lowestoft on Fridays. And an urgent notice which said, "You may telephone from here".'[3]

The fish barrow was 'followed by a grave procession of cats, clothing-club men and penny-a-week insurance men, a baker's van, a paraffin-oil tanker hung all over with tin kettles and saucepans, and – very soon – the accumulator-man for those with wirelesses. Gossips took note of the time which these often larky chaps might spend at a particular cottage.'[4] 'Villages are all stories, of course,'

Ronnie concluded. 'Past and present get interleaved and a drama or poetry or scandal or crime or romance emerges.'[5]

Ronnie loved Acton village church as a vessel for gripping sagas. He was drawn especially to an eighteenth-century family monument of princely ostentation, in which Robert Jennens, adjutant to the Duke of Marlborough, swoons towards death, attended by the weeping allegorical figure of Grief. A missing inscription adds mystery to a cautionary Suffolk tale.

Robert had begun to transform Acton Place into a Palladian palace but his money-lending son halted payment and camped in the basement. When not in London, calling in debts with merciless interest, the Acton Miser lived reclusively down to his name. When breathing his last, in 1798, he was the richest cadaver-to-be in England. Cursing the world, he died intestate – provoking legal disputes among possible heirs and certain imposters for over a century. Lawyers were the beneficiaries. The *Jennens v Jennens* action led Charles Dickens to the interminable *Jarndyce v Jarndyce* court case pivotal to the plot of *Bleak House*.

The Blythe family had their own miser. Agnes Bean, Ronnie's great-aunt, had run a sweetshop at Newman's Green with an iron fist and now lived as a thrifty widow, with a linnet and creature comforts carefully caged.

Set slightly apart from an orchard surrounded by high hedges and a padlocked gate ('more like a fortification than something growing'), her clapboard cottage looked as if it should have been made of gingerbread and smelled enticingly of stored apples from late summer to spring. But visiting children were offered only windfalls. The 'eaters' and 'keepers' in her apple-room were for her alone. Ronnie likened her cottage to 'a kind of Suffolk Eden once sinful boys had been driven out'.[6] Her grave now obliterated in Acton churchyard, she has left her mean mark in a short story called 'The Windfall':

'Aunt used to take me into this orchard and poke about in the rank grass with her polished cane until, suddenly, there was a *clunk*. "One there, Toby," she used to say. The windfall would, as often as not, have a disgusting wet cavity where it had lain on the ground and wasps would scuttle out of it. Aunt would then take it from me, shake it, breathe on its good side and rub it against her skirts. Then she would solemnly pass it to me. All around us were apples. They nodded against the sky and poured down the shiny boughs in pale yellow streams – more apples than Aunt could ever eat, sell or want. But never once did she actually *pick* one for me.'[7]

To this recollected story Ronnie added a fictional plot of the family gathering in Aunt's parlour, with her corpse upstairs before the funeral ('Don't you want to pay your last respects before Aunt's screwed down for ever?'). The boy Toby rushes to the unlocked orchard, aiming to pick one of the apples 'hung singly in fabulous globes and myriadly in flushed cascades'. But he can bring himself only to search for another windfall. Meanwhile, relatives in the house have been seizing objects they claimed were promised to them, until halted by the unexpected arrival of the vicar. He reads out a shocking will: Toby inherits all.

In reality, the rich inheritance of Ronald Blythe would never be measured in material terms.

6

The Coming Down Time

FOLLOWING THE END of the First World War and swift withdrawal of farm subsidies, the rural economy returned to a pattern of decline that would last for fifty years. Far from medieval wool wealth, Suffolk was now among England's poorest counties. Derelict cottages fell into abandoned fields. Hopes were subsiding too.

In 1919 weekly farmworking hours had been reduced to fifty-four in summer and forty-eight in winter, with a half-day on Saturday adding what became a crucial chance for paid overtime. A year later the minimum Suffolk farm wage was 46 shillings (£2.30) a week, barely half the national average rate in factories. It was then cut again – with agricultural workers striking in 1923 for 6d (2.5p) an hour – as rural recession deepened into the Great Depression.

Decline was general across rural England. Much later Ronnie got to know the writer Laurie Lee whose lyrically novelised memoir of 1920s Gloucestershire, *Cider with Rosie*, has been popular since its publication in 1959. The beguiling account was followed by two bestsellers on youthful vagabondage, with Ronnie bridling at the Lee line: 'Young men don't leave a lush creamy village life solely for economic reasons.'

'But there were not many youths, faced with fieldwork and penury, who would have given a thought to its topping of lush creaminess,' he retorted. 'And to give Laurie Lee his due, he never forgot the hardships and limitations which he so famously coated with opulence. He knew what lay beneath.'[1]

In early drafts *Cider with Rosie* had been *Cider with Poppy* and *Cider with Daisy*, the shifting title underlining a fantastic tale unfixed by facts from an author who contended that 'the only truth is what you remember'. The Lee memory was selective. Ronnie had perfect recall – for every imperfection.

Ronnie admired the rural memoir *Early to Rise: A Suffolk Morning*. Its author, Colchester-raised Hugh Barrett, had left school in 1933, at fifteen, to become an eager farm pupil. The teenager was in the ascendant when all around him – apart from plagues of rats, rabbits, wood pigeons and fleas feeding on human endeavour – was in free fall.

The Barrett farm depended on fourteen Suffolk horses with their own personalities, strengths and demands – one a willing puller, another never treading on beet rows during hoeing. They drew the implements for ploughing, harrowing, drilling, rolling, cutting, binding and carting. A solitary tractor was used for heavy cultivating, but neither it nor its driver was well regarded. The annihilating victory of mechanisation – removing people from the land and rendering the Suffolk Punch an endangered species – was yet to come. At that moment no one was winning. Every farm still working was a sea of debt in an ocean of dereliction.

'Everything was going down hill. Arable land tumbled down to speargrass, bracken and brambles, buildings fell about the livestock's ears. Ditches and drains slowly filled, gutters fell, hedges grew tall and wide . . . The smaller landlords were in almost as bad a plight as their tenants – their manor houses and halls lost roof-tiles which were not put back, their gravelled drives grew grass; park rails rusted and scrubby animals roamed among ragwort and thistles and docks, where before fine pedigree cattle had grazed well-kept pastures.'[2]

Farm rents still fell due on quarter days – 25 March for Lady Day or the Feast of the Annunciation, 24 June for Midsummer Day, 29 September for Michaelmas or the Feast of St Michael and All Angels, 25 December for Christmas – when farmhands were also hired and rehired. Farm sales were traditionally held on Lady Day or Michaelmas, but during the depression they cropped up weekly, private ruin rendered pitilessly public. In East Anglia it was called 'the coming down time'.

One Suffolk farmer toiling near the Essex border had two sons

and 150 acres. Both heirs and helpers were taken by the First World
War. The old man struggled on 'straight but never out of debt' until
finished off by two drought years. An implacable tithe holder forced
closure. Everything had to go. The former farmer stood stony-faced
as broken implements were knocked down by an auctioneer, but
when bidding began for his four Suffolk horses, he stroked a mare's
neck and wept. He was to be taken in by a brother, but days later
his wife found him hanging in an outhouse. Suicide was endemic
in rural Suffolk in the year that, far away in Germany, Adolf Hitler
came to power.

'A length of rope over a beam in the barn, a charge of shot from
a four-ten, a cold death in the horse pond; how many farmers took
these ways out? – and how many more lived with the fear that they
too might be driven the same way? The men, particularly the older
ones, were in even crueller plight. If their employers "gave up", or
were sold up, and no new man came to take over the farm, or
coming in required fewer hands, they had the workhouse to go to.
Fear of the workhouse was as real and immediate as it had ever been
– and like their masters many men took a short cut and put an end
to it all.'³

Still, the vestiges of rural vitality and festivity remained. This was
the time of the last great communal gatherings to harvest the English
countryside. The collecting cycle began in June with haymaking.
'There used to be a moment just before the old hay harvest when
it was a crime to walk in a meadow. "You didn't come across the
pasture, did you?" they would ask anxiously. There was a week or
two before the haymakers went in when the meadows reached a
state of scented luxuriance almost impossible to describe. Their
growth by the river was so tall that it closed over our heads.'⁴

And then came the scything. There would be 'rhythmic swishing
and the fall of green stems against the blade, followed by bouts of
honing and little screams of whetstone and steel'.⁵ The drying of
the scythed vegetation was still 'every able-bodied woman's rite
. . . sweaty girls with huge wooden rakes and pitchforks tossing
grass in blazing sunshine. Bare arms and shoulders, but a bonnet
of course.

'Hay once had to be made when the grass was full of growth,
and sappy, then left and thrown about, and only when it was as dry
as a bone made into stacks. Wet hay in a stack would heat up until

it became an internal oven setting fire to the lot. The River Stour
meadows were hay-kingdoms when we were children . . . The hay
was as much wild flowers as grass . . . The air would be heavy and
overpowering, and a feeling of lassitude would run through the
landscape, causing it to droop.'[6]

Harvesting by John Nash.

Now the corn would be golden. After a 'Lord' was chosen to bargain
for pay, children helped parents and grandparents to bring in the grain.
Round and round went the horse-drawn reaper-binder, with rabbits
and hares driven into the dwindling centre – until they dashed from a
sliver of corn, and into the arms or sticks of hungry countrymen or
the jaws of their dogs. Here was the harvest bonus, along with jugs of
beer fetched from the nearest inn. The traditional feast had already been
surrendered and the right to free ale at a time of intensive labour became
another source of tension as the depression hardened.

Ronnie recollected a rush to make the first loaf from a barley field
cut on Lammas Day – 1 August, his parents' wedding day. Men wove
corn dollies from the last sheaf of the field. The strands made a cage
to imprison the goddess Ceres and ensure fertility the following year.
The pagan talisman hung in the beleaguered Christian farmhouse.

Next came the ancient tradition of gleaning the stubble, where
families picked up ears of grain the horsemen and machinery had

left behind. Then, on the Sunday nearest the full moon marking the autumn equinox, when day and night are equal, the Harvest Festival evensong service in Acton church was not to be missed. Even Ronnie's father attended.

'The beloved interior had more to do with amplitude than taste. Thickets of Michaelmas daisies, mountains of fruit and vegetables, the pulpit festooned with hops and grapes, the way to the lectern perilous with what was always politely called garden produce, and the indescribably holy smell of paraffin, starch and plants. A low sun blazed in from the west and mortified the oil lamps. Having walked three miles through stubble fields in short trousers – "Sunday best" – my legs were scratched and slightly bloody.'[7]

In old age, on the phone from East Anglia to Australia, Ronnie and Harold would reminisce about earning boyhood pocket money by stone-picking and weeding. At least they had been allowed to keep the pennies earned, unlike their youthful forebears. 'You have to be old to have lifted a stook,' Ronnie noted. 'They were surprisingly weighty and prickly.'[8]

For all the human impoverishment, before the wealth of post-war agricultural industrialisation, it was a time of wild profusion. Suffolk's verdant hedgerows were loud with linnets and yellowhammers, its marshes with warblers and buntings. Winter fields had enough left-over food for swarming flocks of green and golden plovers, fieldfares, redwings and starlings. In spring courting nightingales and cuckoos were joined by rasping corncrakes – a wake-up call to weary occupants of farm cottages in the middle of the night.

Hardship worsened from late September, with the nadir in deepest winter. One freezing January Ronnie recalled 'the farm labourers of my boyhood as they sugar-beeted at New Year, chopping and kicking the roots from the iron ground, picking them up and trimming them with a tool which was part spoke, part knife. They wore sacking cowls, like monks, and leather mittens, and they toiled in sociable huddles. They were the last of the unmechanised agricultural workforce and if there are still those who regard such lives as an idyll, they should borrow the sugar-beet tool from where it hangs among the bygones in the village pub and try doing a couple of rows across a field on a day such as this. It was killing.'[9]

George Blythe, working in the mud and dust in his army greatcoat and boots, hated the sweat and humiliation of fieldwork. He would have fled back into military service given the chance. So desperate a desire to get out says a lot about George's home life. There was a palpable distance – all those pregnancies notwithstanding – between husband and wife. They had only their children, and poverty, in common.

7

Child of Nature

IN THE END George got as far as Sudbury's cemetery, where grave-digging experience earned him less stressful manual labour. When Ronnie was four the family moved from the Murder House to 2 Gallows Hill, Chilton. Skulls unearthed when the low, grey Victorian terrace was being built confirmed an execution site.

Mr and Mrs Blythe arrived with three small boys, and all they possessed loaded on a horse-drawn dray – a pathetic paucity exposed to public scrutiny. But still their dire poverty was known only within the family. They were so poor that cousins brought straw for the children's bedding.

The ancient village of Chilton, not yet a Sudbury suburb, was a mile and a half from Acton where the migrants were always returning, walking back for church services (George excepted) and family visits. Ronnie, ever punctual for important things, found it excruciating that his mother invariably made them late for Sunday worship. 'They started early,' she insisted.

Final expansion of the Blythe family would force a further move within Chilton – five children walking behind another borrowed dray while Tilly pushed Gerry in a pram. Their new home, California Cottage, was a mouldering clapboarded Victorian bungalow in an overgrown smallholding (kitchen garden plus orchard with apple, pear, greengage and walnut trees). It stood alongside a ruined farm and a derelict brickyard and close to an old chalk quarry.

The scenery of recession was a playground for an imaginative child always seeking hiding places from the sound of his mother's voice pressing him into the tyranny of household chores. He lay in long grass reading or gazing up at the clouds as calls went unheeded. 'My best perfected art was the vanishing trick,' he said. Later, the mysterious chateau in the Alain-Fournier novel *Le Grand Meaulnes* would bring to mind expansive feelings at Chilton. Even when confined, he entered 'the private realm of children's animism, with its magic trees and posts and indeed in my case a fat dark cobble set in a brick courtyard which I talked to when I was six'.[1]

As in Acton, there were fowls to feed and eggs to collect, messages to deliver and a ceaseless fetching of this or that. Now a band of brothers and sisters also needed minding. The butchered pig had been replaced by goats whose milk, Tilly had been informed, was nutritious for children and especially for sickly Gerry. So, the older boys learned to milk them. The goats were stabled overnight, milked in the morning, then staked out in a rough meadow with a water trough. Ronnie and Harold hauled water from the garden well, previously the horse pump – letting down a galvanised pail to a ledge from which icy water gushed when they pushed with all their might to heave a bar round.

Part of the old Victorian brickyard, the goat meadow was covered with listing pug sheds, ekes for drying the bricks and furnaces for baking them – industrial relics over which nasturtiums and wild sweatpeas ran amok each summer. Beyond lay abandoned cornfields with dens for absconding readers.

When free to roam, Ronnie and Harold felt like kings until moated and castellated Chilton Hall, with cannons at the main door, revealed the unscalable walls of a rigid class structure. The Tudor mansion was a country home for Sir Thomas Crisp English, a royal surgeon, who sent them backing into hedges as he passed in his chauffeur-driven Rolls-Royce.

Now Ronnie was given the man-making task of gardening. Directed to carve out his own plot, he chose a site riven with tree roots. The result was exhaustion and despondency – a claustrophobic feeling of being trapped in expectations he could not fathom. Penny packets of lobelia and clarkia seeds were scattered. The reluctant gardener transplanted clumps of wild flowers but they rarely took, so the flowers were pressed in discarded books of wallpaper samples. Much later he reasoned: 'It was thought desirable by country women

Chilton Hall.

that their menfolk should spend as much of their lives outside as was possible and a "good garden", which was a family's most visible asset, indicated social virtue.'[2]

Not that George conformed to this convention. Once a year Tilly badgered him to dig the garden, then she was left to plant and tend the fruit and vegetables which, with much pickling and preserving, helped to sustain the family. Neither did Father do the deed when chickens needed slaughtering: the milkman or breadman had to be persuaded to slice through a fowl's neck with a cleaver, the children watching in fascinated horror as the headless bird ran in circles until finally toppling over.

Ronnie knew the drill with male relatives and neighbours: cottage gardens bursting with jumbled fruit, vegetables and flowers – rhubarb and roses, cabbages and sweet williams, pinks and blackcurrants – were to be inspected and admired, after which the visitor left with a root of this, a shoot of that and edible produce wrapped in newspaper. But this novice gardener longed for gifts from Chilton Hall's unvisited borders: 'When as children we walked along the foot-path which skirted Chilton Hall – there was an ancient right of way to the church – our voices grew quiet and we were on our best behaviour. Not because Sir Thomas Crisp English might descend on us from his battlements with furious cries but because his garden would be holding a green finger to its lovely lips.

'The other day the life-peer who now lives in the Hall welcomed me in and for the first time I saw my first Great Garden in its entirety. Its buttressed Tudor walls, its glittering moat and bridges, its "room" after "room" of beds of flowers and fruit, its artfully enclosed sweetness, its girls on the lawns, its chasing dogs – and its solitary gardener, the slight young man who did it all – the mowing, the digging, the upkeep, the everything. There he stands, Keeper of the Realm. When I explained to him and my host how we dropped our voices when we passed through their garden as children, overcome with awe, they smiled gently.'[3]

Back in boyhood, he decorated his disappointing plot with field flints and old bricks in grey, red and yellowy Suffolk white mosaics. Then, after he pressed black and white seeds into the soil, astonishing sunflowers towered over him in searing greens, oranges and yellows. And willow hoops staking out his garden sprouted in spring – returning, as if by magic, the cultivated and confined to nature. Fresh graves, hooped off while the earth settled, burst into similar shoot with a reassuring message of rebirth.

For Ronnie from seven onwards, spurred at times by a vexed mother crying 'Go to Jericho and don't come back till teatime!', there was the liberation of all-day rambles – with brothers if need be, better yet without. 'We saw some strange sights but we also saw our native territory in an exciting and explorative way . . . It was indeed this childish wandering which told us we were "Suffolk" and laid down our territorial rights.'[4]

'I climbed a road called Gallows Hill every day and never once did it say something agonising, macabre and morbid to me. What it said was freedom, running loose. Gallows Hill was the path to the white violet and cowslip sites – for plants remained undisturbed in their locations for generations then, and village people of all ages saw them as a form of permanent geography by which the distance of Sunday walks could be measured, or where tea or love could be made, or, in my case, where books could be read.'[5]

Believing themselves the rightful owners of every discovery, the Blythe children tasted their freedom: 'We ate fresh hawthorn buds, and called them bread and cheese. We gnawed raw carrots. We were the inheritors of glut when it came to fallen plums. We pretended to enjoy crab apples . . . Best of all, we drank from the spring waters, a hilly meadow stream near our home, and paddled in them, our white feet startling tiny fish.'[6]

A special joy was the golden-fleshed greengage, staple fruit tree of cottage gardens along with old varieties of apple. Originally a Persian wild plum, it was brought from France by Sir William Gage of Hengrave Hall near Bury St Edmunds in the early eighteenth century. A Reine Claude label lost en route, the importer lent his own name. Spreading across Suffolk, the fruit became the birthright of every scrumping child. 'The trees, tall and straggly, had linen lines tied to them, and were thought something you had to put up with, like nettles. But I was enchanted . . .'[7]

Abandoned dwellings – with peeling wallpapers to see, decay to smell, stairs to climb and doors to open – held unmissable drama. The Blythe children could not resist the ruined cottage at Ovens Green: 'We were as children implored, ordered, threatened not to go near it, and all because of its dangerous well. But we did of course, sickeningly thrilled by its clammy depths, counting the feet as our pebbles ricocheted from side to side, and estimating the number of disobedient boys and girls who had fallen in.'[8] Tilly would have been no less appalled by the pillowcases passed by Grandma in spring conspiracies. They were filled with peggle (cowslip) and dandelion blooms for home-made wine.

Medieval churches seemed to prop up the sky above the low Suffolk landscape. Ronnie and Harold conquered towers for bird's-eye views of their homeland. They planted imaginary flags at the summit of Stoke-by-Nayland's church with a commanding vista over the Stour Valley to the sea at Harwich. Climbing spiral stairs at Lavenham, they surveyed and annexed scenery stretching to Chilton until the voice of the verger boomed from far below: 'Come you down you young varmints!'

Looking back on the genesis of his life in churches, he thought it had 'more to do with inquisitiveness and magic than religion and architecture. They were all wide open, morning, noon and night then and I used to wander miles from one to another opening their vast carved doors, climbing belfries, staring, sniffing their strong old scents, reading inscriptions, poking about. They were like stories which one could actually enter.'[9]

It was indeed a grand thing for impoverished boys to own a broad East Anglian view – an affinity and absorption so complete that surrounding scenery could enter their beings as a natural cure. 'I am walking, climbing, or lying on grass, and not necessarily high up, and filled with a great view, and suddenly all that I can see, hear and smell amalgamates and becomes a kind of landscape laser which passes right through me, healing me totally. Never having been ill, I must ask myself, of what? I suppose, in my case, of dullness, of that reduction of my senses brought on by not getting out.'[10]

In woods, too, which the Blythe brothers thought their own, they were surprised by gamekeepers and sent packing. Harold held on to that sense of wrongful eviction from High Wood, since it had been his most prized possession. Decades later an estate agency in Australia made him a millionaire. He called his property empire High Wood.

Stumbling upon lovers, as Ronnie later told his writer friend Roger Deakin, was a woodland tradition. 'All country children were conceived in woods, he said, because the cottages were simply too full of other people. Children, grandparents and others lived hugger-mugger in the cramped rooms, so couples adjourned to the woods for privacy.'[11]

Out after breakfast, home by teatime; then early to bed with a prayer taught by Tilly. Ronnie would still be reciting its four comforting lines in the last weeks of his life:

> Lord keep us safe this night
> Secure from all our fears
> May angels guard us while we sleep
> Till morning light appears.

He slept beneath a print of Holman Hunt's *The Light of the World* – forever his mother's favourite picture. Ronnie found the dark, sepia reproduction forbidding. 'Later, I discovered that it was painted in an English garden – one not unlike mine.'[12] A family snap in the parlour was framed in later memory: 'Ages ago, a . . . lady arranges the four of us in a flowery meadow to take our photo . . . she poses us, a baby sister and three brothers in sailor suits, like a reduced cricket team. One of my brothers is chewing a bit of grass, and the other is, like the Lord, kept from wriggling by a bright object – a bunch of keys.

'Tall August plants waver above us. A few yards away, and out of sight, there is a deep pit in which men dig clay for bricks. The men have been to the Western Front and to Gallipoli. The lady's snaps will be sent to Chester to be developed for one-and-sixpence. After the holidays, she will return to London, to our grief, for we love her, although we have long forgotten her name. But the four children go on sitting in the grass for ever, the restless one stilled.'[13]

Blythe siblings. Left to right: Harold, Bernard, Connie and Ronnie.

In his seventies Ronnie went back to Chilton for a new water purifier and got lost on an industrial estate: 'Gone the deserted lime-pits, the marshy meadows, the weathering timber – "the Logs" – the dark ponds into which we squelched, the remote neighbours on their World War One chicken farms, the green lanes, and come scores of hi-tech buildings, in one of which lurked the water purifier.

'I am now walking on sacred ground, for just under the concrete lies the agricultural ruin of our play-land, the peggles and white violets, the dens and old reapers, the hides and private territories of the old country child. I found my way to the right hi-tech shop by using the church as a compass. For although everything else had been flattened out, there it rose, perpendicular and eternal. My sister Constance had been baptised in it one September Sunday long ago before the corn had been cut, so that her long robe trailed over the wild flowers.'[14]

PART TWO

The Boy in the Library

To enter a book is to escape from a prison or an emptiness.
Ronald Blythe, *A Writer's Day-Book*

8

Creative Dreams

RONNIE STARTED SCHOOL in Acton. Walking back to his home village from the age of five, he was far more inspired along the way than by indoctrination in the classroom.

Tuition began with a slate in a wooden frame, a cloth strung to the base to erase the chalk marks: 'Paper was stingily handed out for decades in village schools such as ours. First, slates, then, dazzlingly, an exercise book and ink.'[1] 'To spoil a piece of paper was unforgivable, so dreadful an action was it that it took real nerve to write your name on the top of a clean page. To blot your copy-book – what a fate!'[2]

The focus was on reading, writing, sums, patriotism and religion by rote ('chalk and talk') learning – a grounding for children from the labouring classes to make themselves useful and dutiful. But there were also nature studies, singing and country dancing. 'People in search of ancient rural noises often forget this regular metronomic infant chanting of Faith, Arithmetic, Duty and English, and how it dominated the adult community round about; the same inflexions for alphabet, Commandments, dates and tables, the same little tricks for grasping the same little facts.'[3]

From an early age Ronnie loved reading; it was the best thing his mother ever imparted. They both worshipped books. The key volume of instruction in the family home was the King James Bible, honoured in two editions. From one Tilly read her daily 'portion'; an ornate tome with a metal clasp was for special holy occasions.

Here, in either edition, was a glorious treasury of stories rendered in the language of poetry. The everyday Blythe household Bible did not end with Revelation but a list of featured plants – giving Ronnie a first lesson in botany. Fascinating too were architectural plans for anyone minded to recreate the Temple. And a map of the Holy Land was a guide to fabulous geography. George, who had been there, looked away.

On 1 April 1930 – April Fool's Day – Ronnie, aged seven, was enrolled at St Gregory and St Peter elementary school in Sudbury. It was no joke that his name in the register was followed by the birth date of a mystery five-year-old. Neither was it a novelty since the Blythes had been misrepresented on official documents for centuries.

The young Ronald Blythe was always being reprimanded and punished for inattention ('Wake up! Did you hear what I just said?' 'Are you still with us?'). Six decades later, when his thoughts went walkabout in village school governor meetings, he found himself 'ever fearful of the County Council whacking me over the knuckles for day-dreaming'.[4]

Eventually, an errant student's concentration was captured and his enthusiasm fired by Percy Leggett, a popular eccentric. Schooled at St Peter's and St Gregory's, Mr Leggett had never left – training as a pupil-teacher and ending as a broad educator and art master. Designing sets for Sudbury Dramatic Society productions in the Victoria Hall, he also presented his own one-man show. Members of the audience were invited to make a mark on a large sheet of paper, which the maestro then magicked into a picture.

The art tutor further championed the home-grown eighteenth-century genius of Thomas Gainsborough and John Constable. It was both miraculous and only fitting for Ronnie that two of the greatest landscape painters Britain ever produced were born barely ten miles apart, and virtually beside the River Stour, in Sudbury and East Bergholt.

Shown reproductions of the work of the twin masters by Mr Leggett, Ronnie set off on a detective trail – matching black-and-white pictures to colourful landscapes and picking up information about the artists and their families. Like him, they had taught themselves by careful observation while absconding in woods, marshes and meadows and along lanes and riverbanks: 'these scenes made me a painter', Constable wrote, while Gainsborough's friend and biographer Philip Thicknesse noted that 'there was not a Picturesque clump of Trees, nor even a single Tree of beauty nor hedge row . . . for some miles around the place of his nativity, that he had not so perfectly in his mind's eye.'[5] Ronnie embraced them both as brothers. Their multitudinous kin – the Gainsboroughs extending to shroud-spinner, cleric, publican and a mad-cap inventor who tried to fly on copper wings; the Constables to farming, milling and controlling trade on the Stour from Sudbury to Mistley – became more real to him than his own relatives.

Such fellow feeling fired a dream that he too might be a painter. This absurd notion had to remain a closely guarded secret: an artistic rural labourer's son in the 1930s could only ever be a painter and decorator. But for a time Ronnie was feverishly drawing and painting until, very suddenly, before his thirteenth birthday, the passion fell away – and a hunger for reading and writing all but consumed him.

In the midst of this maelstrom he was accosted by benevolent Dr Grace Griffith at the local flower show. She asked him what he wanted to be when he grew up. 'A writer or an artist or something like that,' he said, surprised into perfect candour. It was anyway an article of rural faith back then that you had to be truthful to a doctor. And Dr Grace never forgot – laughing, decades later, when reminding the successful author that was Ronald Blythe about the reach of his youthful ambition, stretching somewhere between admirable and incredible. By that point a visual writer was composing image-filled paragraphs like pictures.

A contrasting figure of lasting influence was Mr Berry, the English master. He lent Ronnie book after book – so that an avid eleven-year-old reader could race through the collected works of George Bernard Shaw. Mr Berry, a local historian also in thrall to Gainsborough and Constable, assured his special pupil that the greatest romance lay in stories weaving together knowledge and imagination, with a sense of place far beyond the prevailing social order. And so, very early on, Ronnie's intimate address book came to include the real and imaginary, the living and the dead.

For all the health of an outdoor childhood, massed killers stalked an inter-war era before curative drugs and jabs. Outbreaks of scarlet fever, diphtheria, diarrhoea, influenza and measles forced isolation and took an infant toll, and poor boys and girls in particular became familiar with death as it claimed their contemporaries. The constant epidemic across all ages and classes was tuberculosis. 'You would catch your death from a drop of spittle,' Ronnie said. Members of a stricken family could die one by one until a cottage was empty, then to be either scrubbed out with carbolic and its windows closed, or left to decay, in case consumption was galloping through the wallpaper.

Aged ten, Ronnie and schoolfriend Harry Shaw used to sneak out with their fathers' hammers to break stones in gravel pits in a quest for treasure. Suffolk boys knew back then that certain flints held hibernating toads; if these freed creatures were in turn split open, ingested gems would glister with an emerald light. No one had found such a jewel, or a buried toad even, but the search went on. After a bout of feverish stone bashing the marble-white Harry – his pallor much envied – took to his bed and faded clean away, another casualty of consumption. He died just before Ronnie learned that stones really did contain formerly living things. A survivor then hunted alone for fossils.

Of his grandfather's funeral, in 1930, Ronnie remembered only 'a shuffling of footsteps among the leaves'. Harry's virginally white coffin and a torrent of white flowers remained with him always: 'it was bad enough to know that Harry had "gone" without having to see where he had gone. Not above the blue sky but down into the deepest, muddiest hole imaginable. Down, down he went, the undertaker's men letting out white straps for what seemed like an hour whilst the rector shouted prayers into the wind. Such sadness. We, the other boys and myself, were rushed into mortality, something which previously had belonged only to grown-ups and animals. Our black armbands marked us, as trees for felling are marked, for the earth.'[6]

Harry's deathbed lay in a house beside the Victoria Hall where the Dramatic Society performed and where dance music played on Saturdays, lending him an added glamour. The next call on a tubercular schoolfriend was to a terrace near the railway station. Lily Ward had an ethereal beauty, her skin white and waxen, her long, dark hair uncut since thoughts were already turning to the laying out of the body and how she must look her best for eternity. Graves for Harry and Lily were dug by George Blythe.

With repetition and confirmation, fear of death subsided for Ronnie. Dread gave way to understanding of the naturalness of earthly decay. Bible messages, taken to heart and head, assisted the philosophy of acceptance – while strengthening his faith. The fact that you could die at any moment made life more precious. The point, or counterpoint, to the inevitability and infinity of death was to live in a creative present. And not to fritter a second.

Death was almost a homely business for the Blythes; the children earned pennies from Father by gathering bags of moss for grave coverings. At Christmas they helped him add wreaths of berries, holly, fir and ivy. George bought a new suit each year and wore his old one to work in a display of respect and dignity. He joked that he had 7,000 people under him; yet, true to form, when offered the post of cemetery superintendent, with more pay and a better house, he declined. 'Mum was furious,' Connie said. 'She would have liked him to move up the ladder, but I suspect he refused because of his poor handwriting.'

9

Watchful Vigilance

ONE VIVID MEMORY from Ronnie's childhood was of 'going for walks with Mother and telling her lies about the distance. "No, it's only a little ways further", I would tell her. And we'd walk and walk.'[1] In truth, he wanted to outpace his guardian and go his own way.

Tilly led her children on church-run summer outings to sedate Felixstowe, when they longed for gaudy Clacton-on-Sea. Once, in Maldon for a change, there was the disappointment of alighting to river mud. Ronnie 'sulked and was what they called "quiet", which I knew was hurtful. But this grief did have its positive side for it fixed the Blackwater geography in my memory as accurately as a snapshot, right down to the litter bobbing about under the landing-stages and the texture of the earth on which we sat. It all seemed messy, empty and impoverished, yet, as the day drew on, absorbing in the most private sense. When I got home my pockets were full of things to remind me of it, flowers, sticks, stones and the Swan Vesta matchbox boat I had made and sailed across the salty pool. I miss Maldon as one always does miss places where one has been perfectly sad.'[2]

There were also rare trips to London to see Tilly's sisters in Bloomsbury and take in the sights (St Paul's, Big Ben, the Tower) broadly along the way. On a first visit to the National Gallery, aged eight, Ronnie gazed through the keyhole of an antique Dutch model house at an immaculate *trompe l'œil* interior of furnished rooms. But not for long. Tilly was always in a rush to be back on the coach before nightfall. London gave her the creeps.

Mostly there were meandering walks with Mother to Long Melford and Lavenham, and perhaps the treat of a bus ride home. The latter destination had drifted from medieval might into 'a forgotten, off the map place like a town in a fairy story, all piled up roofs and cobbled streets, plus a palace here and there'.[3] Tilly was still enthralled by the romance of the countryside: 'Walking with Mother long ago, lopping the heads off flowers as we went, I was told what a pity it was to have given birth to such an unkind boy.'[4]

Ronnie may have responded viscerally in that uncharacteristic instant to a moment of shock. His manner gentle and graceful, his hair curled and lustrous, he had an epicene quality which country people would have derided in private as effeminate. Although probably well intentioned, and possibly short-sighted, a woman encountered on an early walk looked at Ronnie and gushed: 'What a lovely little girl!' Those five words resounded in nightmares as a cue for contempt and ridicule. They spurred further retreat into introspection and guardedness, the best form of self-protection being never to give ammunition to the enemy, never to give yourself away. Safety lay in being the observer, not the observed. Watchfulness had always held a note of vigilance. Now happiness rested in solitary adventures with stories for company.

In a letter to the novelist Patricia Highsmith, written when he was fifty, Ronnie recalled erotic childhood love: 'As a little boy I fell deeply in love more than once. There was no sex, not even the childishly explorative kind, but with a school friend named Alan there was a dream of him naked. We were about nine. But I felt the same about a little girl called Priscilla Carter (the first time I have ever written her name). She was killed while serving in one of those women's forces during the last war. I really did feel a deep love for both these children but never became a close friend of either.'[5]

Unscathed by the puritanism of his background, Ronnie was wholly at home in his body. In his hundredth year he informed a chiropodist as a simple matter of fact that his feet had always been beautiful. A little earlier he told a friend that he still had 'the legs for jeans'. More people would notice powerful workman's hands attached to his faunlike figure.

Once a week, aged eight or nine, Ronnie waited at the Big Tree to meet Tilly, returning laden from the market at Bury St Edmunds. She would be tired and in need of help to carry everything home. 'It was a bus-stop on the Sudbury–Lavenham road, a stagged oak on its last legs growing from a little green . . . "The Big Tree, please", all the ladies would say to the conductor, and the bus would shake and rattle under scores of far bigger oaks until it reached this stark and crumbling destination . . . When it rained we stood inside it, filtering its dust through our fingers, and somehow comforted.'[6]

From the age of ten an eldest son's most frequent day out came via the bus to Bury and the burdensome privilege of being Mother's special helper. The burial place of St Edmund was once second only to Canterbury as an English centre of pilgrimage. Now country people poured in for markets where Ronnie was thrilled and chilled by stallholders crying out:

> Polstead cherries! Polstead cherries!
> Red as Maria Marten's blood!

In 1827 Maria Marten had been lured to the Red Barn in the nearby village of Polstead by William Corder with a promise of elopement. But he shot and buried her, in fear she might expose his fraudulent dealings or fury over her pregnancies by other men, including his brother. A murder trial in Bury drew a macabre modern pilgrimage, with souvenir hunters also flocking to the crime scene and stripping the barn and Maria's grave bare. William was hanged and dissected, his skull perused for the cod science of phrenology.

Ronnie was a regular visitor to Bury's Moyse's Hall Museum and the display of items relating to the murder and its aftermath. Alongside a mottled Bible bound in a young man's skin, there was a wrinkled and fissured scrap of leather-like black material: part of the killer's scalp, with one delicate ear still attached. It was made gruesomely clear that punishment could also be a crime and even more revolting. Ronnie was relieved when what remained of William Corder's bones were cremated as late as 2004.

The big local attraction, over three summer days and nights, was Long Melford's traditional horse sale and funfair – though houses beside the green were boarded up in view of the carnival's habit of riotous assembly when afternoons wore on and the intake of alcohol accelerated. Pubs had special licences to open from 10 a.m. At least they did until yearly brawls turned lethal in Ronnie's boyhood and licensing reverted to the still unsober norm.

Tilly took her children early to revel in the horses and avoid the inebriation. Some dealers sold, in often rigged auctions, fifty or more stallions, colts, geldings, mares and foals in every equine form, from Suffolk Punches to ponies and donkeys. As farmers shouted bids in a makeshift ring, barkers bawled out all the fun of the fairground – from swingboat rides and merry-go-rounds with galloping horses chasing garish ostriches to freak and shriek shows, shooting galleries and coconut shies, steam organs, fortune tellers, gingerbread sellers, china stalls and weight-lifting and wrestling contests.

Ronnie loved the way naphtha lights from whirling carousels glittered on a miraculous Suffolk church – always his absolute favourite – as rollicking music churned out on the summer green. He would invariably go inside to see Tudor lords and ladies in stained glass shaking their heads as if at the hullabaloo outside but actually in a last gasp of Suffolk society before the Reformation.

When the BBC's *Songs of Praise* was filmed in Long Melford church, and an elderly Ronnie was interviewed as a celebrity worshipper and architectural expert, the programme dramatised his youthful self cycling to the churchyard. A middle-class boy shown on a leisurely exercise had none of the real Ronnie's ardour and longing.

'My teenage self cycled to the fair . . . the roundabout with its mirror and lights and mad music, the swings with the girls' skirts flying and voices screaming, the passionate glances from strangers, the sordid sideshows, the strange excitement, the moonlit majesty of the vast church above and the Tudor palace below. And then, after only three days, the fair all gone. Just wounded grass and sawdust from the coconut shies.'[7]

There were two encampments of caravans, wagons and tents, one for show folk and one for gypsies. Ronnie gravitated to the latter. His early library loans had included the 1850s novelised memoirs *Lavengro* and *The Romany Rye* by wanderer George Borrow, with their heroine Belle Berners from the Great House at Long Melford. Neither of two stately homes in the village, this was the workhouse.

In her youth, Ronnie's grandmother had watched the customary burning of a deceased Romany chief's caravan on Lavenham heath.

Now he was thrilled by the virile culture of swarthily handsome nomads whom others dealt with sparingly and spurned if they possibly could. He longed to climb into a colourful caravan with a cosy interior for the adventures of the open road with a gypsy guide. The horse-drawn transport of delight would move reassuringly slowly so that everything could be savoured along the way, the stomach happily settled.

He embarked on youthful vagabondage via *The Autobiography of a Super-Tramp*. Author W. H. Davies had lost a leg while hopping a train, so Ronnie sometimes likened him to an uncle who made light of similar misfortune with expert handling of a horse and gig – throwing his reins to the stable-boy at the White Horse in Sudbury on market days.

For all the insularity of his native district, and the ongoing fierceness of old laws against vagrancy, itinerants abounded. Tinkers, tramps, travelling salesmen, gypsies – workforce and idling force – brought dramatic disturbance, a mainstay of rural literature. Tramps were forever traipsing eighteen miles between workhouses to shelter for the night. Everyone could recognise and classify a seasonal stranger: 'gypsies were everywhere when I was a boy. They came regularly to the house, for mother would only have their split ash clothespegs with the little tin band. And they did piece-work in summer, pea-picking, soft fruit gathering, hence the chalked board outside the pub, "No Gypsies, No Travellers". There was a green lane known as the Gull where we found stamped-out hearths and blackened cans, and evidence of ponies. In no time fireweed came to hide the mess . . .

'We knew a woman tramp called Nellie Eighteen and her lover Boxer who refused to sleep in the Spike (workhouse) and who resided briefly in ruined buildings of all kinds, and were accepted as part of the wandering population. Fanciful things were said about them. But they were tramps and not gypsies. We all knew the difference. You wouldn't find tramps pushing a pram.'[8]

Nellie Eighteen became Ellie Nineteen in a Blythe short story, where she shares a poacher's feast with the narrator:

> And then she went into a gorse thicket and soon returned with a big, steaming can. It was matt with smoke-black and swung from a bent wire handle. The smell which came out of it was impossibly glorious. She swayed it like a censer under my nose and laughed.

'The Phasian bird,' she said.

'It smells like pheasant.'

'They are apt to,' she said.

'Is it − is it pheasant?' I asked, guiltily.

'To me, at this moment, it's supper.' She fished the delicious, slippery brown fragments out with twigs. I have never tasted anything so good since. And the quantity! I could feel myself stretching.

'We won't ask each other questions,' she said.

'No,' I agreed.

'Only one thing.'

I looked across at her. She had removed the big, broken hat and her long hair streamed on to her shoulders.

'Folks have to live as they can.' [9]

With all the roaming of human beings, Ronnie used to wonder why animals − horses in particular − tolerated fences and hedges. 'Why didn't they just jump over them and gallop off to Bedfordshire, this county having become for some reason a far freedom in my imagination?' [10]

Cleanliness had been next to godliness in the Blythe household. Friday night was bath night, with six children taking turns to soak in a tin tub filled with pans of hot water from the range. There was much hair brushing and combing − as well as braiding and curling (tying with rags overnight) for the girls. Thickly flowing locks, from dark to whitened luxuriance in later decades, were Ronnie's lasting pride and glory. He knew that in workhouses − or armies or prisons or hospitals − they hacked off your hair. Letting it loose was a mark of liberation.

Mr Mead the barber was the chief villain of his childhood. 'It cost sixpence for him to ruin your hair,' Ronnie said eight decades later. 'I would never let anyone touch it after that. I always did it myself. He used to say that I should have been a girl with hair like that. He sat me on a high-chair and cut it all off, then plastered my head with horrible Brylcreem. Mother used to wash it off. She took pride in our hair but was mindful of what the neighbours might think.'

10

A Pauper Palace

Dᴜʀɪɴɢ ᴛʜᴇ ᴘʀᴏʟᴏɴɢᴇᴅ slump between the wars, poor people dreamed of paradise in a council house – with undamp walls, unleaking roofs, indoor plumbing, electric light and freedom from infestation and sudden eviction.

Refuge dwellings were rising in pairs, rows and estates all over the place, though rents were too high for many rural labourers. George Blythe had a local authority wage as a gravedigger and his name on the Sudbury waiting list, so that in 1937, when Ronnie was fourteen, the family was rehoused in Jubilee Road, a name honouring the 25-year reign of George V. Two short brick and pebble-dashed terraces, behind privet hedges and with long back gardens, now stood in the late king's memory. Twenty houses were available and the Blythes were nineteenth in the queue. Again they hired a horse and dray to convey everything they owned, and the children followed on foot.

This little piece of municipal heaven gave the boys and girls separate sleeping places for the first time. With four bedrooms, there were only two Blythes per room, though Ronnie and Harold still shared a bed. There was also the luxury of piped cold water and an inside toilet and bath. Sixpence in an electric copper heated water for bucketing into the bath.

The new house lay on high ground above the Horse and Groom on East Street – one of nearly forty pubs serving a town of 7,000 people – where George was soon a regular. Best of all for his country family, 22 Jubilee Road gave way to lanes, paths and greenery stretching back to Chilton and Acton.

The Blythes awaited a pauper palace all through the royal dramas of 1936 – from the death of George V in January to the abdication of Edward VIII and the accession of George VI in December. They listened on the wireless, having finally been able to afford a radio set, though it was silenced every Sunday when novels remained unopened. Jubilee Road still hosts a rare postbox for the king of less than a year, with his initials and number and the crown he never wore.

The radio had an electrifying impact. Save for Tilly and vicars, virtually everyone Ronnie knew spoke with a Suffolk accent, and most characters in books could be imagined using the same soft burr. Even if elementary school teachers struck out the dialect word 'shew' in essays in favour of 'showed', they too spoke in the local lilt, with every sentence ending in an uplift like a question. But the clipped tones of the British Broadcasting Corporation – an institution a month older than Ronnie – were a shaming revelation.

Now we might laugh at the plummy voices of pioneering BBC presenters, suggesting recruitment from the outer ranks of the royal family. But in the 1930s this uniform drawl, delivered in a belief that it was understandable to all, irritating to none and geographically neutral, sent out the unspoken message to millions of listeners that they themselves used improper English. Whether subliminally or deliberately, the teenage Ronnie set about changing his voice – if not from snobbery in himself then from a deep awareness of it in others. Above anything and anyone, he desired the classless anonymity of the observer, recorder and artist. Paradoxically, to be taken seriously, he needed to emulate the sounds of the educated elite. Within a decade his disqualifying accent had vanished without trace.

He was also to hide his native poverty in literary and generalised disguises. When questioned on personal matters, he would say that he came from 'an old farming family'.[1] If pressed further, he might add that ancestral shepherds had evolved into 'small farmers', wiping away inherited hardship like a stain. It was not in his humanitarian nature to complain for himself. In a television profile at the age of sixty, which he plotted and presented, he said simply that his family had agricultural roots and in his childhood they had 'apparently lived on air'.[2]

Ronnie was not the only one concerned with how others might perceive him. The Blythe siblings were gleeful when Arthur Boggis, boxer and butcher, roared up from London in his motor car. An ensuing spree would surely feature ice-cream. The bluff and jolly benefactor came with his 'sister' Emily Boggis – Tilly's half-sister. Later they learned that Uncle Arthur was really Emily's son, born when she was seventeen. Such deception was traditional for the Boggises, Blythes and so many other families.

Welcoming party for Uncle Arthur and Aunt Emily in Jubilee Road.

Even with improved domestic conditions, the Blythes were still near the bottom of the social pile. Jubilee Road was in an area of slum clearance known as the Wents. Although partly developed under the Homes For Heroes scheme, it retained a rough reputation; many parents told their children not to play there. Despite enviable facilities and substantial rents, there was a stigma against council housing along with a horror of charity. Self-respect was based on self-support. Not to be able to provide for yourself and your family suggested moral failure.

In Tilly's mind, however, there was still a hierarchy of poverty. She told her children not to mix with rougher neighbours – but also never to be rude. She observed this social rule by greeting anyone acceptable with a formal 'How do you do?' The unaccepted got a curt nod and the word 'Do' while she moved quickly on.

Sudbury had prospered in the Middle Ages from textile industries and, although silk weaving persisted, fine historic buildings remained intact and often untouched through harder times with no funds for restoration and wreckage. For those not living in them, the town had picturesque hovels tilting in streets with evocative names such as Inkerman Row and Gooseberry Row.

Walking, always walking, Ronnie learned the lie of the land and the clinging on of traditional rural crafts and skills. It was taken for granted that children were fascinated by the fiery furnace of the blacksmith's forge, so youthful crowds gathered unhindered at the doors of Mr Hume at Sudbury or Mr Huffey at Lavenham – taciturn men with rolled-up sleeves and braces who ignored age-old questions as to why horses being shod went unhurt amid the smoke and flames. 'Their sparks flew but never their tempers. If we gawped too close there would be little more than a "Mind your backs there." The mare with her foot scorching on the tripod would blink at us benignly.'[3]

Seventy years later, Ronnie retraced his walk to school and recalled the passing scene in perfect order. 'There they still were, the cottages-turned-sweetshops, the modest terraces, the cuts and alleys, the pubs on the corners, the monkey puzzle trees, the letter-boxes with V.R., the doorways, the coping stones where we sat and swung our legs.

'I could hear, though this time in my head, the clang of the shop bells on the C-springs which brought Miss Scott, haunted, silent, unwelcoming to serve us boiled sweets, or Mrs Gilder, a floury Juno, to hand us doughnuts. Miss Scott carried the exactitude of weights and measures to the limit and would, they said, have halved a toffee. Mrs Gilder knew nothing about weights and measures but everything there was to know about hungry children and sent us off with more than we durst expect or could have paid for . . .

'And there is where the blacksmith's should have been but a new road has pushed it over, and there is the Patty-man's shop, so small, however did he get into it. He had a double life as a potato-cake seller and town crier. The handsome Suffolk white-brick terrace where the sweep lived, and the Miss Willises, "Dressmakers" on a swinging card, did their expert business, has come up in the world, and would not be below the consideration of the local commuters. The Miss Willises were identical twins . . . if a school cap was raised to them there would be a double Mona Lisa smile, fleeting, transforming. Not so Miss Baker at Pont's Palings – the artist Dupont, Gainsborough's handsome nephew, had lived there – she would croquet conkers at us through the iron rails with unbending skill but never a smile. For her the lovely horse chestnut which dominated her street garden was an annual penance demanded of her by God.'[4]

The wisteria-covered house that was Pont's Palings, on the corner of East Street and North Street, gave way to a bus station. 'They tore down the railing, cut down the tree, concreted over the garden, and we could buy tickets for five shillings (25p) for the Corona Coach to London.'[5]

On North Street, Ronnie could still walk through the familiar entrance gate to St Gregory's and St Peter's School, below the founding date of 1747. But no hope now that the school would ever honour its most illustrious old boy with a wall plaque. There was neither hope nor walls: the building had been levelled in the 1980s for a car park.

Although Ronnie came to relish a rural quietude, the soundtrack of an industrious Sudbury never quite left him. Revisiting in his eighties, he noted: 'Market day in the small Suffolk town. Brilliant March sunshine. Three times as many stalls as in my boyhood and many times less noise. Instead of shouting and entertaining, the stallholders quietly cower beneath their awnings . . . The faint howl of the sawmill, the thump and splash of the flourmill, the rich reek of the maltings, the marvellous scent of the numerous family bakers and that of many other back-shop trades, the musk and ring of the blacksmith's forge, the piteous cries coming from the cattle-market are no more . . . Thus this recessional quiet.'[6]

Between the wars cattle were still being driven, with many shouts and much lowing, to market through narrow streets, or else reversing the route to pasture on the Common Lands over the river. And there were daily drives between meadows and town dairies for milking. Having concluded their market business, farmers repaired to their customary inn table for roast beef.

The Stour wound around Sudbury and impressed itself upon a

valley landscape in flow and flood. It teemed with traffic. Horse-drawn barges run by the Constable family and painted by the artist were scuttled at Ballingdon as late as the First World War. In the 1930s they could still be seen below the water surface like inert black whales.

While recalling floods from childhood, where water washed in and out of brick-floored cottages leaving little damage, Ronnie always saw danger in the Stour: he had nearly drowned here when he was eight. So, he never joined the groups of bathing boys, jumping from banks and bridges and cavorting among the yellow flags and water lilies like the party in the *Akenfield* film.

Many – girls especially – never learned to swim back then. Water, still carried into houses in pails, was used sparingly. Older generations of the poor brewed beer or tea because water could be lethal; in large amounts it remained ominous. Murky pools known as meres were the preserve of pike and dragons, and lures for anyone with a yen to end it all: 'bad lots, betrayed girls, the usual thing. Plots for Thomas Hardy – not for natural history.'[7]

John Constable's painting *The Hay Wain* – reverie of summer heat, with wagon axles cooling in the Stour; now the iconic image of rural England – unlocked bittersweet memories. 'I spent my boyhood by such water, wading in a bit, bare toes squeezing the mud. It provided my first sense of ennui.'[8]

Sudbury also boasted three grand medieval churches. Ronnie became a choirboy in the oldest and grandest, the former collegiate church of St Gregory. When changing in the vestry, he was watched by the Nut – the skull of patron Simon Sudbury. This exalted son of Suffolk had been the Archbishop of Canterbury and Lord Chancellor who crowned the boy-king Richard II and rashly devised a poll tax to avert a royal financial crisis, inciting the Peasants' Revolt and his beheading.

Now the lofty head behind glass made a mirror for choirboys when they needed to fix their ruffs and comb their hair. The boys 'stared out mortality, lost in our own reflections, eye to socket with the Archbishop'.[9]

As Canon Hughes thundered out the Litany in a Welsh accent, his bald head glistening with the effort, Ronnie's hands stroked the silk-smooth armrests of a choir stall while his thoughts strayed to carved misericords including a likeness of Simon Sudbury's dog. His musings might then drift towards a monumental tomb to Georgian merchant Thomas Carter whose Latin inscription he loved – not least since it helped him, in the most secret part of a self-education campaign through reading, to learn the classical language. And so the son of one of Sudbury's poorest families translated: 'Traveller, I will relate to you a wondrous thing, when the aforementioned breathed his last, a Sudbury camel passed through the eye of a needle. If thou hast wealth, go and do likewise.'

As always, he made the most of a wandering mind and wondering imagination – later, in a sermon, praising childhood daydreaming in class or pew. It faded in maturity except for 'artists, poets and a few saints and the not quite sane'. In his youthful case: 'Trapped birds and butterflies, and once a dragonfly from the Stour just outside zigzagging close enough to the wide summer door for it to escape, which it could not, would preoccupy me. Eventually tremendous praying on my part caused it to zig out to the river. I went with it, leaving my body in the church as cover for my dream flight.'[10]

Amid such dream flights Ronnie's brilliance masqueraded as backwardness. 'You'll be late for your own funeral,' his mother said. Or again: '"Your head is like a sieve" – Mother. Not true. My head is like an attic, full of things that might come in handy. You never know.'[11] Hers was the lead voice in a chorus of accusation and interrogation. Someone muttered: 'Reading's the problem.' Someone else passed a hand close to his eyes and enquired: 'Are you still with us?' Pithily and witheringly, he recalled his silence in the face of pressing enquiry: 'The boy Joseph told his dreams – that was his mistake. "A penny for them," said grandmother, but there was no sale. "Snap out of it," said father.'[12]

While still in the ecstasy of boyhood, Ronnie acquired a liking for melancholy. He transcribed on to the flyleaf of the family everyday Bible, in the loopy copperplate taught at his elementary school, the words of George Matheson's most soulful Victorian hymn:

> O Love that wilt not let me go,
> I rest my weary soul in thee.
> I give thee back the life I owe
> that in thine ocean depths its flow
> may richer, fuller be . . .

Reopening the Bible many decades later, he reread verses he had written out with such care. And then he said quietly: 'I ask you.' Faith in God and nature had been almost at one for such a country child, along with a sprinkling of superstition for good luck. Now browned and brittle, Ronnie's youthful markers for beloved biblical passages were four-leaf clovers. He retained a deep respect for folk-lore, not least as magical stories. Faith and nature were all wrapped in festivals and rituals – notably at Easter:

'First potatoes, football matches and the boat-club row to Henny Swan was Good Friday. A handful of saints would have been scattered across the nave for the Three Hours and all the shops in the small market town would have closed. Good Friday, a day when nobody seemed to know quite what to do, mourn or plant or rush about. Early in the morning, sevenish, we were sent to Mr Gilder or Mr Unwin for the hot-cross buns, and they smelled holy in their paper bags. We devoured them with devotion.'[13]

With a piety that could never be dogmatic, he was only intrigued when the Shrine of Our Lady, originally sited in St Gregory's, was recreated in Sudbury's Roman Catholic church. The commissioner was the priest Father Moir, the donor his Protestant mother. Ronnie later wrote: 'My mother thought he should have been hanged for doing this, although not drawn and quartered, as she was a devout Christian.'[14]

11

Writerly Company

A NEW HIGH School for Girls soon rose in the field beside the
Blythe house – aspirant partner to Sudbury Grammar School
for boys, endowed in 1491.

Such ancient and modern pathways to professions and univer-
sities were still out of bounds for most children. The United
Kingdom had 5.3 million school pupils in 1938. Not even a fifth
of fourteen-year-olds remained in education and far fewer made
it to university; just 9,311 graduates were awarded first degrees and
1,480 higher degrees.[1]

Awards had long been available for some poor children to claim
an elite education. When Tilly was at St Clement Danes School
one student had won a grammar school scholarship. This feat was
so fantastic that teachers and pupils had a day's holiday in honour
of the prodigy. So, Tilly knew that escape through education was
possible even if exceptional. And now she took positive action to
assist her younger children. Once the high school was up and
running, Connie won a scholarship at fourteen – her advancement
was so successful that Eileen was allowed to follow. Gerry then
secured a scholarship to the grammar school.

Tilly made ends meet by making clothes and finding second-hand
bargains – including a piano. Connie, Eileen and Gerry were then
treated to lessons, where Gerry was found to possess real talent.
Such a gift entailed costlier tuition with the organist at St Peter's
church. It also added an obligation to the missionary zeal of Tilly

Connie, Harold, Bernard and Ronnie.

Blythe: Gerry and a portable harmonium fired up hymn singers on Sudbury street corners.

The Blythes were a little better off by the late 1930s, but nothing like enough to explain the disparity of educational opportunity between the eldest and youngest children – especially the glaring neglect of Ronnie. Being overlooked seemed to boil down to the matter of personal behaviour. Ronnie's curious mind, far from being nurtured, was perceived as an impediment to getting on and fitting in – an embarrassing and annoying sign that he was away with the fairies.

The chasm between Tilly and George was not in age but in outlook. However briefly, Tilly had shone at school. She venerated missionary teachers and wished she could have been one herself, or at least married to one. Mother and all the children were fervent borrowers of books from the public library in North Street; Father ventured no further than a local newspaper. Blythe appetites for the lending service were limited only by the twopenny fees, which meant speed-reading in Jubilee Road given the family queue for each volume.

Ronnie raced through Baroness Orczy's Scarlet Pimpernel novels. Set during the Reign of Terror following the French Revolution, the sagas' apparently foppish English hero adopted a dashing secret identity to rescue aristocrats from the guillotine. His symbol was a tiny flower. It wasn't so much that the boy reader in the Sudbury council house had found a romantic hero from a class beyond his ken; he already knew a lot about the art of concealment and could identify with a master practitioner.

Similarly, there was a romantic and erotic reading to the piratical world of *Treasure Island* by Robert Louis Stevenson. And Daniel Defoe's *Robinson Crusoe* was a cue for fantasies of how a castaway far from a desert island might be happily companioned with a fellow misfit. He would learn with glee that Man Friday may have sprung to life on paper in Bury St Edmunds.

Books acquired permanently were precious possessions – Ronnie adding several as school prizes, including *Boswell's Life of Johnson*. Part of the mystery of Ronnie's minimal formal education may derive from what his mother viewed as his fragility. He clearly had an androgynous quality and a gentleness easily mistaken for weakness. She may have wanted to protect him from rising above himself – and out of her power.

Certainly, while always observing the biblical duty to honour his father and mother, expressing polite respect when speaking of them at all, he retained a revulsion against maternal control. In his short story 'Bride Michael', a young man is in danger of being overwhelmed by a religious vocation. But he is most immediately oppressed by an enquiring and affectionate letter from his mother ('I love you because you are a good boy'). It unleashes a furious tirade: 'If loving parents was such a normal thing, would the prophets have needed to mention it so often? The last time he had gone home his mother had taken his face in her hands as if it was a piece of her own property. When it looked as though she might kiss his mouth he had fought back a scream.'[2]

The other Blythe children would look back fondly on the maternal love Tilly extended, having received so little herself. 'Matilda was a good mother, lovely and interesting,' said Connie. 'But their lives were blighted by the Depression.' Harold recalled intrinsic kindness: poor as they were, Sunday roast lunch was shared with two elderly neighbours. Tilly toiled equally on weekdays when the children came home from school for a hot meal, to be joined by George walking down the hill from the cemetery and then back up again.

George was generally silent and distant. Connie remembered him 'jiggling us on his knees, making up a silly little rhyme, with us laughing; but he didn't have a lot to do with us growing up'. Every Friday, George gave Tilly half his wages for family bills, keeping an equal part for his beer and tobacco. For all her disdain of alcohol, and unbending sense of Christian behaviour, she never complained. When Connie queried the division of the money, she answered: 'Well, he did earn it.'

The Blythe children faced different prospects as they finished their education. Connie won her mother's backing to leave school at sixteen so she could train as a nurse in London – an echo of Tilly's own experience, and all the more since the career move led to Connie meeting the man she was to marry. Ronnie and the next two brothers, however, were evicted from the classroom at fourteen with no academic qualifications: Harold became a butcher's assistant, Bernard a mechanic. In the summer of 1937 Ronnie faced making his own way in the world – and adding to the slender family income.

At least Ronnie was apprenticed into the world of literature, albeit at the lowest level. He found a job in what he remembered as a Sudbury bookshop – sparing him a portering post in the cottage hospital still widely viewed as the workhouse.[3] Cutmore's in North Street, next to the White Horse pub, was really a bookshop, stationer and newsagent with a separate range of ladies' lingerie. The miniature department store was later to be replaced by a branch of Woolworth's.

Mercifully, the most junior sales assistant dealt mostly with the books. He enjoyed handling them and talking about them, if not actually selling them. What he really wanted to do was read them. In breaks he was always buried in a book. And in work time he gazed out of the window.

The view took in St Peter's church, on Market Hill, with its guardian griffins on each pinnacle to keep Satan at bay, its processions and resounding voices at evensong. Outside, a drinking fountain had a chained brass cup like a Holy Grail, from which Ronnie imagined 'somehow mysteriously tasting the water in the New Testament'.[4] And then came a thrilling statue of Tom Gainsborough, the local lad who had put Sudbury on the cultural map, 'pitched above the noisy market stalls in a stance of supreme achievement'.[5]

Ronnie never wrote about his bookshop job; indeed, much of

his Sudbury life would be dropped from conversation if not memory, as there was a strong sense that real, writerly existence began with the belated winning of independence. But the 1939 census gave his occupation as library assistant. This new posting went unrecorded in a *Who's Who* entry. When quizzed in his nineties, he looked surprised, then said: 'Oh yes, I did have a silly job in a little Sudbury library.' It was not the principal public library in North Street, but a small subscription lending service.

He recalled 'a kind of corner shop, with immense timbers, and part of an ancient house where John Bunyan had stayed when he came to give the Suffolk Dissenters a piece of his mind.' Ronnie pictured him 'in the timbered room, now lined with novels; or tying his horse to a gigantic nail that protruded from the blackened king-post'.[6]

Now a voracious and omnivorous reader read himself an education, first devouring the literary classics of England and France. Then, as an author in the making, he paid special attention to the contemporary rural short stories of A. E. Coppard, H. E. Bates and H. A. Manhood, for subject matter and style.

The library assistant was also engaged in his first substantial piece of writing. It was a critique of Suffolk poet Robert Bloomfield whose rural cycle, *The Farmer's Boy*, caused a sensation when published in 1800 – shortly before the Napoleonic Wars. Ronnie recognised an idyllic view of life on the land in a piece written for publication in the *Suffolk and Essex Free Press*.

Bloomfield was ultimately a connector to a far better peasant poet: John Clare. From the seismic jolt of first discovering 'The Nightingale's Nest' to directing that it should be read at his memorial service, here was the boy in the library's foremost literary hero. Born 129 years apart, their early experiences were strikingly similar. The 'scant and spare' nest of the elusive bird seemingly made of song was a metaphor for their impoverished, isolated and exultant boyhoods:

> How curious is the nest. No other Bird
> Uses such loose materials or weaves
> Their dwellings in such spots – dead oaken leaves
> Are placed without, and velvet moss within,
> And little scraps of grass – and scant and spare
> Of what seems scarce materials, down and hair . . .

Beneficiaries of everything they lacked, John Clare and Ronald Blythe were untrained and unconstrained – with original voices purified by observation and imagination. And, for all the material deprivation, both had access to literature. The tutors chosen in print obliterated their solitude in writerly fellowship.

'Writers do not retreat into books, they advance. They meet their equals, their betters, their inferiors, but rarely know where they themselves stand. All they know is that they are in good company – the best that they are likely to find. To enter a book is to escape from a prison or an emptiness.'[7]

12

Great Explorations

R APTURE FOR RONALD Blythe was complete when he bought with early earnings a sturdy Rudge bicycle. At last, he could move at speed without waves of travel sickness.

He thought nothing of riding fifty miles from parish to parish with Henry Munro Cautley's newly published *Suffolk Churches and Their Treasures*. Now, a love of the mysterious and magical atmosphere of churches was enlarged by burgeoning appreciation of their role as houses of words:

'These are the walls within which everything was said: centuries of birth words, marriage words, more words, death words, gossip, the language of the hymn poets and the song writers, of the Latin and English liturgists, and the immense Bible translation language. All this language said here in the local accent. This place is witness through the year to the very creation of literary and colloquial English as getting on for a thousand years of sermons battered away at human nature. So it is a house of words as well as a house of wood and stone. No old church can be understood if one omits the eloquence factor.'[1]

Ronnie's bicycle-broadened domain covered ancestral High Suffolk – a clay plateau once thickly wooded and still rife with ancient greens and commons. Eastward from Walsham-le-Willows to Halesworth and northward from the Deben to the Waveney valleys, the native landscape ran to hedged intimacy and sweeping vistas. Here, he felt reborn.

'What I liked and still like is the way in which the panorama dominates me. The land is all view and I am all viewer, and soon the ecological patterns and colours not only spread before me but permeate me, and I become part of what I am seeing. I can see patches of medieval forest here and there among the corn, and although I know that "the woods decay and fall", I also know that in comparison with human flesh they take ages to do so. Thus its ancientness must be one of the healing factors of landscape. High Suffolk tells me that the foundations of my view were laid in the ice-age, and the shape of almost everything which covers its surface was fashioned centuries ago. But simultaneously with its antiquity it presents the very latest crop of flowers, birds, insects and sounds. And so I too, wandering on to Monks Eleigh, have a nice sense of being just born and everything before me.'[2]

Bicycling to Wiston, he passed the East Anglian Sanatorium on a breezy hilltop. Founded in 1901 by Dr Jane Walker, the San treated incurable tuberculosis with fresh air for those unable to afford the Mediterranean or the Alps. Ronnie, in rude good health, was shocked to see grown men lined in long prams. Out in all weathers, black hoods and aprons protecting from rain and snow, the invalids raised thin, pale arms to wave eerie greetings when they caught the slowed cyclist staring.

The East Anglian Sanatorium at Wiston.

In 1917 Grace Griffith, a young Welsh doctor, began a fortnight of relief work at Wiston – then stayed to become a local legend. Arriving by horse and cart, she extended a Bures GP's rounds first on a motorbike and then in a battered car as her practice came to encompass much of West Suffolk. Dr Grace, who probably attended Ronnie's birth, was kindness and firmness combined – her car likely to contain some of her six children plus those of a farmworker whose wife needed a rest after giving birth, or any of the ten refugee Basque boys taken in during the Spanish Civil War. Her word was law, and not just because she was respected: she was loved.

Ever a firm believer in fresh-air treatment, Dr Grace acquired a family retreat at Tiger Hill, part of an ancient wood known as Assington Thicks, eventually stretching to fifty acres. This figure of magisterial gauntness escaped for an hour or two between surgeries and home visits, especially in spring for the nightingales and blue-bells. Her brickmaker's cottage in a clearing had a garden hide for badger-watching. Naturally this haven came to be shared with her patients. Ronnie and his siblings ran wild in a wood named after a tiger believed to be sabre-toothed, and later loaded so many bluebells on to their bicycles that they could barely ride them home.

The need to savour and save natural splendours served, even then, as a call to action. Native Suffolk fatalism was countered first in Assington: 'My own proto-conservationist gesture was to give five shillings towards saving a line of hedgerow oaks threatened by a local farmer. I was about fifteen, and half a lifetime on I pass them with satisfaction. Halting woodland destruction was a very parochial busi-ness then, but one requiring nerve, for it was thought disgraceful to criticise a country neighbour. Petitions such as ours could be grounds for dissent for many years.'[3]

Now Ronnie moved beyond country neighbours via a fifteen-mile bike or bus ride over the Essex border to Colchester – his shining city on a hill and Britain's oldest recorded metropolis. The Celtic and Roman hub called Camulodunum, citadel of Cunobeline (possibly Old King Cole of the nursery rhyme, certainly Shakespeare's Cymbeline), has also been linked to the Arthurian legend of Camelot. For a boy with a headful of stories, here lay the stuff of romance.

Although Colchester was the reputed birthplace of St Helena – mother of Emperor Constantine – its character for Ronnie was

marvellously masculine. A garrison town for two millennia, its streets
still filled with off-duty soldiers in search of a good time.

Here was a great historic layer cake: a Roman temple to the
deified Emperor Claudius (razed in Boudicca's rebellion) led to a
Norman castle and fortifications prompting a devastating civil war
siege. Over seventy-three summer days in 1648 some 800 horses
were eaten. Royalist defenders finally surrendered and in his youth
Ronnie was thrilled by the gallantry of their leaders, Charles Lucas
and George Lisle. Condemned to death, they had kissed 'before the
musket balls tore into their bedraggled finery'.[4] Later, he cursed
them for causing penury and ruin.

Colchester also gave him his best-loved martyr, taken to heart as
a personal saint and perfect subject for a Benjamin Britten opera.
James Parnell had become a Quaker as a teenager after walking from
his home in Retford to talk to George Fox, the dissenting religious
movement's founder, in prison in Carlisle. He returned to the Suffolk–
Essex border to share his faith – a dangerous venture in the 1650s.
'He stood outside parish churches as the congregation emerged and
"disturbed the peace". But there was no peace, only religious rants
and the like. His talk-in-Christ was a kind of poetry, but this was not
wanted. So they put him in Colchester prison, where the gaoler's
wife turned him into a sideshow, eventually murdering him. From
boyhood on, I have paused at his cell. It is an open brick fireplace,
high up in the wall, from which he fell while being exhibited.'[5]

Cycling to Hadleigh and its killing ground on Aldham Common,
Ronnie made pilgrimages to the sites of Counter-Reformation
martyrs, 'who I see stumbling to the stake along Angel Street.
Particularly the great Rowland Taylor, Rector of this wool-town
and pupil of Erasmus, and who, they said, taught the weavers so
well that he made it a little university.'[6] 'I would prop my bike against
the railings and imagine the terrible scene, the fat old man from
Northumbria . . . and the horrible magistrate from over the fields
who had slapped his face for saying his last psalm in English.'[7]

But another seventeenth-century martyr from his home patch
went unmentioned: Arthur Daniels had been born into a Roman
Catholic family at Acton Place in the 1620s and trained as a Jesuit
priest in Spain. Rashly returning to England in the grip of civil
war, he was vilely killed before a huge crowd at Tyburn in London.
Beatified in the 1930s, Arthur Daniels was not a personal saint for

Ronald Blythe. Universally humanitarian, but a seeker of low church heroes, Ronnie knew that during the brief reign of Bloody Mary in the 1550s nineteen Protestants had been burned at the stake in Colchester Castle, just like Rowland Taylor and others in Hadleigh, in the name of the religion espoused by Arthur Daniels. And thus his sympathy, though still running deep, was apparently of a lower order.

Sectarian murders in Suffolk and Essex certainly caused him to ponder his own humane gospel and the evil committed in the name of religion. 'There, where the lovers embrace, Colchester burnt men and women and boys and girls. Once, a dozen of them chained together in a single bonfire. Terrible processions would have come this way. Religion delights and worries me. But then so it did the Lord's friends and enemies, for the worst and best things descend or rise from it. It is the seat of light and darkness, of intelligence and idiocy, of tenderness and cruelty.'[8]

Ronnie's special kind of faith was a form of reverie bound up with stories and landscapes, and with poems and paintings. 'As a boy I dreamed of scholars and saints wandering around markets and cornfields, and of artists and poets sitting under the trees.'[9]

June 1939 saw the publication of Julian Tennyson's *Suffolk Scene: A Book of Description and Adventure*. Ronnie thought it hugely romantic that a youthful great-grandson of the Victorian poet had a passion for the eastern county to match his own. This long love letter between hard covers went into his bicycle basket as Britain moved inexorably towards war. It captured the mood of the moment, when the scene had never looked lovelier now that it was under threat from the Luftwaffe. The reader found common cause with the writer, who gladly trudged more than 100 miles from London to Aldeburgh and thousands all over sacred Suffolk. The best-loved Tennyson walk was in the remote area known as the Saints, between the Blyth and Waveney rivers, where Ronnie added a feeling of ancestral connection when exploring – and getting happily lost – on his bike:

'The wildest and most confusing walk you can possibly take is over that stretch covering the groups of villages known as the South Elmhalls or South Elmhams and the Ilketshalls; here, believe it or not, within a radius of a few miles are villages called St Cross or Sancroft St George, St James, St Margaret, All Saints-cum-St Nicholas, St Michael, St Peter, St Lawrence, St John, St Andrew and St Margaret again. Some are Elmhams, others are Ilketshalls, and I don't suppose that half the inhabitants know which are which. It took me all day to find my way to the Minster at St Cross when first I went there, and about midday I began to amuse myself by asking the worthies, what few of them I met, for the right road to South Elmham All Saints-cum-St Nicholas, just to note their various reactions.'[10]

As Ronnie's siblings acquired bicycles of their own, they wanted to join his marathon two-wheeled journeys. But he outstripped them all. He remembered how, at a certain spot, Connie would jump off, sit on a bank and say: 'You go on. I'll be all right.' So on – and on – he went through the limitless Suffolk lanes, leaving his family far behind him. And never looking back. This was how it was going to be.

All through the summer of 1939, in great heat and mounting menace, Ronnie cycled to see the miraculous happenings at Sutton Hoo. Here a medium had told the widowed Edith Pretty to dig in one of the mounds on her estate above the River Deben opposite Woodbridge. Local archaeologists plus gardeners Mr Spooner and Mr Jacobs set to work. They struck gold. When word of emerging wonders got out, a security detachment arrived in the form of a policeman on a bicycle. Then august Tom Kendrick came from the British Museum. Met at Woodbridge station, he was ushered into the waiting room where a tobacco tin was opened to reveal a stupendous buckle. It bore a mesh of golden snakes, birds and beasts and an ingenious triple-lock mechanism.

But for Ronnie the unearthed story was more precious than the seventh-century treasure. He was enthralled to see and conjecture: 'sunburnt archaeologists, shirtless and dusty, and the plastic sheets bellying out from their poles, looking as though the sand ship was off to Sweden once more. The fabulous boat with a glittering king at the helm would be sliding into the Deben, or whatever he called his river then, and off to Europe for, as his regalia proved, there were no limits as to how far he would go to add to his finery.'

Ronnie's friends Rhoisia and Bridget Copinger Hill, elderly twins whose family had owned land at Buxhall since 1173, would probably be making tea for the team beside the excavation: 'All three of us felt a faintly hereditary interest in what was being dug up and some ownership of the king's glorious chattels. Thus we would bump down Mrs Pretty's field track with the same ease as Lord Tollemache would bump over his drawbridge a few miles south [at moated Helmingham Hall]. The Anglo-Saxon burial site was our family grave . . . For the best inventory of what they found, read Beowulf . . . I can hear the harp being played in the hall, and the ancestral shouts and the whirling gulls.'[11]

13

Gunner Blythe

BRITAIN DECLARED WAR on Germany on 3 September 1939, two months before Ronnie turned seventeen. At first, in the 'phoney' calm-before-storm phase of the conflict, the global calamity was overshadowed by a commotion closer to home. The uproar came when a sober Sudbury mother spied her eldest son leaving a small birthday celebration in the White Horse pub. Admittedly, a minor offence had been committed, since the legal drinking age had been raised to eighteen soon after the imbiber's birth.

Ronnie had been discussing books with a friend over half pints of beer in the inn linked to the Gainsborough family, but Tilly Blythe was sure he had gone to the devil. She would wail warnings whenever he came home smelling of 'ale' – another word for brimstone and treacle. Hellfire and maternal ire notwithstanding, he continued to enjoy public houses – where in his case there would be more talking than drinking, and moments of pure and poetic revelation. Guinness was good for him.

An early conversation about poetry at the bar of the Royal Oak in Sudbury was interrupted by a rotund agent for the Ind Coope brewery. Back in 1915, on a boat bound for Gallipoli, he had been one of six ratings sent ashore at the Greek island of Skyros to bury an officer who had died from an insect bite. They dug the grave of Rupert Brooke in rocky ground – a poet's stony corner of some foreign field that was now for ever England.

It was also at the age of seventeen that Ronnie fully embraced his sexuality. Drawn to men emotionally and physically, he accepted this attraction simply as a fact of nature. He was always at ease in his own skin.

But, in an era of repression, any form of deviation from sexual and social conformity, along with its secrets, denials and lies, was also a spur for subterfuge. Some were driven to suicide when exposed as illegitimate, the now meaningless term 'bastard' being an unspeakable swear word. And to cap such eternal shame, self-killers were denied Christian rites and church burial.

While free from guilt, Ronnie went further in self-defence than mere circumspection. Escape into a dreamworld was spurred by society being at odds with his innermost inclinations. Disdain was the least of it: condemned homosexuals could end up not only as pariahs but as prisoners, serving sentences with hard labour.

He knew his mother worried about him, and what that meant. From her severe point of view – she had just defected from the Church of England to the diehard Plymouth Brethren – the wages of sin were hellishly clear. The message was droned out at three forbidding meetings every Sunday, to which the younger children were dragooned. Eileen would recall time-stopping tedium and 'always having one foot out of the door'. The Blythe siblings, save for Ronnie, would be put off formal religion altogether. But there was a sympathetic side to Tilly Blythe and a valiant attempt at empathy. When she said 'I do understand, you know', Ronnie wanted to run away more than ever.

He was aware of being desired by older men gazing with burning eyes when passing in the street. Mr Kipling, brother of a Sudbury factory owner and prisoner of a harridan wife, cast looks of infinite longing. Now Reginald Hart, an experienced lad, educated him in the coded words of the gay world and added practical tuition. There was sexual release with Ronald Poole in a haystack. And then a blond Adonis called Eric Cutts, living bravely with a fellow civil servant in Birmingham, came home to see his family in Great Cornard. Inviting Ronnie for a walk, he stopped, turned and kissed him hard against a wall, a hank of fair hair tumbling over his forehead and caressing Ronnie's face. A novice felt both elated and unworthy of a beautiful lover.

Private pleasure grew more intense and urgent as Britain faced the enormity of war and defeat after defeat. The swift fall of France in June 1940, following Nazi occupation of the Low Countries, Denmark and Norway, left besieged Britain and a far-flung Commonwealth to fight alone. It was to be a full year before Hitler turned the tide on himself by a ruinous invasion of the Soviet Union, while the United States entered the war as late as the following December with the Japanese attack on Pearl Harbor.

Amid the levelling of the ration book and price controls, the Blythes did relatively well. Besides 'Dig for Victory' produce from a long back garden, an extended clan linked to the land ensured comparative plenty. Not for them the typical restriction to an egg a week. And they already had a taste for rabbit and pigeon. There was also the occasional treat of a trip to the former public library in North Street. It was now a British Restaurant whose cheap, wholesome and morale-lifting meals were unrationed.

Sudbury cheered in April 1940 to hear one of its own on the BBC Home Service. RAF gunner William Lillie coolly related how he had fought off six Junker 88 fighter bombers over the North Sea – downing one, damaging another and forcing four to flee – while his Short Sunderland flying boat was protecting a convoy. Bill Lillie had been a St Gregory's chorister with Ronnie. Now the town laid on a welcome at the railway station for the homecoming hero. Getting wind of the fuss in store, he left the train early at Bures and walked quietly home to his family in Girling Street. He was then marched to the welcoming party by his mortified mother.

The Sudbury Territorial Gunners joined the British Expeditionary Force in France early in 1940. From April, rapid German advances overwhelmed one country after another then trapped Allied servicemen on the Channel coast. During eight days and nights from late May, 338,226 men were rescued from Dunkirk beaches by a scratch fleet of 850 boats – including Suffolk and Essex lifeboats, yachts and trawlers – mitigating the defeat before the Battle of Britain. While that aerial conflict raged in high summer above southern and eastern England, a Sunderland was shot down over the North Sea with the loss of its crew – including 21-year-old Bill Lillie. He never knew that the Battle of Britain was won by the end of October.

Just after his eighteenth birthday, in November, Ronnie received a letter of conscription into the war. The library assistant passed the army medical and was posted to the Royal Artillery – an umbrella band for more than a million men serving in 960 gunner regiments during the course of the six-year conflict. He was sent for training at Catterick Camp, near Richmond in north Yorkshire, the temporary First World War base for 40,000 men in 2,000 huts by then made permanent.

One of the Second World War's most unlikely recruits, Ronnie packed a copy of Virginia Woolf's experimental 1931 novel *The Waves* for protection. The book opened in Suffolk. Its focus on individual consciousness within a stream of human voices suited a lost soul in a barracks. At least Ronnie had never known the luxury of a room of his own. Lulled by the novel's 'careful beauty',[1] he had scarcely finished reading when the author drowned herself.

He had already spotted verses by Sidney Keyes in the *New Statesman*. And soon he felt the novelist's passing best summed up in the Keyes poem 'Elegy for Mrs Virginia Woolf'. Barely a year later, before his twenty-first birthday, the poet was killed in North Africa – raising him to the host of Blythe literary heroes with premature deaths. Eventually the Woolf tribute and other Keyes works featured in Ronnie's anthology *Components of the Scene: An Anthology of the Prose and Poetry of the Second World War*, published in 1966.

Most immediately, amid all the turmoil of displacement into wartime jeopardy, passages in *The Waves* gave glimpses of a creative, ordered and homely haven. Seventy-five years later, long after securing such a domestic paradise for himself, he picked out two paragraphs in an essay:

'"The sun struck straight upon the house, making the white walls glare between the dark windows. Their panes, woven thickly with green branches, held circles of impenetrable darkness.

'"Sharp wedges of light lay upon the window-sill and showed inside the room plates with blue rims, cups with curved handles, the bulge of a great bowl, the criss-cross pattern in the rug, and the formidable corners and lines of cabinets and bookcases."'

'Just as now, this minute,' he added. 'Nothing need be changed in the description. The virtue of such writing is to show us all over again the beauty of the ordinary, the commonplace.'[2] But such a vision was extraordinary to a reader in a vast military network, clinging only as a dream.

Catterick Camp lay in attractive countryside between the Yorkshire

Dales and North Yorkshire Moors – all, and more, now an army training ground. Ronnie wrote to a friend in the 1950s: 'We always tried to head towards Guisborough where there were particularly delicious tea arrangements. Sometimes we went to Robin Hood's Bay, sometimes to Staithes and many, many dismal times to Redcar where I learnt to ride a motor-bike.'[3]

For Gunner Blythe, who would never again ride a motorbike, this militarised terrain was hell on earth. No aggression could be drummed into him no matter how persuasively and forcefully they tried. The complete non-combatant was above hurting the proverbial fly: harming another human being was anathema to him; sacrilegious, even, since God was in everyone. Used to hiding his true character, he disguised his pacifism now. Not that it would have saved him; conscientious objectors in the good-versus-evil struggle with Hitler had a very hard time.

Ronnie came to honour two more war poets – one remaining a fantastical figure and the other becoming a friend. If Sidney Keyes had been 'the explorer of what it was like to die', Keith Douglas was 'the amazing confessor of what it was like to kill'.[4] Douglas survived the North Africa campaign and returned to England – to publish his dazzling poems in literary magazines where they were admired by Ronnie, the non-killer, like bulletins from Mars.

The poetry of R. N. Currey proved much more approachable. As did the poet himself. In 2001 Ronnie would write a long and loving introduction for Currey's Collected Poems, quoting praise from T. S. Eliot. South African Ralph Currey became a veteran teacher at Colchester Royal Grammar School, occupying the same house for over sixty years. But, his tutoring broken by war service in India, his poetic span was global. Through it all he showed what Ronnie called 'a sanity of the imagination' and an enchantment with language.

Before decades of friendship, Ronnie had bought the first volume of Currey poetry, This Other Planet, in 1940. A poem called 'Boy with a Rifle' drew on the school cricket ground's conversion to a shooting range where pupils were instructed by masters. Gradually, as Ronnie noted, the young teacher advanced from gun drill to gun war.

But Gunner Blythe never got beyond gun drill in the worst eighteen months of his life. In all the later erasures, this period of incarceration in a war machine was the most heavily censored. He neither wrote nor talked about it, dodging questions like verbal bullets. When pressed in 2014 in the peace of a summer garden, he mentioned, after a long silence, the 'boredom, futility and silliness of endless drilling'. Then he changed the subject.

The only permanent reminder of a military sentence was a poignant pencil portrait of his newly enlisted eighteen-year-old self. Drawn by G. D. Johnson – 'a fellow soldier, not a lover' – he sent it home to his mother. It is a shocking study in innocence, revealing none of the inner resilience. No wonder that throughout his early life he attracted a small army of unwanted protectors.

Since he was so clearly failing to pass muster as a private soldier, an even more hopeless attempt was made to mould him into an officer – with a training course begun in York (where he could at least marvel at the minster) and swiftly abandoned. From Catterick he was also posted briefly to a coastal battery in north-east Scotland. His next and last billet was Rye, on the Sussex coast, where he yearned to see inside Lamb House – successively the home of two of his favourite novelists, Henry James and E. F. 'Mapp and Lucia' Benson. But the Georgian haven was closed, its garden room, where Jamesian stories were penned in golden summers, bombed.

The raw recruit.

Then his mother, whose loving letters were oddly disconcerting, did a wonderful thing. A book token, enclosed with one typically misfiring missive, sent him dashing to a Rye bookshop. After delectable deliberation, he picked out the gold and blue covers on books by Marcel Proust, a name unknown to him. He bought the first two volumes in the *Remembrance of Things Past* sequence, and found that these reflections from an exquisite homosexual world were exactly what he needed at a time of barbarism and boredom. The complete set would get him through the war.

Apart from Woolf and Proust, the only positive recollection of military service was a lot of erotic action and 'some of the best sex ever with another soldier'. Was homosexuality the cause of his dismissal? Or else a nervous breakdown? Or both? Did army psychologists come to the rescue? Or did the military police pounce? Files – if they exist – are closed. All the former Gunner Blythe would say, in his nineties, was that he had been a fish out of water. And: 'In the end I think I was invalided out, in a way.'

He completed his military service fifty years later when introducing and editing *Private Words: Letters and Diaries from the Second World War*. It contains no confession but evidence, perhaps, between the lines. As in: 'Both the call-up and the various forces volunteer centres, for all their vetting of body and mind, netted some chronically unsuitable specimens. Barrack-room mates, sergeants and eventually the commanding officer himself would find themselves defeated by what at first they preferred to see as something which could be licked into shape but which . . . had no controllable pattern. Army ways came up against a powerful absence of assimilation.'[5]

And in a chapter entitled 'Conchie': 'out of the short-lived popular renunciation of war as a means of settling the arguments of nations, there remained a small group of people whose principles, religion and common sense combined made them stick to their guns, as it were, and refuse to take up arms of any kind. However sincere they were, they often made a poor showing before some examining board or other and were forced into uniform. It was then that to have the courage of one's convictions was to possess very great courage indeed, for to be a conchie in a barracks was like being a sex offender in a gaol, the object of all abuse.'[6]

Ronnie would always appear tentative, and some might construe that trait as cowardice. In fact, he was armed with the fearlessness of the writer on the front line of life – called up to bear witness to the glories and follies of human existence. He had to see, hear and feel what was going on, until he could observe and absorb no longer or others intervened.

But the low point of his life was also a stroke of tremendous luck. If Ronnie had been drafted into the 5th Suffolks – like his father and so many other Sudbury men – he would have been posted to the Far East. The 4th and 5th Suffolk battalions reached Singapore just before a Japanese onslaught. In February 1942 they were part of the biggest surrender in British history.

Some 770 Suffolk lives were to be lost, mostly through execution, disease, beatings and starvation as they slaved to build a 260-mile Burma–Siam railway with its infamous bridge on the River Kwai, or when shipped to toil in Japan itself. Their sufferings were recorded in the harrowing drawings of cartoonist Ronald Searle, who wrote: 'Basically all the people we loved and knew and grew up with simply became fertiliser for the nearest bamboo.'[7]

Emaciated and ghostly survivors who returned to Sudbury after the Japanese surrender in August 1945 were never the same again. True to Suffolk form, abiding terrors went mostly unmentioned.

14

To the Headland

RELEASED IN MAY 1942, Ronnie had saved enough money for a recuperative holiday in west Cornwall. Still only nineteen, and in a last bow to maternal protection, he took his mother. Looking back, he thought the destination appealed because 'it was about as far as one could go'.[1]

Then and ever after, the rail journey from London to Penzance was heaven for him. From a seat on the left side of the carriage, his face was glued to the window, too spellbound even to open a book. He loved the way the train, after a long ride through greenery, almost hit the sea at Dawlish in a kind of fanfare. It then ran along coast and estuary before flying over the Royal Albert Bridge, sky high above the River Tamar, dividing Devon and Cornwall.

And then came the procession of stations named after Cornish saints – Germans, Austell, Erth, Ives – as the locomotive steamed on through woods, moors and meadows. Finally, Mount's Bay and Penzance itself, seemingly far out in the Atlantic, Cornish granite having given way to an ocean of ultramarine stretching away into azure and indigo. It was a world away from the grey and brown North Sea – and light years from army khaki.

But bright colour was a discovery of the next morning, for they alighted in sea fog and a blanketing melancholy amid a blare of fog warnings. Lugging cases filled with a few clothes and a lot of library books, they walked along the seafront to the fishing and painting village of Newlyn. Ronnie had written to reserve two rooms in a

The view from Newlyn to Penzance.

terraced guesthouse on Chywoone Hill above the harbour: bed, breakfast and evening meal, three guineas each for the week.

Their landlady, a 'beautiful dark Andalusian-looking woman of perhaps forty-five', told them about the artists: 'They were every-where when she was a girl. You could not move for them. Everybody was painted. She had been painted herself, by a Mr Stanhope Forbes. A gaunt old man was pointed out as having been painted by Tuke – "only a long time ago, they say".'[2]

Ejected from their guesthouse after breakfast, they had to stay out until 6 p.m. Not that they minded, being happy to read their novels in shelters on the Penzance promenade when it rained, as it often did. When the sun shone, they took long walks, on one of which they encountered the artist Samuel 'Lamorna' Birch at work in the landscape.

The pubs Tilly spurned closed at 8.30 p.m. on Saturday; then huge fishermen with loud voices – having bought each other pints of beer with a 'What'll it be my handsome?' and a 'Here y'are my lover' – congregated outside to sing rousing Wesleyan hymns such as 'O For a Closer Walk with God' and 'Jesu, the Very Thought of Thee'. On Sunday, fisher families crowded into a vast Methodist chapel for further blasts of singing. Ronnie and Tilly joined in with gusto.

Ronnie also set off on his own adventures, sneaking into those seductive pubs and spending a day in St Ives. Just then its greatest artist, the untutored and unfettered former fisherman Alfred Wallis, was dying in the nearby workhouse infirmary at Madron. While looking intently in an art gallery window, the visitor was asked, 'Are you an art critic?' The questioner was the young modernist painter Wilhelmina Barns-Graham. Even if there had been a trace of irony in the opening line, the ensuing talk about the creative spark pleased the artist. She wrote down the budding writer's name and address and sent him encouraging postcards.

As ever, he sought out solitude. His most memorable moment of the convalescent trip was lying close to a cliff edge, looking down on the foaming ocean. He would think of this in sunshine for the rest of his life. 'All I want to do is to lie where the sun can touch me. It reminds me of sprawling above the Atlantic in Cornwall when I was a teenager and becoming mesmerised by the blue tumult below, the regular biff of the water on rock, the crying seabirds, the hot sward, the thinking, "Why ever go home? Why ever go anywhere?"'[3]

Lying by that cliff edge, he was not only looking on foaming ocean; his head was — and more often — buried in a book as his main path to self-discovery. 'My recollections of this Cornwall are vivid, yet inconsequential in the topographical sense. I seem not to have watched birds, searched for flowers, studied churches and cromlechs as I have since, but to have used the still fairly deserted landscape as an aid to discovering the geography of my own interior . . . what little I can remember of it breaks through the isolated and total self-indulgence of a long read on an empty headland . . .

'I think that this youthful Cornwall must now be seen as a window, if not a door, opening upon the direction I had to take, except that, looking back, I can see no plan or resolution. The fuchsia and tamarisk hedges, the superb ferns, particularly the hart's-tongue glossily licking its way through the crevices of moist drystone walls; the jessamine, thrift, navelwort, scilla and all the lavish flora of the headlands; the cement-smeared slates of the farm roofs and a scented wind like that which blows over the Camargue; the tossing mournful seabirds and that underlying primitiveness . . . these were some of the things which occasionally got between me and the printed page.'[4]

Reading and romancing the spirit of Cornwall while trying to find himself were all well and good, but back in Newlyn Ronnie was gladly seduced by a jeweller from Bath. They arranged several assignations in the fields above the village — eliciting memories of one evening path lit by greenish-orange glow-worms and the gleam of sheets laid out to dry aromatically on gorse bushes in moonlight.

At the end of the week the departing lover presented Ronnie with a copy of the *Rubaiyat of Omar Khayyam* – eleventh-century quatrains by the Persian poet as translated by Edward FitzGerald in 1859. The Anglo-Irish translator, himself a poet, had lived for most of his strange life in Suffolk.

FitzGerald, mystical and homosexual, had been cocooned by inherited wealth. Based near Woodbridge, he never needed to worry what the neighbours thought or how he might sustain himself. Indeed, he had gaily sailed *The Scandal* – a boat named after 'the staple product of Woodbridge' – while reserving his literary talent for letters to friends. He lived with portraits of the best of them: between likenesses of writers William Makepeace Thackeray and Alfred, Lord Tennyson hung an image of beloved Joseph 'Posh' Fletcher, a handsome and heavy-drinking Lowestoft fisherman.

After the brief respite of Cornwall, Ronnie was returned to scrutiny in Jubilee Road. Connie, who adored her eldest brother and knew him to be uncommonly brainy, thought he had been recruited by the intelligence services. But his masculine failure in military life was all too evident in a close-knit community with so many fathers, sons, husbands, brothers and lovers still endangered. Before all this, Ronnie had been quietly mocked as a peasant boy putting on airs and graces and a sore trial to his parents. Those with more education but possibly more prejudice used the word 'effete'. Now there was silent hostility, or outright condemnation, for those not doing their bit.

Warship Week in February 1942 had set a national fundraising challenge for British cities to buy battleships and aircraft carriers, towns to pay for cruisers and destroyers, and smaller communities to furnish lesser vessels. Tasked with finding £75,000, Sudbury and Long Melford reached £144,000 – enough to adopt HMS *Scarab*, a Royal Navy 'Insect Class' river gunboat. This revived First World War veteran would see very active service in the Mediterranean. Weathering the war without a single casualty, the crew could expect gifts at every port sent by Suffolk folk, from home-made cakes and biscuits to knitted gloves, scarves and jumpers. Some came from the Blythe family.

Recent military trauma weighed heavily in Ronnie's mind as he learned the *Rubaiyat* by heart as a form of solace. 'Wry and sadly happy, it says: seize the moment – seize it from the moment you wake to the moment you die.'⁵ Savouring a poem heady with wine, friendship, roses and dust, he never forgot best-loved lines:

> Ah, make the most of what we yet may spend,
> Before we too into the dust descend;
> Dust into dust, and under dust to lie
> Sans wine, sans song, sans singer, and – sans End!

The exhortation to live could not lessen the problem of how he was going to make a living. He tried to fill in and fit in with menial labour useful to the war effort. Then, as if a sign from heaven, the perfect post was advertised in the local press. He applied with the utmost care, knowing his life depended on it. His script was cursive and concise. For all its omissions, an elementary education had instilled the art of letter-writing.

Called for an interview in Colchester, the applicant was never so happy as when the postman brought news the job was his. At twenty, he was used to hiding his deepest feelings. But now a reference-librarian-to-be jumped for joy.

15

War and Peace

DRESSED IN FORMAL grey suit and tie, the rescued Ronald Blythe commuted by Chambers bus from Sudbury to Colchester. His sanctuary in a public library should have been the epitome of peace; instead, it was an outpost engulfed in an ongoing world of war.

Built in 1893 beside the town hall and law courts in West Stockwell Street, Colchester library had been designed by Brightwell Binyon as a symbol of late Victorian power and progress. Lofty ambition was disguised in a cosily comforting neo-Jacobean assemblage of brick, dark timber and pargeting.

More than the olde worlde building, Ronnie was impressed that the architect was a distant cousin of poet Laurence Binyon. The writer, who had just died, was immortalised for First World War verses starting 'They shall grow not old, as we that are left grow old'. These lines would be recited every Remembrance Day, though the ceremony was paused for the current conflict.

A larger library by Marshall Sisson had risen in Culver Street in the late 1930s. But it was requisitioned for the administration and the printing of a new book – with wartime coupons for rationed food and clothing. The library transfer would have to wait until October 1948.

When Ronnie arrived, in 1943, doomed shelves were depleted since prized books had been removed to tea chests and basements for safekeeping. Now the silence of the half-empty chambers was broken by air-raid sirens as bombers targeted the barracks and a factory making engines for submarines and landing craft. In February 1944 a Boudicca-scale conflagration gutted warehouses, shops and part of the engine plant. But production limped on and so did the work of the reference librarian.

Now an airfield was hastily laid out from Gallows Hill in Chilton towards Acton. Footpaths Ronnie had taken back to his birthplace, along with landmark trees and cottages, vanished under a concrete plateau. From April 1944 Station 174 hosted the American 486th Bombardment Group – 2,800 servicemen flying in Liberators and Fortresses on 191 missions over the occupied Continent until April 1945. The plane formations made an amazing spectacle above Jubilee Road. A total of 207 crewmen would be killed while 303 bailed out to become prisoners of war. And this was just one of 100 airbases across East Anglia.

Sudbury filled with American accents as servicemen with an average age of twenty-two – the same as Ronnie – flocked to pubs, the Gainsborough and County cinemas, Victoria Hall dances and meals served in a Red Cross club on East Street. Sensing the longing for home cooking, Tilly set up a catering service in Jubilee Road. Eileen recalled: 'My siblings and I would have our dinner first on those nights, and then help Mother prepare a meal for the officers, who really enjoyed themselves. The money they paid helped the

The Blythes, 1944. Left to right: George,
Kip the dog, Gerald, Tilly, Ronnie, Eileen.

family.' There were also gifts bought on the base such as tins of spam (cooked and preserved pork), pineapple or peaches.

Flying crews who might die the next day, and who showered gifts as they sought pleasure in the meantime, exuded glamour for Sudbury girls. Previously such idols had been encountered only in the movies (and indeed, Clark Gable and Jimmy Stewart were now in uniform in neighbouring counties). When Ronnie walked through the town in the evening, he found Anglo-American friendship being warmly extended among couples in darkened shop doorways.

The boy in the library continued to have erotic encounters of his own. Once, cycling down Ballingdon Hill in a high summer Thomas Gainsborough landscape, he passed a young farmworker cycling uphill. They both looked back, slowed and halted, then wheeled their bikes into a cornfield. Ronnie never forgot the feeling of rough corn stalks and hot sun on his bare skin.

All through the dying days of the war he was bound up with the fate of antiquarian books and archival researches, and maintaining the silence of a reduced reference library amid a surrounding furore. In its quiet way, it was the civilisation for which the war was being fought. And for the reference librarian himself, literature was ever more of an escape from menacing reality. Amid mounting evidence of scarcely credible horrors inflicted on the Jews by the Nazis and British prisoners by the Japanese, relief lay in books the totalitarian mind would have burned.

Ronnie was also looking to the future. On 10 February 1944 the letters columns of the *Suffolk and Essex Free Press* included an appeal from Ronald Blythe at the Colchester Public Library. It was entitled 'Museum for Sudbury'.

Dear Sir,

Considerable interest must again be widely manifest by the renewal of the proposal for a Sudbury Museum – an idea which unfortunately is still quite barren of any sign of materialisation.

. . . as it is to-day, Sudbury is still an embodiment of great charm, but the beauty is going fast, and if local interest is not practically reawakened, in a very short time it will have descended to almost mediocrity . . .

Could not something be done for this object after the war? Could not . . . a committee be formed of educationists, antiquarians and artists to meet and begin to make the Borough of Sudbury Museum an actuality?

A museum in Gainsborough's birthplace would have to wait until 1961. As late as 1973 the Sudbury Society was formed after a successful battle to save the historic Corn Exchange from being bulldozed for a supermarket. Ronnie backed both campaigns and was elated when the rescued Corn Exchange came to host Sudbury Library.

D-Day landings in Normandy on 6 June 1944 brought short-lived celebration. In the newspapers he set out each morning the reference librarian read that poet Keith Douglas had been killed, aged twenty-four, near Bayeux. Ronnie mourned a cultural catastrophe. And on top of slow and painful progress for Allied armies across the Continent, there was an unleashing of ever more terrible weapons on the home front. As V1 and then V2 flying bombs rained down – the first like aerial motorbikes cutting out overhead, the supersonic second exploding before the arrival of their sound – the inevitability of victory seemed less certain than the impossibility of peace.

The librarian was biding his time as a chronicler. Ultimately, researches for *Private Words* would be aided by his friend Christopher Elliott. A Suffolk schoolboy during the conflict, Christopher idolised his aviator brother, Donald, who was captured on Java. Forced to build airfields for the Japanese, he vanished on a death march in Borneo in March 1945. Refusing to accept his brother's fate, Christopher fired off letters to the Air Ministry and to village chiefs and sawmills along the route. Donald had left his mark on Suffolk tree trunks: had similar carvings been found in the Malayan jungle? A trail opened: a grave for five prisoners was found to contain an RAF cap with Donald Elliott's name.

March 1945 clouded further with news that Julian Tennyson, author of *Suffolk Scene*, had died in Burma. His rural bible had been reprinted five times by 1944. Dog-eared copies were in Suffolk kit-bags at the D-Day landings; more had been packed off to be read and reread in the Far East. The dazzling writer was destroyed by a piece of shrapnel 'about the size of a little-finger nail'.

The most bought and borrowed poetry book in 1945 was *Other Men's Flowers*, a selection by the Earl Wavell, viceroy of India, Second World War commander and son of Colchester. Ronnie was fascinated that the garden of Archibald Wavell's childhood home abutted that of R. N. Currey. Currey's anthology *Poems from India*, published in 1946, was assisted by John Wavell, the viceroy's soldier son. A love of poetry ran in the warrior family – and war and art merged beneath the civic soil:

'The foundations of their houses went deep into a Roman cemetery and it was quite usual to dig up tesserae with the potatoes. All in all, they were surrounded by some two hundred acres of Roman graves. Below their hardcourts and shrubberies lay soldiers from all over Europe, their wives and children and slaves. One of them was "Longinus, son of Sdapezematycus, Duplicarius of the first Wing of Thracians from the province of Sardis (who died) in his fortieth year . . ." and who was buried by Currey's garden wall. His tombstone in the local museum has enthralled me since boyhood. It shows a cavalry officer riding in triumph over a barbarian, poor man.'[1]

In an injury of ancient history or recent archaeology, Longinus had lost a hand. But half a century after the Second World War ended it was unearthed by builders in the Wavell garden. 'Currey's ninety years fled like an evening gone, as they say, in the light of the discovery. It was a Longinus who pierced the dead Christ, and a Longinus who was an excellent critic in Athens, and a Longinus who was governor of Judaea. After I left the anthologist I walked to the museum to see my Longinus and his victim. Would they stick his hand back on tomorrow? Oh no, archaeological surgery can take years. You see, there is no blood in stone, no nerves, no warmth unless the sun catches it.'[2]

16

Bloody Books

FINALLY, AS CONFLICT in Europe ended on 8 May, Ronnie could set about refilling emptied bookshelves. The first call was to bring in a bequest from Canon Gerald Rendall.

The cleric, academic and classicist had just died after active retirement in Dedham, during which time he continued to insist that Shakespeare was the pen name of Lord Oxford. He left half of his voluminous library to Colchester. Ronnie was exhilarated by the task – keen to know the donor of his school-prize *Boswell's Life of Johnson* through the books he kept for himself.

A removal team was less respectful: 'The library window was wide, and a truck was parked below it, and down it the removal men were sliding his precious books like coals. They were making a start, they said, whistling cheerfully. Beautiful bindings with his crest, fluttering pages, first editions fell from the duckboard in a heap. Shock must have lent my voice authority; for the removal men's carnage came to a sudden halt. I heard one of them say: "You know I don't mind what I do, Bob, but I hate moving a parson – half a ton of bloody books before you start."'[1]

Treasures of the reference library were now retrieved from chests and vaults. The crowning jewel of an eighteenth-century gentleman's library was a copy of *On the Consolation of Philosophy*, written by the Roman statesman Boethius in 523 CE, translated by Geoffrey Chaucer and published in London by William Caxton in 1478. Spared the sunken tea chest treatment, this gem lived in a safe,

wrapped in yellowing spreads from the *Times* newspaper. Ronnie
often pored over the precious text. As with St Paul's letters, Malory's
Le Morte d'Arthur and Bunyan's *The Pilgrim's Progress*, he marvelled
at the creativity of great writers during incarceration.

Books bequeathed to Colchester in 1631 by Samuel Harsnett, for
the use of local clergy, were less eagerly recovered. The gift of a local
baker's son who died Archbishop of York had been boxed and buried,
Ronnie reported, 'in case Hitler got hold of them and became an
Anglican'.[2] Harsnett had earned himself a church window and a town
hall sculpted likeness for benevolence to his birthplace. He had written
powerfully against Puritan beliefs in demons and witchcraft, and his
anti-Catholic diatribe in *A Declaration of Egregious Popish Impostures*
had provided phrases for *King Lear*. Some of his vellum-bound books
had been owned by Renaissance humanists and Protestant reformers
(Erasmus, Luther, Calvin, Foxe). Ronnie handled the great Polyglot
Bible used by the King James scholars with awe.

The British Museum advised rubbing the sticky calf-skin covers
with a foul-smelling preservative, so Ronnie spent long days

Library colleagues.

'polishing them up, now and then catching some spidery hand, perhaps of the Archbishop himself, as it descended in the margin'.[3] The archbishop had flown less high than Ipswich butcher's son Thomas Wolsey, who built Hampton Court for himself and nearly became Pope before losing favour with Henry VIII and expiring just before execution. But Samuel Harsnett died peacefully before the reckoning of the civil war. Ronnie found it hard to admire an irascible priest who served as a literary censor. 'Once, he licensed a book without reading it. But if it was anything like some of the books in his own library, whose slippery covers I was polishing, I could sympathise.'[4]

The seeker of salvation in literature reserved more reverence for a living descendant of Matthew Newcomen, another seventeenth-century Puritan cleric from Colchester. Tilting far from low-church roots, Gilbert Newcomen had known the founder of Aestheticism, Walter Pater. Ronnie was gripped just then by Pater's philosophical novel *Marius the Epicurean*. Now his gaze alighted on Father Gilbert as an object of interest in himself. For the elderly curate wore the Roman Catholic-style cassock of the soutane and, escaping like wisps of flame from beneath a wide-brimmed Holy Joe hat, a red wig.

For as long as anyone could remember, Father Gilbert had assisted Canon Henry Carter in the Colchester parish of St Leonard's – where mean streets ran down to the Roman landing stage on the River Colne. He had rejected all preferment so they could stay faithfully together and become known as the Divines. The couple filled the ancient church with art, music and ritual, and cared for everyone. Refusing to be martyrs to the moral climate of their times, they remained loving partners and models of quiet courage.

At the age of ninety Father Gilbert was introduced to Ronnie in the library. They arranged to meet in the George Hotel, the cleric bringing his library book in a fish basket. Ronnie longed to ask about Walter Pater but the spectacle before him forbade all enquiry. The priest had clearly taken such pains to preserve a youthful aspect that questions about so long ago would amount to cover blown.

So, the two men sipped sherry and ignored the seventy years between them. 'They said his aunt was Lady Londonderry – they said all manner of things, but with affection. About this time I also met two religious women who loved one another and who, too, were saints. Anyone with any experience of the Church who has not observed such love, true and lasting as it is, would have to be blind or ignorant. Theirs has always been a special ministry through the ages.'[5]

Ronnie was a radical to his last fibre. In the general election of July 1945, a month after victory in Europe, he enthusiastically voted Labour. And, though enthusiasm waned, he was never to vote for any other party. Sudbury and Colchester returned Labour MPs for the first – and last – time in his lifetime, as Winston Churchill and the Conservatives were swept from power by a political landslide. While glad and grateful for victory in war, most voters still smarted from personal and family defeats in depressed 1930s peace. Now they wanted fairer rewards after so much sacrifice.

The votes of returning service personnel had barely been counted when an atomic bomb was dropped on the Japanese city of Hiroshima. A second bomb on Nagasaki three days later forced Japan's surrender and raised the spectre of global annihilation. Ronnie, fellow Christian Socialists and many more besides responded in horror with a renunciation of nuclear weapons. Although rarely a maker of political declarations, his pacifist convictions and belief in a universal brother- and sisterhood never wavered.

In June 1946 Ronnie defended the ethic of brotherly love when a Colonel Hamilton raged in a local newspaper over Italian prisoners of war being indulged with cups of tea. Regular contributor T. A. Gillespy echoed: 'The Italians have practically been given the freedom of the country, and they often appear in brown shoes that were definitely not army issue.' What moved Ronnie to action was a final apocalyptic paragraph. Mr Gillespy had emerged from the war obsessed by Armageddon, as the last battle of good and evil before the Day of Judgement, with which he lambasted sinful readers of the *Suffolk and Essex Free Press*. Now he forecast that the looming liquidation of the British Empire would provoke the ultimate mortal and divine conflict.

The voice of reason from Colchester Public Library, armed with the ammunition of deep reading, replied:

We have had it with sugar and with lemon but now we are offered it in a manner quite unknown in Cranford. Mr Gillespy, although gaily acqui-escent at the distribution of Empire, finds himself unable to restrain his

The man in the library.

wrath when his brothers are given tea. For whether men are German Germans or Italian Italians, they must remain Mr Gillespy's brothers. Love and the brotherhood of all mankind are the elementary fundamentals of true Christianity.

To read Mr Gillespy's recent uncharity after being regaled for months by his spiritual protestations and Job-like prognostications, is too much. To end the supreme pettiness of his letter with such clarion concepts of the last days is to brush the fringes of absurdity. Pope, in his 'Essay on Man', wrote:

> In Faith and Hope the world will disagree
> But all mankind's concern is charity.

May I, without impertinence, suggest that Mr Gillespy forsakes his Revelationary pyrotechnics for a night, and reads the true, simple, changeless ethics of Christ-like love to be found in the Gospels. True humanism such as that belonging to St Augustine, Nurse Cavell, Shakespeare and Paulo Veronese (in his 'Darius before Alexander') will ultimately prove a more amaranthine factor in world happiness than all the trumpet bumblings of such prejudice.[6]

Although yet to wear his scholarship lightly, the writer was now wholly at home in the library – with a professional ease that would glide seemingly without effort between West Stockwell Street and Culver Street. As teenage student Alan Cudmore, a future surveyor and Ronnie's lifelong friend, would remember of the latter venue:

'Ronnie had his desk on a dais at the end of the Reference Library where one entered, with the individual desks for readers facing towards him. He was always dressed very smartly, often to be seen in a Simpson's grey flannel suit, well cut to suit his figure and the jacket always buttoned. He moved around the shelves purposefully, knowing precisely where to find the title he was seeking; his movements were elegant, geared to preserving the accepted silence of the Reference Library with the Neo-Georgian windows separating the bays of bookshelves.'[7]

17

Sloth Incarnate

A LIBRARY IS a place of longing, a refuge from the world and a route to enlightenment. As a rich assortment of troubled and questing humanity came to seek the help of Colchester's gently charismatic reference librarian, there was often a queue at the enquiries desk.

Ronnie was aware of the stir he was making among homosexual readers suddenly in need of bookish guidance. Two young artists and embattled lovers, Richard Chopping and Denis Wirth-Miller – Dickie and Denis – did not bother to ask for advice. They brazenly admitted coming in just to look at him. Dickie Chopping, a Colchester miller's son, produced the 1943 book *Butterflies in Britain* before moving with Denis from Wormingford to Wivenhoe and working for seven years on an aborted 22-volume encyclopedia of British wildflowers. The move was punctuated in Denis's case by nine weeks in Wormwood Scrubs for gross indecency – a police set-up, he insisted.

Dickie's best-known artworks were to be dust jackets for nine of Ian Fleming's James Bond novels. Disgruntled by the lowness of his fee, he finally quit, saying: 'I don't mind a bit of sex but there is enough violence in the world without needing to make it more glamorous.'[1] Cue laughter in Wivenhoe where Dickie and Denis were notorious performance artists – staging an endlessly rowdy street, bar and domestic drama like a Punch and Punch puppet show, sometimes featuring their friend Francis Bacon, who for a time had a studio in Queen's Road (the name amused him).

Ronnie was to have one sober meeting with Francis, whom he remembered for 'charming solicitude and impeccable manners' and admired for unremitting dedication to the making of original art. But he avoided Dickie and Denis when not trapped at his desk. Chaos attended them. They were plainly in a drink-fuelled spiral whose main casualty would be creative work not getting done.

By way of contrast, author Sidney Cunliffe-Owen, a forty-something former army captain, was assisted in and then deflected from research for a historical novel. In the air of concentrated quietude, where coded messages were delivered in delectable whispers, he thought he had fallen in love. Ronnie, flattered by the attentions of a published writer, agreed to meet outside the library, where he was not so much drawn into a romance as intrigued by an older man's ardour. Captain Cunliffe-Owen plotted an overnight trip to London, paying for two hotel rooms and aiming only to rumple the bedcovers in one to foil the rules and fool the staff. But he was to be disappointed. Ronnie recoiled from a would-be suitor's presence when it pressed too close.

Lean, suave and noble, the military veteran hid amazement behind a stiff upper lip when, after an innocent introduction, the object of his obsession defected to a 21-stone widower befriended by the captain at Cambridge. Canon Edward John Gaitskell Barnett – John – was known as 'Sloth Incarnate'. Above his gluttonous mouth and stained teeth, what looked like a thin brown moustache turned out to be a nicotine line due to a constancy of Balkan Sobranie cigarette smoke and an insufficiency of soap and water. His voice, however, was beautiful.

The big attraction of John Barnett was his position as rector of Little Easton near Thaxted – not that this unlikely cousin of Labour politician Hugh Gaitskell made much of the role himself. He was the reactionary antithesis of every radical thing the late patroness of the living, Daisy Greville, Countess of Warwick, held dear. A mistress of Edward VII, she had converted from socialite to socialist. The red countess then demonstrated her commitment to the poor so thoroughly that, up to her death at hocked and gutted Easton Lodge in 1938, she progressively made herself one of them.

Ronnie, a frequent weekend visitor to the rectory, and the rector's bed, had entered the pages of a comic novel. He loved the fact that H. G. Wells had written sixty books here. And that the Warwick estate's Barn Theatre had involved George Bernard Shaw and Ellen Terry – the latter honoured with a sumptuous church plaque by Alfred Gilbert, maker of the Piccadilly Eros, near a décolleté bust of 'darling Daisy' in youthful socialite mode. Lady Warwick was also a prolific author, with books on wildlife, gardens, William Morris and memoirs her conservative daughter deemed 'muck'.

All those artful associations, plus the lingering aura of Morris-and-Greville-style Merrie England, meant more than a light fling with a Tory cleric. Best of all was the fact that Restoration poet Thomas Ken had been a hyperactive rector at Little Easton. The words of his 'Morning Hymn' were akin to a call to arms for Ronnie:

> Awake my soul! and with the sun
> Thy daily stage of duty run;
> Shake off dull sloth, and joyful rise
> To pay thy morning sacrifice.

The lyric was an affront to the current incumbent, who rarely rose before midday. But it helped in Ronnie's eventual decision to have his confirmation service here, the symbolic laying-on of hands by the local bishop signifying his deep and deepening allegiance to the Church of England.

A typical day at Little Easton rectory began with Ronnie being woken by Frankie, the chain-smoking housekeeper, with a mug of tea and a hunk of buttered bread to stave off hunger pangs until a gargantuan breakfast. This was served in the kitchen, the only warm room, before Frankie left for a shift in a seed factory, coughing her way up the drive. As for the rector, he believed almost religiously that, at least for himself, Sunday should also be a day of rest.

The congregation now reduced to a few Warwick retainers, the Barnett idea of pastoral work was sketching pastel scenes in Easton Lodge park. When Ronnie returned from a walk to the village, he enquired: 'What is it like down there?' The 'sermon walk' laid out along yew-hedged lawns in the rectory garden, where a line of ambling priests had shaped Sabbath messages, now went untrod.

Apart from food and Ronnie, the parson's pleasure lay in music. His library of classical records introduced a lover half his age to the pre-war French repertoire and to British composers led by Ralph Vaughan Williams. The listener and story collector came to revel in the songs of Reynaldo Hahn, since he was Proust's first lover and partly the model for the composer Vinteuil in *Remembrance of Things Past*.

On Good Friday the canon summoned farmworkers to carry his Steinway grand into the church for a three-hour recital of Bach cantatas. Before each rendition, as for Sunday services, the player rose late, breakfasted long and threw a cassock over his pyjamas. On this special theatrical occasion, he added a cape clasped at the throat by tarnished silver lions biting on a chain. John Barnett was to remain rector of Little Easton for twenty indolent years before retiring to a retreat and ultimately ascending to eternal rest at the age of ninety-eight.

The picture postcard villages of north Essex – close to London while contriving to appear remote – bristled with authors and artists in the 1940s. Ronnie avoided the Dickie-and-Denis-style uproar at Tilty Mill near Great Dunmow, where writer Elizabeth Smart left her four children by poet George Barker in the careless hands of painters, drinkers, lovers and sparring partners the Two Roberts, Colquhoun and MacBryde, while she worked in London to pay the bills. After a binge in Sudbury, MacBryde challenged the Gainsborough statue to a fight. The mill threatened with wreckage every partying weekend was rented from the Scottish poet and novelist Ruthven Todd. His idiosyncratic character and elusive company would have been more to Ronnie's taste.

Friendships were made with artists massing in Great Bardfield – with its Tudorised, Georgianised and Victorianised high street concealing medieval grandeur – since the arrival of Eric Ravilious and Edward Bawden in 1930. Notable talents such as John Aldridge, Michael Rothenstein and Kenneth Rowntree now shone hereabouts. Even in this rather idealised village – with a town crier called Piper, a grocer named Clinkscales, Mr Bones the Butcher and a sweetshop run by Mr and Mrs Fudge – conflicts between congregating creatives also made the case for productive solitude. But Ronnie attended Great Bardfield open exhibitions of the 1950s, in which artists showed their work in houses they had also stylishly furnished and decorated for next to nothing – confirming the practice of art as an enticing and engrossing way of life.

As he commuted from Sudbury, Ronnie yearned to live in Colchester. He was literally frozen out when, in the Arctic start to 1947, snowdrifts made travelling hazardous and at times hopeless. A spring thaw and storms brought severe flooding. Ballingdon Street became a river, and in the low-lying area around All Saints church residents waited in bedrooms for rescue boats.

Now Ronnie grabbed the first lifeline. Daphne, on the library staff, was a weekend walking companion; her mother gave him lodgings. Within weeks he realised that marriage was being planned. 'Daphne became absolutely clinging,' he said. 'I couldn't bear it. I just had to get away.' In a small flat at the top of a 1930s house in Lexden Road, he basked in hard-won freedom at the age of twenty-six. He might express regret later, but the thrill of solitude was for ever: by choice he would never again live with another soul, save for independent-minded cats.

Slowly and warily he was making his own way in life with essays accepted by the *Essex Review* and *East Anglian Magazine*. And yet his workplace remained the centre of everything. In the library he read himself an advanced education with the greatest authors as tutors. The gods of his literary pantheon were his guides to a life in art. He also organised talks and exhibitions. The first show was lent by Colonel Constable and included pictures by his famous forebear plus personal effects including the painter's wedding ring. Ronnie curated the display and wrote, designed and oversaw the printing of the catalogue. On two afternoons each week, when the library shut before reopening in the evenings, he read in the park.

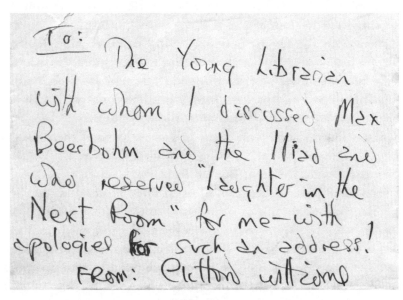

A fan letter.

He was aware of other gay young men, but most were too effeminate for carefree company. There was the constant fear of being found out and ridiculed, or worse. A gay pub in Colchester was depressing and at risk of police raids. Ronnie sometimes went to quiet spots with soldiers but more often with local lads. 'I would go with almost anyone really; sex meant nothing to me: being a writer was everything.' When new to the library, he went home with a man met in the gay pub and woke at dawn with a feeling of desolation. Quietly dressing and slipping away, he wandered the streets until it was time for work. Rooms of his own were always a safe haven.

Given a writer's blending of fact, fantasy and empathy, his own memories were allotted to the town hall's sculpted St Helena. She was pictured remembering 'morning coffee in the restaurants below, the dressed shop windows, the departed elegance, the public library service – marvellous, this – and the gentlemen-only bar at the Red Lion, where a Manet-like lady kept a roaring fire'.[2]

On a visit to the library, retired army officer and future priest Derek Richards advanced on the librarian – taking him to lunch at the Red Lion and then home to bed. Later there were invitations to stay in Wales, where Ronnie was photographed naked on the beach. Back at the house, his host told him to stay away from windows in case of prying eyes. Even naturists lived in fear of exposure in those days.

There were also regular outings to London, less than an hour by train from Colchester, to soak up sights and sensations. Wonderful walks began at Liverpool Street station for someone alert to the sediments of past and present. First a ritual crossing of Old Broad Street to say a prayer in St Botolph's, Bishopsgate. Better even than an East Anglian saint, John Keats had been baptised there. Then perhaps a saunter to the stranded gravestones of writers William Blake and Daniel Defoe in Bunhill Fields.

Soho lured him. Once, in the French Pub, he stood at the edge of a rampageous throng of writers and artists with his customary glass of beer. Then the voice of George Barker boomed from the bar: 'Why is that boy so sad?' But that singular boy was just drinking it all in. On opening another promising pub door, he retreated from the sight of Dylan Thomas, morose and alone at the bar; already blotto and waiting for someone to buy the next pint.

From one gay haunt a well-dressed young man took him back to a bedsit of indescribable squalor. He followed another lonely lad more successfully, but when he awoke and lifted his host's watch from the bedside table to check the time, a hand clamped his wrist to thwart a theft. Trust was no easier to find than love among the marginalised and criminalised.

Late one night, missing the last train home, and with no prospect of a nocturnal embrace, he tried to sleep in the crypt night shelter at St Martin-in-the-Fields. On a wire bunk with a thin blanket, his wallet under a pillow, he put up with the torch shone in his face hourly. But by 4 a.m. groaning men were too disturbing. So, he walked to Covent Garden where traders and porters were already at work.

Gritty experience was all grist for a writer's mill. Never afraid or appalled, Ronnie was only intrigued. 'Whatever the troubles and challenges of life, writers preserve themselves,' he said.

18

The Pied Piper

ONE HEART-STOPPING AND life-changing morning, Miss Osborne, a senior librarian, pointed out a tall, slightly stooped man in his forties with a silvery voice who she said was a poet. James Turner certainly looked the part.

Ethereally thin, his white skin appeared all the paler against cheeks flaming red. A shock of wavy hair fell over his long face and a pipe protruded among pens from his corduroy jacket pocket. The image of a masculine martyr, he was at once a figure of wild romance. Ronnie was transfixed.

James Ernest Turner was one of five surviving children of a rich surveyor and architect, the family ferried by Rolls-Royce between two servanted houses in Kent. His middle name memorialised an older brother who died in infancy and in whose blameless shade he proved a perpetual disappointment. True, the bar was set mountainously high: Father's ice axe, used in conquering Mont Blanc and the Matterhorn, hung over a mantelpiece, challenging the children to rise up and make their own way in life. The eldest remaining boy was further hampered by those romantic and poetic looks, evident so early, since they betrayed the gnawing presence of pulmonary tuberculosis − a cross to be bravely borne and never mentioned. It was a long time before Ronnie could piece together his tortuous and tortured story.

Frequently ill and generally flailing, James felt called to religion until losing his faith at Oxford where he read English but failed to take a degree. After working briefly as a teacher, artist's model and bookstore assistant, he was given £2 a week *not* to enter his father's London office. The perk was a small price to pay since this distracted son's sinecure post cataloguing old correspondence had led to a basement fire from a discarded cigarette. Following a spell in a Devon nursing home, where he was tended by his future wife, Catherine, he turned to agriculture – first with an unpaid post in a Sussex tomato nursery (where he mutilated 200 plants on his first morning). Then he steered his own mushroom-growing business to bankruptcy before rubbing along as a chauffeur and publisher's reader while finding his feet as a writer.

The Turners arrived in Essex on New Year's Eve 1941, James having been set up in another nursery by his father. The couple rented Layer Marney rectory whose incumbent lived in London with his partner, Tom. James's sister, Dorothea, had long shared rooms with Enid. But no questions were – or could be – asked. Even in this outpost of supposed bohemia, propriety rested on a prevailing silence. Just as the poet kept quiet about his own consumption, any perceived debilitation was not to be discussed: illness and weakness were similarly impolite. The best James could manage was to dedicate to his courageous sister a book on British eccentrics.

James and Cathy.

At Layer Marney a poltergeist was fatefully encountered. As James explained: 'keys and pieces of coal were thrown about and the lavatory chain was pulled at two o'clock in the morning when we were alone in the house and in bed.'[1] That fixated them and forever unsettled them. Barely unpacked in one old house when plotting a move to the next, they now embarked on a series of false starts in doleful properties where supernatural antennae detected fresh apparitions – and profitable makeovers.

Catherine Turner – aka Cathy – was born Lucie Porter; but James, in thrall to the drama of *Wuthering Heights* when they met, discerned the heroine of his future life so awarded her an appropriate name. Farmer's daughter and cat lover, she defended her husband like a lioness and was ultimately exhausted and embittered. Along the contorted way, she often drew the line. 'James!' she exclaimed with an air of finality when deciding he had gone too far. Ronnie thought of a dog being called to heel. The author's wife was also credited in print for their state of perpetual upheaval. 'Cathy was always one for a change,' James said disingenuously. 'She had a recurring desire for new curtains.'[2]

After three swift Essex shifts, James veered briefly from wraith chasing and built a bungalow beside the nursery to his father's donated design. It was only just complete when, in April 1947, house and business were sold and the Turners bought into the hoax of nearby Borley Rectory – claimed by psychic investigator and conjuror Harry Price to be the most haunted house in England. Although the main building had burned down in 1939, the address remained a tourist trap and, in James's magpie mind, a source of potential income. Life in a grim coachman's cottage would give him a plot and celebrity. He made sure the local press reported his arrival. When first observing James Turner in the reference library just after the move to Borley, Ronnie was entranced by a restless spirit and published poet. As a life model, however, he left a lot to be desired.

Undeterred by bankruptcy from the same pursuit, the poet was busy building mushroom sheds on the residue of Borley Rectory and cultivating a four-acre orchard. But it was the business of the ghosts – a lovelorn nun delivered by spectral carriage and headless driver, to walk in the garden or write on walls announcing her burial in the cellar – which really mushroomed. As a result, the Turners came to rue the fact that the rectory was indeed haunted

– by hordes of nocturnal visitors. What went bump in the night were uninvited ghost-hunters crashing into things and each other, until one solved the problem by rigging up a spotlight in a tree. At the same time, James Turner was re-entering the spirit world by regaining his religious faith – aided by Clifford Henning, Borley rector and ghostbuster.

Examining the parish church, the two men decided that a slab covering the entrance to tomb vaults and perhaps secret passages was the altar stone dislodged in the Reformation. They would reinstate it and have a good poke around over the Whitsun holiday. News spread so that sightseers included pressmen probably alerted by James. He had certainly invited the newly met Ronnie for tea. Walking from Sudbury in spring sunshine, Ronnie arrived to find his host digging up bones amid a disorderly crowd in the chancel. 'The church should have been closed, of course, to all visitors and we should have been less unseemly,' James recalled. 'I think a peculiar madness infected all of us there that day, perhaps due to the heat.'[3]

Heat and madness notwithstanding, Ronnie was wearing his habitual jacket and tie, and his recurring ironic smile. Following that first tea-time entertainment, he guided the Turners on motor tours of East Anglia and stayed with them at weekends. 'He was extremely witty, knew about books and authors and delighted, as we did, in afternoons spent looking at a church in some out-of-the-way parish,' James wrote. 'He had as fine a collection of "dotty" parsons as I did . . .' Their new friend was deemed to be an idealist still growing in ideas and life. 'But Ronnie had the ability of seeing into people's motives and, later, the talent to put these people and their motives down on paper with great success.'[4]

In the meantime he was sorting the transfer of the reference library to the Marshall Sisson building in Culver Street. Delivery – and, it seemed, deliverance – lay in a light and lofty place of work and learning promising a bright future and looking to last for ever.

James Turner was to prove an invaluable connector to inspirational books and people. In ways he did not always approve, or understand, he opened Ronnie's world and enriched his existence. The poet with the sharpened silver tongue became the most important and troubling man in Ronnie's life: 'It was Turner's form of conspiracy which meant the most to me at this time, his very English mixture of fierce opinions and delicacy.'[5] James accepted an acolyte's devotion as his due. Always near to broke, he allowed Ronnie to pay for rounds of tea or beer and accepted gifts of razor blades.

When they met, the latest costly Turner scheme for raising cash was to grow anemones commercially on wasted ground between his fruit trees. Ever prone to seek expert opinion and then ignore it, he consulted Sir Cedric Morris of Benton End, a nearby artist's garden and art school, whose playful, diffident manner masked a fecund creativity. Both men grew their own tobacco – Cedric had a barnful of it drying from the rafters. As the two wayward grandees stretched long limbs and smoked amicably together, James preached in his beguiling voice on the marvels of mushrooms while Cedric urged caution with anemones.

After careful study, the socialist baronet pronounced Borley soil unfit for the current Turner craze. James, in defiance, ordered 10,000 corms and spent a week planting them. None came up. (Next he tried flax, which rippled in a lovely blue-mauve amid a sea of wild flowers, but was ruled not worth the lifting from weed-stricken fields.) His most useful introduction to Benton End, barely a week after the bone-rattling tea party in Borley, was Ronnie.

19

Cedric and Lett

Painted red, like a warning or provocation, Benton End lay in gorgeous gardens overhanging the River Brett on the edge of Hadleigh. Cedric Morris reigned in the outdoor kingdom while his partner, Arthur Lett-Haines – known as Lett and less appropriately as Father – ran the bohemian house together with its (in)famous art school.

James Turner, turning a blind eye to what might be going on in bedrooms and possibly the potting sheds, was impressed by Cedric's success as a propagator. He appreciated the flowering spectacle and still more the scent of money. Plants seen from a distance turned out to be quite different from the usual garden variety. 'Cedric had been at it again, cross-pollinating until he produced a plant that would figure in the seedsmen's catalogues as *new this season* and costing a fortune.'[1]

The spell cast instantly on Ronnie was all the more potent in early June when Benton End looked its iris-blooming best. Floral show-offs, ultimately to include ninety Benton End varieties, were on bawdy parade in box-hedged beds. Bearded beauties stuck out tongues in a raunchy kaleidoscope excluding only 'knicker and salmon pink'. Ronnie's recollections came to 'float about in a kind of Giverny haze. There were orchid-pink *Cordelia*, and *Strathmore*, the greatest pink iris in Britain, there was *Paprika*, a flower the colour of tarnished gun-metal, there was the ravishing *Fandango* which danced in the Suffolk winds, there was *Coronet*, a flaring

Iris Week at Benton End, 1940s.

near-gold bloom and some said the best yellow plicata iris in the world, there was *Susan*, all white and brown with exquisitely etched falls. There were *Beatrice*, *Abbot*, *Opal*, *Faustus*, *Apollo*, *Mocha* and the lilac-grey *Diane*, and many more. Many Benton End students were immortalised by a polleny paintbrush.'[2]

Cedric presided in a private heaven with that polleny paintbrush summoning colourful casts of plants and painters into exuberant existence. Not that there were ever formal lessons: students found their own vantage point, picking up surrounding inspiration and a liberated attitude to life. The master set an impossible example by starting in the top-left corner of a canvas and working diagonally across it until a mosaic-like composition was miraculously complete. 'His Benton End doubled as Art School and connoisseur garden, the two creativities becoming inseparable. Each sphere lent the other a singular authority. It was the painter as much as the gardener who gently transferred the pollen from anther to stigma, just as it was the botanist who made the canvases bloom with a kind of, at times, aggressive life-force. Watching him, I witnessed the moth-wing touch of omnipotence.'[3]

Arriving with a shy and prim air, false impressions as he knew so well, Ronnie never forgot a first brush with his true sensualist nature. 'Nobody has such a good time as a good-time puritan,' he remarked, of Cedric Morris and himself. 'After a brief taking stock of me, Cedric led us into the celebrated brilliance of his "iris week", and I was initiated into a realm of flowers, botanical and art students, earthy-fingered grandees and a great many giggly asides which I didn't quite get. He had just inherited his father's baronetcy and this seemed to add to the comedy. The gardeners wove their way round easels propped up in the long grass and the artists, of all ages, painted peering visitors and dense foliage in the exuberant Morris manner. The doors and window-frames of the ancient house glared Newlyn blue and there was a whiff of garlic and wine in the air from the distant kitchen. The atmosphere was well out of this world so far as I had previously witnessed and tasted it. It was robust and coarse, and exquisite and tentative all at once. Rough and ready and fine mannered. Also faintly dangerous.'[4]

Ronnie gained an indelible impression of a big scrubbed table with wooden platters in an ochre kitchen crammed with lustreware and bold oils of seabirds, formidable women dressing salads and discussing plants, knowing youths, candlelight, cats (one of the women was Orlando the Marmalade Cat creator and Lett's former lover Kathleen 'Moggy' Hale), a single electric bar heater before an eighteenth-century bread oven and an overall sense of 'spartan grandeur'. All a kind of bliss. 'The enemy was the bourgeoisie and his – in Suffolk, at the time, more likely her – values; for Cedric and Lett-Haines were very old and very witty about ancient struggles . . . I imagined old whiffs of garlic and red wine, turpentine and paint, the old voices – somewhat grand – telling tales out of school.'[5]

Staying for a communal meal, Ronnie was astounded by the Mediterranean feast concocted in a former Suffolk bakehouse. In between smoking, drinking and regaling, Lett was a stupendous cook. When the food was dolloped on platters to be wiped 'clean' with bread, and the wine glasses filled and refilled, he became a racy raconteur.

Ronnie was given to understand that Lett and Cedric had met in Trafalgar Square on Armistice Night in 1918; Lett had abandoned the last semblance of fidelity along with a marriage as they moved to East Anglia via London, Cornwall and Paris. No longer a couple, the pair remained side by side despite the ravine between their characters – two rulers with often discrete, sometimes overlapping and occasionally warring courts in their French-style and garden-focused East Anglian School of Painting and Drawing.

Lett and Cedric's first art school, at Dedham, had burned down one night in 1940 after students Lucian Freud and David Carr left burning cigarette butts in a bin. Next morning all the students were painting the smouldering ruins when Sir Alfred Munnings – Dedham-based symbol of painterly reaction – paused in his passing car to cry 'Down with modern art!' Both culprits continued to be welcomed at Benton End until the disruptive and destructive Lucian (house-burner, heart-breaker) was finally told to stay away. Even here there were rules, usually unspoken, to defend the primacy of creative labour.

From that first meal in a setting he found 'curiously stately' – with the long table laid by model-turned-housekeeper Millie Hayes, who was 'a mite unsteady by seven o'clock' – Ronnie was unfazed by larger-than-life Lett. Looking back on the teller of salacious sagas

Cedric and Lett with pet parrots, c.1936.

he wrote: 'The tales were either scandalously about himself or floridly about their travels and encounters, and were designed to shock and inform. If his facts were often inexact, his gist was transparent. Occasionally Cedric would step in and straighten out some curly bit of tale without condemnation or fuss, or with one of his bouts of glee. Lett talked through a big wicked smile like the wolf-grandmother in Little Red Riding Hood. With his large frame and rearing, scarred bald dome, a legacy from the Western Front, and his mocking courtesy, he made no bones about dominating the scene.'[6]

He also made no bones about fancying Ronnie – practically licking his lips and startling false teeth as he relished a treat in store. Cedric, meanwhile, got down to business. Since Ronnie had readily admitted that his longing to be a painter was long since passed, and that writing was now his goal, he was recruited as the art school's unpaid scribe. He would pen and edit catalogue notes and press notices and be admitted to the productive paradise on equal terms with the artists.

James affected to notice nothing untoward in Lett's lascivious leer, and indeed so used was he to ignoring the obvious that he was probably none the wiser when staring into the co-host's lupine face. Certainly, a shock awaited in the car on the drive home. 'Well, what did you think?' James asked. Ronnie would repeat this question several times in print and, although appearing to answer it variously, he never wrote down the exchange which actually followed. 'I'm just like them,' he said quietly, meaning sexually. Stopping abruptly, as if affronted by a wasp, James snapped: 'You can't know us then.' He started the car again. The rest of the journey was spent in stunned silence – borne of acute disappointment on one side and disdain on the other.

Ronnie *was* able to continue knowing the Turners, provided awareness of personal matters went unacknowledged. Although thinking themselves radical, their opinions could be furiously reactionary – and they were close enough to Alfred Munnings to attend his birthday dinner. Turner mentorship made for lop-sided friendship which nevertheless, save for one break and occasional outbursts from both James and Cathy against fearsome homosexuality, lasted until death.

Subterfuge could be exhilarating in such blinkered company. Early in the friendship, during an evening of heavy book talk and light drinking in Colchester's Waggon and Horses pub, Ronnie was followed to the lavatory in the yard by a lad from the bar. Wordlessly they tore off their clothes and made love under the moonlit Roman city wall. Then they dressed and returned to their respective parties. No one had noticed a thing.

On a subsequent solo visit to Benton End, of which there would be many, Lett made full use of the view over the drive from his bedroom. Spying a lithe figure approaching, he waylaid him at the door and led him briskly upstairs. Amid the turmoil of a room heaped with books, empty champagne bottles and biscuit wrappers, Arthur Lett-Haines made yet another sexual conquest. Just the once. Although to Ronnie it was all perfectly natural, and practically meaningless, sex was an aperitif for a feast of friendship. But impressions linger, and Ronnie was eventually to be informed by the next owner of Benton End: 'We had to have Lett's bedroom exorcised − TWICE.'

Also on one occasion only, Ronnie agreed to being driven by Lett in his 'newly acquired but far from competently managed motor-car' to the Marquis of Cornwallis pub in Lower Layham, scene of many a Benton End shindig. The inept chauffeur wore a new tweed suit which 'looked as though it was made from old carpet'.[7] Another time, Lett presented Ronnie, as a promising young man of letters, with a typed poem. The gift was a five-page ballad he declaimed into the staid Suffolk air when Benton Enders proved disappointingly unshockable. It was 'Eskimo Nell'. The recipient enjoyed the ribald joke and kept it among his literary papers.

Gradually Ronnie came to understand that, for all the garrulous and bisexual capering, Lett was essentially lonely − and that this mournful state had nothing to do with the absence of other people. The man who worked flat out for the house and art school, for Cedric and the students, was a thwarted Surrealist parted from his true calling as an artist − adrift from the muse whose company Ronnie guarded at all costs.

Cedric was never known to have ventured into the town of Hadleigh, or, as he called it, 'the village'. When the art school closed in winter, he painted and plant-hunted abroad. Lett retired to the exclusive Brown's Hotel in London citing 'reasons of economy'. Really, he needed a deluxe convalescent home to recover from toiling for the balmy life of Cedric Morris. 'Cedric was a pagan who liked the sun on his back and the day's colours in his eyes, and the tastes and sounds of Now . . . I was always intrigued by his cat-like satisfaction with present time. It caused his days to become so long that, in spite of a stream of visitors, an enormous amount of painting and gardening – and teaching – managed to get done.'[8]

When the divergent but mutually dependent masters of Benton End were dead, and just before the Tate's 1988 Morris memorial show, Ronnie wrote: 'Much, much later, sitting with [Lett] during his last illness, at ease and fond of him, I tasted little surges of regret about my early self which, contrary to what was generally believed, was neither prim nor charmingly shy, but steely . . . But even then, as the pair of old friends complained their way out of a world which they had taken every advantage of, and which they had greedily enjoyed, I still found difficulty in telling either one of them, and it should have been Cedric, how grateful I was that they had deflected me from too much safety.'[9]

After the Whirlwind

FOREVER TRYING TO harness raging discontent to rewarding energy, James Turner was briefly in tune with a burst of wild easterly weather. In the summer of 1948 he and Ronnie swapped first letters after a storm swept through Essex and Suffolk. The exchange set the companionable, literary and churchy tone of their friendship. It formed a calm centre in the lives of both correspondents as Ronnie's social and literary circles widened excitingly:

The Library, Colchester. After the Whirlwind.

Dear James,

All the preparations are made for Crabbe [James was giving a library talk on the poet] and I have invited a number of distinguished ladies and gentlemen to hear you.

Today I met Canon Jack pushing a basket attached to a walking stick along the High Street. He said that if he were invited to be Archbishop of Canterbury now he would decline the honour, so entirely felicitous is Colne Engaine . . .

Also, still ecclesiastically speaking, yesterday I met the Rev Sparling and he wonders if you would come to Langham on Wednesday and read a poem. I am going to read one. It is all very simple. Mr S will write to you. Also will Cathy and yourself have some coffee afterwards with the Bishop (who is also reading, but from the Bible)?

Cedric Morris asked me to say how pleased he would be if you were
his way, if you would call. 'Your friend who talks so well' he called you.
Well, no more. See you soon.
Love to all,
Ronnie[1]

While mushroom mania lasted for James Turner, Ronnie was
caught in the wake of a human whirlwind. 'I helped turn the horse
manure in the dark stables. It steamed in the blackness whilst the
mushrooms themselves gave off a psychedelic glow. We picked the
mysterious fungi which seemed to come from nothing overnight,
with a smell that was both deathly and promising, and filled the
rush punnets. The London hotels, James told us, were craving for
them. His enthusiasms were our gospel.'[2]

James was also consulting Christopher Perkins, a painter from an
engineering clan who had lived in France and New Zealand and
now owned a Sudbury mushroom factory. Ronnie was drawn into
the cosmopolitan orbit of the Perkins family – Christopher and his
flamboyant wife Berry, her composer uncle Martin Shaw and, most
of all, their daughters Juliet and Jane. These two very distinctive
characters would be lasting friends.

During a party hosted by Christopher and Berry in their historic
Sudbury house, Ronnie danced with a circus performer – a muscular
young woman from an acrobatic act called the Garcia Three. Whirling
round the floor, he shared his love of the *Titus Groan* and *Gormenghast*
novels of Mervyn Peake – his and James Turner's passion of the
moment. Back came the astonishing answer: 'I know him.'

To prove her much doubted point, Ronnie and James were invited
to the informant's Bulmer cottage the next evening. There, below
framed posters of the Garcia Three's equally acrobatic parents entertaining the crowned heads of Europe, they found Mervyn Peake
– 'tall, with sunken violet eyes' – sitting on a sofa. He was an artist,
illustrator and poet whose intended quartet of surreal Gormenghast
novels would be hampered then halted by early onset dementia. But
for now: 'Meryvn said that he had so hated being in the army that
he had created an alternative world – Gormenghast, into which he
could flee. This world was a kingdom-sized castle. There was a
women's unit nearby where he met the two sisters whose bodies

were like those of boxers. They modelled for him. They became friends – hence his being here.'[3]

Ronnie struck up a literary correspondence, and when he was agonising between the library or full-time writing, Mervyn Peake encouraged him. Meanwhile, Ronnie and James were able to explore the vast, Gormenghast-like attics of the Perkins family home and to imagine fresh chapters for a fantastic story.

Around this time James spied a stranger at the gate where he had hung a tin plate warning that TRESPASSERS WILL BE PROSECUTED. Not that it had any effect. Now he was nettled, at first, to find a smart young man turning over the notice with a walking stick. The manoeuvre was all the trickier since the intruder was trying to perform it with eyes shut – so he could claim, almost truthfully, never to have seen the message.

The elegance and comic arrogance of Tommy Frankland won James over – and the Cambridge student was invited in. For many years he would be a baroque adornment to the lives of the Turners, and still more of Ronnie. Most immediately, he brought friends for ghost hunts, after which he stood guests and hosts regal lunches at the Bull Hotel in Long Melford. With stiff collars, tight suits and eighteenth-century imperiousness, Tommy modelled himself on Sir Thomas Frankland, a naval adventurer to whom he was probably unrelated. Funds for his acts of impulsive generosity were cadged. But he had the wit to carry it off entertainingly so that James, fooled over the money, found him 'utterly lovable in his absurdity'.

What James and Cathy most wilfully overlooked was that Tommy was ostentatiously – Oscar Wildely – gay. They were unaware of the all-male dinner parties in grand London flats to which Ronnie – enjoying the Frankland joke as they did and understanding it far more – was often invited. Homosexuality would not be decriminalised until 1967 within a severe definition of privacy, just in time for Ronald Blythe's forty-fifth birthday. Until long afterwards, such a gathering risked prosecution if fantasies spilt into the facts of life. Any frisson of excitement came at a cost of demeaning furtiveness. Ronnie was less a participant than an observer – a writer at the party making mental notes.

And if private houses were not wholly safe from the police, sexual encounters elsewhere were perilous. Ronnie was horrified by the 1948 trial of a sixty-year-old Cavendish GP apprehended on a darkened

Tommy Frankland.

country lane while in the back of his parked car with a prisoner of war. Dr Crowther, claiming language lessons which could not take place in his home due to a housekeeper's anti-German sentiments, was charged with gross indecency. A character reference from a retired general, and the defendant's age, led the judge to deliver a 'lenient' sentence: the doctor was bound over for two years. But the real and dreadful punishment was coverage in the local press. Books were so much safer.

In 1949, when turning twenty-seven, Ronnie founded the Colchester Literary Society, formalising a programme of book talks. One helper was Kay Gilmour, sister of composer Gerald Finzi, who had lost three brothers on the Western Front and memorialised them each year in the *Times*. In the wake of another world war she was about to publish a book called *Committee Procedure* – hoping common rules would aid global reconciliation. Ronnie, who would serve on so many committees down the decades, compiled the index.

Peggy Kirkcaldy, with limited means but splendid style, threw dinner parties after literary society lectures. Both she and her lover, medic Bob Sauvan-Smith, cast beneficent eyes on Ronnie. There would be a pattern in which he was companion to an older couple, almost like an adopted child.

When Bob and Peggy treated themselves to a French motor tour,
Ronnie went too. The May meander to Burgundy was his first
voyage abroad, and – since they paused en route in Paris and returned
via Chartres and Versailles – worth the miseries of travel sickness in
the back of Bob's car. By now the passenger was immersed in the
French literary classics, and so Paris was an open book. And Vézelay,
a fortified town around a once mighty abbey, was a picture on
Ascension Day.

'We had arrived there in the dark, so that I was amazed when
the shutters were opened wide the next morning to reveal a swallow-
soaring heaven and a sacred uproar below. L'Ascencion! Youthful,
laughing priests-to-be lifted their skirts as waiters-to-be watered the
flagstones. And there was this urgent calling to prayer from the grey
and gold basilica . . .'[4]

Ronnie's call to veneration was also an awareness that he was
deliciously close to Saint-Sauveur-en-Puisaye – and the garden of
the goddess Sido, who implored her daughter only to 'Look!' The
observant child became the writer Colette. Ronnie was seduced by
passionate memories she had begun to publish in the year of his
birth – the perfume of flowers seeming to be released when he
parted her lyrical pages. As she wrote:

> My childish pride and imagination saw our house as the central point of
> a mariner's chart of gardens, winds, and rays of light, no section of which
> lay quite beyond my mother's influence . . .
>
> 'I'm really rather worried. I can't remember whether it was a family
> of crocus bulbs I planted there, or the chrysalis of an emperor moth.'
>
> 'We've only got to scratch to find out.'
>
> A swift hand stopped mine. Why did no one ever model or paint or
> carve that hand of Sido's?[5]

By the time he reached Colette's Burgundy, Ronnie had already
paid homage in the arcaded park of the Palais-Royal in Paris, knowing
that somewhere above him the fabulous author, now elderly and
arthritic, lay bedridden in a noble apartment like some literary
dowager empress. Just to be near was enough.

21

Personal Gods

K AY GILMOUR HAD been to school with Marie Stopes whose father owned a brewery on Colchester's East Hill, and now she persuaded the birth control pioneer to speak to the embryonic literary society. People came flocking to be titillated by a broadside on sex – but got outspoken views on sonnets delivered in a whisper.

Ronnie later wrote of a Queen Elizabeth I-style figure 'sheathed' in celebrity: 'She appeared to be more embroiled than dressed in quantities of luxurious old russet fur, out of which her head rose, arctic and imperious. Her hair was plentiful and was dyed a rich conker red. In spite of her furs and her jewelled chains, her throat remained emphatically naked. That she was a romantic was obvious, that she was fearless was history, but that her voice should be so far removed from a sounding brass as to recall nothing as much as tinkling teacups was disconcerting.'[1]

A frustrated full house dispersed 'baffled and abashed' while the unlucky elect went on to dinner with Dr Stopes courtesy of Peggy. 'Our guest crouched forward on her fragile chair, looked daggers and kept us hesitant.' Conversational topics were raised and crushed. James Turner was snubbed when venturing a view on sonnets, 'the inference being that if she had not already exhausted this theme, it had certainly exhausted her'. And when turning to contraceptives they 'chattered too emancipatedly and were reminded, although not in as many words, that it was Love that made the world go round, not caps'.[2] The perceptive generosity of Ronald Blythe was plain in his conclusion: 'Looking back – it was all ages ago – I can faintly see her point.

'She had made up her mind to fail us because we had quite decidedly failed her. She had been on the defensive for too long and now she found it quite impossible to concede a jot. Her world was sharply divided between midgets and giants, those who feared emotion and had common thoughts, and the throbbing, rapturous chosen ones. She was sick to death of us all as we tried to insist on a sensible stance between these poles. She had taught the man in the street to heave overboard the prurience and taboos of centuries so that he could soar up into the ultimate fulfilment of bliss – and what had he done? The oaf had used her gift like an extra gadget in the lavatory.'[3]

Ronnie himself used a parting gift, a hefty *We Burn* volume of poems signed by the authoress, as a gadget in the garden. Writing outside in fine weather, he found the incendiary tome gave firm support to the notebook on his knees.

More successfully, if scarcely less peculiarly, Dorothy L. Sayers came from her home in nearby Witham to address the literary society. Speaking without notes, but with white gloves and a monocle, she made no mention of her popular Lord Peter Wimsey crime novels. Her serious literary work, she insisted, ranged from translation to theology. Her Colchester audience was treated to a lecture on the Roman emperor Constantine and his mother, St Helena, to lend a local legendary note. If an air of regret attended the choice of subject, at least they could hear what she said.

Osbert Sitwell, along with companion David Horner, took a shine to the secretary and invited him to visit when in London. Ronnie wrote to a friend: 'I received him at the top of the stairs and could not have been more apprehensive if it had been the Pope. He was very gracious. I threw him to a handful of poets whilst I went and made a speech to the vast throng then I went to fetch him, concluding with "I will now ask Sir Osbert Sitwell to join us." This said very portentously. When we came through the door, everyone clapped and thundered. Osbert looked *very* pleased and bowed, not unlike Queen Mary. He stood at my desk on the dais and read for a whole hour *brilliantly* . . . At 9 we descended to an enormous Daimler with a chauffeur reading a Western in the front and were taken to Bob's for dinner.'[4]

Although failing to entice T. S. Eliot, Ronnie was tickled pink to greet Edmund Blunden. For all the power of his poems, he was a greater advocate for poetry itself – resurrecting the talents of fellow First World War poets Ivor Gurney and Wilfred Owen; guiding Sidney Keyes, the short-lived poet of the second global conflict, while teaching him map-reading. Best of all, in 1931 he had published *Sketches in the Life of John Clare by Himself*. Ronnie had discovered in a library copy a boyhood very much like his own. He would go on to read everything by Clare – poetry, prose, song lyrics – as it was brought back from long oblivion following the author's death in Northampton Asylum in 1864 and later confinement of his manuscripts in Peterborough Museum, with undying gratitude to Edmund Blunden. Together they became Clare's champions.

As for Blunden himself: 'I recall him chiefly for his sensitivity towards a young man who aimed to be a writer but was not able to say so as we waited for the train on Colchester station.'[5] That poetic sensitivity was best expressed in the gifting of his lecture notes. 'His handwriting was a present in itself.'[6] Perhaps such a gesture was also tacit recognition that a young book group organiser longed for a more substantial life in literature. It was as if the poet sensed the poems and short stories taking shape in Ronnie's flat and so far shared with no one.

The person he most wanted to read his work was of course James Turner, but adulation was always tempered by caution. He discerned from the outset the limits of his guru's interest and forbearance. For all the literary engagement, they could see things so differently.

After a shared outing to the bedraggled church at Denston, Ronnie relished a masterwork in decay: 'Quite what they were thinking of when they founded this collegiate church just before the Reformation one cannot say, but they filled it with running hares and harts, hounds, birds, lions – even an elephant. They scamper around the clerestory and snooze on the stalls and benches . . . It always pleases me to see how much of nature manages to get into a church.'[7] James, on the other hand, perceiving a place of 'ghosts' and 'strange sounds', declared it 'a melancholy visit!' Downcast spirits lifted at a pub door. Pointing to an iron water butt, Ronnie said: 'Big enough to cook a missionary in.'[8]

But it was amazing how much chaos managed to get into the life of his guru. Low-flying aircraft brought down shelves in the

Borley sheds as the mushrooms were coming on to crop. Sensing a cosmic curse, the Turners cut their losses and rented a rat-infested cottage in Belchamp Walter for £80 a year. The rootless writer left with a £70 advance for a novel and a gardening job at Belchamp Hall. He spent £50 on renovations and wrestled with another jungle garden, leaving what remained of the rectory on the market at an optimistic £4,500. Cashing in on property was the Turner way of life since writing brought in so little and other fundraising schemes made losses. They convinced themselves that each move was for the better. When able to settle down, James could write some good poems. More often his energies were consumed by a gnawing need for sustenance and ensuing frustration and envy.

Ronnie had long explored the new district of the Turners on his bicycle. Elizabethan scholar Arthur Golding, translator of classical authors including Ovid, whose lines were used by Shakespeare in *The Tempest*, had lived at Belchamp St Paul. Miss Oates could still be seen in the garden of Over Hall in Gestingthorpe, where her dashing brother, Captain Lawrence 'Titus' Oates, had lived before vanishing with the Scott expedition to the South Pole in 1912. She worshipped at Liston church on condition she chose the hymns. Inviting Ronnie to tea, she lent him the silver wedding outfit of a Georgian forebear for a fancy dress party. The ghostly suit from 1749 was a perfect fit.

Then the Irish poet W. R. 'Bertie' Rodgers came to live at Purkiss Farmhouse in Borley with his Danish wife Marianne, the former spouse of his ex-boss at the BBC. Their marriage and rural retreat had followed the deaths of the poet's parents and his first wife, a schizophrenic. In what might have been the middle of nowhere, the convalescent newlyweds were down a lane from the village pump where the Turners fetched water – loading buckets into the back of their car.

James took champagne as a house-warming gift and further bottles to writerly meetings continuing in nearby pubs. He took Ronnie too. James and Bertie added to their allure in wreaths of pipe smoke – the aroma of masculinity. Ronnie had tried a pipe when he was twenty-one but could not keep the tobacco alight. It was another prop – another possession – not needed for an aspirant life as a writer.

Bertie Rodgers, a thick-set man with grey hair, always wore a grey suit – a dour presentation offset by an engaging smile.

Contradiction was key to his character: he appeared luxurious when always close to broke; his sobering assessments ('men and women are as honest as the day is long and no longer') were delivered when rolling drunk.

The former minister, scorned by parishioners as 'the Catholic Presbyterian', had just left a BBC post but continued to broadcast. Raised in Belfast, his talk was all of Dublin – of Synge and Yeats and Lady Gregory. Ronnie hung on beguiling stories delivered in a barely audible murmur: the commanding orator really needed a microphone.

It was in itself electrifying that the whisperer had just been elected to the Irish Academy of Letters to fill a vacancy caused by the death of George Bernard Shaw. In Suffolk, Rodgers pondered his homeland from afar. His recorded masterpiece 'The Return Room' was broadcast in 1955. A montage of voices, music and soundscapes evoking 1920s Belfast would have a great impact on Ronnie as he laid down impressions for the future harvest of *Akenfield*.

Meanwhile, there was a memorable episode when he and three revered poets – James Turner, Bertie Rodgers and Ralph Currey – spent a day visiting Suffolk churches and discussing the short life and deathless writing of the seventeenth-century poet-priest George Herbert. Ronnie was initiated into a lifetime of devotion.

From one country pulpit Ronnie read aloud to his literary holy trinity from an open Bible while wishing he could recite one of the stories he was secretly writing. But the worshipper did not presume to confess to his personal gods that he longed to be like them.

Christine and John

IN JUNE 1951, during the Festival of Britain, a first UK production of Mozart's opera *Idomeneo* was presented at Glyndebourne. That same month a tall woman in her mid-fifties with a Bloomsbury voice, shaded glasses and dancing steps sought a miniature copy of the score in Colchester Public Library.

The enquirer – Christine Nash – was also wearing the activist's outfit of a Women's Voluntary Service uniform. She conversed warmly with the reference librarian and returned the next day to borrow *him*. They had mutual friends in Lett and Cedric, she understood. Would he care to come for tea to meet her painter husband?

John and Christine Nash lived at Bottengoms in Wormingford, an address suggesting a fairy tale. On his next free half-day, Ronnie got off the bus at Tin Chapel Corner. There was no sign of a chapel, or the studio of a noted artist and newly elected Royal Academician – only a sea of corn. And the ford in the river from which a Saxon village had taken its name, an origin now lost to a dragon legend, was invisible too.

The visitor walked a country mile along a tree-lined lane and farm track. Although in Essex, much of what lay visibly before him was familiar Suffolk – from the church tower at Stoke-by-Nayland to the slope down to the Stour at Bures where, on Christmas Day 855, fifteen-year-old King Edmund of East Anglia was crowned.

The scene contracted into a tunnel of greenery – the track snaking towards the river with hazel hedges meeting overhead. Finally, an East Anglian longhouse came partly into view in a dell. It stood amid four ponds and numerous collapsing outbuildings – barns, byres, sties, chicken coop, cart shed, greenhouse, garage, earth closet – an orchard and a germinal plantsman's garden.

Christine Nash had first made this journey eight summers earlier, meeting in the verdant tunnel an old man with a bag and stick. 'Good morning,' he said. 'I'm the postman. My name is Death.' Bottengoms was not for the faint-hearted.

The teller of the tale would become Ronnie's confidante, muse and surrogate parent – though that last disquieting word could never be openly acknowledged. Ronnie found Christine 'enchanting' from the outset and, once accepted into the Nash circle of 'dear ones', he became part of the enchantment. Half German and half Scots, Dorothy Christine Kühlenthal had been a student at London's Slade School of Fine Art in its heyday, just before the First World War, training alongside Dora Carrington, Stanley Spencer, Mark Gertler and Paul Nash, then joining Roger Fry's Omega Workshops. She married Paul's younger brother John, a book illustrator and landscape painter, when he was serving with the Artists Rifles.

Slight in stature, with strong aquiline features and a stronger will, John Northcote Nash had originally wanted to be a writer, then a cartoonist. Moving from words to images, he heeded his brother's warning that artistic training might harm his special gift. There were parallels with the unguided creative path of Ronnie, though the younger man had no other option. John's life and genius were now summed up by two great paintings: *Over The Top: 1st Artists Rifles at Marcoing, 30th December 1917*, a record of a push by eighty men near Cambrai in which the artist was one of twelve not killed or wounded; and *The Cornfield*, his first non-war picture painted on returning – a rural celebration and declaration of future intent. The former hung in the Imperial War Museum; the latter was heading to the Tate Gallery.

Their marital homes would have room for one artist only: him. Scouting the scenery her husband needed to draw, Christine also created the domestic regime necessary for the ensuing paintings – perhaps those pictures should have had two signatures. But a wifely eclipse as an artist was dictated mostly by glaucoma. Hence the tinted glasses. Christine's two finest, Slade-made paintings – *The*

Picnic and *The Nativity* – remained in Bottengoms. Evoked with a lightness belying heavily symbolic scenes, the artist stared from *The Picnic* with the direct gaze poor eyesight no longer permitted. A sandwich was being proffered like a votive offering and on her head she had balanced an apple – a symbol of St Dorothy. An affecting picture about a discarded name and a lost talent was suggestive now of sacrifice.

It was Christine's abiding belief that parents must be set aside along with Victorian values and period first names. John had learned this lesson with youthful trauma when, the security of a middle-class home suddenly shattered, his mother was committed to an asylum after attacking him with a knife. Christine would later reveal to Ronnie the tragedy of her own motherhood – begging him never to mention it to John.

After problems with pregnancy, she had finally given birth to a son, William, in 1930, when they lived in rural Buckinghamshire. One November day, nearly five years later, Christine and the boy were returning in the car after driving John to a train station. The passenger door had opened when they turned a corner. It was an era before seat belts. Christine grabbed at William's coat, but he slipped from her grasp and slid over the leather seat. All this time – a lifetime of seconds – she was braking hard, so that when the infant plunged through the open door the car had almost halted. Christine rushed to the verge to comfort her son. But he had hit his head on a grating and never regained consciousness.

Further attempts at conception failed and, for all her bohemianism, Christine vetoed John's desperate plan to father a child with another woman who would share motherhood. Henceforth they would nurture John's art together amid a company of cats, and Christine would be adored by a brood of godchildren.

Christine had led John to Wormingford on a sketching trip in 1929. They stayed in a cottage adjoining the mill – ignoring Walter Sickert's expostulation that Gainsborough and Constable had left the Stour Valley a 'sucked orange'. Wrapped up in his own scenic vision, John was also undeterred from returning when, on a second visit in 1930, mill and cottage burned down and pictures were pulled from the flames. After all his First World War agonies the English countryside could only be an idyll for him.

When Christine first walked through the green bower to

Bottengoms, she was unable to approach a house rumoured to be for sale. The timber-framed farmhouse of around 1600 with beams from an older building had become a double-dweller before abandonment in the 1930s when fields running to a hundred acres were absorbed by a neighbour. Thatch had been replaced in Georgian times by an undulating peg tile roof descending to four feet from the ground at the back and known in East Anglia as a 'cat-slide'. Not that a cat, or a lick of ground, was visible when Christine came to view.

The forlorn farmhouse was almost overwhelmed by two wild acres of former garden and orchard. A spring-fed stream still plashed across the floor of the old dairy in a Tudor idea of a desirable residence with running water. The decayed plot tilting towards the river was a reserve for rats and nightingales. 'The nettles and elders were right up to the top of the ground-floor windows,' Christine noted. 'There was no trace of a garden, no sign of a path. So I continued down the track and sat for a long time under a willow tree by a barn and I thought it was the most beautiful place I'd ever seen, but absolutely impossible to contemplate as a house to live in.'[1]

Undaunted by the absolutely impossible, Christine returned with John and a path was beaten to the house so they could ponder how ancient rooms might be revived. As it turned out, only Christine had done the pondering by the time the decision was made to buy. John, now a war artist for the second time and bent on peaceful recuperation, stayed in the garden. Sifting earth through his fingers, he exclaimed: 'Yes, yes, this would do, this would be perfect for my purpose.'[2] There were several kinds of soil – good earth, soggy marsh, sand patch – and ponds thrown in. A deal was struck with the farmer, who saw that £700 was of more use to him than a vanishing ruin.

By the time Ronnie arrived, the plot had been knocked into basic shape by garbage removers and other jobbing labourers – among them German prisoners of war who adored Christine for her kindness and fluency in their language. They tended the edible as well as the visual, with nut and fruit trees and a kitchen garden. Much later, when Ronnie lived at Bottengoms, an ancient man appeared who had grown up there in the 1920s – he drew a picture of productivity, with chicken coop, pigsty and a watercress bed in the stream.

Bottengoms, 1950.

The capable hands of John Nash were more those of a gardener than a painter, though as the Bottengoms plot thickened and coloured over the years Ronnie, a biddable garden hand, never saw the plantsman lift a spade. But a true botanist valued the wild and the cultivated. John welcomed invasive marestail around ponds dredged and planted with flag and marsh marigold, and introduced balsam, bamboo and gunnera. Glades of lawn floated romantically around islanded beds – the most prominent palette-shaped – and among tall grasses and old roses.

Planting bore out the cool passion in John's illustrations for the 1927 book *Poisonous Plants: Deadly, Dangerous and Suspect*. Here was consolation for a childless man who need not mind the menace. 'His garden was always plentifully supplied with henbane, hemlock, monk's hood, foxglove, meadow saffron, spurge laurel, datura, caper spurge, herb Paris, Helleborus foetidus and other such species which he had often been found staring at, much as one might at a murderer. He was proud, not only of their robust growth, but of their capabilities.'[3]

By now there had been the barest overhaul of the house interior save for one big intervention: the stream was diverted around the building but still poured, or sometimes dribbled siltily, from taps.

Wartime restrictions, as well as low funds and love of simplicity, forced the arts of making-do, mending and recycling. Fine furniture from Buckinghamshire – including a Steinway grand piano – came on a horse and cart. The horse died on arrival.

Old china in Christine's brightly painted Bloomsbury-style corner dresser now gleamed through cat hair, cigarette smoke and cobwebs. Glaring electric light was long resisted for the glowing pools and accentuated shadows cast by oil lamps and wood or coal fires. Smelling of paraffin heating and underlying damp, the snugly stifled air was redolent of 'grand squalor'. Bottengoms as Ronnie first knew it was Christine's creation. 'She swept it out, ran up curtains on her Singer, scrubbed its bricks, lit its grates . . . She admired the way an occasional leaf would deck the bathwater and encouraged bind-weed to climb the saucepan-stand.'[4]

After further invitations to tea, Ronnie began to spend weekends in Wormingford and lend his labour. 'Keeping the winter outside was a full-time occupation here, with the result that sometimes a Tudor fug was brewed inside. There were heavy velvet curtains at windows and doors, a coke stove like a grenade in the studio, Aladdin lamps everywhere, a blazing coal fire in the drawing-room, and plenty of cosy cigarette smoke wandering from ceiling to ceiling. Draft excluders (or sandbag bolsters) were placed where one might least fall over them. Hot cats were welcome to laps. We dressed up to go to bed, or at least the artists did, in fleecy pyjamas and bedsocks . . . "Don't let the warmth out!" was the cry should I open the front door. The back door could not be closed for it was stuck in a pile of house-martins' droppings. A second, interior door, massively bolstered and draped, kept us airless.'[5]

In this difficult setting, Christine served four substantial meals daily. After a full breakfast, John painted from 10 a.m. sharp. Lunch at 1p.m. was preceded by sherry, then it was back to the studio until 4 p.m. high tea. The artist might stroll in the garden while Christine cooked from 6 p.m., changing her clothes before dinner at 8 p.m. Groceries were delivered and domestic cleaners doubled as vegetable peelers. Otherwise, Christine did it all.

John's admiring view simply blotted out the challenges. He referred to Bottengoms as the 'old homestead' in a lightly mocking tone. For all his pictures of the garden and surrounding landscape, he never depicted more than a shadow of the house.

A spring- and stream-blessed hollow, probably attracting human habitation for millennia, was held in a spell of calm even as tempests raged overhead. Starting with the front step, there were swathes of sun-trap seclusion where it felt a shame not to be naked. But from the outset Ronnie was treated as a budding writer who, temporarily salaried at the library, had to produce his proper work in free time. 'There was anxiety about where I should write, where I might not die from cold. What sometimes worried me was all this carefully contained fug not sending me back to sleep.'[6]

When the Nashes went away, a space was cleared for writing in John's frowsty studio, where piles of fag ends reeked in cocoa tin lids. A table in the garden was more enticing. And as the car rattled down the track, clothes were discarded. For Christine, to whom the beauty of Bottengoms neither eclipsed the burden nor prevented her clouded eye from picturing an easier life elsewhere, Ronnie was an emotional, intellectual and practical godsend. She was relieved to leave house and cats in his care during working holidays – John sketching landscapes she tracked from Scotland to Cornwall.

They all adored cats. A Bottengoms cluster began with Wewak, wartime evacuee from Shepherds Bush improbably named after the Japanese garrison in New Guinea bypassed by General MacArthur in 1944. Her kitten Mad Doll became mother to Queenie. More mogs wandered down the track or were brought by neighbours. Ronnie attended periodically to this feline company amid contrasting Nash notes. Christine: 'Water pot plants! Blackie eats Pilchards with the back-bone removed . . . the vet is coming to see Queenie this evening . . . Pratt is paid 6s an hour, his son (if he comes) 3s an hour and Ruth 4s an hour. Ruth will be coming for gardening but not for housework.'[7] John: 'Look for an occasional strawberry in the kitchen garden.'[8]

In next to no time Bottengoms, makeshift and magnificent, became Ronnie's true home. 'A car battery started the pump if you were lucky. Paintings swung on nails. Books rocked on shelves. Pot plants and botanic specimens filled the windows. Should in summer the bathwater fail, John would seize a towel and jump in the pond. There was a great deal of music and much hard work. Old chaps and boys toiled outside. Eric Ravilious's widow contributed the greenhouse. Mountains of vegetables and fruit came in from the wilderness. I cleaned out the ponds. Jams and pickles boiled away.

Ron from the village shop brought the order. Doors were never locked – no keys anyway.'[9]

A hive of fruitful industry lay in a hard-worked landscape. In late summer an encampment of tents appeared just beyond the garden as itinerant farm labourers and their families came to pick beans. Here was another source of the odd-jobbers who made Bottengoms happily habitable.

Ronnie was relieved that the Nashes never wanted to be treated as a married couple, but as two people conducting separate strands of friendship. He would write sitting on a bank or in a meadow while John fished or sketched. He weeded the garden to John's direction. After dinner they played piano duets to him or he read novels to them while Christine, with strong glasses and lamplight, worked on the costumes she was endlessly cutting, pinning and sewing for her amateur drama group.

His interest in them was intense and penetrating – as was theirs in him together with a Bloomsbury raciness and candour. They appreciated the witty acumen of a writer's eye and ear. The trio

Christine dancing.

became, tacitly, a family. Although each had reasons for avoiding the word 'parent', Christine's care for Ronnie was near to maternal. She had tried and failed to become a novelist: now she backed his writing goal to the hilt. She was first reader and foremost critic for his nascent flow of short stories. Postcards went to Mr and Mrs Nash, but letters were for Christine alone – and she wrote more in return. Ronnie's tone of deep affection was masked by teasing humour. Only once the armour of humour allowed him to acknowledge his 'mother-confessor'.

Christine was promoter and protector. While making it clear she would prefer the putative author to occupy Bottengoms with a friend of his own age and inclinations, instead of remaining alone in her absence, she was appalled when Ronnie continued to pay overnight visits to louche old Canon Barnett at Little Easton. In the end she put a stop to it by driving over one Sunday and spiriting him away.

23

Storm Tides

THERE WAS A sensational sunset in the chill late afternoon of
Friday, 30 January 1953, as Colchester Public Library prepared
to close. Ronnie walked back to his flat lifted by the drama and
blissfully unaware that Colchester was about to face a new siege –
from the sea.

On Saturday, across the eastern counties, snow began to flurry,
winds to wail and trees to fall. The Nashes, buffeted in their car en
route to a dinner party in Manningtree, and feeling the substantial
house of their hosts trembling all evening, took a long detour home
to avoid blocked roads. 'Every time we passed a tree we felt it was
coming on us,' Christine wrote in her diary. 'It was like a dangerous
game of musical chairs.'

Bottengoms creaked and shuddered all night, and they woke to
news of a storm-driven deluge on both sides of the North Sea. By
afternoon the Women's Voluntary Service called Christine into
action. 'At 4.15 Miss Western rang up to say would I go at once to
Harwich, that the whole town was under water, & that Jaywick was
even worse, & Canvey Island worst of all. In fact the sea had come
in everywhere. At Aldeburgh, the Alde had altered its course &
come out at Slaughden. Southwold an island. Yarmouth cut off &
so on, up & down the coast.

'We set off just before dusk. The storm was perhaps not quite so
rough, but enough to shake the car. As we got nearer the coast we
began to pass ambulances on their way to Colchester. At Dovercourt

all food shops were open, with the words "Open Emergency" chalked on the windows, we found our way to the police station where really tired & grimy looking biddies & police were working by the light of oil lamps. Water was lapping round the building & 3 boats were tied up to railings, the road in front sloped away into the water. We were sent back to the Transit Camp, where an evening meal was being prepared, we went into one hut, where the beds were up: a group of "refugees" were huddled round a tortoise stove [in] shawls, blankets and head scarves . . .'[1]

Down the eastern coast of Britain from the Orkneys to Kent the devastation was immense, with 307 people drowned in the worst of the inundation, from Lincolnshire to Essex. The carcases of thousands of farm animals littered a scene of carnage often stretching for what had once been many miles inland. In some places ground had given way permanently to water. Surveying the altered coastline and sodden landscape, James Turner thought of his next money-making scheme and how Ronnie might help. James now hectored his publisher – an old school friend – to commission *The Rivers of East Anglia* (Cassell, 1954). Ronnie was researcher and guide for what became an exhaustive motor tour of the recovering region – the pilot's recurring queasiness never mentioned along with the driver's abiding ill health.

Even more than the waterlogged landscape, they shared a love of its literary links. While exploring Woodbridge they had tea at Farlingaye Hall, where Edward FitzGerald had hosted Tennyson and Carlyle until a crowing cockerel spurred their return to London. The fowl sound of ill luck was still the dominant note in the soundtrack of rural Suffolk. They visited the FitzGerald tomb at Boulge, then drove to the ancient dead oaks and giant holly trees of Staverton Thicks, where James expected to meet a friendly ogre. Ronnie loved the tangle of nature, history and mythology (this being one rumoured site for East Anglian martyr-king Edmund's last battle with the Danes). A word to Christine led John Nash to a place of lasting inspiration.

But the social climate of the times remained inclement. The second Elizabethan age, ushered in from 1952 with a young queen's pledge of public service, and crowned in pomp and glory the following year, was also a new era of persecution. Winston Churchill's Conservatives had returned to power in 1951 and incoming Home Secretary Sir David Maxwell Fyfe was a man with a mission. He had applied a formidable legal brain to a lethal cross-examination of Nazi war criminal Hermann Goering at the Nuremberg Trials – securing the death sentence which the convict applied himself by ingesting cyanide. Now the new minister employed similar vigour in the hounding of homosexuals.

Police forces were exhorted to prosecute gay men wherever they were found to be practising their unspeakable vice, in public or private. Entrapment through sting operations, agents provocateurs – notably the plain-clothed copper lingering in the public urinal with an unzipped fly – and house searches with or without warrants raised conviction rates.

Those hauled into court in 1953 included popular novelist Rupert Croft-Cooke and newly knighted actor Sir John Gielgud – the former to be jailed for consensual sex in his own home, the latter fined for indecency in a Chelsea lavatory. Even then, public opinion was turning against a punitive law. When news of Sir John's trial broke, he was paralysed with fright in a Liverpool theatre dressing room. Co-star Sybil Thorndike clasped his hand, said 'Come along John, darling, they won't boo me', and led him on stage to a standing ovation.[2] The Gielgud career survived, but not without cost. The judge had told him: 'See your doctor the moment you leave here.'[3] He had to soon enough, after a nervous breakdown.

Prosecution of Lord Montagu of Beaulieu was the biggest sensation. Britain's youngest peer was among three men charged after a beach party with two airmen. Another of the accused was his cousin, Michael Pitt Rivers. With the proceedings reported in prurient detail, the trio were jailed for 'consensual homosexual offences'. The case – and particularly the fact that the third defendant, journalist Peter Wildeblood, changed his plea to guilty and dared to invoke a right to personal freedom – was a watershed in British social history. Slowly but surely, public opinion pushed the law towards the view that what consenting adults did in private was pretty much their own affair.

But 1954 marked a peak in the prosecution of 'practising' homosexuals, with more than a thousand in jail across England and Wales. Gilbert Nixon, a former lieutenant colonel decorated with the Military Cross in the Second World War, was among fifteen sentenced in a Somerset trial. Year-long imprisonment ended after a few hours when, like Goering at Nuremberg, he swallowed cyanide. That year a similar fate awaited codebreaker Alan Turing, arrested after reporting a young lover over a burglary at his home. His penalty for 'gross indecency' was chemical castration. A man who had done so much to win the war lost his security clearance. He killed himself, at forty-one, with cyanide in an apple.

Ironically, 1954 was also the year when the homophobic Home Secretary unwittingly launched a process of liberal reform by setting up the Departmental Committee on Homosexual Offences and Prostitution under educationalist Sir John Wolfenden. The founder expected the deliberators to think as he did. They were certainly disdainful, with the chairman proposing early on that, to spare the feelings of the women in the room, hearings should adopt the term Huntley and Palmer after the popular biscuit maker. Huntley would stand for homosexuals and Palmer for prostitutes. And as it was, only three Huntleys dared to testify – one being Peter Wildeblood.

In 1957 the Wolfenden Committee concluded that homosexuality was not a disease and 'homosexual behaviour between consenting adults in private should no longer be a criminal offence'. The panel proposed a legal age of 21 for consenting homosexuals, compared with 16 for heterosexuals. It would be another decade before Wolfenden's recommendations passed into law under Labour Home Secretary Roy Jenkins. Meanwhile, prosecutions and prowlings continued. How could stable relationships weather such a punishing climate? Small wonder Ronnie played safe and lived alone. And headed periodically towards some physical warmth – and occasionally some smoke and steam.

Ronnie knew a central London circle of relatively safe houses – pubs, clubs, saunas – in which a criminalised subculture could unwind. He visited the Savoy Turkish Baths in Jermyn Street where patrons could spend the night in curtained cubicles for less than the price of a hotel bed. That night might be spent alone or in company.

Between the gay cruising grounds of the parks and the Eros statue of Piccadilly Circus, the baths were the haunt of guardsmen killing boredom and augmenting the low pay of the armed and still conscripted services. Here Ronnie recognised closeted actors such as Alec Guinness and the popular pianist Russ Conway, with whom he once shared a cubicle. Public figures lounging poolside included Tory politicians. Ronnie had a liaison with Treasury minister Edward Boyle and glimpsed future prime minister Edward Heath, whose officially sexless state as a 'confirmed bachelor' safeguarded his career.

Ted Heath's friend Ian Harvey – familiar to Ronnie – was less fortunate. One night in November 1958 the Foreign Office minister, married with young children, was caught in St James's Park with a guardsman. He tried to escape and was beaten in an ensuing fracas. When they appeared in court, he gallantly paid two £5 fines, then left to find the world he had known crashing around him. In 1971, with homosexuality legalised in strictest privacy, flagging the distance from full acceptance, he wrote in a sad memoir: 'The branded homosexual, although no longer liable to the same punishments as he was in the past, is punished both by society and himself. He is weighed down by shame and guilt . . .'[4]

While Ronnie regarded sexuality as a fact of life to be accepted and enjoyed, he had no intention of being ambushed by it: everything in its place. Beyond legalised injustice and still hostile swathes of public opinion, he recognised a greater peril within himself. Most of the men drawn to him were older and controlling, mistaking his gentle nature for malleability if not a positive desire to be dominated. They, too, failed to see that inner steel.

The feline younger partners Ronnie favoured were a threat to writerly priorities. So, he kept an emotional cut-off point, ensuring that no encounter or affair could stray beyond the pleasurable and casual and into demanding, draining commitment – still less into muddle or chaos. 'I always knew that in the end I would be the one washing the socks,' he said. The one writing the books had to remain alone.

PART THREE

Song of Innocence and Experience

I was free. I only had to work. I felt so relieved I could have wept.

Ronald Blythe to Christine Nash, 31 August 1955

24

Times by the Sea

Ronnie was beginning to sell features and short stories with wide-ranging rural themes sent speculatively to newspapers and magazines, an exhilarating process edging him towards another kind of life in books. Cat-sitting at Bottengoms, he wrote to Christine with unconvincing nonchalance:

> Have done some writing – but more lolling. It is such a *lollable* place. Sold a short story to *Chambers's Journal* (a very lumpy magazine) for 14 guineas last Wednesday and finished two more *Observer* essays.
>
> Kindest wishes to John.
>
> Love to you,
>
> Ronnie[1]

He was nearly thirty-two and chafing at the confines of library life. Now he wrote to Roy Tracey – a former grammar school boy who credited Ronnie with the mentoring which got him into Oxford University to read English: 'I am back in Lexden Road again. They are taking up the tramlines outside. The operation is curiously dental. I can hardly bear to see the tortuous iron worms prised out of the ground and hear the huge drills. I long for Bottengoms and wood pigeons . . . Life continues much the same. One reads and eats and works and sometimes looks at the sky and thinks of Crete or Xanadu or Oxiana or Skye.'[2]

After posting that letter the writer sent himself to Skye, on what passed for a Hebridean holiday. In truth it was a reconnaissance mission: tipped off by Christine, he was trying to fathom whether he could write on a remote Scottish island – like the late George Orwell, who had completed *1984*, his last novel, on nearby Jura five years earlier.

Ronnie set out with his guidebook, *The Journal of a Tour to the Hebrides with Samuel Johnson* by James Boswell, blithely assuming scenes would be little changed from the visit by the doctor and his disciple in 1773. He was anyway seeking directions of another kind. He also packed *Boswell's Life of Johnson*. Pressed bog cotton, campion and heather came to stain its pages. His elementary school prize was forever his favourite book because 'opening it is like walking into a room full of old friends'.[3]

The experiment was a useful failure. He adored the wild landscape and wilder climate but the puritanical nature of Hebridean culture was crippling. Returning from a long Sunday walk, and confessing to going barefoot on the beach, he was berated at his guesthouse for breaking the holy sobriety of the Sabbath by sea bathing. He resisted the obvious answer that he was saved from a full immersion in sinfulness by being unable to swim. But in the wake of such interference he knew he had to make a writer's life much closer to home ground.

It was Christine who took the decisive action. A Quaker friend, Mrs Foljambe, had bought a Victorian bungalow above the beach at Thorpeness near Aldeburgh for her two sons. But one had drowned while wildfowling on the Essex marshes and the other never came. So, Christine negotiated a winter lease on an exposed house with a green corrugated-iron roof and the deceptive name of Fairhaven. Rent: 30 shillings (£1.50) a week.

Ronnie was pressed to quit the library to work on a much discussed first novel by the sea – 'The world won't come to an end' – as he fretted over jettisoning a secure position and pension for writerly uncertainty and a house lease ending in May. Christine was 'the kind of woman who made sure that you wouldn't plunge out of your depth before she pushed you off the diving board', he said. 'She had a gift for making cautious people momentarily incautious when it was absolutely necessary.'[4]

Working out that by cashing in his pension for £300 he could survive on £3 a week for two years, he had already handed in his notice when he told his mother. 'Can't you write in the evenings?'

she asked, aghast. Giving up a 'regular job' was madness to Tilly. Even then, what she saw as better judgement was overlain with love. Declaring devotion, and signalling surrender, Tilly presented Ronnie with a costly Parker pen. But he used thin-stemmed dipping pens. The fat fountain pen felt unwieldy, and he consigned it to a drawer.

James Turner deemed Aldeburgh air toxic to a fledgling writer. Ostensibly a model of loyalty, the guru's adherent quietly went his own way. And so, in December 1954, he quit the municipal confidence of the Marshall Sisson library and what proved to be false security. When part of the vacated building was relaunched as a Waterstones bookshop, decades later, a feted writer was invited to open it: Ronnie, of course.

But in January 1955 the prospect looked grim when Ronnie's brother Bernard drove him to Thorpeness in a blizzard. The car was loaded with more books than clothes, plus paper, ink, pens, an Olympic typewriter, a dismantled bicycle and small items of furniture donated by Christine.

The brothers unpacked in a sleeting gale. Bernard, the mechanic, reassembled the bike. They were met by the caretaker, who agreed to do the laundry for 5 shillings (25p) a fortnight. Then the siblings shook hands and Bernard, plus the caretaker, drove slowly away. With a sinking feeling, Ronnie watched the car vanish into whiteout. He had never felt more alone – or more disorientated.

Closing the door, he looked around a frigid interior resembling a dislodged outpost of the British Raj. Lloyd Loom chairs, bamboo card tables, ashtrays, bright rugs, chintz and Benares brass suggested a clubhouse in the Simla hills emptied of light, heat and people and drifting to wintry East Anglia. The one warm spot given any sign of sunshine would be a conservatory on the seaward side soon hailed by Christine as the Solar. Sea-glistening sun would flood this reading and writing room from south, east and west. Even on that bleak first day there was a ray of literary light.

Lying on a window sill, a random leftover from summer reading, was Christine Weston's Anglo-Indian novel *Indigo*. The castaway opened it and read: 'An age had rolled over him, he felt stranded on a reef of loneliness.' Ronnie explored this psychological saga of friendship, prejudice and cruelty – reading on as if trying to decipher a message in a bottle from a faraway beach, in a foreign language, meant only for him. As he later reflected: 'Although I seem to have stayed put I have always been enthralled by travel and I like its imaginative use in literature. It was here . . . that both the local and world view became far less separated than they are usually imagined to be.'[5]

Unrolling a damp mattress, and adding over his pyjamas a thick fisherman's jersey which might have belonged to a drowned man, he felt warmed by the book's colour. He would ultimately look back on this pivotal period of his life in a piercingly evocative memoir called *The Time by the Sea*, written and published as late as 2013:

'I read [*Indigo*] in small snatches with the waves thumping the shingle for my attention. I had never slept so near to the sea before, not even in Cornwall. It was marvellously monotonous and apparently safe, unable to make the few yards to where I lay, a sea on a cosmic leash, rushing at me then pulling back. Yet it plucked at my pillow and clinked its shingly trinkets at my ear. It bayed and hissed and implored, and would do so for ever. I felt it dragging my new purpose from me.'[6]

In the transformation of morning, he began to get his bearings and recover his resolve. Later the taut shape of the Suffolk coast between Orford and Southwold would be likened to a longbow, 'with the slight bulge of Thorpeness forming the grip'. By then he had trekked across a unique hinterland formed from 'an ancient agricultural pattern of warrens, denes, dingles, coverts, heaths, decoys, marshes, meres, sluices, thinly-soiled barley fields, flats and pastures called the Sandlings'. His walks had taken him to five old ports (Orford, Aldeburgh, Dunwich, Walberswick, Southwold) and the banks of seven rivers from the Butley to the Blyth.[7]

But on that first day he strode out to size up the sea – an immense marine wall with Rotterdam–Harwich shipping riding its horizon – and his new niche in the universe. With snow no longer swirling but 'cold beyond belief', he trudged northward in his duffel coat, muffled in yards of woollen scarf knitted by his mother. Gathering Robinson Crusoe-like resolution, he collected driftwood – bits of painted boats and Southwold's broken pier – to dry in a shed for salty-blue fires.

When walking south to Aldeburgh, he found a rundown town with rolls of barbed wire and broken concrete blocks. Relics of war and flood suggested a battered community still on the defensive as he began to write in 'strange limbo'. 'Friends wrote to say how brave I was, as if I had volunteered to carry the message across the minefield, others said that they would give me six months.'[8] In letters to his benefactor, he tried to sound buoyant:

Fairhaven, Thorpeness, Sunday

My dear Christine,

The fire is glowing, the books sit in the bookcase, papers sprawl, the typewriter yawns. I have cooked three meals, yesterday a very late, light luncheon or a very early heavy tea; this morning a most substantial breakfast which I was able to eat in the Solar, the eye of heaven beaming bright, and another light lunch to compensate for the extremely large supper I anticipate tonight.

When we got here the wind blew the rain from the sea in a terrible horizontal tempest. We staggered into the house with my 'effects' – Buhl commodes, Tanagra figurines, early editions of Ecclesiasticus etc. Tins of soup, loaves of bread, pats of butter, rolls of paper – indeed all that one needs. Mrs Westrop was already in the house and had opened it up Something Wonderful! I have reason to believe that she is not indifferent to me. She did however show a morbid interest in my health and left the name of a doctor fixed into a picture over the fireplace. 'If you need me sudden,' she said anxiously, 'ring Aldeburgh 10 and I'll come *at once!*'

. . . Today I rose at 9 and walked along the shore. It was glorious. The sea blue and glittering, the sky opalescent and enough driftwood lying about to keep me warm for ten years . . .

Well, more news soon. Believe me, I am very happy. Thank you for your most practical help in my *vita nuova*. James rang up last night. How good my friends are.

Love to you both,
Ronnie[9]

All the land for miles around, along with many buildings, belonged to the Ogilvie family, who were among the grandest and oddest strands of the Scottish migration to East Anglia. Glencairn Stuart Ogilvie, playwright and barrister, had formed a farming estate hereabouts and then, just before the First World War, reconfigured Thorpe hamlet as Thorpeness, a fantasy holiday camp for colonialists on furlough.

Between the sea and the Meare, a boating lake inspired by J. M.

Barrie's *Peter Pan*, model cottages in Tudor and Jacobean styles were to be served by a tennis club, golf course and twig-line railway. Prosperity and popularity had now peeled away. The House in the Clouds – a water tank disguised as a cottage and then converted into an aerial retreat for children's writer Mrs Malcolm Mason – needed a lick of paint. Ronnie broke his solitude in the post office. But he was usually the only customer at the Dolphin bar where a poster for Stuart Ogilvie's play *The Meadows of Makebelieve* remained framed on a wall like a faded brochure.

Out of season and era, he set down the first words of a first novel. It was 'not unlike putting a toe in the North Sea when the weather warmed up. How far dare I go? There was a page of Quink then a page of Olympia typewriter letters. I saw that I was methodical if nothing.'[10] Although the weather never did seem to warm up at Thorpeness, this was his writing practice ever after: a page or two of neat script then transcribed and lightly edited into pristine type. Just for now he planned a literary tale in the manner of E. M. Forster or Elizabeth Bowen. He could not yet afford to trust his own voice.

His ambiguous lovers in a thinly disguised Aldeburgh on the verge of the Second World War would 'lie to their mothers, tentatively explore each other's bodies and emerging characters and take a long time to grow up'.[11] The anti-war hero would be deflected from love to literature, like the novice author himself – the bond stressed further when the protagonist's name changed from Tom to Richard Brand (sharing the author's initials).

The novel published five years later as *A Treasonable Growth* would take its title from Wordsworth's poem 'The Prelude':

> And, worst of all, a treasonable growth
> Of indecisive judgements, that impaired
> And shook the mind's simplicity.

But the book was held up less by indecision than the greater urgency of money. With half of the budgeted £3 a week lost on rent, Ronnie felt compelled to make up a perceived shortfall with stories, sent out hopefully but with postage stamps to cover the return cost of rejection.

Shortest stories went to V. S. Pritchett at the *New Statesman*, longer ones to John Lehmann at the *London Magazine*. Others were scattered as far as France, Italy and America. Most produced not rejection slips and spent stamps but cheques – for 5 or 10 guineas, even £25 – so that Ronnie could pay his way from the start. Spending little, his earnings would exceed expenditure until his ninety-fifth year. Not that this brought security for decades to come. A photo from this time shows Ronnie leaning out into an abyss of adventurous possibility – braced for elemental exposure like a ship's figurehead in a gale.

In 1878 the Polish mariner Józef Teodor Konrad Korzeniowski had jumped ship in the Suffolk port of Lowestoft to join the British Merchant Navy and learn the language of his adopted land, poring over East Anglian newspapers while steaming up and down the east coast. Eleven years later he began a career as the masterly English novelist and short-story writer Joseph Conrad. Reviewing this

Ronnie at Thorpeness, 1955.

hard-won achievement via a volume of the author's letters, Ronnie felt a common cause:

'There is an acute species of melancholy attached to the early days of authorship which is often all too lightly dismissed by biographers as teething pains. The worried Conrad of *Youth*, *Heart of Darkness*, *Lord Jim*, etc. could not have imagined the Conrad of *Chance* and its revered and lucrative successors. The letters of the new man of letters are those of risk and loss, the familiar concomitants of the first freelance years. His very blessing, a wife who could type as well as create the high standards of domestic order he needed, their first son and, from the very beginning, the inestimable friendship of Edward Garnett, prince of publishers' readers, were themselves a reproach, for they had to be justified.'[12]

Although literally out in the cold, Ronnie had his characters chattering in his head for company. And always the sound of the sea. He would write a story about a woman going crazy over shingle, but the ceaseless churning as it resounded through a draughty bungalow was consoling:

'And threading through its chinks the everlasting timpani of stones, millions of them in endless movement, raking, clattering softly, wearing each other into spheres, which I found quite wonderful and missed terribly when I left. This shingle spit petered out just below me.'[13]

25

It Has Begun

Setting off to Aldeburgh for supplies one week later, Ronnie was partly blinded by another whirling flurry in a whitened wasteland. Suddenly an elderly man in a tweed coat and flat cap stepped out of the blur like an apparition. The approaching stranger was instantly familiar.

Edward Morgan Forster, now seventy-seven, still moved with the quick, light tread of youth, like a last vestige of the poised and purposeful novels he had long ceased to write. With no acknowledgement, the two men continued pressing forward against the eddying snowflakes. But when Ronnie returned to Fairhaven, a note on a torn-out diary page had been thrust under the door.

> 4 Crabbe Street,
> Saturday
>
> Dear Mr Blyth,
>   If you are free tonight and can come in for a drink, we shall be very pleased to see you.
>   Yours sincerely,
>   E. M. Forster[1]

Ronnie was bewildered. It was as if Forster had appeared in person to serve a novice writer with a suit for breach of copyright when his homage was barely begun. How had he known Ronnie was there? The question was never asked. It was evident by now that the boy from the library had a way of being noticed.

Filled with foreboding, Ronnie went to 4 Crabbe Street – Crag House. This was the Aldeburgh house of composer Benjamin Britten and tenor Peter Pears, where Forster was making himself at home while the owners were away. He greeted Ronnie at the door, shook snow from his duffel coat before hanging it up and then ushered him into a disordered sitting room. Every surface, including the absent master's piano, was covered with paper slips on which he and a companion were evidently working. The friend was introduced as Sebastian Sprott, the name he had used when a youthful member of the Bloomsbury Group; now, he was better known as psychologist and professor of philosophy W. J. H. Sprott. He was also, Ronnie would discover, a former lover of economist Maynard Keynes.

The meeting would have been doubly daunting had the two titans – he could scarcely envisage them as Morgan and Sebastian – not been so immediately disarming. They were gentle and charming, though distracted by the task before them. E. M. Forster's work in progress was a biography of his great-aunt Marianne Thornton, whose money had given him financial freedom. Spread all around them were the makings of an index. Since indexing was part of his stock-in-trade as a librarian, Ronnie offered help and soon had the job done.

The Forsterian response, as he gathered up the perfectly ordered slips, was not exactly rewarding. 'We eat at lunchtime,' he said, fetching sherry and dry biscuits. Ronnie, now ravenous, was feeling rather glum. Next came the inevitable question of what the visitor was reading just then. Rather than the honest answer of Forster's *Howard's End*, or the intellectually impressive Camus, he found himself saying 'Elizabeth Bowen'. Since his novel was to be in her style if not in that of his host, the prompt may have been subliminal. A brief meeting of Sprott and Forster's eyes compelled him to defend an author who had delighted him with *The Death of the Heart* and *The Heat of the Day*. Then they praised her too.

'I felt shy and vulnerable, immensely hungry, and unable to explain myself. I wondered how and when to leave. At about nine Forster helped me on with my coat and said that they couldn't thank me enough for my assistance. Starving and cold, I went to the White Lion Hotel and sat by a great fire, feeling that I had failed some kind of test.'[2]

The following week, however, when shopping in Aldeburgh, Ronnie passed the Britten house and Morgan Forster came hurrying out to greet him. He carried Ronnie's straw fish basket on a round of calls. '"Now the fishmonger's did you say, Ronald?" Now the baker's on the corner. Now the observing glance.' Ronnie returned that observing glance and listening ear. 'His voice was disconcertingly youthful, his features rather foxy, although with fine eyes behind the glasses.' Also the camouflage of the watcher and listener wanting never to draw attention to himself. 'Forster's clothes were a miracle of drabness, I used to wonder where one could buy them. They were so careful in having nothing to say. But his talk!'[3] Now they spoke of literature and themselves. Forster expressed a hope that he was looking after himself and a wish – though it was nearer a certainty – that he would not always live alone.

Apart from notes and letters, almost everything Ronnie wrote from now on was published. The exceptions were minimal shopping lists and accounts of meagre spending – calling at the fishmonger had been a rare occurrence since he normally bought a basin of herrings from fishermen on the beach for a shilling. Rationing, begun during the war and worsened in some respects after the conflict, had officially ended in July 1954, but for Ronnie shortage persisted. His diary was essentially a book of appointments. But after this heavenly encounter, he went home and added three triumphant words: 'It has begun.'

Far more than a writing style, Ronnie copied from E. M. Forster creative integrity which made literature a sacred endeavour. And the romance of it all was captured in a copy of Forster's *Alexandria: A History and a Guide*, which he found on a second-hand book rack. First published in 1922, his birth year, Ronnie read the tale of a cosmopolitan Mediterranean city on Aldeburgh beach, treasuring an introduction to the Greek-Egyptian poet Constantine Cavafy.

During the war Forster had presented a radio profile of Aldeburgh poet George Crabbe, who avenged himself on venal neighbours with a group portrait of savage candour called *The Borough*. In Californian exile, Benjamin Britten, a Lowestoft dentist's son, had read the script in the *Listener*. It began: 'To talk about Crabbe is to talk about England.' Britten tracked down a copy of *The Borough* and was struck by two lightning bolts of self-realisation as he read it; he knew at once that he had to write an opera and return to his native county. The results were *Peter Grimes* and the Aldeburgh Festival.

Forster attended the *Peter Grimes* premiere at Sadler's Wells in June 1945. The opera's reception was so resounding as to herald the recasting of England as a musical nation for the first time since the reign of Elizabeth I. And it further signalled an artistic renaissance after the exhaustion of two world wars and the depression between them. While Forster endorsed the eerie glory of music conveying the Suffolk sea and climate, he was shocked by liberties taken with the Crabbe text in the toned-down libretto of Montagu Slater. When collaborating with Eric Crozier on words for Britten's opera *Billy Budd*, premiered at the Royal Opera House in 1951, he made sure that Herman Melville's inspirational novella was more faithfully followed – or at least, matched in dramatic impact.

Eric Crozier had championed and even instigated Britten's music with promising ideas and the drive to see demanding projects to fruition. A year after directing *Peter Grimes*, he premiered its follow-up, *The Rape of Lucretia*, at Glyndebourne, with Kathleen Ferrier in the title role. Another year on and he was librettist for

Eric Crozier and E. M. Forster, Aldeburgh, 1949.

the comic *Albert Herring*, with a Suffolk setting and a role for Nancy Evans, his wife-to-be and co-founder of the English Opera Group. The company could have been called the Opera Group of Great Britten.

In 1948 Crozier had joined Britten and Pears in launching the Aldeburgh Festival as he continued to seize every opportunity to pay inspired tribute to the composer's genius. But then it all fell apart, as working relationships around the Suffolk master so often did. He hated suggestions. Although it was never quite clear how the chasm had opened, by the time Ronnie arrived, Eric – and therefore Nancy too – had been cast out of the charmed circle. They had retreated a few miles to a cottage refuge in Great Glemham provided by the charismatic Countess of Cranbrook – Fidelity – who chaired the festival in its first decades and scooped up many of the broken pieces. For the exiles it was both a model village and a Suffolk Siberia.

Ronnie felt an outcast too. Looking back at sixty, he said: 'Considering that a number of important friendships were getting themselves established at this time, it is strange that I still see it as full of isolation.'4 He would have a peculiar way of feeling isolated in a particular place while a familiar of its most notable people.

In what they jokingly likened to a Montague and Capulet union, Ronnie's Sudbury friend Jane Perkins was now married to Aldeburgh-deriving Denis Garrett – though their rival clans of engineers and agricultural machinery makers had long since dispersed and dazzled in new ways.

As Ronnie recalled: 'The Garretts *were* Aldeburgh. In the nineteenth century the family had built Snape Maltings and the Leiston Ironworks. Newson Garrett's daughters Elizabeth Garrett Anderson ("cousin Lizzie") and Millicent Fawcett ("cousin Millie") – would go on to change the world for women. Elizabeth Garrett Anderson was the first woman doctor and first woman mayor; her sister would become Dame Millicent Fawcett who frightened the politicians as a formidable advocate of women's suffrage as well as helping to found Newnham College.'5

Now Denis Garrett was a Cambridge don with a chair in plant pathology for eradicating diseases in corn and rice. But there were regular returns to Suffolk. Ronnie and Jane looked up in churches while Denis looked down in churchyards. On sea walks, they all

The Garretts and Turners.

gazed around their feet at the secretively rich ecology of the shingle (horned poppy, sea holly, sedum, spurge, sea pea). When Ronnie stayed with the Garretts in Cambridge, he shared a key to the botanical gardens, but also to culture and academia. As he told Christine:

I had a lovely Cambridge. Jane and I went to hear 'Dido and Aeneas' at the A.D.C. theatre. It was terribly touching because all the cast were so young and the tragedy was so mature. Dido alone was quite grown-up, not beautiful – she looked like the Queen of Holland – but she was dressed in the snowiest robes and should have had one 'orb-like' breast exposed, but this was impossible, of course. Aeneas was handsome but dull; when Dido sang the exquisite farewell 'Remember me' one imagined him to be the type who would tie a knot in a hankie . . .

Finally saw E. M. Forster at lunch [in Trinity College]. He looked
desolate, hooked-over like a fern, old and tired in the midst of the young
and Protean.[6]

Then Jane's artist sister Juliet bought a house beside the Brudenell
Hotel and facing the Aldeburgh sea. Painting the walls in glowing
Bloomsbury colours (green, cobalt, gold), she served red wine with
nightly heaps of spaghetti bolognese – cooking on a gas stove which
also stood in for central heating since rarely turned off. Juliet's
husband, Leon Laden, was a writer of work 'so exquisite as to be
invisible', Ronnie told Christine. Their new home at Brudenell
House promised to be another haven in any pending storm, and
their Hillman Minx an all-weather taxi.

But, as James Turner was less than reliable, the reassuring company
Ronnie most craved was Christine's. In an early letter from Fairhaven
there is pleading beneath the playful tone:

How could next week do for your visit? Would it not be just the right
thing to do after all your concentrations? Any day. Or Two Days or Three
Days. Do let me know. You will like Fairhaven. It has a drawbridge and
an orangery in the later manner of Inigo Jones. You shall have the small
state room which was refurbished for Queen Charlotte by the 8th Duke.
The wing is full of Americans, I'm afraid. But we must live with the
times. There is a Solar – I'm sure you remember that. I'm sitting in it
now, writing a novel and looking at the sea . . .[7]

26

Ben and Peter

ON A FREEZING Suffolk coast that spring May loomed ominously, given its eviction order from Fairhaven. And the dread month dawned with Ronnie receiving a summons.

An account deficit of £25 was deplored by Barclays branch manager, Mr Cullum. Told that this very sum was due from the *London Magazine*, the bank official continued to see red. In a pinched corner of frugal East Anglia, debt was a four-letter word.

Ronnie was left so shaken that when he ran into Juliet Laden, and told her of his predicament, she wrote out a cheque for £25 on the spot. Back in the bank he expected jubilation: 'Instead I received an even more anxious look. Not only was I the kind of new customer who was going to bother him, but a swift borrower to boot. He was now worldly-wise in Aldeburgh ways, the insecurity of people like myself, the flimsiness of our lives.'[1]

In fact, Mr Cullum could not have fathomed the depths of Ronald Blythe's insecurity. Four months had passed since the cashed-in library pension raised £300 and the plan to live, at worst, for two years on £3 a week. Exhaustive monthly accounts confirmed tighter thrift, with total spending in March as low as £10 11s 5½d (rent £6, grocer £1 6s 9½d, butcher £1 4s 4d, wireless licence £1). Amid an influx of cheques for short stories, the £300 squirrelled away in a savings scheme stayed untouched.

For all the unpleasantness in the bank, an undefended old age was far worse a prospect for a worrier in his early thirties. When again accused of wastrel ways – this time by Leon Laden (irate that his wife's charity should extend beyond himself) – he forwarded the *London Magazine*'s £25. But another solution was needed for getting by if he could not bear to dip even briefly into his savings.

And now he was facing eviction. Christine paid one last visit to the bungalow in the sand dunes. On a spring day of rare sunshine she swam languidly in the North Sea – wearing a straw hat and puffing on a cigarette in an amber holder. Then she reclined feline fashion in the Solar. Her presence would always be calming. Shortly afterwards, with his possessions scattered among friends, Ronnie recuperated at Bottengoms – and looked after John, house, garden and cats while Christine was away.

The Aldeburgh Festival was in crisis. General Manager Elizabeth Sweeting had just received a note that her services could no longer be afforded. With the future of the enterprise rumoured to be in doubt, desperate schemes were being pondered. As Ronnie wrote to Christine:

> I reached Bottengoms at 8 and after supper went straight to bed. The extraordinary news came the next morning. This is it . . .
>
> The Aldeburgh Festival (of music & the arts) is not closing-down. Nor is it going to be a long weekend. This is not generally known, indeed, is quite *un*known outside the Glemham Circle. It is possible that you know all this. But the facts are that certain people are of the opinion that the present Festival Manager should retire. And her Ladyship, acceding to these wishes, has gone about the world finding out more facts about myself. She has asked me, through an intermediary, whether I want to be Festival Manager. She says that the salary is nominal, but there would be a little flat & so, security.
>
> I have pointed out my limitations, my ignorance of music etc. But they say there are a number of people in Aldeburgh who think of nothing but music and the Festival Manager is needed to put people in the right seats and take care of distinguished visitors and write thousands of letters. Nothing is cut & dried. That Bless'd Pair of Sirens have to be consulted. I am to wait perhaps a fortnight. I have permission to tell all this. Well![2]

But it was not to be. The Bless'd Siren that was Peter Pears most probably foiled so fanciful a notion spread by Fidelity Cranbrook. Elizabeth Sweeting was replaced by Stephen Reiss, an art dealer who advised Peter on his picture collection and exuded organisational calm and skill. He would take the tactful title of Honorary Secretary given sensitivities over a summary sacking, and he needed assistance. Ronnie, the only name put forward, was won over by the £150 annual fee – the sum he had worked out he could live on if all else failed.

At the Crag House interview Stephen Reiss blinked through his glasses as the would-be assistant, wearing tweed jacket, green corduroy trousers and tie, faced the gaze and knees of Britten and Pears – both fresh from the tennis court. Fidelity, carrying serious matters lightly, 'laughed and tossed her hair'. The aristocratic arranger with film-star glamour was now dispelling tension while making the introductions. The Cranbrooks were old friends of the Nashes and Christine had sung Ronnie's praises as an exhibition and lecture planner.

'As Britten could only love or hate, it was said, and did not possess a detached view on anything, or anybody, I suppose he should not have been present. But he was . . . and would be at even the most mundane affairs affecting the Festival. The question at this moment wasn't so much "Can you help?" but "When can you start?" The room was dominated by bare legs, Peter's so white and plump, Ben's so ochre and knobbly. Doors were wide open fore and aft and a fresh breeze poured from the sea into Crabbe Street. So that was that.'[3]

The error of the appointment was lost on everyone except Ronnie and Stephen Reiss: 'What poor Stephen needed was not a young man who had run a literary society and hung a John Constable exhibition but a competent office worker. What he got was a financially illiterate novelist.' All at sea, the new recruit was sent off to say hello – and goodbye – to Elizabeth Sweeting. He found her packing up in a work room behind the Wentworth Hotel inundated by box files and with dark stains from the 1953 floods. The tiny office resembled an epic battleground. 'It was terrible!' Elizabeth said, summing up the water damage and possibly far more. Ronnie noted 'an element of thankfulness regarding her departure'.[4]

Cash – a constant problem – had been less key than a personality collision. The 1953 flood had been followed by the surge tide that was Imogen Holst, daughter and disciple of Gustav Holst, who was now Britten's assistant and confidante. The two women clashed; but for Ronnie, Imogen – Imo – was another life-saver. She found him a little flat called Crossways, in Victoria Road.

Although wrongly supposing that Ronnie's dedication to the

Ben, Imo and Peter.

festival and its composing founder matched her own, the admirable Miss Holst honoured him with a recognition that he was already a writer. 'The best encouragement comes from those who don't give advice or a noticeably helping hand, but who somehow glimpse the future in the beginner,' he wrote.[5]

It was Christine who continued to elicit his confidences: 'Imogen has just left. She wouldn't have tea but she danced in my bedroom and who could ask for more? It was about the charity concert for Elizabeth on Sunday. She wanted to know if I could work the lights and curtains! I <u>ask</u> you! I said yes anyway. The fuss they make. One would think it the Albert rather than the Jubilee Hall.'[6]

And, a week later: 'Would you like to hear about Elizabeth's benefit? . . . Every ticket was sold and twenty people were obliged to sit at the back of the stage. I was in a state pushing chairs forward, pulling bouquets in, soothing Imo, dazzling Ben, putting the lights on and off, smiling at her Ladyship in the front row, dying with fright because of the hypocritical speech she was about to embark on during the interval. In contrast, Elizabeth made a brilliant speech, cold as icicles, polite as Lady Troubridge, perfect as could be, indeed, shattering. She was given £100 and a bunch of daisies. The concert, which up to this point had been thoughtful, morose even, then broke into skittishness with Belloc songs. Peter sweated and Ben snarled.

'The Festival work is never ending. Last week I wrote about 40 letters, typed endless agenda, ran a dozen errands, had 2 committees and typed the instruments and who were to play them for every concert in next year's Festival. Tomorrow is the full Council for which I have had to hire the Moot Hall from the Mayor. There will be 17 people present. It's about as bad as the library for £150 . . . But I am philosophical about it and will do all I can for a year by which time I should be getting established. No wonder Ben is so pleasant!'7

For all his wry humour and sense of being put-upon, Ronnie came to see the magnificent conviction behind the music – and the melodrama – of Aldeburgh. He perceived that Benjamin Britten's character carried all the complications, for himself and others, of 'ruthless kindness'. And that together Britten and Peter Pears were models of creativity and courage. As an unstinting composer and uncertain singer, they had become enmeshed in 1937 when sorting the possessions of a mutual friend killed in an air crash. Their ensuing union, professionally and far less privately than they would have wished in a different world, was lifelong.

Innuendo and insult were challenged, if not scotched, by valiant confession. The first song cycle Britten composed for Pears in 1940, 'Seven Sonnets for Michelangelo', was a declaration of their illegal love. Already under attack as returning pacifists from America, they premiered the cycle in war-torn London in 1942. Stricken with nerves before any performance, the composer and pianist felt as if he were 'parading naked in public' at this one.8

When the Aldeburgh gala was founded (in what the singer envisaged as 'a modest festival with a few concerts given by friends') there was no disguising the heart of the musical – and moral – purpose. The opening offering written and played on the piano by Ben and sung by Peter was Canticle I, 'My Beloved Is Mine', op. 40. The text was based on the verse from the Song of Solomon, 'My beloved is mine and I am his: he feedeth among the lilies.' It might equally have been entitled: 'This is who we are and will be. Get over it.'

The Britten–Pears absence when Ronnie arrived in Aldeburgh was due to the London premiere of Canticle III, 'Still Falls the Rain', op. 55, with words by Edith Sitwell. It was performed in a memorial concert for the Australian pianist Noel Mewton-Wood, who had killed himself after his male partner died following an appendix operation. Both Ben and Peter knew their good fortune and how narrowly it was shared. At home and abroad they were fearless and tireless champions of their own kind.

Of course, there was sniggering and worse in Suffolk and beyond – at one point Ronnie reported to Christine that 'dozens of well-printed posters came out all over Aldeburgh advertising a new opera to take place in the Martello Tower and called "My Love is a Bosun's Mate"'.[9] But the strength, quality and sincerity of the Aldeburgh Festival overcame all.

Fidelity Cranbrook – from a Quaker background like Peter Pears, and with a brace of gay brothers-in-law – was key to winning the venture a broad acceptance. The inaugural meeting she chaired drew in the great and good: mayor, vicar, the Wentworth Hotel owner and Margery Spring-Rice, social reformer, author and granddaughter of Newson Garrett. Snobbery added Aldeburgh's yachting and golfing fraternities (privately dubbed 'the antibodies' by impish Fidelity). The aristocratic element was enhanced when the Earl of Harewood, the Queen's musical cousin, was recruited as president.

With this coalition in place, the rather unlikely and very daring festival by the sea, in a small town at the end of a branch railway line (lopped by 1963), came to command an international reputation when it could count on only a 300-seat Jubilee Hall plus a cinema, church and chapel for concerts, and a Tudor civic Moot Hall for exhibitions. When Ronnie arrived, the trawl for musical venues had spread as far as boats bobbing on the Meare at Thorpeness. And such a socially embedded cultural enterprise could enjoy royal approval – even when Benjamin Britten was allegedly being interviewed by the police in the mid-1950s witch-hunt against homosexuals. No further action was taken. Never was a life so consumed by music, said the composer Michael Tippett – a verdict overlooking only Imogen Holst.

A craving for the company of adolescent boys was assumed by many to have a predatory aspect. But Ronnie noted 'a "pity" for boyhood which would so compulsively run flame-like through

Britten's work, and throughout his life'.[10] He was to observe moments of private exhilaration when the composer uttered strange war whoops and cried: 'I'm thirteen!' Always possessed by the muse of music, a harried adult sought relaxation in a carefree youth he had never known.

Moreover, a shy man driven to compose, and to present himself on a public stage as a pianist, struggled with anxiety, depression and exhaustion – and with physical ailments his partner thought psychosomatic. At times an unrelenting creativity left its vessel sick of the sight and sound of himself – and others too. A pacifist horrified by confrontation ultimately froze out offending parties in an emotional permafrost more devastating than a verbal or physical fight.

Once other people grated on frayed nerves, tipping points could be trivial. And thus, as Ronnie gathered, what finally did for Elizabeth Sweeting was that the composer could no longer abide the way she walked.

Approach to Bottengoms.

Bottengoms in winter.

Dining room with corner cabinet painted by Christine.

Dining room with sculpted head by Jon Edgar.

Ronnie's study.

Garden room in summer.

Mr and Mrs Andrews by Thomas Gainsborough, 1750.

Dedham Vale with River Stour in Flood by John Constable, *c.*1815.

The Nativity by Christine Kühlenthal, 1912.

The Picnic by Christine Kühlenthal, 1914.

Wild Garden, Winter by John Nash, 1959.

The Barn, Wormingford by John Nash, 1954.

Ronald Blythe in his Study at Bottengoms Farmhouse by Toby Wiggins, 2008.

27

Along Crag Path

O N EVENING WALKS in Aldeburgh, Ronnie wandered along the promenade of Crag Path, with its view over the shingle and the sea. Usually, he was en route to Brudenell House for a warm welcome and a hot meal with Juliet Laden.

Swiftly past the back of Crag House, and then the Jubilee Hall, Ronnie slowed at the lighted windows of no. 32, home of popular novelist Margery Sharp and what he saw as an idyll funded by fiction. In fine weather the authoress might be on the balcony, drinking wine and playing chess with her husband, Major Castle; framed in lamplight, secure in her publishers and readers. Behind them, in a clapboard villa, Wilkie Collins had written his best novel, *No Name*.

At no. 38, after an introduction from Imogen, Ronnie embraced a family of Jewish exiles. Kurt Hübschmann had given up a Berlin photographic studio after Hitler came to power, to be reborn as Kurt Hutton, pioneering photojournalism in Britain for *Picture Post*. His wife Gretl had been a dress designer in Vienna. Ronnie basked in their culture, affection and joyful creativity. Several of Kurt's pictures grace this book.

Located between the Castles and Huttons, Strafford House brought thoughts of Victorian banker-author Edward Clodd, and the Whitsun weekends he hosted for fellow rationalists. The Darwinian gatherings of eminent men included writers George Gissing, George Meredith and Ronnie's beloved Thomas Hardy – who upset the party by

Crag Path window.

attending services in Aldeburgh church. Ronnie relished Strafford House being built 'on what they called the Crag Path . . . because it is made of Coralline Crag from the Pliocene period which I have always thought was a good address for Victorian evolutionists'.[1]

Now a would-be novelist, already deflected by festival labours and short stories, began to imagine a radio play dramatising one of these Aldeburgh assemblies. He ran the idea past Imo, who was encouraging and then astonishing – with news that Clodd's widow was still alive and sharing a deluxe bungalow by the golf course with a companion. The address was in the phone book.

Mrs Clodd had been Miss Rope, the forward thinker's secretary, who married him when he was an elderly widower. Ronnie received an invitation to tea. Seated in Hardy's chair from Strafford House, he was served literary reminiscences by 'a bag of bones in a pretty summer dress'[2] and fruit cake by her companion, Miss Grant-Duff. Neither wanted him to leave, as if his presence put off something ominous – boredom, he assumed. Amid so kind a reception, the proposed play drew scant enthusiasm. Days later, the two women left a note telling the gardener not to go into the bedroom but to call the police, then concluded a suicide pact. The radio drama went unwritten.

More promisingly, thanks again to the Nashes, Ronnie was drawn into the giddy social orbit of Lance Sieveking – a sloping giant striding along Crag Path. The radio producer lived just outside Aldeburgh, at the White House in Snape, with his third wife Maisie and their small son. Kinsman of Gainsborough and the writer Gerard Manley Hopkins, Lance was a towering figure in every sense: as a teenager he had begun a first novel illustrated by G. K. Chesterton.

Enlisted in the Artists Rifles in 1914 alongside Paul Nash, Lance first thought a watercolour by his future friend 'the work of a child who hadn't yet "learnt to draw"'.[3] But looking at Paul's pictures would be listed as a favourite pursuit in *Who's Who*, together with reading old letters. His own surreal missives revealed the maverick wit of an establishment misfit – and a sense of everything not being what it seemed.

Lance and his second wife Natalie Denny had been alarming figures to Christine, their restless spirit best – or worst – expressed at parties where people shouted, drank too much and launched into messy affairs. Natalie's liaison with boorish Randolph Churchill – Winston's only son and a man 'utterly unspoiled by failure', as Noel Coward quipped – for example. Christine would not have liked the romantic note in Lance's madcap letters to Ronnie.

While raw emotional material might be woven into the stuff of fabulous fiction, for Ronnie the exhausting nature of conjugal relationships was heavily underlined. Even friendship could get alarmingly out of hand . . .

Juliet Laden's open house often included her friend and painting companion Peggy Somerville, who had exhibited with the Royal Society of Drawing as a three-year-old. Ronnie would remember her 'as fresh as a Renoir . . . bright face, Horrocks cotton dress and her voice a seabird's wail as she catches sight of me'.[4] A sensational and ruinous reputation as a child genius had reached a zenith when Peggy staged a sell-out 'retrospective' show at London's Claridge Gallery aged nine. Novelty then faded into obscurity. But the wistful figure Ronnie knew had never stopped painting. Her mature watercolours, pastels and oils displayed a breezy impressionistic talent few now noticed.

For a while Ronnie, Peggy and the Ladens formed a companionable quartet, with outings to the funfair or the medieval splendour of nearby Newbourne Hall, where the Somerville family assembled for New Year's Eve. Then tensions between Juliet and Leon erupted in anger and anguish. He spent thwarted days in his study 'working' on an ingenious and ever invisible thriller; she, painting while light lasted, dreaded the marital bed.

All four of these singular characters existed primarily in private fantasy. They were brought to earth with a jolt when Juliet expressed a hope that Peggy would marry Ronnie. Only really at home painting Chagall-like pictures, she had yet to wish for herself a divorce. The incompatibility of Ronnie and Peggy was already glaring. 'Peggy arrived on Tuesday, laden most kindly with groceries. I took her to tea with Juliet, then we had a tensile evening, about as cosy as cuddling up to a porcupine. She stayed the night, was polite, but I fear, uncomfortable . . . Having satisfied herself of the way I live, she won't come again. She says that she is ill with her thyroid and other treatments. She is quite lacking in all tranquillity.'[5]

Peggy moved northward to Stone House in the village of Middleton, where she cared for her blind and bed-ridden mother while continuing to paint. She died at fifty-seven of cancer, leaving a treasury of unseen pictures. Much later, waiting for a train at Darsham station, Ronnie ruled out a short walk to her grave when art and nature were still on track.

'Best to watch the wild flowers flourishing between the lines and to imagine her painting them. Or setting pastel drawings of them, first giving a petal here and there a little finger smudge as I so often saw her do. Death is such a strange business. One goes but never leaves. Artists and poets in particular will hang around at halts along the line.'[6]

Meanwhile, Ronnie privately bewailed the drudgery of assisting Stephen Reiss compared with the priority of his novel:

Festival Office,
Aldeburgh,
Suffolk
(Don't tell Ben)

Dearest Christine,

Really, *Tom* goes on apace. It's far, far from all it should be, or perhaps, might be; but practice is certainly making the sentences fly. Also, I'm into it again – you know how something put away grows out of knowledge – or at least out of sympathy. I have stricken Mary's horrid mother down with a stroke and she lies all day in a shuttered room making things very difficult. Mary and Tom went to Edinburgh and there were *deeds* not words, which although not asterisked, were only touched upon.

Now I'll tell you of a very delightful happening. E. M. Forster walked up from Crag House to Crossways to see me . . . The charm of it! Well we met for three times in all and he left for Cambridge this morning. He asked about a thousand questions, looked very frail and was doing the proofs of a new book called 'The Clapham Sect'.

It would be absolutely lovely to have you here soon, but it *is* most frightfully cold. Nothing will really warm Crossways and after the Festival I intend to think of somewhere sunnier. My plan is simply to finish this book as soon as possible and to the best of my ability, then get the festival over and take a look at the future. Mr Forster says I shouldn't hesitate to go to Greece – or to somewhere – not to settle, he says for a few years more. It sounds splendid, but probably isn't so easy!

Everything about the festival is fun – except S. R. We simply don't like each other. Good manners prevail, but I am suspect; I know too many people – as if that matters! But it does to S. R.! The trouble is I'm good at arrangements – but a mediocre typist! We have got a great deal of work done . . .

Well, my dear, an early night I think. If you were here I would sit up and talk till midnight, but in the circumstances I shall retire and think about a bit more of *Tom*. Then sleep.

Much love,

R x[7]

Fidelity Cranbrook was fondly referred to as 'Fidele' or 'Her Ladyship' in letters passing between Ronnie and Christine. She remained an active and sometimes mischievous agent on Ronnie's behalf. As Ronnie reported to Christine:

My dear,

Let me send you a letter from my office – an odd office where nothing is addressed to me where, in fact, I don't care to move a thing.

Her Ladyship called this morning. Fortunately I was working hard at my desk in the window and not sunbathing or gossiping, so made a very good impression. There was a whole car-load of other ladyships, mostly unrecognisable, who waved from various apertures. I am working hard on my book and quite suddenly have the highest hopes. People are beginning to go 'round' and not just lie flat. I have done about 30,000 words.

I have had no letters for two days so desolation. Even a bill would make a break. I did so enjoy my Bottengoms this time, more, I think, than ever before . . .

Her naughty ladyship is already taking sides. S. Reiss has no place in her heart and she already compares us, I hope not in Crag Path circles! or the fat will be in the fire.[8]

In retrospect Ronnie saw how heroically Stephen had held everything together – to be rewarded with the dedication for Britten's opera *A Midsummer Night's Dream* before the almost inevitable fall from grace. He recalled the sad, pale face, the noble manner and an attendant air of tragedy not borne of administrative burdens alone. Mrs Reiss had been passionately involved with a hotelier. In a small and snooping town such as Aldeburgh, no human affair was wholly private.

Seeing Ronnie's talents wasted, Fidelity engineered a defection to Imogen Holst and the duty of compiling, and partly writing, the 1956 festival programme book. 'When I was with her everything changed,' he said.[9] Dynamo Imo was the consummate artist and so an ideal role model. She practically skipped along Crag Path, lips pursed, bright eyes fixed firmly forward – making it plain that the seriousness of her musical mission precluded all interruption.

A substantial composer in her own right, Imogen Holst was also a riveting conductor: rapt attention could lead to rapture. 'Conductors achieve their best results very variously,' Ronnie wrote. 'Sir Thomas Beecham obviously believes in a certain amount of terrorisation! Sir Malcolm Sargent gets his best results through his ruthless urbanity, and Benjamin Britten . . . by an equally ruthless kindness. But Imogen Holst is the only conductor I have seen who appears to be "audience-free". She is a suppliant at the rostrum. Do it for *me*, she seems to say – and, of course, they do!'[10]

'Her stiff fair hair was centrally parted and fixed in a tiny bun,' he added in a posthumous tribute. 'When she conducted with a wild dancing movement which could be comic as well as dead-serious the smooth curves of her hair would come a little adrift and make her look especially vulnerable.'[11]

Their shared labours gained in intensity when Ben and Peter left for a lengthy foreign tour at the end of 1955 – leaving Imo in charge of the 1956 festival. 'We sat at her big desk [on which Gustav Holst had composed *The Planets*] and edited the articles, notes and programmes, whilst all around our feet sprawled the orchestrations she was doing for Ben. At about ten she would make us a little meal and about midnight I would walk home with a long list of queries.'[12]

The little meal – probably scrambled egg on toast: so quick, so filling – was eaten on a dining table conjured up from a board laid over the bath and brightened with a check tablecloth. With no notion of work time or leisure time, the task in hand continued to be plotted as they ate, though Imo's modulated voice might now break into raucous laughter. Making art was an awfully big adventure.

'I do remember an exultancy about her which was catching. Trailing up the stairs to her flat she called out, "The Festival is everything – *everything* – dear, isn't it?" And I felt a warning. But she set me up to work on the Programme Book and, given a free hand with it, I was also aware of a rise in my status, or rather the realisation that she had, mercifully for him, stolen me from Stephen Reiss. Could Kurt Hutton take the pictures? Could John Nash do the line drawings? Might I discuss the printing with Benham's of Colchester?'[13]

That exultant sense of creative purpose rubbed off on Ronnie too. He had often wanted to convince Christine that he was happier than he really felt. Now he wrote in genuine joy: 'Did you see my *Sunday Times* article sharing a page with Sir T. Beecham? Well, there's fame if you like. And the proofs of another *N Statesman* article arrived today – one on E. M. Forster.

'A strange thing happened this morning. I suddenly thought as I sat up in bed with my morning tea (an almost adulatory addiction . . . I share with the Nashes), that this was the life I dreamed of when I was twenty. My bed was littered with proof sheets. I had had four articles published in a week. I had been reading Montaigne since seven. I was free. I only had to work. I felt so relieved I could have wept.'[14]

28

Dappled Hemlock

THE 1956 ALDEBURGH Festival was an artistic triumph − with Ronnie, now thirty-three, more than editor of an erudite programme. This member of a metaphorical and literal chorus was everything from chair arranger to security guard.

He sang in Britten's 'Saint Nicolas' cantata conducted by Imogen and, most thrillingly, acted as Forster's amanuensis for a lecture on Alexandria. Sir Kenneth Clark had borrowed J. F. Millet drawings from Paris for a Moot Hall exhibition on condition they were never unattended. Who would take the night shift? 'Ronnie,' said Ben.

So, he slept on a camp bed below portraits of Aldeburgh mayors and French peasants much like his forebears. Waves roared and rats scampered as he dreamed of Peter Grimes's Moot Hall trial for lethal handling of orphaned apprentices. Each morning he bought two herrings on the beach and went home to roll the fish in oatmeal and fry them for breakfast before working on his novel. Herrings were teeming in almost the last of their annual migrations around the British coast from the Orkneys to Cornwall. When hard-pressed, Ronnie ate two more of the 'silver darlings', kippered probably, for supper.

'What there was not was wages,' he remembered, 'just little handouts and big improvisations. Simplicity was the thing. I walked and biked everywhere.'[1] Almost everywhere: he caught a bus to Blythburgh, to bring in the church known as the Cathedral of the Marshes as a festival venue. Learning that the vicar lived in

THE NINTH

Aldeburgh Festival

OF MUSIC AND THE ARTS: 15-24 JUNE

1956

COMPLETE PROGRAMME BOOK : 5s.

Walberswick, he walked a seven-mile round trek back to the bus stop. It was worth the effort: over tea an aged cleric, polite but puzzled, was converted to concerts of sacred music by the sincerity of the petitioner. And he went by train to Saxmundham to meet Edith Sitwell and escort her to Aldeburgh, carrying the hamper containing the clothes for her performance.

At the Jubilee Hall presentation of Gustav Holst's chamber opera *Sāvitri*, Ronnie sat in the front row between Imo and Forster. As they rose to leave, he spotted the author's cap on the dusty floor, picked it up and banged it on his knee. Forster was miffed rather than grateful and thoroughly rankled by the sight of a NO PARKING sign outside Crag House. But when they met later for a splendid Wentworth Hotel dinner, as Imo's guests, all was well again.

Only when returning to his gloomy flat alone could Ronnie be dislodged by doubt: 'Sometimes Ben would drop me off after a Festival meeting in his Rolls, and all at once I would feel troubled and lonely. Unsure of myself and "far from home". Although the

question was, "Where was home?" And where should I be going?
And, maybe, who with?'[2]

He tried to cheer up bleak surroundings – the sale of a short
story to an American magazine for the dizzying sum of £100
prompting a buying spree at an Aldeburgh auction. He wrote in
triumph to Christine: 'The Sale was a great success. As the hour
for it got nearer and nearer, I got more and more apprehensive,
envisaging a waste of chipped saucepans, decollated plaster figures,
lousy bedding, arthritic chairs, unstable tables, punctured cushions,
Tortoise heaters – just the thing for a vestry, cavernous sideboards
– just the thing for her Ladyship's chickens, crestfallen carpets and
unsatisfactory commodes. But the *difference* – and it shall have a new
paragraph.

'In all I spent £29 and for that I have completely furnished the
flat. The difference is fantastic. I bought a huge, beautiful carpet for
the sitting-room for £6.10. It was the best thing at the auction.
With it there were underfelts. Also I got a vast bundle of magnificent lined curtains & pelmets which fitted exactly. (I fear you won't
believe this, but it's true.) And a number of chairs, period stuff,
although nothing they would be acrimonious about at the U.S.A.
Also the essentials, such as an 1860 coffee-grinder . . .'[3]

Now he could count on a wide supportive network for a literary
life. Many books were borrowed from Aldeburgh public library, with
advice from Miss Redstone whose friend, Miss Howe, was the
daughter of Edward FitzGerald's housekeeper, a typically Ronnie
connection. More were lent by Norah Nichols, widow of the poet
Robert Nichols. Nancy Firbank added witty novels by nephew
Ronald Firbank and a note offering love, towels and sheets.

Bertie Rodgers turned up to whisper words of wisdom in a noisy
bar. 'Can you hear me, Ronnie?' he asked in the habitual murmur.

'No, Bertie.'

'If you'd had the drink you could.'

But now he listened intently because the poet was launching him
as a publisher's reader – at 30 shillings (£1.50) a manuscript. To be
paid for reading was a dream come true, even if the first manuscript
sent to this distanced son of a discontented farm labourer was *The
History of the Pig*. He would plough diligently through scores of
unpublishable novels before discovering gems by the likes of David
Storey, Stanley Middleton, William Trevor and Edna O'Brien.

For many years the letters passing between Ronnie and James Turner discussed their hard labour as publishers' readers. James fumed over the 'trash' he had to read, and publishers so often wanted to publish, when his own efforts drew tepid reviews at best and sales so small that books were never reprinted. Recurrent illness irritated an irascible nature. Ronnie was shaken to hear that his guru had been rushed to hospital in Braintree. Christine learned after the crisis: 'I cycled to Belchamp last Sunday in tropical heat. Cathy took me to Braintree by car. James is now home and well enough to ring up and tell me that he can't make head or tail of my stories. You have no idea how welcome such a crabbed opinion is. It proves beyond doubt that he's himself again.'[4]

Being himself again, James could be worse than belittling – as Ronnie told Christine after a moment of self-doubt. He had suffered agonies of tedium in the George Hotel in Colchester with former library colleagues including 'Hunt' ('who is so nice that every word he says cannot help but inflate my remorse'): 'Then the parents. And the Hunts and the Uncles. I have visited them all. How many times have I not said, "*Don't* worry!" – and each time thought, that is what they should say to me. Everything is so disappointing – the weather, my work, which I haven't enough confidence in, James Turner, in whom I trusted and who retold all my confidences to – of *all* people – Leon. Then suddenly the sun comes out – it has now and is dappling the hemlock – and I read a bit of last week's work and don't care a bit when they (James & Co.) mock at what they call its "finish". Why *shouldn't* it have "finish"?'[5]

But James had already performed one of his most helpful acts by linking Ronnie with a literary agent – a junior partner in the firm of Pearn, Pollinger & Higham named Paul Scott. Like many other authors – notably John Braine, John Fowles and Elizabeth David – Ronnie found this affable and imperturbable agent a model of scrupulous efficiency and sympathy.

A first visit to the agency, impressively sited above the offices of the *Lady* magazine in Covent Garden, was modest enough. 'Mr Paul Scott received me in an office of Victorian gloom, sat me in a greasy armchair and we talked happily for half-an-hour.'[6] Lunch at the Epicure came later. Paul Scott was plotting novels of his own which ultimately culminated in *The Raj Quartet*. He would write full-time from 1960, after seeing Ronnie's novel into print, companioned by a daily bottle of gin; his wife moved to a women's refuge. Ronnie was flabbergasted when Hilary Spurling's *Paul Scott: A Life* came out in 1990.

Meanwhile, in the autumn of 1956 the writerly distance Ronnie still had to travel was summed up when Christine apologised for misspelling his name in a previous letter. She 'had never seen it written and had in mind Bligh of Bounty fame!'⁷ Christine read his character like no one else, however. She bought a reading lamp for his thirty-fourth birthday – so he could work on his proofs in bed. It also illuminated 'the most astounding letter' from Alfred Knopf 'about the biggest publisher in New York' asking to see a novel after a tip from John Lehmann.

This golden invitation led the feted author-to-be to the shocking discovery that *A Treasonable Growth* was two-thirds unwritten. 'But at the same time – like a revelation – all the rest of the book occurred to me . . . I am saved.' Or, at least he intended to be – concluding: 'I don't write *half hard enough* and really must get into the habit of writing *all the time*.'⁸ He also saw in Imogen Holst how collaborative exultation could lead to exhaustion, which he would later diagnose as the destructive cost of her own compositions not getting done. That and the debilitating impact of the weather.

No sooner had he expounded on the joys of winter in the *Observer* than he felt perished on an Arctic coast. 'Aldeburgh is *silent* with cold. It is a curious feeling. All the sea-birds have left and gone inland: houses are boarded up. The Brudenell Hotel has rolled-up towels along every window to keep out the wind-knives.' Fidelity, at a festival committee meeting, looking 'gloriously well, very Ingrid Bergmany', came to the rescue with a weekend invitation to Glemham. "It's lovely and warm, *ducks*," said her Ladyship.'⁹

Out of the icy blue the editor of *John Bull* magazine wrote hoping that Ronnie might become a short-story fixture, but the first samples were rejected. '*Too* damn good,' wrote the journal chief. 'Do you want our readers searching their heads?' Asked for snappier and more soothing rural tales, he tried to comply for the prospect of ready money; even these were deemed too complex.

But the judgement of 'damn fine, and memorable', when 'Immediate Possession' went to the *Paris Review*, was a different story. The judge, Eugene Walter, became a flirtatious penfriend: he himself could have been the hero of a vagabond novel. Raised partly on the streets of Mobile, and partly in the company of Truman Capote, he kept in touch with his home ground by carrying a box of Alabaman red earth on travels from New York to Paris and Italy. Along the tortuous way, eventually leading back to destitution in Mobile, he was by turns a poet, short-story author, screenwriter, actor, translator, editor, cryptographer, puppeteer, costume designer and chef.

At this point Eugene was being poached from the *Paris Review* by the American-born Princess Marguerite Caetani to co-edit *Botteghe Oscure* – her multilingual literary magazine named after the address of her palace in Rome, which the conscript was also to share. After falling out with the princess, he moved into movies as translator for Federico Fellini and as Nina Rota's lyricist for 'What is a Youth?', the theme song to Franco Zeffirelli's *Romeo and Juliet*. In a pack of cards, he would have been both an ace and a joker.

Accepting Ronnie's story 'The Common Soldiery' for *Botteghe Oscure*, Eugene praised its 'elan, energy & some extra sense of language' and then tempted Ronnie by praising Rome with some extra sense of drama. The tip was passed on to a holidaying Fidelity so that Eugene could report a 'perfect' evening with 'your Cranbrook treasure'. But he pressed on, in vain, for Ronnie himself:

> If only only only you would get a Somerset Maugham prize or something of that ilk and come to Rome where you ought to be anyway, anyway for a year . . . I go every morning to Ostia to splash in the Mediterranean and toast my carcass a little: three summers in the Caetani family prison have left me pale as a bean sprouted under a rock and not that appetizing! Mahogany is my ambition: I'll achieve golden brown oak at least.
>
> Come and join me: there's iced caviar and pale greenish Salaparuta wine and lovely melon. We could talk (will when we meet) 48 hours without stopping.
>
> Mille fleurs,
> Eugene[10]

But Eugene Walter's Rome, like E. M. Forster's Greece, was rebuffed. The thousand flowers to be cultivated were on paper or in a Suffolk cottage garden.

29

A Country Estate

Now the Turners bought an uncomfortable house in the village of Grundisburgh, close to Woodbridge, in anticipation of an inheritance and views over the Vale of Hasketon. True to form, they had a big impact on Ronnie.

Cathy ran up a new set of curtains and James waxed lyrical with the usual transient enthusiasm. The psychic duo had discerned one more setting for supernatural disturbance. And James, still milking Borley fame, was setting himself up as author and editor of ghost stories. Ronnie contributed to several anthologies with enigmatic tales never fitting the spine-tingling bill. While grateful for small fees, he was obliging a needy friend. He was also catching itchy feet.

Over Easter 1956, while full pelt on the June festival, Ronnie plotted an escape from Aldeburgh back to the Suffolk countryside. He feared his overriding goal of being a writer would be over-whelmed by organisational faff and furore. The Crossways lease was passed to an Anglo-American couple with a car. 'I didn't mention the winter and, anyway, if it gets too icy they can always live in the car. So now the die is cast and I must go.'[1]

What promised to be the idyll of Church Cottage in Great Glemham had been offered by the kind Cranbrooks at a peppercorn rent, with impressive alterations thrown in. Christine was told:

> It is quite certain that I am to live at Glemham. I am terribly happy about
> it. This flat has the most curious effect on my spirits and I can never view

it with any degree of permanency. I went over the cottage yesterday with Jock [Lord Cranbrook], his Lordship armed with a notebook and a most obliging pencil which wrote things like 'partition down' and 'window lengthened' and 'floor made-up'.

The garden is huger than I first suspected but has infinite possibilities, not to speak of infinite sun . . . I am going to work upstairs in a room very like John's; that is, on the end, with a little window staring across the park. This will be wonderful. No gaping faces passing by, no traffic to speak of and the hot-water system all about me . . .

I see the Master today at 6.30. We are to go through the Programme Book. Ben is wreathed in smiles and is delighted with the enormous progress that has been made under the new arrangements. And now that S. R. and myself have been 'separated', we seem to get on much better. But not so Imo. What *has* happened to make her so much like a half-munched celandine? Her Ladyship says 'Well out of it, my dear, well out of it!'

I am now the Fiction Reviewer for the *New Statesman*. The first batch of novels arrived last Tuesday.

I am being made a fuss of in New York, appearing in the glossies under the heading 'The Editor's Guest Book' and 'please will I send relevant facts and some informal photographs?' Mr Stevens, the chemist and choir-master took the photographs, not over well, although he was not unaware of the eminence they might well receive, possibly being squashed between Dior and details of the next heavyweight fight to take place in Madison Square Gardens.

On Friday I walked across the marshes to Fairhaven which was bolted and barred and peculiarly desolate, but with all its shortcomings it was a better place to work in than this here Crossways![2]

Cross ways summed up the state of things behind the scenes at the festival. The vicar, Rupert Godfrey, was a reluctant recruit, wishing for the holiness of his church to be unsullied by applause and for 'less rape' in Britten's *The Rape of Lucretia*. While others mocked, Ronnie reflected that, as a former Japanese prisoner of war, the parson was perhaps the only member of the company who had seen rape; he honoured the Godfrey asceticism – partly sharing it himself.

When Mr Cullum – the bank manager who had resigned as festival treasurer over Elizabeth Sweeting's sacking – became mayor of Aldeburgh, Ronnie reported: 'This has thrown us all *completely* out.' Stephen Reiss remarked: 'We now have Church and State against us!'³ Ronnie loved such wit even when he felt that the weight of a seaside arts festival was being mightily inflated.

For all his sympathy with the absorbed Ben and Imo, he was more in tune with the distance of Peter Pears had he but known it. Nearly sixty years later he wrote: 'All I can recall of him was a quiet watchfulness as Ben spoke, a nervous smile, a self-protective courtesy.'⁴ Aldeburgh was not the natural home of Peter Pears. More likely than his partner to be away on tour, and more certain to be tempted by other liaisons, the singer had expressed a personal hope in envisaging only a modest festival when it all began. As the production grew, he could remain a key player thanks to frequent flights abroad and back to the metropolitan milieu in which he was most at ease.

Ronnie's mind might be forever roaming but physically he was essentially static. He moved in September with extreme reluctance – telling Christine: 'Nearly everything is packed up. I can't bear moving. Outwardly I am all commonsense, efficiency. Inside I am rather sick! Never mind. Crossways is a sorry sight – those reproachful shadows where things have been!'⁵

A return to a Suffolk village, though in far grander circumstances than he had ever known, was to mark the start of Ronnie's real life as a writer. He quit the Aldeburgh Festival that summer, its salary eclipsed by payments for short stories and essays, publishers' reader reports and reviews for the *New Statesman* and *Observer*. He was also planning to work with Kurt Hutton on illustrated features. The main aim, however, was to finish his novel.

In December Kurt photographed Ronnie in his new abode: aged thirty-four and brimming with confidence, the transformation to the life he had always wanted was now complete. Removal expenses had been met with £30 for a story in *Homes & Gardens* magazine. And due to his own good taste, loans from friends and that bonanza in the Aldeburgh saleroom, his cottage resembled a wing of Great Glemham House. As Christine eventually learned:

This is a tardy thank-you after so great a kindness . . . I alternate between the most exhausting cottage-work and the most exacting typewriter-work with a contentment which is marvellous to behold. Those giving . . . odds and ends have made all the difference. I now have a modest bedroom

. . . and an immodest sitting-room. My *dear*! said Fidelity, and Cathy sniffed . . .

I did my Hutton work and delivered it yesterday. Kurt very pleased and said we would use this article as an example . . . I am being prodded mercilessly about my novel, but none of the prodders could be worse than my own conscience. Everything is going to the wall now, and I am going to finish it, pack it up and cross my fingers.[6]

Christine Nash would always be Ronnie's rock. But she was worn down by the hard slog of domestic management, and the wearying affairs of John Nash, as well as the Women's Voluntary Service and amateur drama. While her letters were all sagacity and sympathy, her diaries could be stonier through sheer tiredness. She took an unfailingly practical view of life and expected it in others; moreover, she mostly kept her troubles to herself. Here are her private thoughts of Ronnie at the end of pressured days in 1957:

An immodest sitting-room.

20 February: Outing to Ipswich: Home to find J & Ron greatly cheered
after having had the Studio chimney on fire, & 4 firemen down here
full of high spirits. I was gratified to find that all my cautions about
Jackdaws nests & twigs in large chimneys more than justified by events.
A spark from the newly lit fire ignited a mountain of twigs. And so a
much less gloomy evening.

21 February: J to London by the 9.43 to visit Mr Smith for tooth extrac-
tion. He takes the car & after R & I wash up, R starts away on a big
Life Talk. I cannot move, even to make bed, until 12.30. The difficulties & loneliness of living alone are gone into & possibilities of
companionable marriage & so forth & so on. I have to be brisk. I
manage to hem up the gold velvet curtains meantime. Then quick
lunch & put him on the 2 o'c bus.

10 March: See Ronnie at his cottage. He seemed more cheerful & has
made great strides in his garden which begins to take shape.

11 March: Take R back to Bott. Rush to get lunch, which we have in
the garden, the house ice cold & temp outside 65 . . . Tea with Ron
& much chatter on 'life & love' & so on. Walk up track & put him
on 5.40 bus for Sudbury.

8 April: Ronnie rings asking if he may come Tuesday for the night, bang
goes my one free evening.

9 April: Ron arrived at 5 o'c. He was in much more cheerful mood,
although we had a lot of grumbles over parents – still that's natural.
Nice dinner & a great deal of conversation. A phantasy of a Doll at
Glemham! Insist on bed by midnight, tho it sounds cruel. It seems he
has not yet got a publisher for his novel.

9 May: J starts away directly after breakfast to the Selection Committee
of the Contemporary Art Society & I prepare for Ronnie who was to
come to lunch & talk. Cold Bacon & Salad. He is living at Sudbury
because his Mother cannot cope alone. I try to work out the feathers
on the wing, but cannot concentrate owing to spate of talk, so sewed
gold lace on the robe instead. R. wishes life to be 'gay & charming'.
What does he mean by that?

3 July: With Ronnie. V. hot again. Lunch in garden, cold bacon, salad,
cheese. Made list early of all to be done, because his talk is so incessant
I cannot even think. Bring sewing to every meal, so that I can work
inconspicuously . . . force R to work while I pick rasps & red currants.
Tea, more talk & sewing. Made R shell broad beans.

1 August: Decide I must ask Ronnie over for the day . . . Ron comes

on 2 o'c bus. Make icing cake. Sit in the garden mending towel &
listening. Tea in garden . . . Cook dins, & more & more listening . . .
we get late, sitting & chatting over our wine, & R misses bus. I take
him to Sudbury.[7]

It would be another two summers before unalloyed joy lit up
Christine's diary – when, after a day in London, she luxuriated in
a balmy evening all to herself. 'I got back here at 9 o'c, & quickly
did the watering. The Temp was still 68, so I took my dinner &
ate it in the garden in the after-glow. It was wonderful . . . When
it got too dark to read I brought out 2 candles, & they burnt without
a single flicker. Oh what happiness. These are the moments that
make one's life.'[8]

Meanwhile, in a move which would have far-reaching consequences, Ronnie was directed by Jock Cranbrook to become
churchwarden of All Saints, Great Glemham. He was awed by a
church where George Crabbe had been rector. There were few
Sundays when he did not hear the Suffolky voice of the poet-
botanist-doctor-priest. 'The parish had got four professionals for the
price of one . . . in summer he would take the whole congregation
round the village after service and instruct it in botany. The Hall
gardens were flooded with his snowdrops still.'[9]

At Great Glemham.

The start of Ronnie's Anglican activities also included writing and producing a guide to Aldeburgh parish church for free. The printer sent a calendar by way of thanks – to the wrong address. This 1957 labour of love might have recouped the annual fee lost with the festival posting, but for the actions of Canon Oram, Rupert Godfrey's successor as Aldeburgh vicar. He entered the guide in a national competition and a future Poet Laureate awarded it a prize.

'I wasn't told about it and went to a City church in London to receive my second prize – £150. John Betjeman sat in the crypt beaming behind a pot of flowers. There were refreshments, wine and canapés on a table. The barrel ceiling was studded with marble tablets. The author of the first-prize church guide could not be present so his rector accepted it for him. When John Betjeman gave me the second-prize cheque Canon Oram snatched it from my hand and put it in his pocket with, "I think this belongs to us" – i.e. Aldeburgh. John Betjeman rose and pointed to me. Canon Oram gave me a hug; but not the cheque.

'Walking to Liverpool Street station I began to rehearse the preliminary rites of Canon Oram's unfrocking. I was later told that at the PCC meeting he had said that if it had not been for his entering my guide for the competition no one would have heard of it, I being so hopeless about such things. And he wrote me a letter of thanks for my generosity. And the guide would sell for half a century. I gave a copy to Ben but did not put two shillings in the box.'[10]

30

Family Matters

THE 1950S COMPLETED Ronnie's move from his blood family to the creative clan of his choice. A complicated emotional process became a simple fact of geography.

It began when his sister Connie married Ken Willis, who was raised near Lavenham but had seen and liked Australia during war service in the Far East. They sought a better life as Ten Pound Poms, emigrating with two small children via a subsidised settlement scheme. Ronnie and Tilly saw them off at Southampton, with Tilly as distraught as if at their funerals. Connie was so seasick on the six-week voyage that she vowed never to return to England whatever she thought of Australia. Returnees within two years had to repay the full £120 cost of their misadventure. That economic disincentive, and experience of Australian sunshine, higher salaries and freedom from war ruination, rationing and class discrimination, cured most emigrants of homesickness. Or, at least, they learned to live with it.

A Town Like Alice by Nevil Shute was a bestseller from 1950. The author, who had served in the Suffolk Regiment in 1918, wrote the Second World War romantic saga after settling in Australia. Harold read it and was inspired to follow his sister. To leave Tilly more bereft, Gerry decided to go too. They sailed from Tilbury on 6 February 1952, and during the night, while they were in their bunks in dormitory cabins for twelve migrant males, George VI died in his sleep.

A million Britons used this assisted passage scheme to populate Australia in the 1950s and 1960s. While most thrived, or at worst weathered life in a far-distant land, a quarter came back in costly disillusion. Happily, the transplanted Blythe siblings took to their new lives and prospered. For the two brothers it began with a journey into wonderment. Gerry played piano with the ship's band, and, as the vessel with its 1,300 one-way trippers glided towards the Straits of Gibraltar and the Mediterranean, there was dancing on deck. Already a world away from his father's voyage to Gallipoli, the star-struck player wrote in his diary: 'The deck was lit by coloured lights and, what with the moon and the music, it was like the films I have seen and now I am no longer in the audience but up on the screen.'[1]

Soon after arriving in Sydney, Gerry met and married a recent migrant from Essex. Then Eileen, as her marriage to an American GI fell apart, determined to leave New York and follow her siblings in making a new start Down Under. Poor Tilly. With four of her children committing to Australia – and Ronnie seemingly on another planet or, even worse, clearly in the orbit of Christine Nash – only Bernard, the mechanic on course to run his own garage, was understandable and available. The emptying house in Jubilee Road, shared with the mute gravedigger, felt like a morgue.

In 1956 Tilly was driven to an act of desperation. A woman who had never ventured as far as Felixstowe without asking God for 'journeying mercies' booked a passage to Australia. The ship's register listed her as an emigrant. Whether it was an administrative error, or she thought better of breaking her marriage vows, she went back to Sudbury after a lengthy visit.

Tilly returned to nurse a dying man: George was now succumbing to lung cancer. His brother Fred had been fatally gassed on the Western Front, though the poison had taken nearly a decade to work its lethal impact when combined with tuberculosis. George was finally gassed by decades of tobacco smoke. All that summer and autumn he listened to bulletins from the Suez Crisis – as a disastrous Israeli and then Anglo-French invasion of Egypt followed President Nasser's nationalisation of the Suez Canal. The territory and folly were familiar. He suffered his memories and malignancy wordlessly.

Ronnie spent much of 1957 back in Sudbury as a nursing assistant. Dutiful towards his parents in their distress, he nevertheless regretted

Tilly and George.

deeply the loss of writerly freedom. He missed his estate cottage and the company he preferred to keep. 'I shall go to Glemham on Tuesday,' Christine was told during one prolonged vigil. 'There's not much I can do, alas, in a day or so. It is such a waste of time, and I flinch from having to explain myself so frequently to my august neighbours, who must think me a very odd person to be living like this for so long.

'Home affairs trickle along, taking up more and more time, with constant and sad interpolations from my father "not to let him go into hospital". He is gradually weakening. When I draw his curtains in the mornings I think he must be gone. Yet gradually (remorselessly, I almost wrote) something flickers in his pale diminished skull and then, disconcertingly, he is talking away quite naturally, although with a fading voice . . .'[2]

Talking away quite naturally meant with a rolled-up cigarette between his lips. He never gave up this primary pleasure, but his last wish was not granted. A few weeks later, a month after his mother, Martha, had breathed her last in Sudbury's Walnut Tree Hospital, at the age of ninety-one, George died in the same building as unhappily and uncomplainingly as he had lived. He was fifty-nine – and still, after forty-seven years of loathsome labour as farmworker, thatcher, soldier, steelworker, brickmaker and gravedigger, six years from a pension.

For all the conventional respect and affection holding the divergent Blythe family together, there had always been a chasm of incomprehension between George and his eldest son – on the father's side, at least. But as the dying man talked away in that fading voice, he found in Ronnie the attentive listener he needed, almost like a priest hearing a last confession.

And so he unburdened himself of all he had suffered. The writer-confessor committed everything to memory before setting it down on paper. This first and final act of familial partnership was the greatest gift for both parties. A decade later the *Akenfield* record of Suffolk life from the late nineteenth century would be taking shape – opening with the devastating testimony of an old farmworker and Great War veteran. Since 1969 the camouflaged story of George Blythe has never been out of print.

Both George and his mother had pleaded to be spared Walnut Tree Hospital because of its long history as a workhouse terrifying Sudbury and surrounding Suffolk and Essex parishes. Taken over by West Suffolk County Council in 1929, it had evolved into a hospital funded by local charity until absorbed by the National Health Service – like so many similar buildings with a dreadful past – in 1948.

George and Martha thought the workhouse ongoing with good reason: some of the inmates had never left. One, Lily Ambrose, had been born the same year as George. In 1914, when they were sixteen, she was sent to the workhouse and he went off to war. He eventually came home again; she never did. Lily's offence was to 'fall' pregnant with an illegitimate child. She was still in the Walnut Tree, institutionalised into infantilism, when Blythe mother and son were dying there in 1957. The last of its 'workhouse women', Lily Ambrose died in Walnut Tree Hospital as late as 1985, having lived there for seventy-one of her eighty-seven years. She was still clutching the doll she had been given when her newborn baby was taken away, and from which she refused to be parted.[3]

Ronnie's own sense of belonging, to the family of his choice,

was underlined on the day of his father's funeral by a letter from
Christine hoping he might get away for a few days to Bottengoms
the following morning. She sent her love on 'a typical funeral day,
damp, dark & a horrid smell of "Chrysanths"'.[4]

Within a month of George's funeral Tilly sailed for Australia.
If not necessarily for the better, it was certainly for good. Ronnie
helped her pack, saw her off and posted George's last Donegal
tweed suit to penniless Bertie Rodgers. In return he received a
formal dinner suit once owned by poet Louis MacNeice, the
formality fading as the august relic acquired down further decades
a sinister green tinge.

Ronnie, left to clear and clean a house which had never felt like
home, wrote to Christine on Boxing Day: 'The most miserable
moment in my life was when I returned to that half-dismantled
Sudbury house after my mother's sailing. I slept on a sofa and except
for the sleeping, did nothing but scrub, pack, heave, dig, dust and
despair for 3 whole days. By the end of that time my belongings
were mysteriously transferred from Sudbury to Glemham and the
roses and lilies of Jubilee Road had become the roses and lilies of
Glemham Street. Then James, kinder than all the saints, arrived and
bore me off to Grundisburgh where we had a placid Christmas, and
I felt like somebody recovering from a long illness . . .

'There is an enormous amount to do in the cottage, but the few
extra things are going to make it very cosy, and so fitting for when
you should stay. The only thing I did was to plant all my currants,
roses etc. The rooms are in a shambles . . .

'I have a quite groundless idea that 1958 is going to be a *good*
year. My resolution is to be really selfish where work is concerned
and to get a good flow of it in circulation round the publishers.
(The Turners' Christmas pudding weighs optimistically within me,
you observe.) I'll write no more than this, except to add that I value
your love and interest above everything.'[5]

Tilly broke the marathon voyage in Ceylon with a joyful visit to
Sister Joan's mission school. Her journeyings late in life were also
to take her from New York to New Zealand. She lived with Harold
and his family until surprising everyone by marrying a fellow member
of the Sydney Plymouth Brethren. Ronnie would never meet his
stepfather or know anything about him, save for the fact that he
owned a car. This stranger could give his mother, a rather lost soul

so far from the Suffolk scenery she had once loved, a previously inconceivable mobility. Grandchildren were a growing consolation.

Although there would be regular correspondence, long avenues of their lives were now closed off from one another. Ronnie, in his nineties, would recollect that Tilly had never encouraged his calling as a writer. While she expressed enjoyment of his letters, newly published books sent across the world went unacknowledged. The inscribed first editions were received by an avid reader in – baffled, hurt or embarrassed – silence.

In genuinely affectionate letters and later phone calls, Ronnie was forever Ronald or Ron to his mother and siblings. Significantly, his blood family never used the name he chose for himself.

In the garden, Great Glemham.

31

Ronnie's Folly

AT GREAT GLEMHAM by early 1959, at the age of thirty-six, Ronnie was finally able to complete his novel, *A Treasonable Growth*. It was dedicated to Christine. On the day he signed the publishing contract in London, he also pondered delivering himself to the capital – at least for a year.

A feudal village had fallen short of an idyll. He could be desperately lonely – all the more so in neighbourly company. His garden edged that of Eric Crozier and Nancy Evans, the Aldeburgh exiles appearing over the fence like ghosts.

The five lively Cranbrook children had inspired Benjamin Britten to write *Let's Make an Opera*. But family jollity could be wearing to a writer whose nature was essentially solitary even if he sometimes thought himself in search of Mr Right. Before moving to Church Cottage, he had written to Christine after a weekend stay with what now read as a premonition: 'I don't really want Fidelity to lead a stuffy life or a splendid one. Neither would suit her. But there must be some civilised mean between these and the pudding-slinging sessions at Glemham. But they thrive and are enchanting and if their guests occasionally have shattered nerves – then it might be a salutary reminder that the English aristocracy are still the toughest breed on the island.'[1]

The Earl and Countess of Cranbrook were staunch public servants. Jock served concurrently on parish, district and county councils, in the House of Lords and briefly in national government, as well as assisting worthy bodies including the Zoological Society of London.

Fidelity, an even keener magistrate than her husband, used their travels to investigate local equivalents of borstals: knowledge of juvenile delinquency had helped in managing the Aldeburgh Festival. Her contacts led Ronnie to a revelation in Maidstone Prison. His ensuing depiction was like an illuminated image of purgatory in a medieval book of hours:

'I had expected the men to be bitter-eyed and have sweaty resentful faces; and instead they were just thin, pale people methodically guillo-tining the fore-edges of massive registers which would one day be filled with the names of other thin pale men. Everywhere one looked, pris-oners were pressing, gilding, tooling and sewing fat folios and bland quartos for the High Court of Justice, the Central Criminal Court, the Director of Public Prosecutions, the Receiver's Office, the Patents Appeal Tribunal, the Master in Lunacy, the Probate and Divorce and Bankruptcy Courts, and all the other institutions which make a good living as a result of the Fall; and it seemed a very salutary thing for them to have to do, like fetching more ink for the Recording Angel.'[2]

For all the serious purpose, Great Glemham House held an over-riding sense of fun – and constant preparations, as it seemed to Ronnie, for the next exhilarating and exhausting party. When a crowd gathered, he retreated into himself. If strangers asked 'What do you do?' he said 'I work for a publisher' and hoped that would shut them up.

The choice before him seemed to be Glemham or London, though longing looks were also cast at Cambridge. Christine set out pros and cons of the main options:

LONDON

FOR	AGAINST
You are 'in the centre of things'	Expense
Access to libraries	Noise
'Life!'	Distraction from work
Invisibility	Again expense
Visits to publishers etc.	Gas or electric heating

GLEMHAM

FOR	AGAINST
Economy	Loneliness
Garden	Self-consciousness
Warmth i.e. solid fuel	Inconvenience of no transport
Appliances	Being overlooked

'You see, I can't find much in favour of the country from your point of view,' she added. 'My lists would be different. You go, if you can. You'll never be content till you do, don't make excuses, just go. Only don't do it too often. I mean don't make a habit of thinking things will be better or different because the place is different.'[3]

The last of Christine's objections to Glemham prompted swift intermediary action. The 'being overlooked' was not so much missing out as being on display in a gilded cage. So Ronnie went to lodge nearby, in a flat of Dallinghoo House belonging to an amateur artist ('no canvas is too large to daunt her alas') while working out what to do with himself.

Christine had thought him resolved on finding a more permanent base in the Woodbridge area when news came that he was leaving for London: 'Maisie Sieveking has forwarded a note from their friends Nest and Douglas Cleverdon, offering a tiny unfurnished flat high up over Regent's Park.

'Last Friday – after signing the contract for my book – I went to see the flat and because the Cleverdons are so nice (our kind of people) and because the sands were running out, I took it. My plan is to stay for a year and then to settle as economically as I can in the country. It will not be possible to stay much longer than this because this bit of Regent's Park is being pulled down in a year or two . . .

'The flat is not at all beautiful or elegant, and its only real attraction is a roomy balcony hanging out over the park. There are two cottage-like rooms with tiny windows and low ceilings, a kitchen as big as the cupboard in my sitting-room and a tall skinny London bathroom. It is absolutely filthy, but the Cleverdons – seeing my horrified face – say they are having it properly spring-cleaned! It is £4 a week. This is a lot compared with Glemham, but Glemham is abnormally cheap.

'It would be foolish to say that I am looking forward to all this. The garden is full of things coming up. And the success of the book has filled me with a new energy. All I want to do is to work . . . Everyone is convinced that a year in London will do me good. It might. There are lots of things I shall enjoy. But I have never realised so strongly before, how much I belong to the country . . . Jock says the flat will be very useful for him to stay in when he goes to meetings at the zoo. I can see life is going to be very complicated.'⁴

Radio producer Douglas Cleverdon had coaxed *Under Milk Wood* from Dylan Thomas during seven years of alcohol-broken labour. When the manuscript was complete, the poet proceeded towards Douglas's BBC office via a prolonged bender in Soho – arriving minus *Under Milk Wood* and any memory of where he might have left it. Douglas then sprinted off on the likeliest pub crawl, finally spying the treasure Under Bar Stool.

All so intoxicating for sober Ronald Blythe. Better yet, the Cleverdons' bow-fronted Georgian house was in the vicinity of Elizabeth Bowen novels. A dull flat glittered with literary lustre. But, in a shell-shocked district, the Albany Street terrace had been slapped with a clearance order. There was a sense of living on borrowed time – on what would be bulldozed, at some unspecified point, for the brutalist edifice of the Royal College of Physicians. Many writers would have blossomed in an end-of-the-world-as-we-know-it atmosphere, but Ronnie was not among them. He needed firm foundations. A temporary rental was rescinded before it even began.

The solution presented itself during a return to Great Glemham for a Cranbrook party. Another guest wanted rid of the final year of a lease on a farmhouse at Debach, a few miles away yet seemingly far deeper into Suffolk. French's Folly – Ronnie's Folly to Christine and Imo since in the back of beyond – was just what he wanted. It was hunched beside a long, straight Roman road on which he had often bicycled. And as if to prove the rightness of the move, the phone was ringing in an otherwise empty house when he walked in.

A Treasonable Growth had just been published – on 22 August 1960 – to heartening reviews for a first novel, not least from Osbert Sitwell. The *Times Literary Supplement* offered muted congratulations for 'a small drama of meanness and futility in the shadow of anni-hilation'. Ronnie wrote: 'I couldn't have put it better myself.'⁵

Now, prompted by the novel's period flavour, publisher Hamish Hamilton was calling with a proposal for the book which became *The Age of Illusion: England in the Twenties and Thirties* – a portrait of the inter-war era. These were the two decades in which Ronnie had been raised in such unpromising circumstances. His own story would be omitted from the panoramic picture.

Suffolk matinee idol.

Related via fifteen penetrating, poignant and hilariously original essays, this was Ronald Blythe's first masterpiece in the literary form he would make his own. The episodic saga researched in public libraries ran from the burial of the Unknown Warrior in Westminster Abbey to the coming of Churchill, by way of Amy Johnson in her flying kit and Harold Davidson, the defrocked rector of Stiffkey, mauled to death by a lion in Skegness shortly after the Abdication Crisis.

The chameleon author would stay put in French's Folly for the next sixteen years. A spasmodic plotting of possible lives elsewhere was a recurring daydream. As he wrote: 'I still occasionally speculate what it can be like to live somewhere where the signposts are not all pointing to the towns and villages of childhood. It is not as if, as some writers have, I made a vow to stick to the home ground; for I never did, and I have often thought that there could be benefit in giving it the slip for a decade or two.

'I could say that it had some kind of pull etc but inertia comes into it. On the other hand, I justify myself, if a writer has stayed at home, there is no doubt that he suffers certain home pressures and his way of coping with such stresses and strains can be the strength of his work.'[6]

In the hard-won life of Ronald Blythe, the work came before everyone and everything.

32

Cornish Romance

WHILE MOST OF his immediate relatives were finding themselves on the other side of the planet, Ronnie's idea of romantic travel focused on the far west of England. His love of Cornwall would be lifelong.

There were 1950s holidays with the Turners exploring coast and countryside around Falmouth, with an especially happy visit in the summer of 1958 and an end-of-jaunt call at the Bell and Steelyard pub in Woodbridge. Regaled with love of all things Cornish, the landlord produced a snapshot of Primrose Cottage, in a hamlet near Padstow. He was selling it for £3,000 and the turn-again Turners duly bought it. The traditional stone and slate cottage within sight and sound of Atlantic breakers would set a new gardening challenge since the vendor had covered part of the plot in pink concrete.

Waving goodbye and good riddance to Grundisburgh the following Easter, James took away the bitter memory of a north-easterly gale blowing through the Vale of Hasketon for twelve wearisome weeks. The superior weather of Cornwall would be one settled point in their wandering mantra for the rest of their windswept lives.

The haven at Trethias was a stroll from the Cornish Arms pub 'full of huge Cornishmen who dance to an accordion and another Cornishman with bells on his calves' – a foretaste of Padstow's May Day folk carnival when the 'Obby 'Oss horse is lured from winter sleep and teased through the streets by swaying and singing crowds. Ronnie was urged to follow the Turner lead with praise for a small cottage for sale in St Merryn. Cathy added: 'Can you be tempted?'[1] This too would be a constant refrain.

In early July James wrote from his attic study in dazzled delight that 'we are straight at last'. He was looking out over a hayfield being cut: 'The hedges are encrusted with valerian & honeysuckle falls in fountains into mackerel, caught at five o'clock in the morning. In fact paradise can scarcely be more heavenly, or if it is, then it will really be something.'[2]

In December, writing with plans to meet Ronnie's Christmas Eve train at Padstow, he mentioned having to go to hospital three times a week by private car. This news was imparted only because of an interesting encounter on the journey, 'one fellow passenger being an old lady who said her mother used to have a villa outside Rome and, as a girl, had lived on the Isle of Wight. "I remember the Old Queen at Osborne. How gay the balls were at Christmas." She had seen Tennyson "every day. What joy!"'[3] The now down-at-heel Miss Matthews was to go 'quite dotty', James reported – convinced, when dying in Redruth hospital, that she was 'staying in a spa in Baden-Baden in about 1900'.[4] It was due to stories like this that Ronnie continued to revere him.

He loved his guru's passing passions and, that Christmas, enthused to Christine over the latest obsession: 'It was the strangest thing to be journeying to Cornwall in the winter, looking out at all those places which one normally equates with June. And very exciting, too. James & Cathy met me at Padstow Station and drove me to their house. It is very old with thick walls and a broad slate terrace lets the garden descend in a series of lavender-smothered steps. From upstairs there are lovely wild views towards Treyarnon and Constantine Bay. No sooner had I arrived than the most tremendous gales blew up and spume from the sea hung in the tamarisks like fat lumps of detergent.

'On Boxing Day I went walking on my own to Trevose Head in such a thunder of wind, Atlantic rollers and hail that I was almost deafened. I had never seen a sea like this before. It was just a great boiling cauldron of titanic water – really rather frightening. The Bull rock threw up the waves to more than a hundred feet and the sea burst into the coves like shot. Coming back I found a broad, shallow stream had sprung up where I had walked, so I had to take off my socks and shoes and wade – up to my knees – across

Constantine Bay! The water was warmer than Aldeburgh in August. One could have bathed. All the hedgerows are dense with daisies, hart's tongue, wild wallflowers and a beautiful little round leaf, which I don't know.

'We have had a delightful Christmas and each night I lie in bed and listen to the sea . . . James and I have just returned from walking to Porthcothan and it is absolutely lovely – even in a gale!'⁵

A pattern was being set: the wildness of the weather; diminishing walks in Turner company; long explorations alone. But for a year there would be a break in the friendship, on the face of it due to humdrum housekeeping.

The fracture had been anticipated when Ronnie wrote to Christine of his first Cornish holiday with James and Cathy (and, on this occasion, her mother). From Mylor, near Falmouth, he reported: 'We were enchanted by the cottage. Quite roomy and tastefully furnished with a great many mod. cons. Plenty of hot water, despised by the Turners but delighted in by me. James is wonderful. So equable and kind and warm to appreciate things. I like a certain eagerness in life. But the Turner ladies are too voluble in their domesticity and already I am tired of kitchen comparisons and conversation like a shopping-list. I am aware more than most men of the importance of such things but I can't think with so much talk about washing-up. I would do it myself, and *silently*, if they would let me. But they rejoice in their burden.'⁶

In September 1960 the Turners, inviting themselves to stay at French's Folly, in the spirit of their own generous hosting, were undeterred by Ronnie's honest reply of being beset by work. They would be 'easy guests since out a good deal'. James left an account of the ensuing debacle.

'Nothing seemed to go right. It was true, I think, that we did not understand the touchiness of such young men as Ronnie who live alone and look after themselves.' Cathy, having offered in vain to shop and cook, had gone into the kitchen to help with pointed lines of enquiry such as where's a sharp knife? and why don't you get yourself a modern cooker? 'They were the kind of remarks often made between old friends,' James asserted. 'Ronnie rounded on her with "All you bloody women are the same. Always complaining about my lack of this or that." He was obviously very angry.'⁷

At the dawn of the 'permissive' 1960s the pattern of marriage in

Britain was still set along Victorian lines. Many more women had careers by then, but most would abandon them – by choice or, more likely, compulsion – with the wearing of a wedding ring. Men brought home the money for the bacon and women bought, cooked and served it, also clearing and cleaning. Apart from household repairs, male participation in domestic labour was seen as exceptional if not exemplary while gardening remained a manly thing.

Hitting a nerve in Ronnie, Cathy provoked one of the rare explosions in his life. Mostly he was able to restrain himself amid the barbs. As when, passing Cathy on the stairs and catching the aroma of her perfume, he said: 'You smell nice.' To which she shot back: 'I should!' Somehow it was an affront to a traditional notion of masculinity and femininity even for him to have noticed.

An offer for Ronnie to stay in Cornwall that Christmas was fobbed off with an excuse of work, and communication ceased for many months. The painful breach for both sides was finally ended by Ronnie writing – 'What is more I can't stand this *listening* silence for another minute' – when James was also on the point of sending a conciliatory letter.[8]

All of this and more was written up by James in his memoir of 1970, when Ronnie was famous for *Akenfield* and an impressive name to brandish in print. Ronnie recoiled from such exposure, but that was not the worst of it. James could write in one voice only – his own – and his fiction was lightly cooked from raw emotion and experience. Ronnie recognised a character in one novel, who had found literary fame through youthful good looks, as a projection of himself distorted through the prism of authorial resentment. Deep hurt healed in silence.

From now on the bare bones of the old friendship would remain, through affectionate familiarity running over many Cornish reunions, without ever again touching his heart. But gratitude to James Turner would be unceasing. As Ronnie said on turning ninety: 'I based my life on his freedom.'[9]

33
Little Bird

IN JUNE 1960, at the start of the decade in which he found fame as a writer, Ronald Blythe took a day trip to the National Gallery in London. He wanted to see a newly acquired Thomas Gainsborough painting of a young couple in their country seat near Sudbury.

The Auberies estate in which the newly wed Mr and Mrs Andrews, Robert and Frances, were pictured in 1750 was almost unaltered by the passing centuries, save for an accumulation of myth. Locally roaming spirits had long reported that the stone cats on the gateposts changed places every midnight.

Now, just like the painted figures, the visitor was formally dressed, though he carried a briefcase rather than a huntsman's gun. And who could say what Frances Andrews, the trophy wife, might have been holding – bag, baby, fan, pheasant? – since her hands were wrapped around an unpainted patch on her lap. The enigma extended to the sitters' faces – the bride shrewd, perhaps; the husband's countenance broad and open as the East Anglian landscape while at the same time giving little away. A mystery makes a story and, for the gallery viewer from Suffolk, stories were the stuff of life.

Late in the afternoon of the painting's first day on public display, when approaching a small crowd gathered in the vestibule of honour, the countryman remembered that briefcases were not allowed. He thought, as he wrote to James Turner, 'oh hell what does it matter, I'm only going to look at one picture . . .

'I noticed that the attendant had reached his hand half out to direct me to the cloakroom, then he stared and said, "Good afternoon, sir." I was a bit nonplussed at this and went to look at the Gainsborough, which is wonderful . . . A big, tweedy man who looked a bit like Vaughan Williams looked at the painting and then looked at me, and then he looked again. And again and again and again. Meanwhile, everyone stopped talking and began to watch me and I thought something was wrong with my zip or worse.

'At last I escaped and crossed the vestibule and stood in front of the only other picture in it, a big blowsy Madonna. Immediately there was a touch on my shoulder and there was Vaughan Williams looking over me and saying, "Do forgive me, Mr Andrews."

'Well, after I had explained to him that I had, as a matter of fact, lived a good part of my life within a couple of miles of this landscape . . . this had the oddest effect. He looked disbelieving and bewildered. We shook hands and I left the gallery. Everyone turned round and watched me go and the attendant saluted.'[1]

In that same summer of 1960 fifteen-year-old Margaret Hambling, who wanted only to draw and paint, mustered the courage to take her pictures to Benton End for advice and, she hoped, acceptance. She was admitted and her life changed for ever.

The supplicant was the daughter of a Hadleigh bank manager and Conservative Association mainstay, and her defection to the 'glowing oxblood farmhouse' on the edge of the stolid Suffolk town would be absolute. The French-style atelier for liberated art and life was 'known locally as the "Artists' House" and for "every vice under the sun"'.[2]

Students at the East Anglian School of Painting and Drawing were drawn to either one of the masters, Arthur Lett-Haines or Cedric Morris, whose advice could be contradictory. The Cedric people painted like him; the Lett people painted like themselves. While loving Cedric, the promptly renamed Maggi was decidedly a Lett person. The scary mentor paid his youngest protégée the compliment of showing her no mercy. After a first month of fault-finding, she was close to tears, seeming to do everything wrong, even when chopping a carrot. 'You don't pick holes in a rotten apple,' Lett said reassuringly.

'He was the one who said the important things to me,' Maggi remembers. 'Such as: "If you are going to be an artist you have to make your work your best friend. Take to it whatever you are feeling and have a conversation with it." And: "It's no good being an artist without imagination."[3] Those crucial lessons have already been learned by the company she will keep.

Now high tea is laid out in a high-summer garden. Paints and easels are abandoned in the flaming flowerscape, where John Nash and Cedric Morris, plantsmen first and painters second, have been deep in botanical conversation for hours. The party may well include the Colonel's daughter-turned-painter Joan 'Maudie' Warburton and Welsh artist Glyn Morgan (known as the Little Prince since so good-looking), gardener Beth Chatto and garden writer Tony Venison.

And here, wholly at home in his patrician aspect, is Ronald Blythe. He carries a weight of wisdom lightly. His first novel is about to be published, his short stories are coming out in a collected volume and he is researching *The Age of Illusion*, the book declaring his genius.

Interviewed for this biography sixty-two years later, Maggi recalls Ronnie as being 'rather like a delicate little bird who darted about; he seemed to be always on the move though always rather concentrated. He had piercing eyes and was quite giggly and always smiling. Not overawed at all. But he was also slightly removed from everything

Cedric and Ronnie.

– occasionally pitching in with a witty comment but always observing, observing: a little bird looking and listening from a distance.'

Even here, at the sociable table in the artists' garden, he is on the edge of the picture. Both Cedric and Lett are evidently fond of him. And he, possibly alone within the gathering, is in neither directorial camp. In some unspoken way he is somewhat aloof: his own person; an artist looking on.

Told that he knew he could give a false impression of being shy and prim, Maggi says: 'He did have the air of a Sunday school teacher. Always rather smart. Everything Ronnie did was very precise; his voice was rather posh.'

Reflecting on their enduring friendship – with mutual affection but with neither party being in the other's inner circle – she says: 'I never saw Ronnie with anyone. I always imagined he was gay but without any evidence. He wasn't physical in the sense of giving you a great big hug or even pecking a kiss. He was reserved, watchful.'

Surprised when enlightened, Maggi especially loves the idea that the formally dressed figure was a lifelong naturist. And she is astonished by the depths of his early poverty, the lack of formal schooling and the jettisoned peasant burr. Then, after musing in a long silence, in which new pieces are slotting into an old mental image, she says: 'So, he was a complete invention, like Noël Coward. How amazing.'

From that first meeting with Maggi Hambling in 1960, Ronnie visited Benton End regularly over further decades. He witnessed the art school as it flared then faded and closed, and the garden as it gradually receded into a hayfield lit up with showy but slowly choking blooms.

During many stays at Bottengoms, John Nash announced late of an afternoon: 'Let's drive over to see the Boys.' 'Oh do, darlings!' Christine exclaimed, glad for some time to herself and a break from cooking. A welcome would be guaranteed, with warm amity as John and Cedric picked up a perennial conversation about the life of plants.

After Lett's death in 1978, Ronnie, alone or in company, continued to call on Cedric, as he went, complaining bitterly, from bright sunlight into the shuttered night of blindness. For all their friendship, the vigour and candour of the Morris creative vision was too much for John Nash at times. But Ronnie was similarly unflinching:

'He had an understanding of plant mortality which affected his human portraits. An "all flesh is grass" statement to accompany the vigour of vegetable and human life. "Watch out", John Nash would say. Cedric would reach for a flower and look into it, his brown fingers, painty and nicotiny, their nails rimmed with soil, caressing its stem. With flowers, as with birds and men, he wanted them to give a truthful account of themselves.'[4]

And such a reaching out for truth had revelatory results. 'In one way or another all of us "flowered" at Benton End,' Ronnie concluded.[5]

Near to his death, in 1982, Cedric invited close friends to choose keepsake pictures. Ronnie selected a breezy view of the Algarve with washing blowing on a backyard line and a pear tree blowsy with blossom. The artist was too sightless to sign it, so Maggi brushed on a perfect facsimile of his name.

Ronnie last saw Cedric when calling in with Glyn Morgan after an outing to Sizewell in torrential rain. He hung drenched jeans over the Aga while Millie, the housekeeper, fetched an ancient three-piece Morris suit, which he wore stylishly for supper, only minus a shirt and socks. As they said their farewells Cedric took 'a curious sliding tumble through his overcoat to the brick floor on which we met thirty years ago'. He was lifted to his deathbed where Maggi drew him still reaching out for truth.

'I thought, now there must be a gap, a great vacancy, the shattering of the first circle. But no, and for the simple reason that when people are in their nineties, as Cedric was, they stop taking up the full human space. "He's not all there!" the village boys used to shout at some persecuted creature of their own age, and for some months past it was plain to me that, although he was in his chair at dinner, or trotting down the backstairs at Benton End, or cutting into the talk with all the old amusement and relevance, vital aspects of Cedric had already wandered off to their own devices, leaving us just enough of his personality to trick us into thinking that he was still here and could be for ever.

'He knew differently. Last Christmas, when the first deep snow had fallen, he said to me, "Do they touch your sleeve like this?" giving a little attention-drawing pluck to his jacket. Well, they don't, to be honest. Not yet. But if I manage to be ninety I dare say they will.'[6]

At Benton End the biggest scourge was not convention but

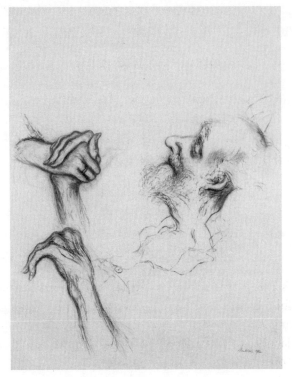

Cedric by Maggi Hambling, 1982.

boredom, though they often combined. 'Not a boring thing' had been Cedric's highest praise for a plant picture – and a person also. He cared nothing for contradictory and contrary opinions, given the courage (and support) simply to be himself. 'The lasting influence that Benton End had on me was a sense of openness, honesty and intellectual freedom. Not to give a damn!'[7]

Shrewdly self-aware, Ronnie concluded: 'Although so unlike him, I was drawn easily into his conspiracy of laughing judgements and solid work, although, alas, I was too much myself to achieve anything approaching his freedom.' Taking away exactly enough for his own personality and purposes, Ronnie absorbed 'a whole range of new attitudes and ideas to my existence which gave it just the right amount of carelessness it needed in order to survive'.[8]

'At Benton End I was taught somehow that you could do everything for yourself. They never gave any lessons, you simply took an easel. It was £3 a week – bring your own sheets.'[9]

34

Break in the Elms

FRENCH'S FOLLY WAS named by its farmer owner, Harold French, in rueful memory of the bill for even the most cheapskate restoration. Facing north, and huddled against an arrow-straight Roman road, the Jacobean farmhouse now looked to some like a curled up hedgehog on the verge of being squashed.

Ronnie loved it at first sight and ever after. His study window squinted over a hedge to elm trees – bearing wood for floors, chairs, bookshelves and coffins – and then across rolling, pond-rife fields. Set amid low wooded hills and quiet valleys between Woodbridge and Framlingham, Debach – pronounced Debbidge – was the epitome of workaday Deben Valley villages. Eminently missable, it presented no cause for pause on any passing journey. But the elms gave – or lent, as it turned out – a touch of grandeur even in winter:

'Back at the house I walk into a scene which has little to date it. Small, typical East Suffolk fields screened by elms, and icy here and there with spreading ponds. It is what I see every morning from my upstairs desk. Daily, I observe it all emerging from the night, moving phosphorescent islands which are my neighbour's sheep.'[1]

What Ronnie's friends thought the middle of nowhere was bang on the divide between the Sandlings of coastal Suffolk and the clay plateau of High Suffolk. The new resident would always revel in borderlands. Here cornland lay beside a plain of concrete – the remains of wartime Debach aerodrome, which Spitfires had again ceded to skylarks. Crevices were still yielding evidence of military occupation, messages from the departed spurring an attentive walker on fresh researches into war poetry, stories and diaries.

A break in the line of elm trees nearest to French's Folly had been caused by a crashing and burning plane. Neighbours related in matter-of-fact Suffolk fashion how the collision had decapitated the pilot. While digging a kitchen garden Ronnie unearthed a lot of blackened and rusted metal – warped and jagged thin panels, instruments full of worms – which he solemnly reburied.

Harold French had squandered on French's Folly a small fraction of his compensation for aerodrome land. He lived with his sister and together they splashed out on the standard symbols of wealth: swimming pool, Jaguar, racehorses (Debach Boy and Debach Girl). But mostly the siblings held fast to frugal ways. When a hotel booked them a double room, the mistake was never rectified since it brought a lower bill. They took the Jag blackberrying – Ronnie watching a slow, purring progression from bush to bush.

French's Folly supported Ronnie's view that people of slow-moving ages built houses next to roads for the stimulation of seeing and hearing the world go by. 'The road in front was a kind of clock: half-past-six the farm men and the road men on their bikes, half-past-eight the school children on theirs and office workers' cars going to Ipswich, and all the seasonal traffic of course, drills, pea lorries, harvesters. A few yards away at the back it was totally different, no time at all, just these ditches and vast uncut may hedges which surrounded the fields belonging to the house when it was a farm.'[2]

Borderland again. On a kind of frontier, the former farmhouse was hunched around a large old horse pond with mallard, moorhen, carp and tench. The horses had gone but occasionally the garden was still trampled by marauding cattle.

At long last Ronnie was in his element – and, for all his love of privacy, open to local people hiding curiosity in helpfulness. The admiral living on one side and the general on the other kept a dignified distance, but the appraisal began with the prompt appearance of 'an ancient man with sky-blue eyes to "give you a hand with the grass", i.e. to find out who I was. Very wise.

'Rumour having been put about that I wrote books, he was mildly awed. Then, spotting a typewriter, it was "Aha!" Any fool could write books with a machine. He himself had never written a word in his life, nor read one. What is more, they – he meant a succession

French's Folly.

of scribbling vicars – had failed to put him down. What did I think of that? I congratulated him. Later, he would take me to a barn to show his 14-year-old handprint in the plaster and declare triumphantly, "That's all!" He meant evidence of his existence. I was taught some wonderful local history by this unlettered neighbour.'[3]

In time the existence of this unlettered neighbour would be marked out in deathless words, though posterity would know him only as 'Davey' – and even that was not his name. He was a kind of outcast but, given that Debach had a population of barely eighty, people round about were anyway thin on the ground: 'On Saturday afternoons the village football club played visiting teams in the meadow next to the house with almost no spectators.

'I used to laugh and say that the house and its surroundings were minimal situations which encouraged a writer like myself to fill them out with my imagination. But this was just a sort of defensive thing one tells people. Nothing around here was minimal to me. This place was a full and intricate restatement of everything which my family had heard and seen and understood for hundreds of years.'[4]

Tiny Debach was dwindling into a hamlet. Ronnie became churchwarden at All Saints church just before the Victorian building designed by Gilbert Scott on a medieval base was converted into a house. The first service he led was its last evensong, after which he was directed by the diocese to distribute ornaments and furnishings among nearby churches. Then he redistributed himself to the larger village of Charsfield, to serve as churchwarden alongside road mender Ernie Cole. The vicar – Dubliner Cecil Fox, once, so romantically to Ronnie, rector of Killarney – and his wife Addie became friends.

In many ways a rural congregation was his natural community ('Mrs Martin on the harmonium and the holy simple man they all cared for in his regular place').[5] Sundays brought a break from writerly solitude. Anglican allegiance leavened routine with ritual and festival, the church calendar joining the seasonal cycle in mapping out the year and putting a freelance writer firmly in his place. He loved the order of the Liturgy – matins, evensong – in which his mind was still inclined to wander.

His spirituality would never be doctrinal. For him it was all about the stories, landscapes and people and the connecting of past and present in a chain of life. The pew was also an excellent vantage point. As he said of fellow churchgoers: 'I'm fascinated by their personalities and by something which is unreachable which might be called their spirituality or their prayerfulness. And I see them Sunday after Sunday . . .

'I suppose it is the writer in me which becomes enthralled by them. I never ask them questions . . . I just can't help but see them and their children or their backgrounds. They had these beginnings in the old field work and if they are very old sometimes in service or perhaps in the big house and not in service at all but rather grand. But there they all are in church, sometimes kneeling at the rail, taking the chalice which has had the lips of people touching it since the time of Shakespeare. And it is very poetic.'[6]

Walking and cycling from church to church, he found 'the simplest, most sacred building' in his lifelong personal guidebook dedicated to St Andrew and St Eustachius at Hoo ('rubble walls, Early English windows, more Tudor bricks, an altar like an hospitable tea-table, a brick floor like a larder').[7] Here Ronnie worshipped with Mr and Mrs Buckles – she leaving boxes of eggs in his bicycle basket, he spinning out biblical readings in a broad Suffolk yarn. 'Hoo, for me the loveliest of all field-churches, where at Whitsun only the tips of the tombs could be seen dipping like grey boats on an ocean of Queen Anne's Lace. I had an old farmworker friend there who read the lesson. When it carried him away, as it often did, he would pause then say, "That was very fine. I'll read that agen." He would have been perplexed had he known that I still hear him as one of the great oracles of God.'[8]

But further distancing from his blood family was confirmed when Tilly Blythe visited from Australia. 'I saw myself writing quietly at a desk with a nice old lady doing embroidery or knitting by my side. Alas, it was far from this. She dislikes the country; it frightens her. She enjoyed spending long days in Woodbridge and Ipswich and going on about a score of brief visits to relations. But Debach rather floored her by its being merely a house surrounded by meadows.'[9]

Each late April he cycled eight miles to Framsden as the guest of Queenie Fox – queen of the snake's head fritillary. Everyone was invited. 'For a few spring Sundays her meadow had become her front room. There were nightingales, and a chilly wind blew, and I

Hoo church.

imagined the flowers rustling as they swayed. We were welcomed into the field, not asked to walk around it. Dotted here and there among the blooms were other guests awkwardly trying not to tread on them. Almost immobilised by the flowers at our feet, we became trapped like figures in the floral margin of a book of hours. Queenie had no such qualms. She strode around picking handfuls of both purple and white fritillaries to press on us.'[10] Largesse was the old country way when it came to flowers, rooted in the old wives' certainty that the more you plucked the more they grew.

Amid an ongoing cycle of the living and the dead, Ronnie remained haunted by the shade of Edward FitzGerald. The translator-poet had been unabashed by his own idiosyncrasy, but his family had buried him in Boulge churchyard with an epitaph by way of an excuse: 'It is God that made us, and not we ourselves.'

'My favourite churchyard when I lived near Woodbridge was Boulge, where Edward FitzGerald lies under a rose from Omar Khayyam's tomb in Iran,' Ronnie wrote. 'I would cycle to it and lie in the tall grasses, listening to Mr Anderson's sheep blaring through the hedge and smelling the bull-daisies, and thinking of a short story . . .

'There were mown paths between summer thickets, illegible names, done-for dates. Lady White's husband. I would have tea with her. Thin, shallow cups, warm, fresh scones. A butler.

'She was fragile, almost not present, her hands like skeletal autumn leaves that blow along the lanes. "Where did you leave your bicycle?" She knew folk who knew Fitz. "A very odd man. But then it wouldn't do if we were all alike!"'[11]

Ronnie took his place among what was then the large bachelor-hood of the countryside. Why so many men remained unmarried was a rural mystery with a note of poignancy. Wheelwright Clifford Arbon of Monewden said with bleak Suffolk humour: 'Those who knew me didn't want me and I didn't want to disappoint a stranger!'[12]

The writer lived between past and present, fact and fiction. One friend driving over for supper at French's Folly began a discussion of Regency country life as portrayed in Jane Austen novels, where parties were aligned with full moons – when, save for clouded skies, it was safest to send out carriages. The guest was then left speechless on learning that Ronnie still took the lunar calendar into account when responding to social invitations. Blythe night vision was unusually attuned for cross-country rambles. But a full moon was best for a merry bicyclist wheeling homeward along unlit and potholed lanes.[13]

As time passed Ronnie was accepted into the local scene as a singular figure rather more elevated than eccentric – and ultimately a fitting personage to hand out prizes for home-grown produce at the Debach and Boulge Show. In earthy Suffolk natural phenomena could be spectacular: 'Cycling back to Debach from Framlingham I saw a great oak in the middle of a field blazing like a torch or an immense sparkler letting off its own thunder. When the rain fell, not daring to shelter under a tree, I stood in a ditch and wisely distant from my shining bike, literally wet to the skin and yet somehow exhilarated and "elemental".'[14]

All too soon the grandest trees began to die from Dutch elm disease. Ronnie was aware that in East Anglia 'elms propagated themselves by runners, travelling along farm hedges, and they perished similarly, death running from one to the next until they all vanished'.[15] Neither sentimental nor nostalgic, he embraced the nature of earthly decay.

And besides, even as the elm trees disappeared, he knew their species had not really died. They remained as shoots and saplings in thousands of hedgerows – succumbing only when large enough for split bark to let in lethal beetles.

Elms, like hope, spring eternal.

35

Intensities of Love

THE SUCCESS OF *The Age of Illusion*, the first Blythe book to be published and acclaimed in America despite all the hopes for his debut novel, sealed Ronnie's literary career when he was forty. Like an East Anglian elm on its runner, fresh growth was generated. Most immediately, the author was inducted into the Penguin English Library as a selector, editor and introducer of classic texts.

A first subject, Jane Austen's *Emma*, involved euphoric sessions with the first edition held by the Victoria & Albert Museum. Published in 1966, the Blythe tribute ran through twenty-three reprints until launched as a Penguin Classic in 1985. Later he would present Thomas Hardy's *Far From the Madding Crowd* and *The Awkward Age* by Henry James, whose heroine was last seen in the Suffolk town of Beccles.

Now, and best of all, Ronnie chose to champion the writings of William Hazlitt, the Georgian radical with whom he found a common cause. He loved both the wayward life and the wildly free-wheeling work – being drawn to a boy who had hidden in the long grass from the sound of his mother's voice summoning him, in vain, to conformity. When not gazing at cloud formations, Hazlitt had found himself in books, and especially in the essays of the French Renaissance philosopher Michel de Montaigne.

Commissioner Tony Godwin welcomed a compelling subject who was a model for the 1960s counter-culture. 'Hazlitt leaves no one neutral,' Ronnie would write. 'Disturbed himself by every ecstatic, political and tragic aspect of the human condition, he could never believe that there were those who managed to get through life without feeling and knowing these things in all their intensity.'[1]

For Richard Mabey, Hazlitt was not so much Ronnie's hero as his alter ego: 'The two have so much in common: they are self-educated countrymen – "village intellectuals", passionate liberals, Romantics in love with language and their fellow humans, of whatever situation. But Hazlitt was burdened with baggage Ronnie has mercifully escaped. He was bitter, subject to mood-swings and outbursts of violence, intemperate in just about every possible way and incapable of not wearing his heart on his sleeve.

'By contrast, Ronnie's work, though deeply personal and often autobiographical, is intensely private. Do not expect disclosures or revelations. The man who has written so sensitively about others' travails and illnesses and loves, is silent about his own. If you were to ask him why, the answer might be that robust East Anglian response to nosiness, "Never you mind!" Time enough for that when the biographies are written.'[2]

Crucially for Ronnie, Hazlitt lit a path in writing: 'An essay means to assay, to go forth, usually rather recklessly; to keep a subject in the air as thought follows thought. Hazlitt was a great racquet-player on the St Martin's Street court – where the [Westminster] public library now stands – and a dab hand at keeping a ball in the air. When his essays began to be published in the *Morning Chronicle* in 1812, his enemies were terrified. Where might not his truthfulness fall? He, of course, acknowledged his master, Montaigne. In taking up his pen, he did not set up for a philosopher, wit, orator or moralist, but he became all these by merely daring to tell us whatever passed through his mind. All the best essayists give us a piece of their minds in brief, brilliant helpings.'[3] As with Michel de Montaigne, so with William Hazlitt. And so, too, with Ronald Blythe.

Where Hazlitt was improvident, forever falling into debt, Ronnie was prudent to a fault. To make ends meet, as he believed, since he had a blind spot where his healthy bank balance was concerned, he gave pieces of his mind more laboriously as a publisher's reader. In 1963 he read three manuscripts in an average week. Then there were books for review – scores more of those. That May's deal with the Penguin English Library brought congratulations from James Turner followed by the self-serving thought that Ronnie would no longer have time to be a paid reader and it would *hardly be fair* to other writers who needed the money. In case the hint was missed, the writer of the letter added that he could do with extra work himself.

While Cathy dreamed of a rich Ronnie wintering in Bermuda, shared Christmases in Cornwall continued, as did spring or autumn visits. The complaining and consoling letters poured through every season. Ronnie was asked to write Turner blurbs, edit his manuscripts, review his books, sympathise over his frustrations and rejections and press his case wherever he could – all of which he did. He also continued to assist Turner anthologies, from ghost to gardening stories. James, seeing profit in more permissive times, plotted an anthology on adultery. He related every thwarting thing – a polite note from Iris Murdoch regretting she did not write short stories, a rude one from Graham Greene saying he was very careful of the company he kept; H. E. Bates had an ill wife and L. P. Hartley could not decide either way while in Italy. Ronnie meekly sent a story and gave the collection its title (*Thy Neighbour's Wife*).

On the beach.

And then, in spring 1964, the Turners took flight to another 'dream' cottage. Converted and conveniently sized, Treneague had a fine barn and south-facing views over woodland. It was a ten-minute walk from Wadebridge and a snip at £4,800. Primrose Cottage (mortgaged for £2,750) was put on the market for an ambitious £7,500. A would-be buyer, arriving from Surrey with his pregnant wife, said he too worked from home – raising for James the spectre of writerly competition. But the home-worker was composer Malcolm Arnold, who had made a fortune from film scores including *The Bridge on the River Kwai*. He paid the Turners more than they had really expected and became a friend into the bargain.

Ronnie gladly toured the new house and district that Christmas, and also met the Arnolds. Then and later, Malcolm was most often to be found in the Cornish Arms or the Metropole Hotel in Padstow, drinking and cursing – until thrown out and on to a pub crawl. After one chucking-out, he fell in the harbour. Another time, fresh from the Metropole, he kissed Ronnie on the mouth. 'No, Malcolm! No, no, NO!' shrieked James. Homosexuality had a nasty habit of creeping up on him. And for Malcolm Arnold it may have been the latent key to an unruly nature. Ultimately, wrecked by alcoholism and psychosis, he was rescued by a male hairdresser, who cared for him lovingly for the rest of his life.

Still more than the love that dared to speak its name all too often, James Turner was haunted by failure. This demon was aggravated by the Penguin English Library. After Ronnie's winning debut, he suggested his guru as another contributor. James sent sample books to James Cochrane at Penguin, who brusquely replied that he did not have 'enough of the necessary talent'. 'What, I ask in passing, is so bloody special about them anyway?' James fumed. 'I admit I liked your introduction to *Emma*. I have seen others which are nothing but fourth form.' Were it not for money, he would prefer making the garden. 'But alas, one must work.'[4]

So the literary chores kept on having to be done. Ronnie was roped in for an anthology of love stories, with two tales per contributor from male and female points of view. He sent 'Bride Michael' and agreed to its being halved to fit the brief. Mercifully, the fine Turner voice and forthright opinions led to regular work as a local guide and literary critic on regional television and national radio. But, ever short of cash, James then got Ronnie to press for a civil list pension. Sending a list of names to canvass, he added: 'I rang up Malcolm Arnold who was delighted to be asked, especially as he had just set the P.M.'s wife Mrs Wilson's carol to music.'⁵ The chorus convinced: the pension was granted. Ronnie was then prevailed upon to petition the Royal Literary Fund for further help, which was also forthcoming.

One day the Turners and Ronnie returned home from an outing to find a balladeer waiting in the garden. This was Charles Causley, who became a mainstay of Ronnie's visits. They shared a reverence for the writing of John Clare. While training as a teacher in Peterborough, Charles had cycled to the nineteenth-century poet's childhood haunts in and around Helpston – writing a poem with the title of the village name which Ronnie now saw as a place of future pilgrimage. Charles also helped James to secure his pension, making up for Turner upset when the younger man was awarded the Queen's Gold Medal for Poetry.

In old age Ronnie looked back on Cornish Christmases – with 'chilly churches, vast empty beaches, wild pubs, roaring headlands and an out-of-season landscape that stretches before me at this minute, untouched by time, blowy, enticing. It is only by the greatest self-restraint that I don't lock my door and set off at this very minute to Paddington. Except that, when I reach the Bodmin Road, the little car won't be there to meet me. And strangers will inhabit Treneague, and the other guests will be scattered, like James's dust, on Bodmin Moor, high up by the Cheesewring. And Malcolm Arnold won't be buying rounds in the Cornish Arms. Yet all this does not sadden me because the Cornish Christmases themselves stay full of life . . .

'Goodness knows how many of them there were. They began at Dawlish, where the train hugged the coast and the west of England ran into view. Excitement would fill me then. The tails of the brace of pheasants which my Suffolk landlord had given me would twitch on the luggage rack.

'Then I would come to the granite bedroom and the gulls howling outside, and James, swathed in an immense dressing-gown, with the morning tea. And the early service in the barrel-roofed church, meekly shivering on our knees. And then . . . those local parties, each like a chapter in a novel when seen from this distance. And the drives through the deep lanes in which the spring flowers already

showed themselves. The days of my visit were carefully allocated
. . . one for Charles Causley, one for me to be on my own on the
thunderous cliffs . . .

'Charles Causley would take us on a mystery tour, once to see the
rectory of Sabine Baring-Gould [eclectic writer of 'Onward, Christian
Soldiers') at Lewtrenchard on the Devon border, and to places that
only a native Cornishman would know. He had a dry wit. His life
was divided between schoolmastering and caring for his invalid mother.
Somehow, between these conscientiously performed tasks, would come
masterpieces such as "Timothy Winters".'[6]

Driving to a talk in Felixstowe, Charles phoned French's Folly and
jaunts were hurriedly hatched. Ronnie guided him to FitzGerald's grave.
'It was midnight and also Charles's birthday,' he wrote. 'The car glittered
in the moonlight. We could see to read the inscription . . .'[7]

Charles had lost his father in boyhood, but his mother lived to
a great age. Carers were minimal; Charles did it all, often writing
his poems in her room. Ronnie ended letters 'And love to your
Mother'. When Mrs Causley died, an only son and sole carer was
poleaxed and then distanced from James Turner, who blurted about
a happy release and burden lifted. Ronnie wrote: 'People do not
understand the varieties of human love and their intensities.'[8]

36

First Friends

WAKING UP AT Bottengoms was a special joy for Ronnie. Christine, who rose first and liked time to herself downstairs while mustering the energy and strategy for all her duties of the day, brought tea to the guest bedroom and opened the curtains on another instalment of happiness.

She sat on the edge of the bed as they talked about anything and everything. Sometimes she carried a photograph album with tiny black-and-white snaps from her early years as an art student, friend, lover and wife. There were images of a young woman with bobbed hair, often barefoot and always with a far-away look. 'Her name was Dora,' Christine said. 'But we called her Carrington.'

Christine also showed Ronnie her youthful sketchbooks in which there was a pencil portrait of Dora Carrington with her hallmark cropped hair and loose clothes but with the face left blank – underlining the impression of a personality impossible to pin down. Her evident magnetism was also hard to explain even if Christine had cared to try.

Gradually Ronnie came to grasp the complexities of John and Christine's defining relationships into the 1920s, and the intricate mesh of freedoms and obligations with which their partnership began. And this was what they had then strived – and Christine at times struggled – to continue. Rebelling against Victorian bourgeois origins, they had gravitated to the fringes of the Bloomsbury Group and fully embraced the bohemian coterie's espousal of free love. Snatching passing passion became all the more potent during the

First World War, given the prospect of premature, violent death. But rejection of sexual conventions was never really free: it came with an implied acceptance – far easier to calculate in theory than manage in practice – of any attendant emotional cost.

Ronnie was able to place key pieces of the story only when heir to Bottengoms. Years passed before he could go beyond filing Christine's copious diaries in library order, to read them. Eventually he opened a Victorian bread oven to find a long-concealed trunk. Inside were letters returned to John and Christine after Carrington's suicide: painful reminders pushed out of sight. John had fended off Bloomsbury historians with the falsehood that evidence had been destroyed and memory erased by time.

The correspondence between the Nash brothers, Christine and Carrington showed all four to have been engaged in an impassioned artistic affair. Setting their hearts on fresh and vital portrayals of the British landscape, they had supported each other's efforts while pressing forward with their own.

Creative engagement had involved tense entanglement since all three of her correspondents had also been emotionally and physically aroused by the elusive Carrington. As Ronnie observed: 'Paul was romantic; John was just randy.'[1] Carrington had eagerly backed and even engineered the courtship of John and Christine, not least for the freedom their marriage left for herself. Ronnie had once dared to ask John whether he had slept with Carrington. 'The nearest I ever got to her was when we shared a mackintosh apron on the top deck of a London bus,' he said.[2]

Christine, whose youthful lovers included Carrington and Norah – her companion in *The Picnic* painting whose identity has never been established – did not smother a bisexual nature when she became Mrs Nash. Her empathy with Ronnie drew on experience and a belief that sexuality was essentially fluid. She had slept with Norah before and after the latter's marriage to Charlie – the third painted picnicker – with his apparent approval.[3] A sexual charge in the picture was belatedly rather clear.

A mutual androgyny had been addressed by Christine after she and John first made love in a Chilterns wood. Writing after his posting to the war in France, she told him not to worry about a 'lack of muscliness (curious word that). I have certainly a lack of femininity (even curiouser) so we meet in the same place.'[4]

John Nash.

Also, homosexuality was a fact of life within the Nash family. John's sister Barbara ran a plant nursery with her life partner, Norah Hill, and their status as a couple was accepted by John and Christine as a matter of course.

And yet John had always been tormented by Carrington, who could begin a belated missive: 'I am sorry to have been so long answering your letters. But it was such a whacking long one last time that I thought a little rest would be pleasant for you.'[5] Her love for the homosexual writer Lytton Strachey left John outraged by his own ostracism. Carrington and Lytton lived complicatedly together from 1917 until cancer killed him, and she killed herself, fifteen years later. John, bound to Christine, remained in impossible pursuit. As Ronnie wrote:

'From now on until she died all his dealings with her were dominated by his insistence that the threads which once held them together must not be severed. It was a testy, wounding business on his part and he knew her well enough to know that it was everything she disliked, but he could not let her go.'[6]

John had been the first to break the initial monogamy of his marriage. Christine had then embarked on a consolatory affair with the etcher Francis Unwin, standing vigil at his deathbed in a Norfolk tuberculosis sanatorium in 1925. Much of the Bottengoms furniture Ronnie so admired had been his.

The great physical love of Christine's married life was John Langston; she attended his wedding in 1936, and supported both partners, and their children, after the divorce. With dark good looks and enormous appetites – hence the fond soubriquet of 'Hog' – he was charming, promiscuous and diabetic. Lovemaking would lead to caregiving, as it generally did with Christine. Langston stays at Bottengoms were matched by visits to his homes in London and on Skye. Other amorous attachments came and went for Hog, but Barbara Fell, his Central Office of Information colleague and lover, became a fixture in all their lives.

John Nash aged into a party pest, forever pursuing what his weary wife called his 'dolls'. When her tolerance was tested to the limit, she named her stupidest cat Mad Doll. John's long-running affair from the mid-1950s with Monica Bingley, bored wife of the Flatford Mill Field Studies Centre director, was spiked by the return of Nora Meninsky, whose late painter husband, Bernard, had ended their dalliance twenty years earlier. Christine disliked Nora's straining melodramas but could not resist satisfaction in the discomforting of

Nude Figure on Couch by John Nash, 1920. Christine was the model.

'mischievous' Monica. 'If only they could have 6 months on a desert island the thing would cure itself,' she wrote in her diary. 'What is the good of a love affair unless it gives happiness, & if one is married, one must accept that basic fact, & use the other as the cherry on the cake.'[7]

Christine was aghast when Nora then 'took up a kind of retrospective passion for Paul! I imagine as a jealous-making manoeuvre & she made an attack upon poor Ronnie Blythe – with the same end in view'. To break the tension, she arranged for Nora and John to spend twelve hours alone. 'Somehow, after that a more cheerful attitude obtained & I noticed a spate of letters to any & every other doll. Very healthy. It's terrible how very observant one is bound to become.'[8] Ronnie observed the corrosive impact of misspent passion on creative work – though the burden of maintaining a bill-paying flow of paintings took the heavier toll on Christine. Again it was the cost of partnership he counted.

Often depressed, John could be grouchy and disconcerting. While Ronnie always felt at ease in Christine's company, John was 'a father figure manqué'.[9] There was also a distance between Ronnie's inherent radicalism and creeping Nash conservatism. In 1956 Christine noted that Ronnie was 'very anti-Eden', deeming his criticism of the Suez Crisis 'muddled thinking'. But when the Cuban Missile Crisis raged, six years later, and cold war almost heated into armed East–West conflict, they were of one mind as they dealt with fallout among their 'dear ones'.

In November 1962 Barbara Fell sent the Nashes a letter marked 'before reading this could you both please take a tranquillizer'. Inside came news that she was to be tried for showing secret documents to a Yugoslav embassy press attaché, her former lover and ongoing friend, with whom they had all holidayed on Skye. She had been trying rather naively to encourage pro-Western views, and the secrecy of imparted information was low-level. But, given the international atmosphere, and accusations of official complicity and incompetence in former British espionage cases, she expected a custodial sentence.

'John and I love each other more than ever before, and somehow I will make it up to him,' she wrote. 'I think I mind telling you two more than anyone. You have been my dear friends for so long and given me such happiness. You must try to forgive me the pain and beastliness which is going to break on all our heads . . . we must meet soon to arrange practical things about the old boy's welfare if I go to prison . . . please forgive me and go on loving me.'[10]

Ronnie wrote to Christine when the story broke: 'Barbara's is a swift, passionate personality that despises the pettifogging aspects of life. When she is successful, she is richly successful, and when she makes a mistake it is a big mistake. But she isn't bad, only fallible in the most calamitous sense. She will need all the warmth and trust she can get now. The trial and the awful publicity will leave her naked and vulnerable – which ever way the verdict goes . . . the absolute and unchanged regard of her friends is now the most important thing in the world for her.'[11]

Barbara and the now blind Hog spent the weekend before the trial at Bottengoms, and Hog was back for Christmas after Barbara was jailed. She served sixteen months during which time Christine escorted Hog on prison visits and welcomed the prisoner for a weekend in Essex after vetting by the probation service. When allowed to work in York University library, Barbara returned each night to a cell alongside 'several dismal abortionists, two jolly prostitutes, a mixed bag of embezzlers, shoplifters, a murderess'.[12] On her release, there was a prompt wedding and, in June 1964, the happy couple hosted a dinner party to celebrate John's CBE. The stays on Skye continued.

Christine, John and Ronnie felt that Barbara was unfairly treated, not so hard to do perhaps since even the judge said her actions left national security unharmed. But all three lived by E. M. Forster's dictum that if forced to choose between patriotism or loyalty to a friend, friendship should prevail.

37
Ron and Pat

From Great Glemham, Ronnie wrote to Christine: 'And now a bombshell – I have a cat (die katze, I fear). It was foisted on me when I was not quite myself at a dinner party owing to the wine. It has lived in amity with me for the past month and is called Maud. She is brindled with white feet and white ruff, very long stiff whiskers, a mottled face, bushy Persian tail and very cosy ways. My American girlfriend feeds her when I go to London.'[1]

The bombshell was the American girlfriend. That mystery woman would vanish from Ronnie's story almost before entering it. But she remains as a premonition of an all too real American girlfriend and one of the most unlikely couplings in literature.

'Dear Pat', Ronnie would say in later life when asked to describe the noir novelist Patricia Highsmith. He fondly recalled the shirts and the map of the stars she bought for him in Venice, and the gondolier's outfit brought back for herself. Of a shared outing to Cambridge, he remembered the ravine opening between them as he guided her round the marvels of King's College Chapel. Out on the street again it was explained away with typical terseness. 'Huh, Art!' she said.

Dark of hair, skin and eyes, and a year older than Ronnie, this inimitable artist was a slim and handsome Texan who liked dressing as a cowboy. Moccasins gave a glimpse of the split personality so marked in the rest of her life. Her face suggested Native American and African ancestry, ideas dismissed when raised by others but possibilities she herself investigated. In a certain light, before her features coarsened with alcohol, she looked delicately Chinese.

On holiday in Italy, the writer of *Strangers on a Train* and *The Talented Mr Ripley* had fallen for a married Canadian woman with a twelve-year-old son. With a habit for pursuit akin to stalking, the besotted author followed her encouraging quarry to Suffolk and a weekend home in Aldeburgh. She rented a house in the town to keep a watchful eye and wrathful attitude on her lover's family ties and frequent absences in London. But when left alone she was best able to write.

There was also a scriptwriting collaboration with Richard Ingham, a Woodbridge School teacher and acquaintance of Ronnie's. They all met up at the kind of social gathering where Patricia – with striking honesty and killing wit – was reduced to hysterics on encountering a sherry-sipping Colonel Julius Caesar. She followed with a typed note:

27 King Street,
Aldeburgh
30 January 1963

Dear Mr Blythe,

Am writing this just so you will know I have not dropped dead or anything. I am hard at work just now after quite a lot of visitors since and including Christmas, and probably you are working even harder. But if you are around Aldeburgh way, please knock on my door (two doors, one down a short alley). I am never annoyed by this, and we might have some tea or a drink.

When things shape up in a few days I will extend you a proper invitation . . .

Very best wishes,
Pat Highsmith[2]

In her second note, he was Ronald. It was Ronnie by April and love was extended from May. She would write regularly for the rest of her life. They shared writerly successes and problems and mutual devotion to cats, gardens and night walks.

If Patricia Highsmith was practically a stalker, she was also stalked by her own backstory. Her artist mother had tried to abort her by drinking turpentine – finding it funny that she ended up liking the

Pat and cat outside Bridge Cottage.

smell – then divorced her illustrator father nine days before giving birth. Craving maternal approval in vain, a lonely only child took her stepfather's name and fantasised from the age of eight about taking his life too. Like a vengeful twist in a Highsmith story, both wayward guardians would seek psychiatric help over the trauma she gave them back for the 'little hell' of her childhood.

Killing off past lovers in her bestsellers, Pat thought her neurosis might tip over into psychosis. Telling Ronnie she 'embraced the dark', she was given to flashing torchlight in her house at night like an intruder; to calm inner tension a piece of wood was attacked with a saw. But it is too simplistic to say that Tom Ripley, social charmer and serial killer, was really the author herself. For a start she was awkward in company – and dis-eased in her own boyish body. She preferred the company of hermaphrodite snails. They rasped openly on lettuce in a glass tank and travelled with her incognito, snug in her handbag or bra. In her writing they could gain in size, intelligence and appetite until capable of gobbling humanity.

Her speech, exact and ominous and smoky from cigarettes, was like the sparse commentary for a crime documentary. For all her candour, she had preferred to have *The Price of Salt* published under a pen name in 1952 due to its lesbian theme. Disparaging the book as 'sentimental' and 'soppy',[3] she gave Ronnie a copy nonetheless. In her disturbed life, the novel and the friendship were two rare elements with happy endings.

The murky psychological novel she plotted when they were intimates in Suffolk, *A Suspension of Mercy*, ended unhappily but almost without a murder. Near the close the protagonist, wrongly suspected of killing his late wife after burying a rolled-up carpet, forces her lover into suicide. To think herself into such emotional intensity, Pat buried some snails.

In April 1964 she bought pink-washed, seventeenth-century Bridge Cottage in the picturesque village of Earl Soham – two knocked-together labourers' dwellings with old-fashioned roses in a garden above a stream. It was, she informed Arthur Koestler, 'very good for working, due to the extreme English quietude'. That peace was waiting to be broken.

This was also the year when Edmund Blunden retired, from teaching in the Far East, to Hall Mill in Long Melford, thanks to the kindness of fellow First World War poet Siegfried Sassoon. The globetrotter still roamed each lunchtime as far as the bar of the Bull Hotel – it was only next door – where Ronnie sometimes joined him. Roving conversations were most likely to linger on John Clare, whose lyrical cry for freedom, they both agreed, had now soared from long enclosure as the sanest voice in the human madhouse. With the arrival of Blunden and Highsmith, a remote corner of rural England claimed a global literary pantheon.

Ronnie cycled the eight miles from Debach for Pat's dubious hospitality and compelling company. Bridge Cottage was clean, orderly and warm – but, besides whisky filling the fridge and cigarette cartons stacked in the kitchen, meanly supplied. 'It was as if she had just gone out and got the basics,' Ronnie told Highsmith biographer Andrew Wilson. 'She wasn't at all a good hostess – she was rather bad at it really – but she liked to invite me over for supper. After a while, however, it was obvious that she wanted her life back to herself again, to go back to her typewriter and work. That was her reality more than anything else – the act of writing made her happy, gave her something that nothing else could.'[4] She confessed that writing, making 'a good thing of every catastrophe of my life',[5] was her only means of feeling respectable. *In extremis* she was extremely endearing.

But one Saturday supper began perilously when drops of water plopped on the table. Ronnie looked up and saw a glass-bowl lampshade overflowing from a trickle penetrating the ceiling. 'Leave it,' snapped Pat. 'Someone is coming in to fix it.' Clear that this must mean from Monday, Ronnie rushed upstairs to adjust the ballcock in the lavatory. Pat shook with anger. 'She was annoyed that I disobeyed her,' he said.

She camped out in her own life; the only comfort lay in the Gothic mansion of her writing, in which she could wander at will. It was both a dark place and a safe space – where authorial freedom to break every rule resembled that of a psychopath. 'Sometimes when I was with her, we strayed without words into the world where you did what you liked, so you were free as if you were a criminal. Although I didn't understand the psychopathic side that shows itself in her novels, now and again this despair and distress would overcome me; all we were doing was sitting there together in a room. I don't think she was connected to what most people see as the "real world". She was cut off from what we think of as ordinary life, cut off by her genius.'[6]

The drama of dinner at Bridge Cottage was heightened when Pat took a call from Alfred Hitchcock, whose film of her *Strangers on a Train* had made her famous. Still miffed about her movie fee, she was now wealthy and stingy. Fancy shirts from Venice aside, she was disinclined to help the dear and needy. Ronnie fretted over her former lover and faithful friend in America, toiling as a waitress as her health faltered. Pat related these problems in many letters while never writing the cheque to sort them. Her estate would be left to a writers' retreat.

It did not make for easefulness of an evening that Pat could start off drunk and then get drunker. She drove over to Debach in her little Volkswagen, bringing only a bottle of whisky in a paper bag – for her. Ronnie drank sparingly in those days. A wholesome meal could turn into an ashtray. Yet there was a warm affection to the friendship, with Pat staying over she had had too much to drink; Ronnie slept at Bridge Cottage on sensing her unhappiness. 'I thought she was rather attractive in a strange way, so unlike anyone I'd ever met before. She had beautiful manners . . . she was well-bred and had a kind of elegance. Yet her loneliness showed in her face – a cloudiness, an ugliness really – which would go when she laughed, a strange, low chuckle.'[7]

They would share a bed, talking before sleeping about gay love and the unsatisfactory nature of some of their romantic friendships. Once or twice the bed-sharing ended in lovemaking. Both were intensely curious to find out what it felt like to play for the other side. Pat had already speculated in a letter about a fling ostensibly with another gay male friend: 'If any sexual thing happened, it would certainly be with affection, which makes it a bit different. All very hard to explain, so I'd better stop.'[8]

Ronnie saw himself as a good lover, and he liked to imagine the situation from Pat's position, making love to him. With her hipless body and masculine hands, he likened her to an adolescent boy. So this inconceivable couple in their forties became two exploring teenagers. When their heterosexual experiment concluded, they did not refer to it again; it went unmentioned in Highsmith diaries. She never corrected her statement that sexual intercourse felt like 'steel wool in the face'.[9] The experience neither drew them closer nor prised them apart. It was raw material for writing, the thread which bound them.

'She liked the idea of suspense and she was fascinated by amorality. We used to talk about books and our work . . . although her novels didn't really appeal to me at first, they intrigued me and eventually I saw how they reflected her. She had a great memory for details and often she would write out bits of conversation we had had in her books. One did feel sometimes as if one was subject matter.'[10]

Ronnie responded by being unusually confiding. While researching in the British Museum's Reading Room, he had an amorous encounter with a young poet from Barbados. An ensuing affair was charted in letters to Pat. 'He sees himself as an author's personal assistant but he would drive me mad in a week!' Ronnie wrote. 'But I had not fully comprehended the extraordinary quality of negro beauty, its perfection, the poreless skin, like silk, and the brilliant eyes. It is quite comical where this friend is concerned how, in my reactions to him, the erotic is constantly overcome by the aesthetic. He thinks I'm mad, of course. And I am, though not for any reason he would understand. It's that I know at heart the basic inadequacy of these relationships and could, if I were a cynical person, which I don't think I am, smile sadly at the repetitive pattern they follow.'[11]

Besides providing source material, Ronnie was soothing – lamp and radiator against the chill of a Suffolk winter and the Highsmith psyche. How different from the visit of Pat's mother. After locking herself away to finish a synopsis, the writer emerged to an attack by an enraged parent with a coat hanger; both women were prescribed sedatives. Their tortured relationship terminated in estrangement and disinheritance. And after a final row with her married lover – and ire at having to retake a driving test – the restive Patricia Highsmith moved on. Suffolk seemed jinxed when Bridge Cottage flooded before it could be sold.

A hunted huntress tried a house near Fontainebleau – shifting several more times in the neighbourhood before two final unrestful places in Switzerland, where she died in 1995. 'I've a knack for moving from one slum to another,' she wrote. The last staging post, 'built to my orders', was the closest she came to control outside her writing. It was 'comfortable and quiet, also sunny – the latter not always easy to arrange in Switzerland, where the mountains interfere'.[12]

Sending confessional love to France, Ronnie wrote: 'We are both fundamentally on our own in life and this, I suppose, makes the closeness . . . the realisation of it.' Pat referred to 'our consolation, lonely, solitary work sometimes, but a sort of laughing satisfaction, a real joy, when we have brought off a book that is decent, which is praised by the critics, the public and a few friends. This makes up for all the loneliness.'[13]

They swapped books and praise. Pat wrote: 'You are making your reputation as the most reliable non-fiction writer of our era. No fiction writer is reliable, of course, one doesn't expect it.' Ronnie admired *Eleven*, short stories introduced by Graham Greene with praise for 'the poet of apprehension'. In literary style they both strove for concision, and excision, with a necessary ruthlessness spilling over into life. ('They are wonderful stories, Pat, witty, tender, strange, sometimes very terrible and never once any of these things obviously.') And again: 'You are such a total artist, it makes me love you.'[14]

Ronnie was assiduous in helping other writers. He lent his Highsmith letters to another biographer, Joan Schenkar, who returned them with a covering note: 'These letters are warmer and much more relaxed than most of the other letters I've read. And I've read – a long sigh of fatigue here – thousands of them by now. I did make an attempt to re-order the letters chronologically, but a sudden gust of wind scattered them all over my desk and I just couldn't find the resolve to re-sort them. Do excuse me.'[15]

38

Village Voices

As 1967 wound on a hippy trail towards the Summer of Love, some headed to London's Hilton Hotel, or even India, to sit at the feet of the Maharishi with flowers in their hair – and with hallucinatory drugs, perhaps, to heighten the visionary experience. Ronnie was walking to evensong, writing and gardening.

Deep in Hazlitt, he was also stepping warily into a new literary venture by Penguin in London and Pantheon in New York. Swedish writer Jan Myrdal, allowed into Maoist China, had detected in a single rural settlement a vast society in microcosm. The success of the resulting *Report from a Chinese Village* suggested a sociological global series, but the Ronald Blythe volume would prove unique.

At first Ronnie was nonplussed. He always denied being a social historian, and now felt unsuited to the allotted task since definitely no sociologist. No matter, commissioning editor Tony Godwin responded: do it your way. His way was truthfulness in fine writing. He accepted but remained uncertain – considering a Welsh hamlet before looking about him. 'I walked around the village boundaries, which are ancient ditches: very deep, dug into the clay, and full of torrential yellow winter water. And the idea came to me of the fundamental anonymity of most labourers' lives . . . Yet when you come to talk to them you realise how strong they are and how unbelievably rich their lives are; also subtle and various.' His book bearing their witness would express 'the poetry of the ordinary'.[1]

After the diversion of another ghost tale for James Turner, the diverter wrote to say that on such evidence Ronnie's talents were being wasted. 'You must get going on a novel soon, surely? From your letter of this morning, it does not look as if you'll have much chance to do anything but the Village book and the Hazlitt.'[2]

The 'Village book' became *Akenfield: Portrait of an English Village* and it outsold and overshadowed the sum of everything else Ronald Blythe ever wrote. Published in May 1969, and translated into twenty languages, it has never been out of print; at the author's centenary, UK sales alone would exceed 400,000 copies. A forensic focus on a small community from Victorian to new Elizabethan times, chiefly via the lens of compellingly introduced 'interviews', the book was an unforgettable portrait album by way of startling stories.

Here was a history of hardship: of children toiling in fields and old people confined to cupboards; of starveling men who shot up on army rations and lighter labour; of servants facing walls so as not to

Akenfield book jacket. The painting used is
Blythburgh, Suffolk by Edward Seago.

see their lady employer. A magistrate looked back twenty years to
when she joined the bench in a simpler age: 'It was just after the war
and this part of Suffolk was very basic. There was incest and bestiality
on the one side, an American soldier getting drunk and driving into
a brick wall on the other, and people riding bicycles without lamps
in the middle. We get much more variety now.'[3]

A veteran gravedigger, sure of his part in burying people alive,
planned to be cremated. But for all the harrowing revelations,
Akenfield was also a record of myriad skill and recondite knowledge,
of rootedness and connectedness in a living countryside. A thatcher
prospered; a blacksmith had three apprentices mastering ornamental
metalwork. A village of 400 people had sixty clubs and societies.

'I was delighted as always with those who bent the rules, dodged
the system and who managed to be "different" within the rigidities
which rural communities like to impose,' Ronnie explained. 'There
is no place like the countryside for the most imaginative – and
blatant – nonconformity.'[4]

The nonconformist that was Lana Webb would delight reviewer
Tom Driberg. She lived cheerfully with her gran in a converted
railway carriage, a non-victim of chronic incontinence, 'wet as a
ditch, day in, day out', knickers and sheets forever on the washing
line. But Ken, her 'wonderful' young man, drove her to Ipswich
every Saturday night sitting on back copies of the *Daily Express*.[5]
'Incontinence is a way of life,' the doctor said.

A rural dean mused on the limitations of religion: 'Fatalism is the
real controlling force, this and the nature gods, the spirits of the
trees and water and sky and plants. These beliefs seem to have no
language, but they rule.'[6] Yet so much was on the point of erasure.
Most pasture had already been ploughed, and now familiar landmarks
– trees, hedges, wild flower swathes, ponds, paths – were endangered
by the pesticides and bulldozers of intensive, worker-light agriculture.
Animals were vanishing into the closed units of factory farming.

'On a clear day – and they are mostly clear days in this part of
the world – you can see as far as you can bear to see, and sometimes
farther,' Ronnie wrote.[7] Within weeks of publication, hundreds of
millions of people around the world watched on television as the
first man walked on the moon; but, even as change abounded,
neither the author nor his characters could envisage the coming
transformation of English rural life. A group study in landscape

became, rather swiftly, a period piece wrought less in black and white than sepia. By Ronald Blythe's centenary, the alteration since first publication – the dramatic disconnection with the land – was more sweeping than changes charted in the book.

But a period account retains its power through poetic truth, delivered in remarks such as 'I have these deep lines on my face because I have worked under fierce suns' and 'It is thought poor manners to destroy a martin's nest while he is abroad.' The veracity of such lyrical phrasing would be questioned, but Ronnie insisted on their essential truth.

Based largely on Debach and Charsfield, the semi-fictional Akenfield lay close to the actual village of Akenham. The name was designed to suggest the generic acre-field and the old Suffolk slant on the words 'oak' and 'acorn'. No book was ever more local, and yet the title hints at anywhere and everywhere – drawing us all in.

For nearly a year into autumn 1967 Ronnie was marshalling voices with or without a borrowed cassette recorder. As he wrote later: 'To be any kind of writer where one was so deeply rooted could be an awkward business – still can . . . John Clare and Thomas Hardy had everything they required for their inspiration to hand, and they knew it. Yet to translate such common stuff into the finest rural poetry and the finest rural novels in the language carried with it a personal exposure which was hard to bear. As we know to this day, there is a fugitive aspect to every village.'[8]

There was a strong element of wishing to protect himself and others – the club foot of the district nurse went kindly unmentioned – but still more of writerly purpose. When the manuscript went to a young defamation lawyer in London – Andrew Phillips, a future peer and friend of Ronnie's in Sudbury – it was approved without amendment.[9] No living person could be offended since none could be identified. It was a legal ruling on a work of disguised documentation. That satisfied the publisher, but the author was less journalist than alchemist. To hold its magic, a created masterpiece must keep a core of mystery – and *Akenfield* continues to raise questions as well as answers. Who were these memorable people? Not one could be found in any official document.

Names were changed to tombstone lettering and sometimes that was that. The village poet was, of course, James Turner, who received a questionnaire in faraway Cornwall. The lenient magistrate, who thought punishment could compound the harm, was Fidelity Cranbrook. The Scottish sheep farmer was Mr Anderson from Boulge, and so on. 'Framsden, about eight miles from my small farmhouse, was where I saw Hickey, the fancy dancer in *Akenfield*, take the floor and where I sat in the churchyard to write it down.'[10]

But, amid hostility from oral historians reproducing interviews virtually verbatim, Ronnie hinted down the decades at a more personal viewpoint. From: '*Akenfield* was a combination of witness: my own witness and that of three generations, and what you might call the home-fed imagination.'[11] To: '*Akenfield* is a kind of auto-biography in many ways.'[12]

At the book's heart lay a Blythe family biography – and an auto-biography too. The author had always been watching, listening and remembering: now he was writing it all down, the characters and cadences and the extraordinary nature of everyday life best conveyed in a work of art. 'I felt it was legitimate just as a painter might want to paint a portrait of a man to turn some of the things he said into literature rather than something taken down by a reporter. It was a written book, as Hardy might have done it.'[13]

His friends could not imagine him so impertinent as to ask a direct question of a stranger. It was never his habit with an intimate either. He would bequeath his papers to the British Library, but what of those possibly taped interviews? Suffolk historian Norman Scarfe, among many to tackle him on *Akenfield*'s elusive technique, was told he had been unable to afford tapes so had used one repeatedly.[14]

A man so frugal seemed to be taking extra care – artfully, almost slyly – to cover his tracks while stressing the sensitivity of a writer's ear. 'By listening to a particularly individual pattern of words, catching some tell-tale emphasis or by being able to realise that something is being said which the speaker may not have been able to say before, the writer is hearing all those infinite possibilities and experiences which lie just under the surface of things.'[15]

The Blythe style of 'perceptive observation' was supported by the veteran American oral historian Louis 'Studs' Terkel, who recorded an interview in London for his Chicago radio programme. Ronnie defended a conversational technique. 'A straight question doesn't necessarily get a straight answer,' he said.[16]

As it was, he had a modest enough view of *Akenfield*, setting out the manuscript on his kitchen table and 'only hoping and praying that it would do'.[17] The publisher was more confident, sending a proof copy to Aldeburgh for an endorsement. Benjamin Britten read with admiration and unease – as did John Nash, the dedicatee, whose rosy pictures were a far cry from this written portrait composed, in part, in blood. Calling to offer congratulations, the composer asked: 'Are you against our farmers, Ronnie?' 'How could I be?' Ronnie replied – answering without an answer; leaving his book to speak for itself. Britten then wrote: 'Mr Blythe's acute observation of the village and its inhabitants, skilful questioning and sympathetic editing of the answers have made a unique picture of contemporary village life. It is amusing, disturbing and reassuring by turn.'[18]

Penguin gave the author half a launch lunch in an Ipswich hotel, the prudent investment shared with Paul Jennings, author of *The Living Village*. The publisher's agent touring the bookstores of East Anglia met with initial indifference. But once a shop was persuaded to take a copy or two, repeat orders for ten or twelve swiftly followed. A bandwagon rolled on laudatory reviews ('Ronald Blythe has produced perhaps the finest English social document since Richard Gough composed his "History of Myddle" in the seventeenth century' – *Guardian*; 'What riches! What diversity! What a book!' – *The Times*) and word-of-mouth recommendations.[19]

In London, Hatchards presented a Piccadilly window display complete with a model village and W. H. Smith on Liverpool Street station tempted East Anglian travellers with a tower of books. Ronnie heard of a Suffolk farmer who bought a copy for the homeward journey but threw it from a train window long before Ipswich. That partial reader could not believe his lovely county had ever known such miseries. And a pained Lord Stradbroke wrote: 'Surely it is nobler to illumine the mass of gold rather than to blow up the specks of mud into dunghills?'[20]

Adrian Bell's warm review in the *Eastern Daily Press* regretted only a scarcity of the earthy humour – 'punning, allusive, inventive' – he heard as a farm apprentice. 'Perhaps, speaking to a mature man of education, they would bate their rich and bawdy wit,' he wrote, unaware that Ronnie's education was grounded in the fields.[21]

Since thirty-nine of the forty-nine *Akenfield* witnesses were men, Mary Chamberlain was provoked into making recordings for her book *Fenwomen* in the Cambridgeshire village of Isleham. It launched Carmen Callil's Virago Press in 1975. With a twin aim of reviving forgotten female fiction, Virago went on to republish some of Ronnie's favourite novels.

Patricia Highsmith read the Suffolk saga 'sitting (lying in bed) up many pleasant late nights, and enjoying every word'.[22] Charles Causley wrote: 'The words – particularly of the farm-workers, the kind of people I come from – absolutely burn themselves on the mind for ever.'[23]

Buffeted by a summer of acclaim in Britain, Ronnie was bowled over by an autumn reception in the United States. James Morris – already transitioning into Jan – praised a 'horridly enjoyable' book about a 'dour and unbeguiling' place.[24] As Ronnie wrote to Patricia Highsmith in October: '*Akenfield* came out in New York about a fortnight ago and got wonderful treatment – a whole page in *New York Times* Book Review, 20 minutes on NBC, and about fifty other large notices. The result being that Simon & Schuster have paid $12,500 advance on my new book – about the Fabians – so your poor old Suffolk bicycling friend is now rich. What a year. Seriously I don't quite know what to do, I mean how to live. I get worried about this going on all alone in the middle of nowhere and hate myself for not even trying to really love someone – as opposed to making love to him (a pleasantly regular occurrence). It is being 46 I suppose. Self, self, self, I tell myself.'[25]

By the end of November there had been positive reviews in 150 American newspapers and magazines, including *Life* and *Time*. Amid critical success, sales and advances, Ronnie quit as a publisher's reader and tried to resign himself to a disquieting life in the public eye. One of the first of the profile writers to trek to Debach wrote: 'He looks young, with an open, slightly surprised face, sports a light blue polo-neck sweater, and might be an actor resting. He seems *intensely* private, mild but strong . . .'[26]

As journalists came and went, there were the makings of writerly friendships. Angus Wilson made contact after praising *Akenfield* as 'penetrating, extraordinarily unprejudiced, yet deeply caring'.[27] Born in 1913 into a dysfunctional upper-class family, the *Observer* reviewer was the youngest of six brothers, three of them gay. The youngest was also the most outrageous in the boarding schools and hotels where the boys grew up. His career as a British Museum librarian was broken by wartime intelligence work and a nervous breakdown. Writing to ease a troubled mind, he was acclaimed for short stories and novels when leaving the library to write in Suffolk at the same time as Ronnie.

Brilliant and blatant, the future Sir Angus was a high-living socialist and literary panjandrum partnered by the faithful Tony Garrett. They had met in the library. 'He could have been so many things – and naturally I have this feeling that I've swallowed up someone's life,' the writer said.[28] Tony had been forced to resign as a probation officer when his employers received a tip-off that he was 'living with a well-known homosexual'. Their disastrous flight to France in the Thatcher era ended in dementia for Angus and destitution for them both – final chapters then played out in a Bury St Edmunds nursing home funded by charity and friends, and a little billet in the town for Tony, a short walk from a beloved cathedral where Ronnie often saw him. For a solitary author it was one more cautionary tale about the cost of coupledom.

And another novelist wrote from Dorset:

> I found I couldn't read *Akenfield* straight through, any more than I could get to know the landscape by helicopter. As with all villages, the characters hide behind their candour. I thought about them, went back to them, found them different on the second reading, on the third. One thing I like especially about the book: it blows sky-high all that oo-hoo nonsense about the community. The mud on their boots is their community . . .
>
> I hang my head that I have not written before. I have had a great deal on my hands and on my heart this summer.
>
> Yours ever,
>
> Sylvia Townsend Warner[29]

That weight on hands and heart was due to the dying of poet Valentine Ackland, who had borne out her name by looking like Rudolph Valentino. The two women lived together from 1930, tumultuously at times, with Sylvia writing steadily through Valentine's depression, affairs and alcoholism. Sylvia would visit Ronnie later, but her widowed devastation was beyond his comprehension. Writing inured him.

But literary fame upset his Suffolk life. 'All the privacy has gone,' he told Patricia Highsmith. 'The position isn't helped by the fact that I am in the middle of Akenfield, as it were, which has become a kind of centre for visitors. All the TV companies, newspapers, sound radio etc. have arrived. Of course, much of the response has been marvellous and there is a very real comfort and relief in having some real money. At the moment, I do nothing with it. Just pop it in the bank and loll against it, a nice crackly cushion.'[30]

More than forty years later Ronnie told an interviewer: 'When it came out, there was a terrible hullaballo. I walked down to the village, to the shop, and an old farmer's wife was standing by the gate. I thought, "Now I'm for it." She beckoned me over and said, "Oh, my dear, you should have come to me. I could have told you much worse than that."'[31]

39

Home Movie

Flying into London in October 1969, Hollywood stars Paul Newman and Joanne Woodward announced their hope to make an *Akenfield* movie.[1] But, as it turned out, that filmic plough was already in the furrow.

On a crowded commuter train, the tornado that was Suffolk-born Peter Hall had taken along *Akenfield* to avoid any idle moment. He was in tears on arrival, having heard the voice of his grandfather while reading the saga of his own childhood and exile. 'I had spent 35 years leaving,' he wrote. 'Now I wanted to go back.'[2]

A railwayman's son, with uncles still close to the land, Peter had been born in Bury St Edmunds and raised in stations along lines to Cambridge, where he fell in love with drama. In 1969 he had lately ended a decade as founder-director of the Royal Shakespeare Company, and was now working internationally across cinema, theatre and opera. *Akenfield* would be his home movie.

Author, director and an eager editor and co-producer named Rex Pyke quickly agreed that the full book, being a story in forty-nine episodes, was unfilmable. They aimed to preserve the essential atmosphere in a new tale whose bare outline would be plotted by Ronnie – a storyline flexible enough for an improvised production. Although the writer said the director 'didn't know wheat from barley' he had gleaned Suffolk fields as a boy and was mentored by a gamekeeper.[3] And he began each frenetic day calmed by farming news on the radio.[4]

Ronnie and Peter Hall.

In line with a Hall vision inspired by the raw films of Robert Bresson, as well as *Man of Aran* by Robert J. Flaherty, Pasolini's *The Gospel According to St Matthew* and Vittorio De Sica's *Bicycle Thieves*, Ronnie devised a modern Hardy story in a twenty-page synopsis. It began: 'The village – very early in the morning. May-time. The church high on an escarpment above a little river. The corn tall and green and the hedges tangled with honeysuckle and wild roses. Everything very clear, no haze. Promise of a hot day. The church-yard quivering with grasses, sheep's parsley and bull-daisies, though a square patch has been levelled by a rotary scythe. Jaunty old tombstones. Martins diving from the tower. Brightness and clamour. Life, not death. But clods whirling out of a grave. The earth flies from the hole with an almost comic vigour . . .'[5]

What was provisionally entitled 'The Road from Bethany', after the name of a farm, would chart the lives of three generations of farmworkers. Each was named Tom Rouse. Their stories were woven together in flashbacks on the day of the grandfather's funeral – a man who had tried and failed to leave the village save for atrocious army service in the First World War. Middle Tom had gone off to be killed in the second global conflict and now young Tom was torn between marriage in a tied cottage and escape to Australia.

Over three hectic years for Peter Hall, the capital was not forth-coming – one American financier saying cash would flow and Jon Voight star if the action switched to the Mid-West; a British funder wondering whether Albert Finney or Alan Bates could 'do Suffolk'. Peter was succeeding Laurence Olivier as director of the National Theatre and moving the show to a South Bank war zone: his riveting published diaries would be subtitled *The Story of a Dramatic Battle*. He might well have abandoned *Akenfield* but for the persist-ence of Rex Pyke and the dread of letting Suffolk down. 'Rex is a marvellous but alarming man who has never heard of the word impossible,' Peter noted in his diary. 'Half the time he is of course wrong: it *is* impossible. But his determination frequently dispirits the Impossible to such an extent that it cringes away defeat.'[6]

Amid the long wait, Ronnie was approached by film, television and theatre companies wanting to adapt the book. All were told of his loyalty to Peter Hall. Editor-turned-director David Gladwell was especially disappointed that he would not script *Requiem for a Village* – a rival film to be shot in Suffolk.

Ronnie had appeared to pull off an early coup by persuading Benjamin Britten to contribute the score. Although the composer was absorbed in his opera *Death in Venice*, an unused piece of music – 'Hankin Booby', intended as the third movement of the *Suite on English Folk Tunes* – might be extended for the film to fit around. Perhaps the petitioner had been emboldened by the car arriving at French's Folly with copies of the weighty programmes for the first twenty-five Aldeburgh festivals, and a note from Ben asking him to 'turn them into a book' to help revive Snape Maltings Concert Hall following a fire. *Aldeburgh Anthology* was published for Christmas 1972, and Ronnie went to the festival office to sign copies with Ben, Peter Pears and Imogen Holst. Afterwards, coming slowly down the stairs, Ben, purple and puffy, let Peter and Imo go ahead. 'I can't do the Akenfield score. I am ill,' he said, tapping his heart. 'I have to have an operation. I'm sorry.'

'We walked along the Crag Path in silence. The towers were as normal. Fishermen lounged as usual. The gulls cried perpetually. After a few steps he hugged me and went ahead. It was the last time I would see him other than as the grey shade at the rear of the brick Artistic Directors' box in the Maltings, where, usually in an overcoat, he would enter just before the performance, the ghost of his own reality.'[7]

Casting and shooting finally began when Cyril Bennett, programme controller at London Weekend Television, pledged the lion's share of a £145,000 budget – for a film to be delivered in a year, no other strings attached. Rex plotted a co-operative structure where everyone worked for minimum rates or nothing at all in return for a cut of any profits; cheques were issued to meet union rules but not cashed. Equity, the actors' union, allowed an amateur cast after a plea from Peggy Ashcroft. Use of Vera Lynn's 'We'll Meet Again' for a Second World War dance scene was approved by the singer but blocked by the Musicians' Union without payment for twenty back-up players. So, Dame Vera suggested another recording, with voice and organ only.

Before the camera rolled, Ronnie wrote to Patricia Highsmith: 'Peter Hall has been staying here and, while infinitely thoughtful and kind, is infinitely busy for at least 16 hours out of the 24. So that when he departed I actually sat in the garden for a whole day, getting my breath back.'[8] Peter, who would continue lodging at French's Folly and keep hitting his head on low beams, had looked out at 'a very old country, tilled and worked and sweated over by centuries of back-breaking effort'. He added: 'I don't like Suffolk: it frightens me. But because of my childhood, I am always deeply affected by it.'[9]

A notice in the *East Anglian Daily Times* invited non-actors to audition at Farlingaye High School in Woodbridge. Peter marvelled at Ronnie's subtle way of getting people to talk about themselves. Ex-pupil Garrow Shand, a farmer's son who knew how to plough, turned up with the thought: 'It'll be a laugh, won't it?' Picked to play the three Toms, he became the heart and soul of *Akenfield* – a pensive and ambiguous figure seemingly oblivious to the camera, a handsome face hauntingly between that of Peter Hall and Ronald Blythe.

Driving instructor Lyn Brooks was chosen for Charlotte, the lady's maid who becomes old Tom's wife, and supporting characters were essentially Suffolk folk playing themselves (Ida Page as Aunt Ida, Ted Dedham as Ted, Charlie Whiting as Charlie). Ronnie was the vicar he might have been. The embodiment of young

Tom's widowed mother, Dulcie, was met at Charsfield Flower Show, flushed with success after several first prizes. Peggy Cole, well known to Ronnie as the wife of his fellow churchwarden, chattered away while selling raffle tickets. When Peter said he wanted her help in a film, she thought she would be making the tea. As late as Valentine's Day 1973, Peggy and Garrow went to London for a trial scene, where they were told to have a row. 'I thought this was a rum do,' said Peggy. 'Well, anyway, I'd got two boys, you see, so it wasn't hard!'[10]

'In any 20 or 30 men and women, there are a couple who still have the instinct to play – as children play,' Peter Hall explained. 'They are not actors: they cannot easily repeat their inventions without lapsing into self-consciousness or artificiality. But put them into a situation that they know because they have lived it – a harvest, a school lesson, a funeral service or a family argument – and they can fantasise richly, rather as if they were in a charade.'[11]

To capture the seasons, filming was to take place over nine months of weekends due to the weekday jobs of cast and crew. Harvest scenes would claim their summer holidays. Peter was running the National Theatre, filming Harold Pinter's *The Homecoming* and directing a space-fiction musical in New York. Ronnie was to be on set at all times as a guardian of authenticity, with some tension arising. 'Slight difficulties with Ronnie,' Peter wrote in his diary. 'He gives the characters marvellous background information. But he also tends to suggest what they might say. I've had tactfully to stop this. They can't say lines. They can only invent them.'[12]

Embracing the austerity of the budget, Ronnie finally had to accept a cheque from Rex towards his costs. 'You keep on saying you don't have any expenses, but for over a year now you have been housing and feeding half the unit, taking taxis all over Suffolk day and night, and endless phone calls and letters all over England.'[13]

The Techniscope film format, used on Sergio Leone's cult spaghetti westerns, brought a wide screen and a grainy, documentary look. It was to demonstrate the artistry of cameraman Ivan Strasburg (hired over Lord Snowden) in achingly beautiful shots of the broad Suffolk countryside contrasting with the claustrophobic harshness of the story and captured with virtually no artificial lighting. Peter and Rex dashed to Munich to learn a new technique of drizzling anti-flare on the back of the lens to diffuse light and soften colours for period sequences. The metropolitan art director Julia Trevelyan Oman came and went, replaced by set dressers Ian Whittaker and Roger Christian to reflect the modesty of scale.

A high-hedged field was bought for ploughing, sowing with unsprayed barley and harvesting along 1911 lines. A broken binder was restored by Clifford Arbon, the Akenfield wheelwright, and pulled by Suffolk Punch heavy horses from the borstal farm at Hollesley Bay. The Low House pub at Laxfield provided step-dancing and Woodbridge fire brigade hoses rain for the blacksmith's forge scene. Ronnie's beloved Hoo church hosted the funeral, though the bell tower was at Monewden. Sally Bacon excelled at wardrobe thrift: when khaki uniforms ran out for the heart-rending First World War service, she put Rex Pyke in a mock sailor's kit, angling a cap to hide the words 'Kiss Me Quick'.

'Nobody knew the "story" so there was no attempt to tell one,' Ronnie wrote. 'We simply said, "It is a wet day long ago and you can't work and you won't get paid", or "It is a Saturday night dance in the village hall in 1943 and the bombers are going out from Debach aerodrome." Those brief statements formed the basis of improvised dialogue and action.'[14] But he guided the crew with detailed treatment notes for truthful settings.

Such was the precision that Barbara Tilney, the teacher playing the martinet Edwardian schoolmistress, was taught to modify the accent of her native Waveney Valley with a more Deben Valley burr. Her class of small children were shocked by her unaccustomed severity – the smallest, Frank (Sean Wood), bursting into tears. When the class erupted in cheers and jeers as the tyrant was toppled by Tom's rebellion, the little boy wept again and stole the scene.

Peggy Cole – who also shed real tears at the funeral since wearing the clothes she had worn for her father's send-off and hearing the same hymn – outdid everyone in the art of pitching in. She found props and costumes and brought in home-made cakes to jokes that Elizabeth Taylor could learn a thing or two from her. When Robin the gravedigger said he would be held up by working on a real grave, Peggy and her husband filled it in. Peggy did the rabbit-skinning for Lyn Brooks in one scene, also providing the rabbits. Twice the butcher obliged but the third time she could find only a poor creature with myxomatosis on the roadside as she drove to the shoot. 'I stopped and clonked it one,' she said. 'I thought well, I've put it out of its misery, and I took it back and skinned it . . . the liver was a bit spotted; they never knew.'[15]

Peggy surpassed herself for the wake – where strict Baptists unwound into sit-down comics after the tea party when invited to sample 'something stronger'. 'Peter knew I made home-made wine . . . so I took a gallon down – parsnip, gooseberry, wheat. Well, they'd all had a tiddle of this before we started the scene. By the time we got through the scene there was two or three gallons went because I know I had to send my son home to get some more. That was gone. They were well oiled. And the tales were coming out.'[16]

The best joke came from tanked-up Charlie. 'Two women walking away from a funeral, one has just buried her husband. "He was a fine man . . . Every Sunday morning we would lie in bed listening to the church bells. We were up with the ding and down with the dong, and if that bloody fire-engine hadn't come along at that time, he'd be alive now."'

Final footage was shot near Peter's home in Oxfordshire, with a kindly Second World War policeman played by Reg Hall – the director's father. His children had appeared as extras or assisted as crew. Although Ronnie had crafted the closing scene, where young Tom slips away in the early morning, starting a flight to London if not to Australia, much like a Blythe brother, it depicted the saga of Peter Hall. *Akenfield* would remain his most personal work.

For all the originality, there were nods to other rural heroes: a courtship scene where Charlotte steals Tom's watch as he swims in the river and he chases her into the woods while naked was borrowed from an H. E. Bates short story; the harvester who stepped on a bird's nest echoed the Thomas Bewick woodcut used in the classic book by Suffolk oral historian George Ewart Evans, *Ask the Fellows Who Cut the Hay*.

That Ewart Evans homage proved bittersweet when it was learned that another film was being made in and about Suffolk: David Gladwell had pressed on with *Requiem for a Village* guided, it was said, by the oral historian hostile to Ronnie's 'fictional' book. In an exchange of letters, David argued that his film differed by being about the death rather than the adaptability of a rural community. Also, he was using actors for the leads and a fantasy sequence where villagers climbed out of their graves like a Stanley Spencer painting springing to life. The latter was unknown presumably to literalist

George Ewart Evans. Anyway, it was agreed that Peter and Ronnie's film would come out first.

On 24 October 1973 Ronnie reported: 'Now it is all over bar the cutting, which proceeds apace in London.'[17] In fact, turning 43 hours of film into 98 screen minutes would take another nine months and late delivery confounded the one condition of London Weekend Television. Ronnie followed progress in Peter's penthouse Barbican flat, as a portrait of earthy Suffolk emerged in a tower of concrete. During editing it was clear that the drama needed a connective voice, so Suffolk actor Peter Tuddenham narrated as old Tom, lifting mellifluous and harrowing lines from the book relating the terrible times of George Blythe. Now the film's title had to be *Akenfield*. Ronnie only regretted that Edmund Blunden had died in Long Melford before he could see it.

The finishing touch, five years after writer and director first met,

Committal cast.

was the music. Benjamin Britten was given one last chance to contribute, but his heart surgery had been followed by a stroke. Elgar's *Symphony No. 1* was considered and then rejected as too portentous and grand. Peter had directed Michael Tippett's opera *The Knot Garden* and was smitten now by his *Fantasia Concertante on a Theme of Corelli* for string orchestra. As was Ronnie when he heard it. Sharing Suffolk roots, with a boyhood in Wetherden near Stowmarket, the composer might have written his scintillating and poignant piece for the home-grown movie.

40

After *Akenfield*

O N 18 NOVEMBER 1974 *Akenfield* was well received as the first British film to open the London Film Festival. 'It is without doubt not only Hall's best work but one of the best films, and certainly the most unusual, made in and about England,' Alexander Walker wrote in the *Evening Standard*.

A rough cut had pleased film-makers John Schlesinger and Harold Pinter. But Peter Hall's biggest nail-biter came with the Ipswich preview for the cast – Ronnie already reporting that after long months of editing many felt they had laboured in vain. 'We all filed into the cinema,' Peter wrote. 'I said a few words hoping they would like it, for if they didn't, God help us. Then the film. It was very much a Suffolk day out and a Sabbath to boot. At first, very respectable, very reserved. Best-clothes atmosphere. But by the end of the second reel they had warmed through and were really getting the points. They laughed at the jokes, were held by the atmospheric scenes, and my blind terror gradually subsided . . . The cast and their friends took the picture to heart and warmly applauded it at the end. They were very, very moved. And so was I. I was accepted.'[1]

They were preparing for the experiment of simultaneous release on big and small screens. Critic Kenneth Tynan wrote cynically in his diary: 'P Hall's mastery of public relations surges relentlessly on: for weeks now it's been impossible to turn on the radio or TV or pick up a paper without reading something radiant about Akenfield.'[2]

It was reasoned that a film lacking stars and marketing budget would stall at the cinema unless kick-started by an admiring audience on television. With only three channels, and no replay option, it was reckoned that if 5 million Sunday evening viewers induced a further million to see it in the cinema, they would have a hit. Transmission on 26 January 1975 was trailed by a documentary on the filming and a ticket in the *TV Times* with the words: 'Take your seat for a world premiere in your own home.' Nearly 15 million people (over a quarter of the population) did indeed take their seats. Peter Hall leapt from his, at a Chelsea party, to field questions after the debut at the Paris Pullman cinema.

The next morning he was congratulated by a taxi driver and 'Princess Margaret phoned to say she'd liked it but didn't understand why one or two critics had complained it was difficult to understand the dialect. She hadn't found it difficult at all. "Though of course", she said, "one did grow up there, in Norfolk at any rate."'[3]

Reviews ranged from 'mundane clichés' to 'a masterpiece'. The *Guardian*'s Nancy Banks-Smith enthused: 'It is a sort of passion play of their own captivity.' *Private Eye* mocked 'Akenballs'. Controversy was stirred when George Ewart Evans objected in the *Listener* to 'a new strain of romanticism in "country" writing'. Ronnie replied: 'I am neither a sociologist nor an oral historian, honourable though those trades be. My book is composed of talk about the society into which I was born, and was supplied by close friends, neighbours and some strangers, none of whom is fiction.' The contrast with Mr Evans, a Welsh schoolteacher who reached Suffolk when nearly forty, was clear.[4]

A row can be good for business but bad news came from twelve trial cinemas. *Akenfield* was a one-night success which interested people had already seen. The exquisite cinematography of Ivan Strasburg was diminished on the small screen: a ravishing and radical film was belittled from the start. Despite a much praised March premiere, no American distributor saw profit in taking it on. But Rex Pyke said: 'After the *Akenfield* breakthrough it was possible to get finance and participation from television, making films which might otherwise not have been made. *Akenfield* was the model used when we campaigned to get the proposed new ITV2 channel to be a "publishing" channel turning to independent producers, rather than making their own in-house programming, hence we got Channel 4.'[5]

While filming *Akenfield*, Ronnie had been asked to script the defrocked rector of Stiffkey chapter in *The Age of Illusion*; he felt overwhelmed and the invitation was not reissued. Afterwards, he told Patricia Highsmith: 'It was terrific making the film but totally interrupting and everything connected with one's normal existence just piled up . . . We formed a little company called Angle Films to make it and we are keeping this company in existence to make Pinter's *Landscape*.'[6] Ronnie, the unlikely company chairman, was an interested observer when the one-act Harold Pinter play – a two-hander with Peggy Ashcroft and David Waller, directed by Peter Hall for the National Theatre – was filmed in the Buckinghamshire mansion of Pinewood Studios. Although Ronnie would script documentaries on John Constable, John Nash and himself for other television producers, a cinematic affair had ended.

Never copyrighted, 'Akenfield' was claimed by an egg producer, a building company and a Rottweiler dog breeder. It became a close, a peel of church bells and a lot of rural housing. French's Folly was a B&B for a while after Ronnie left it, with a book in every bedroom and the writer's study recast as the Akenfield Suite.[7] The made-up word ended up as hackneyed as a Zorba taverna in Greece.

The annual report for Angle Films at 31 July 1976 put *Akenfield* production costs at £145,932, against net liabilities of £167,180 – and this after some creditors had settled for 50p in the pound. The bankrupt company was wound up in 1989.[8] London Weekend Television, which had taken on distribution when Angle Films ran out of cash, was persuaded by Rex to pass all rights to the Akenfield Trust in 1990. Split ownership, between sixty-five makers and creditors, remained a scenario for inaction.

There was a thirtieth anniversary revival at the National Film Theatre, to coincide with an *Akenfield Revisited* documentary by Rex Pyke, and another in 2016 when the film was remastered for a DVD. Sir Peter Hall, now resembling an aged Buddhist sage, greeted Ronnie at the latter reunion with: 'Why do you never get old!' On his death, a year later, the *Times* hailed 'the most important figure in British theatre for half a century'. He had given up movies as a bad business. 'As a director in the cinema, you don't make films – you hustle,' he said. But some of the last sounds he heard, on a loop in hospital, were from the Tippett score for *Akenfield*.[9]

Rex Pyke was forever focused on Suffolk and the film they had made there, even when retiring to Scotland. Art co-director Roger Christian won an Oscar for his next project, the first *Star Wars*. Garrow Shand bought a digger with his pay and prospered as an agricultural contractor. *Akenfield* shaped his life: he met his future wife, Helen, in the harvest scene. They attended Ronald Blythe's memorial service in St Edmundsbury Cathedral in March 2023. So did Jenny Hall, Peter's daughter, who had appeared as a stone-picker in the film and was set now to direct a stage version of the book.

Most of the *Akenfield* cast carried on with lives caught on camera. The player whose life changed the most, though she remained exactly the same, was Peggy Cole. She named her council house Akenfield and raised £60,000 for local charities by opening her garden to the public. One morning Peggy took a call from Lady Prudence Penn, of Sternfield House near Saxmundham. Her weekend guest was an *Akenfield* fan and would like a garden tour. Lady Penn and Princess Margaret were duly shown around the Cole estate, then served tea in the sitting room. Whereupon the princess pulled a pack of Gauloises from her handbag. 'I didn't allow smoking in the house but I could hardly tell the Queen's sister that,' Peggy said. 'So I just found an ashtray and she lit up causing a right old stink!' The royal visitor signed the guest book, and Peggy loyally stuck an aromatic fag-end alongside.[10]

Ronnie was also drawn in as Lady Penn strove to keep her returning royal guest amused. He led a tour of Blythburgh church and accepted invitations to dinners with a baffling mix of informality and deference. The assembled party ate only while the princess was eating; when she jumped up to throw another log on the fire, they all stood too and stayed upright until she sat down again. But a determined writer was able to limit social distractions by hiding behind his lowly status as a non-driver. He failed a driving test before riding a moped briefly until updating his old Rudge bicycle for a Raleigh. 'I thought he was very clever,' Peggy said, 'because whenever anybody wants him, they've got to go and fetch him.'[11]

Peggy drove herself for talks across Suffolk and beyond – also talking on the *QE2* before a chatty tour of the United States. She became an author, newspaper columnist and MBE. Her reflections on rural life were lapped up until her death, in 2016, aged eighty. Then came astonishment that the matriarch of *Akenfield* had been thirty-seven during filming. Ronnie, the boyish vicar, had been fifty.

The past is indeed a foreign country: they look different while doing things differently there. The cottage where young Tom had lived with his mum had been lent by two brothers at Letheringham. It had one plug and a backyard pump, but the film deal included installation of modern electrics, plumbing and a bathroom. When Peggy visited later the bath was an onion store.

Ronnie himself was affected chiefly by the *Akenfield* book. In 1970 he was elected a fellow of the Royal Society of Literature and won the Heinemann Award. He took Christine to the prize-giving dinner. She wrote in thanks for 'splendid Dins at Wheelers'. And added: 'I felt so proud of you, & so delighted that hard work & the ability to stick to it has been eventually rewarded . . . Both you and John seem to bear out Mr Churchill's famous saying . . . It is not in the beginning, but in the carrying out until the end, that lies the true glory.'[12]

The following year the carrier out received a Society of Authors travel scholarship – enjoying the intimation that the author of the ultra-localist *Akenfield* needed to get out more. 'Do you think they can have heard about my bike rides to Wickham Market?' he asked Patricia Highsmith. 'I have accepted the prize but said that I can't go anywhere until I have finished my present work etc. They don't seem to mind this nor do they insist on a book being produced out of the travelling. Only where shall I go? You are a great traveller, so you must advise me.'[13]

Pat advised a joint trip to Rome or Venice. Pursued in several letters, neither idea was enacted (just like the invitations to visit her in France or Switzerland). The Society of Authors has no record that any foreign travel – and, indeed, a trip of any kind – was ever taken.

Disciple to Mentor

WHILE SETTLING INTO life at Debach, Ronnie had kept up the habit of escaping to London for a day or night – often to dip into the gay social world revolving around the self-confessed brigand that was Tommy Frankland.

Tommy was at his picaresque peak when partnered with the urbane Richard Broome, a Lloyd's underwriter whose father had been master gunner at the Tower of London. Their flats in Manchester and Montagu squares were gay boarding houses and dinner party hubs, an old Rolls-Royce parked outside as a style statement. They flourished entertainingly, for a time, on Tommy's largesse and Richard's money.

It was through Tommy and Richard that Ronnie enjoyed one of his most ardent affairs – with a beautiful young man named Brian Colley, picked up by Richard on a train. Fascination dwindled beyond the bedroom and, as usual, an affectionate attachment drifted towards tedium whenever domesticity loomed. Ronnie found Brian a clerical job with the publisher Faber, not least to keep him at a safe distance in London. That didn't last either.

The momentous meeting via the Tommy and Richard gay circle came one evening when table chatter was on matters sexual and material, save for a quiet corner where Ronnie was talking books with James Hamilton-Paterson. They shared the same birthday, nineteen years apart, and a passion for writing, though their differences looked more striking. James 'was – is – tall, fair, patrician and unprovincial', Ronnie wrote fifty years later. 'Free of those things which have tied me to a small scene.'[1]

James Hamilton-Paterson.

James was the son of London medics. His late and loathed father, a neurological physician, had treated the Aga Khan and provided the inspiration for the poem 'Disease' with which James had won the Newdigate Prize while a student at Oxford. He was about to embark on a lifetime of travel – with a year in Libya before venturing into Suffolk. Writing would be his only fixed point, though his books would cover a remarkable range. Ronnie was instrumental in getting him started and sustaining him on the journey.

When finally reaching Debach, James looked around the garden and said: 'I could be happy here.' Ronnie's heart sank – needlessly, since one self-sufficient singleton was merely recognising and saluting another. They were lovers for a while, but 'neither of us was the other's ideal, so it didn't last', James said.[2] Writerly friendship did.

Ronnie was father figure and literary guide for James, whose talent was also appreciated by Patricia Highsmith. As Ronnie told her before James came for Christmas in 1967: 'He is very unhappy because he can't get abroad. He wants to teach or live in Malaya, though heaven knows why. The main reason seems to be because it is a long way off. I tell him that it doesn't matter what he does in order to get some money or where he lives, provided that he works at his writing . . . He is at the moment working as the theatre porter in a big London hospital and tells me gruesome tales about carting amputated legs off to the incinerator. And just before he left he had to put the leg-less body of a 60-year-old woman into the refrigerator. Until her funeral. Ugh.'[3]

James himself could scarcely have been more amazed when Ronnie took him to meet a grand old lesbian friend who lived, in formal style, at Snape with a young dungaree-clad handywoman called Nick. He was introduced to Molly Kirwan – the mother of his moral tutor at Oxford. Nick led him to the Gateways lesbian night-club in Chelsea where, as Ronnie said following a visit of his own, the last butch-femme couples, remnants of Radclyffe Hall's *Well of Loneliness* generation, 'took their pleasures sadly'.

By the autumn of 1969 Ronnie reported to Patricia Highsmith that James had published a children's novel and was covering erupting troubles in Northern Ireland for the *New Statesman* while working on a television film about volcanoes. They would explore Debach airfield together where James revealed a fascination for aviation. And on walks along the North Sea shore he was nurturing an oceanic passion. This was eventually to be expressed in *Seven-Tenths: The Sea and Its Thresholds*, a book bearing out Ronnie's faith and love:

'To most Europeans, at any rate, the "seaside" is no mere littoral, a bald geographical margin where land happens to stop. It is too closely bound up with the past, with summer holidays, once-yearly pursuits, even erotic adventure, to be an indifferent location. We delve into a cupboard in a winter month, looking for something, and come up instead with a pair of shoes from which sand trickles as from a snapped hourglass. At once we are flooded with memory. We almost hear surf break outside the window in waves which have crossed fields and city streets to find us.'[4]

A Debach regular from the time of Ronnie's *Akenfield* researches, James helped to knock house and garden into better shape. They shored up each other's creative resolve. The younger man was cosmopolitan and intellectual, with the survival skills of a latter-day Robinson Crusoe – ultimately writing what Ronnie regarded as a masterpiece, *Playing with Water*. It related how and why he could live for a quarter of the year by shelter-building, spear-fishing and foraging on an uninhabited Philippine island. Deeply musical, he long contemplated a novel about the elderly Elgar's voyage up the Amazon to the opera house at Manaus. The book to be called *Gerontius* was worth the wait; winning a Whitbread prize in 1989, it was dedicated to Ronnie.

Blythe books were dedicated in turn to James and his mother, Ursula – the latter getting *First Friends*, the story Ronnie made from the youthful letters of the Nash brothers, Christine and Carrington. She was less thankful to receive the news that Ronnie had been the lover of her youthful son. As James said: 'He was an odd mixture of extreme discretion and then moments of not being discreet at all.'[5]

As Ronnie and James ascended as writers, Richard Broome embarked on what Ronnie regarded as a slippery slope from high finance to interior decoration. 'He has left Lloyd's and is doing the usual thing – doing up flats, in other words,' Patricia Highsmith was told. 'I have such a prejudice against otherwise nice gay boys who will keep dashing about with colour schemes and rolls of curtaining.'[6]

Once parted from Richard, Tommy Frankland crashed between indolence and debauchery. 'Tommy is lolling around in London, abusing his phenomenal constitution and getting worried in case it outlasts his capital,' Ronnie related. 'He stays with rich friends all over the place, doing nothing, talking about his temperature and being (fortunately) very charming. "Tommy's trouble", remarked one of his rich hosts, "is how to make two week-ends meet."'[7]

That phenomenal constitution finally exhausted by cravings for alcohol and masochistic assault, Tommy was to die in a dingy attic aged forty-nine, in September 1975, having gone on a rampage in bishop's attire, smashing windows with a crozier. At a lofty London funeral, in the Queen's Chapel of the Savoy, Ronnie read the lesson from Corinthians about bodies sown in weakness and raised in power. Tommy had dreamed of a knighthood for services to charity and the sanctity of a Franciscan monk's burial on the holy island of Iona, where his ashes were surreptitiously scattered to the winds. After a squandered life which had read like a morality tale, Ronnie and James ritually burned obscene diaries lacking literary merit.

Ronald Blythe's life after *Akenfield* was immeasurably enriched when 28-year-old Richard Mabey used his position as a Penguin editor to meet his heroes. Proposing a new version of the village book for secondary schools, he was invited to French's Folly. 'I went on that pretext and got carried away by other things,' he said. 'Ronnie made a cake, as he always did; it was early winter so we didn't get a walk in. Very rapidly the conversation became discursive as it was to continue for the next half-century.'[8]

An Oxford graduate impassioned by the countryside, Richard was an appealing mix of erudition and enthusiasm. Dynamic good looks resembled the romantic image of the young Franz Schubert, which hung on the Blythe study wall as a gift from Imogen Holst. Richard was too young, shy and heterosexual to realise that he was instantly (and lastingly) Ronnie's physical and emotional ideal. Theirs was to be a platonic love affair played out in walks, talks and books – with an undercurrent of unrequited desire which for Ronnie was occasionally overwhelming.

While Ronnie was far stronger than he appeared, Richard was the opposite. An upbringing in the lovely Chilterns had hidden mayhem at home. Suffering from alcoholism and heart disease, his father punished the family from his sickbed by refusing to pay power bills and trying to prevent Richard attending university. Deliverance came with a doughty mother forging cheques and admission letters.

Ronnie was a safe harbour in a storm. 'Here was a grown-up man whose way of life and thinking I could utterly respect and underneath that of course was the bliss of his writing,' Richard said. Ronnie was in turn enchanted when Richard's searchings on their long meanders to local pubs were served up in his first book, *Food for Free*. The father figure was 'fantastically encouraging' for what became a shelf of acclaimed Mabey volumes on nature and culture. In 1986 the Whitbread Prize-winning biography of naturalist Gilbert White was dedicated to Ronnie for 'constant inspiration'.[9]

In his relationships with James Hamilton-Paterson and Richard Mabey, Ronnie transformed at last from disciple to mentor. As his Anglican faith deepened, it mattered not a bit that his literary soulmates were atheists. The two younger men became ever more crucial as an old idol finally failed.

By 1971 the Turners had made the house and garden at Treneague perfect in Ronnie's estimation, and so now they determined to leave – cashing in as usual and chasing the myth of a better life elsewhere. They fancied something picturesque in Fowey or Falmouth but bought a gaunt Edwardian villa near Camelford, with a tiny garden lost in the wild expanse of Bodmin Moor. Cathy confided that

James was growing lazy. Ronnie, joining them for Christmas, made all the encouraging noises. He knew the score by now and even found comfort in a familiar litany of Turner complaint.

Given the faithful nature of Ronnie's love, he was touched by the frailty and fallibility of dear ones without being really moved. He could see a certain pathos when James Turner, the thwarted artist, supported Mary Whitehouse campaigns against the permissive society – all that rot aired and praised while his own grand talent festered. And when James fell from a London bus, then learned in hospital that a pet cat had been run over, Ronnie wrote with telling sympathy. Having dealt briskly with a double calamity, he concluded: 'Is there a good library at the hospital? I do hope so. Nothing is worse than having nothing to read and one needs great quantities of books in hospital.'[10] The recipient would have understood. Life itself depended on great quantities of books. This was the one point on which they could agree absolutely.

The year 1975 opened brightly with the *Akenfield* film premiere and then clouded in May with the death of James Turner, at sixty-six, following illness unmentioned but practically lifelong. The Royal Literary Fund assisted with ensuing expenses. Invited by Cathy to take a book, Ronnie picked *Centuries* by the ecstatic seventeenth-century poet and theologian Thomas Traherne. James had introduced Ronnie to Traherne, though the bliss they shared sadly eluded him.

'Needing to think of happiness, I think of Thomas Traherne,' Ronnie wrote. 'I find his *Centuries*, the copy that once belonged to my first poet-friend, James Turner. There is a snapshot inside of him reading it. He has come out of hospital and is in a deckchair, the green volume in his hands. I find the page.

'"When I came into the country, and being settled among silent trees and woods and hills, had all my time in my own hands, I resolved to spend it all, whatever it cost me, in the search of Happiness, and to satiate the burning thirst which Nature had enkindled in me from youth. In which I was so resolute that I chose rather to live upon ten pounds a year, and to go in leather clothes and to feed upon bread and water, so that I might have all my time clearly to myself . . . So that through His blessing I live a free and kingly life, as if the world were turned again into Eden."'[11]

James Turner had also led Ronnie to the special desolation of Cornish moors – Black, Breock, Breward, Bodmin. They drove one

day to St Juliot, on the moor above Boscastle, where a young architect from Dorset had arrived in 1870 to 'restore' the medieval church.
Thomas Hardy fell for the vicar's sister-in-law, Emma Gifford, and
filled his novel *A Pair of Blue Eyes* with their courtship scenes. Forty
years of joyless marriage followed. Finding a fragment of Emma's
memoir, a widower was then propelled back to Cornwall for heart-
wrenching poems on love and loss. 'He is the poet of regret, of
what might have been,' Ronnie said.

In 1974 Ronnie was invited to help edit the New Wessex Edition
of the works of Thomas Hardy. The novel chosen for him was the
almost forgotten *A Pair of Blue Eyes* – a public project becoming a
private epitaph for another troubled affair of the heart.

42

View on Winter

WHAT LOOKED TO be a steady trajectory of literary success hid the fact that, after sending *Akenfield* to the publisher, Ronnie embarked on a prolonged wild goose chase.

He chose to follow an unclassifiable classic with a formal history of the Fabian Society. The late nineteenth-century socialist think tank co-founded the Labour Party in 1900, also setting up the London School of Economics and the *New Statesman* journal for which Ronnie was chief fiction reviewer. He signed up to an intellectual cause he had always admired from a distance.

There were many trips to the archive at Nuffield College, Oxford, each journey by bus, train, Tube and train again a marathon effort for a non-driver from Debach. Lodging with the Wordsworth family, descendants of the poet's brother, was a bonus. His letters were filled first with enthusiasm, then grit and then the cries of a man drowning in a sea of papers also dry as dust. For all that inherent radicalism, politics lay nowhere near his heart. And economic management went over his head entirely.

One morning in November 1972 he came suddenly to his senses and ditched the Fabians. 'The release!' he confessed to Patricia Highsmith. 'Sometimes it is delicious to give in. I wasted God knows what time and sweat on that book. But it simply didn't happen. I spent weeks at Oxford and in London researching and months here writing, but . . . it was like trying to write about Beethoven without being able to read a note of music.'[1]

Ronnie was flattered to be considered for the much coveted position of biographer for playwright and Fabian polemicist George Bernard Shaw, but the idea did not outlast tentative discussions with the author's estate. The plum task fell to Michael Holroyd, whose £625,000 advance[2] exceeded the entire Blythe career earnings. A lost prize proved all to the good, however: his forte lay in capturing myriad life in condensed and digressionary style rather than comprehensive biography.

His notes were passed to academics Norman and Jeanne MacKenzie and acknowledged in their 1977 book *The First Fabians*. Now Patricia Highsmith learned that, as well as working on a volume provisionally called *The Art of the English Diarist*, 'commissioned by Gollancz ages ago', he was replacing the Fabians with 'a kind of *Akenfield* about old age. Not sociology or geriatrics, simply talk from all kinds of people about being 80-plus.'[3]

Advance payment for the Fabians was diverted to the new book as negotiated by agent Deborah Rogers, successor to Paul Scott. And Ronnie went gladly back to Penguin having dutifully followed Tony Godwin to Weidenfeld & Nicolson. Authorial freedom of action was restored when Tony moved again, to New York, and an older loyalty could reopen. Ronnie was always at his happiest on old ground.

The View in Winter: Reflections on Old Age started with a leftover piece of *Akenfield*. Ronnie had revered elderly people as living history – witnesses to a world before his birth. Now he talked to the Charsfield district nurse, who lived alone in a damp cottage, and although he saw her every Sunday – she was church treasurer – he realised he had never really seen her. At her deathbed in the newly labelled geriatric ward of Ipswich hospital, when in her nineties, he knew he had met an explorer.

Great age was a new phenomenon. Life expectancy in England at Ronald Blythe's birth was 56 for men and 59 for women. In 1979, when *The View in Winter* was published, longevity reached 70.3 years for men – finally surpassing the biblical span of threescore years and ten – and 76.4 for women. The novelty of living for fourscore years and more had been pioneered by his grandmother. At ninety, Martha Blythe spoke less of aches and pains than pleasures and achievements. What intrigued her keenest listener was not how the aged were perceived – that could be barbarous – but how they felt in themselves. 'It's a great experience of its own, like youth,' he found.[4] He also came to believe that this revelation made for the best of all his books.

'Lots of people told me that they would like to talk about their senescence, but that it was far too daring a subject. My book *The View in Winter* is a collection of travellers' tales from the country of the very old. Only those who have lived a very long time can say what it is like to be journeying through this land.'[5]

A Chicago conference on longevity had appalled him with words such as 'gerontology' and 'geriatric'. And he was similarly shocked by the harrowing *Old Age* account by Simone de Beauvoir, atheist and Marxist, of what she called 'Society's secret shame'. He was no less compassionate and infinitely more positive.

A new friend, radio producer Hallam Tennyson, sole surviving brother of Julian Tennyson, could tell him about the beloved author of *Suffolk Scene*. Better yet, Hallam was a route to their father Sir Charles Tennyson who, when nearly a centenarian, recalled the Victorian poet with crystal clarity. This was pure romance for Ronnie, who was also deflecting sexual advances from Hallam, a married father of two, as a long-suppressed gay nature was suddenly liberated.

A gathering of fresh interviews saw another set of changed names and a further mingling of record, observation and memory in a search for deeper truth. The author scanned town and country, talking to miners and craftsmen, engineers and mechanics, medics, teachers, soldiers, priests, housewives and home helps. Some remained 'stamped in heroic terms by the tragic and transcendent happenings of their youth'. One colliery village couple, seventy-three years into their marriage, were 'genuinely intrigued by the sheer casualness with which everybody under sixty accepts abundance'; a First World War veteran coolly reported: 'The other day, while driving my car, with my leg bent up, I felt a small, hard, rough scrap of something between my knees and my trousers. Another bit of shrapnel had worked its way out.'[6]

The reverse of a dismal old people's home was a monastery where every monk, aged between 28 and 95, felt purposeful within an atmosphere of reflection and generosity. Almost anywhere else the community spirit burned on the energy and expertise of people deep in retirement. While every life was unique, and expressed views ranged from positivity to perplexity and resignation to despair, the best defence in extreme old age lay in activity and philosophy.

Like Ronnie himself, the monks were saved from loneliness and grief. This mutilating state was summed up in the testimony of a lesbian academic unhappily returned to her native Welsh valley after the death of her life partner. 'For her, home is not where one comes from, it is where one arrives, and she arrived there in the company of someone who gave her an entire universe of art, travel, literature, love and enthralling work. Among the remnants of her origins she is a displaced person.'[7]

Ronnie was in his fiftieth year, and not halfway through his life, when embarking on *The View in Winter*. A born stoic had lost any fear of death in youth. Telling friends 'I will live to a great age', he was looking ahead, with uncanny accuracy, to his future. He was also acutely aware of the good fortune of writers and artists who, spared futility in retirement, went on reinventing the world every day.

Research overlapped with concern for Christine and John. A pattern of alternate Christmases with Turners and Nashes had been broken by a return to Bottengoms for jollier festivities in 1970. 'It was, as I knew it would be, a beautiful, memorable Christmas, & I *do* thank you for all that love and hospitality,' he wrote to Christine. 'In retrospect, I'm glad we were weather-bound, for this created the specialness of the holiday.'[8]

Two years later he was back with the Nashes in their eightieth year. 'We shall be very quiet, talking round the fire and driving out to see the neighbours,' he told Patricia Highsmith. 'It is the nearest thing I have to going home to the family.' In truth, his old friends were slowing in any weather, Christine more relieved than ever when able to stay at home.[9]

Ronnie continued to enjoy strenuous and recuperative stays in Bottengoms, looking after house, cats and garden when the owners were away, and helping to hold everything together when they were at home. The loveliness of the place still required unremitting labour. Although electricity had been connected for Christmas 1961, oil lamps and heaters were kept – and gleefully revived during power cuts in 1972.

Most of the human warmth was generated by Christine. She was adored by visiting children – ever solicitous, ever inventive, carefully vigilant during games among the poisonous plants. When one little

Bottengoms in snow, 1972.

girl broke away to fall into a pond, Christine comforted her and conjured up a fairy outfit from the costume store. Mishap was metamorphosed into magic. With Nash finances always tight, and John's reliance on Royal Academy Summer Show sales never abating, Christine was unstinting with love but careful with accounting. Ronnie paid for bottles of wine and fractions of grocery bills. After receiving an invoice for £1 11s 4d and a confession that 'we are so mean and stingy over the phone', he took to leaving a blank cheque to cover any eventuality and embarrassment.

When Ronnie used *Akenfield* royalties to acquire a major John Nash oil – Edale glistening in yellow – he wanted the Nashes to share his reward. 'The picture is extraordinary,' he wrote. 'It seems to have taken on an extra dimension which I can only describe as Wordsworthian. And it is not only because of that Derbyshire hill. It looks simply wonderful and dominates the room – which had to have every other picture shifted about in order to accommodate it. I really do love it. I must also pay John for it.'[10] Christine promptly sent a bill for £500.

But at some late point it was clear to them all that Bottengoms should – and would – be left to him. After relating in a letter to Christine a fresh resolve to buy a house, he ended: 'It was lovely to see you for a few days and to be at dear Bottengoms which, if you will forgive the liberty, comes more and more to seem like my home. A part of me.'¹¹ A loaded hint is inconceivable given the character of Ronald Blythe. The topic had already been discussed.

As it was, the tenant of French's Folly was finally seeking to escape uncertainty and parsimony, albeit with a comic edge. Renovation had been so bodged that one night Ronnie's bedroom window fell into the garden; the landlord nearly fell to the ground also when told it would cost £36 to put back. One rental payment had been left in an inscribed copy of *Akenfield* when Harold French was away. The returning farmer came running over the fields, waving the unopened book and crying 'Where's my rent!' The gift had been taken for a low offer in lieu of cash.

Several times Ronnie tried and failed to extract a formal lease on French's Folly or to buy it. Now he faced eviction to make way for farmworkers. Once again, he was proposing to find a property for sale near Woodbridge. But six weeks later he got a valuation of the house he had vowed to leave, offering the sum – £18,000 – to the unyielding farmer. An impasse had been reached. Friends thought the folly of the place was the tenant's persistence in trying to keep it.

Ronnie wrote to Christine more explicitly – typing for the first time to make his position clear: 'A long, long time hence, venerable and with a sense of rightness of purpose, I hope I shall be typing away on a table in Bottengoms' garden and feeling entirely at home.'¹²
A plan was practically in place.

Nash care became more consuming. John, struggling with arthritis, gashed his head falling on the perilous Bottengoms stairs and grew lame from a dodgy hip. His sister, Barbara, went to a nursing home in the old sanatorium at Wiston. Her partner Norah had finally died of shock after being the driver in a car crash which killed Paul Nash's widow, Bunty. Barbara's health then shattered.

Christine, arranger for everyone, suffered her own travails in silence. Back in August 1966 she had ended a long gap in her diary: 'I have been more or less ill the whole year, until the beginning of this month; but not that anyone noticed it. I felt the whole time as if I was recovering from flu without ever having it. I could not write a word. I was so listless that I spent hours on the sofa doing nothing but watch the clouds, or small branches waving, while my eyes filled with tears.'¹³

Her weakening sight could not be missed. Operations for glaucoma left her wearing a green visor for terrifying bouts of driving the Austin 1100 Ronnie called 'an ashtray on wheels' and having to avoid the sunlight she still loved. There was heroism in ongoing treks to France and Skye and biting the bullets of soaring train and plane fares.

Ronnie spent Christmas 1974 alone, quite happily, due to Nash and Turner frailties. He ate a turkey and all the trimmings for a week before reducing the carcase to stock and flinging the remnants as fast food for a host of gulls and rooks. The next Christmas was also spent at home.

John's hip replacement coincided with the 1976 drought, when Ronnie found an octagonal Georgian pewter inkwell among the detritus in his dried-up pond. He wrote in delight on learning that his friends were booked for Skye in September – adding: 'I water in a desultory way but the whole thing has got beyond me. Two weeks of solid pouring rain could hardly have an effect. One of the fascinating effects of the drought is that the outline of many outhouses and ancient farm buildings are marked on the lawns as plainly as if they had been drawn with a ruler . . . It is a year to remember.'[14]

It was indeed. In November Christine collapsed before preparing dinner; an ambulance hurried her to hospital where she died from a heart attack. Ronnie met with befuddlement at Bottengoms after fifty-eight years of marriage. 'What did she mean going off like that?' John said. 'There are some sausages in the fridge.' It was the month they had hated since the death of their son.

At dusk on an autumn afternoon, following Christine's cremation, a Wormingford churchwarden made out a mystery figure digging near the churchyard hedge. It was Ronnie burying a casket of ashes. No permission had been sought. Neither Christine nor John were church attenders – religious faith having been exploded by the First World War – but Ronnie secured the best spot in the graveyard for the person he loved most.

The Langstons flew down from Scotland for the funeral, and days after returning the blind Hog suffered a fatal heart attack while walking with his guide dog. Barbara had just sent John a group photo from their recent visit and written: 'My old boy and I feel so privileged to have known Christine for so many happy years, she was so gentle and loving and had such a gift for friendship . . . I have never known anyone grow old so gracefully.'[15]

Now a widower needed full-time care, and Ronnie quietly moved in to provide it. When French's Folly was burgled, remaining possessions were secreted in Bottengoms' barns: John never knew. The caregiver was writing an introduction to Leo Tolstoy's novella *The Death of Ivan Ilyich*. 'Bloody old Tolstoy!' said jealous John.[16] In the story, the painful and protracted dying of a worldly judge is a nuisance to everyone save for a peasant boy servant, who alone does not fear death and so provides truthful comfort and lets in love. An element of irony was not lost on Ronnie.

And, as it was, a myth was kept alive that the old normality would be returning, so an ancient, ailing artist even talked of remarrying. But Christine was irreplaceable. 'The lynch pin has gone,' John said.[17] He mused on interment in the garden, the churchyard or Buckinghamshire ('where our boy is buried'). And finally he made a will – legalising the long-intended plan to leave the house to Ronnie.

It was to be only ten months before Ronnie finished digging a double grave by the churchyard hedge. John had continued painting and staying with friends for spells passed off as convalescent. Ronnie had cooked for him, cleaned his false teeth, washed his truss. Taking morning tea to the studio bedroom, where one bed leg was a pile of paperback whodunits, he saw a rodent head peek from the pocket of a tweed jacket hanging on a chair. Sleeping under a missing roof tile, the artist might share his pillow with snow. But still he rose with assistance to a cold bath – his yells rising too as the water temperature plummeted.

Otherwise, it was a time of calm companionship until a final decline in Colchester hospital. Together they watched a news report of Benjamin Britten's funeral on television. Ronnie had felt unable to leave a dear old friend alone to attend in person.

'What will you do down here all on your own when I'm gone?' John asked near the end. 'Look after your garden,' Ronnie answered.

Arranging John's funeral service, on 30 September, and reading both lessons, Ronnie then went for a long walk during the wake at Bottengoms, feeling he could do no more. While accolades had poured in for a great artist, dead at eighty-four, a medic friend sent Ronnie a private tribute: 'You made the closing times as good as they could be through infinite generosity of spirit, and a patience amounting to saintliness.'[18]

PART FOUR
The Bard of Bottengoms

Bottengoms is beautiful, wonderfully inconvenient and no spot to get eighty in, but I close my eyes to its many impracticalities and enjoy its isolation.
    Ronald Blythe to Patricia Highsmith, 7 November 1988

43

Postponed Possession

WAKING UP ALONE, on the morning of 1 October, the new owner of Bottengoms felt a wave of elation: in a place of his own; free at last to be himself. Henceforward, this would be the month for starting a new book, but first he finished *The View in Winter*. From this moment in the dying season of autumn his sap of creativity surged.

However, he woke in the guest room as always. Occupying the main bedroom seemed a step too far, since it had been John's studio too and needed major overhaul. Making a study from Christine's bedroom was easier, as she had nurtured his writing, though it felt impertinent to dislodge forty pairs of shoes from a big German press for a growing stack of manuscripts. He placed a chair at his desk from French's Folly, looking to the view of the garden, trees and hedged hilly meadows. But eventually a back would be turned on distraction, so that a writer faced his library and let his imagination fly.

Ronnie had been left the house and most of the contents, including pictures on the walls; but much of the art had been willed to dealer David Wolfers to sell for the benefit of godchildren. A drastic removal proved positive as outgoing paintings gave way to incoming books. More orderly and fastidious than his benefactors, Ronnie began gingerly to clear and clean. A gaggle of helpers had aged and died with the Nashes, save for one gnarled garden hand, but a month from his fifty-fifth birthday the new resident of Bottengoms had the energy, and sense of economy, to do every routine thing himself. He aimed to write each morning and garden each afternoon, and this ambition was pretty much enacted for the next forty years.

A mundane village from the perspective of the road had fine views and fascinating discoveries from footpaths, so the bicycle was abandoned. It took a pleasant walk of a mile to fetch milk and papers, and rather more for the bus stop. And it was two miles for the village shop, which did at least deliver and deal with laundry. In a century of active life, Ronnie was never to possess a washing machine – a fact compounding his horror at being the party in any domestic partnership who would end up soaking the socks.

In Wormingford most doors went unlocked and pinned with temporary notices along the lines of 'Back Thursday. Leave groceries in shed.' Fearless in solitude, isolation and darkness, Ronnie had the comfort of an inherited pet. After Maud died on the lane at Great Glemham, he had foregone feline company since French's Folly was beside a busier highway. Now he enjoyed the undemanding presence of Stripey, the last of the Nash cats.

Outbuildings had been crumbling and tumbling around Bottengoms since the 1920s, with the Nashes doing nothing to stem the slide. Ronnie continued a neglectful tradition as final farmyard structures turned to rubble in the undergrowth. The Eric Ravilious greenhouse was reduced to a stack of glass panes and the grain store imploded on its straddles after yielding a cache of John Nash oils. A garage tilted ever more precariously into a listing building was the last to go. Sentimentality was always marked here by its absence.

As with his land-working ancestors, outdoor exertions ran to hard labour – such as a fresh diverting of the stream further away from the house. But Ronnie never had the passion, time and help to maintain a plantsman's domain. With a drift into a charming country garden, invasive species marauded and hardier rarities clung on in creeping swathes of wilderness. Visiting experts including Beth Chatto and Tony Venison ensured that prized plants – such as John's favourite tawny yellow Gloire de Dijon rose climbing the house facade and ultimately framing a memorial plaque for 'John Nash RA & Christine his wife' were replenished. It all grew into the special beauty and poignancy of a ghost garden.

The house remained a mighty challenge. There were structural issues, but Ronnie's priority was to consider the sacred clutter and let in light and life. All far harder than a vigorous attack on the plot's edges, to lessen the bosky privacy of a defensive enclosure, for a more seamless flow to the landscape beyond. He was the true native here: the Nashes were transplanted exotics. Beyond circles of dear ones and useful ones, they had been exclusive. Ronnie the solitary welcomed the passing world – in passing.

He also felt immensely protective. He designed the Nash gravestone with an inscription from the Song of Solomon: 'Lo, the winter is past, the rain is over and gone; the flowers appear on the earth'. It would have been an odd choice of words for a painterly poet of snow, save for blessed release from that titanic task of keeping Bottengoms warm.

Friends of Christine and John came to pay last respects to their house and found them still in occupation. Admiring the shine on the shrine, Barbara Langston wrote: 'Thank you so much for my delicious evening of drink, food and gossip in such a clean, polished, pretty Bottengoms which nevertheless retained so much of the old atmosphere. You are right – in a quite unsinister and placid way it is POSSESSED. The Old Folk seem to be all around one all the time.'[1]

An inheritor began to feel an intruder beyond curation of a museum or, worse, a mausoleum. He missed French's Folly and independence within the Akenfield community. On Valentine's Day 1978 Patricia Highsmith wrote: 'I do realize that the Nash experience was disturbing to your equilibrium – but the latter is stronger in you than in most of us. I feel sure you will get it back. It is only because you are conscious of it, that it matters so much. Most people in the world are merely silly, glad of a windfall, with no inner life.'[2]

The following January he was resolved to sell up. Fidelity Cranbrook sympathised after a visit: 'It's sad about you having to abandon Bottengoms: but how right – you will have made it all *so* nice by the time you leave – that's the pity of it *really*. I looked in the *East Anglian Daily Times* when I got back and saw several houses in Woodbridge advertised! I think you ought to do it – take the plunge – before next winter when it will all look so pretty and romantic.'[3]

That summer felt far from romantic when former Tate Gallery director John Rothenstein, forever vain and demanding, stayed to research a John Nash book. Each tiresome day began with the wake-up call of a peacock performing callisthenic exercises. But in

July the death of Barbara Nash, whom Ronnie had been faithfully visiting in the old sanatorium on the hill, eased the bequested burden.

Ronnie now tried to write himself into a sense of belonging. Choosing a *Places* anthology, for a 1981 Oxfam fundraiser, his own proffered essay on Bottengoms proved he was still an outsider. 'I never so much as come back from a walk without feeling that I have to break my way into it, although winding grassy paths give access in all directions.'[4]

The anthology confirmed his place among a scattered community of writers. He picked texts by Philip Larkin, John Betjeman and Jan Morris, then commissioned forty more. Friends R. N. Currey and Richard Mabey were enlisted, along with his publisher's reader discoveries Stanley Middleton and William Trevor. And the selector was thrilled to connect with two especially admired writers, Orkney poet and story-spinner George Mackay Brown and novelist Barbara Pym. The latter link came in the nick of time: an essay for Ronnie – 'A Year in West Oxfordshire' – was extracted from diaries as Barbara lay dying in Oxford's John Radcliffe Hospital.

Rescue for the beleaguered resident of Bottengoms came via James Hamilton-Paterson's digging-out of the past. Flimsy partitions had left dark, dank cubicles where Christine's dressmaking materials and costumes for village theatricals mouldered alongside picture stores. As he advanced in the excavation James uncovered 'a great nodding fungus which had sprung up between the bricks on the floor like a visitor from Betelgeuse Alpha trying to get a stealthy toehold on planet Earth'.[5] Much was dumped. Damp etchings by Francis Unwin and others from the Nash circle were spread on lawns to dry.

Then the partitions downstairs and in John's bedroom studio were demolished as 'Ronnie danced nervously at the sound of screeching nails'.[6] James exposed Tudor beams and an end-wall fireplace saved from falling to bits by some emergency DIY. This would not be the only temporary measure to stretch towards permanence under Ronnie's laissez-faire stewardship. A lesson from James in cement mixing was too optimistic.

But the lasting result was an airy room of noble simplicity, with a floor of creamy yellow 'Suffolk white' bricks laid on earth. Ronnie is forever pictured here in a transcendent 1986 photo by John Hedgecoe. The writer-in-residence sits at John Nash's paints table,

In the garden room, 1986.

now an outdoor desk. A sense of a room half in the garden, especially when the front door stays open in summer, is compounded
by a line of veteran implements. The useful assembly will spur one
visitor to ask whether the author collects antique tools.

Richard Mabey said: 'The impression I had when I first went
there was that of going into a bell jar. It was a place full of resonance
and echoes but also marvellously humdrum, with no particular frills
outdoors or in.' Bottengoms enshrined not just a sense of reverence
for recent and distant history but 'a continuous stream of invention
and dwelling' running into the present and future.[7]

Aesthetics plus persistent austerity halted a grand plan to create
a farmhouse kitchen. The sink stayed put in a tiny hallway between
the dining room and formal sitting room – the only passage apart
from the stairs in a three-up, three-down house where one room
ran into another. And Christine's Rayburn long remained like a
Victorian kitchen range in the central fireplace narrowed in the
nineteenth century. Talk over decades about exposing the original
Elizabethan fireplace with presumed brick benches came to nothing.

Clearances in the bedroom studio allowed Ronnie finally to claim occupation. Pointedly, he moved from a double to a single bed – the enlarged and emptied space now seeming to host the last vestige of a monk's dormitory. At last he could sleep almost on the level – in the guest room, with floorboards tilting this way and that, his feet had been twenty degrees higher than his head. And he could wake to a view stretching back to Suffolk: the Cuckoo Hill of King Edmund's crowning; rural writer Adrian Bell's farmhouse – where his broadcaster son Martin was named after nesting martins; the house where Martin Shaw penned the hymn 'Hills of the North Rejoice'. Ronnie would never wish to be rid of historic and poetic associations, but for now James was adamant that past times needed purging in flame.

'He reluctantly agreed and together we hauled a lot of decrepit things outside and made a bonfire of them. They included a moth-eaten and wonky chaise-longue. Its stuffing caught fire with acrid smoke accompanied by Ronnie's belated cries of misgiving, "But that belonged to Dora Carrington! Virginia Woolf would have sat on that. And Lytton Strachey, Maynard Keynes, E. M. Forster . . ." "They're all dead," I said briskly, "so they won't be needing it and neither do you . . ." By the end of that day the ashes of it all had made Ronnie extremely cheerful. Bottengoms was finally his, updated to the here and now.'[8]

Within the sanctuary of Bottengoms, Ronnie did more than keep a window on the world. As cold war deepened, with Britain under Margaret Thatcher replacing a Polaris nuclear arsenal with more powerful Trident missiles, he joined the 1983 Book Action for Nuclear Disarmament's Read Around the Clock for Peace vigil on the steps of St-Martin-in-the-Fields, in whose crypt night shelter he had once bedded down. His political activism never more than sporadic, he remained a supporter of Oxfam and Greenpeace and the radical spirit generally. He took the *Guardian* newspaper along with the *Times Literary Supplement* – and never saw the Church of England's *Church Times* even when its star contributor. Television was kept chiefly for the news, which he followed almost religiously, so that reunions with Richard Mabey would open with current affairs before turning to more timeless topics. He disliked the word 'optimism' for a positive outlook formed by his philosophy of faith and the sheer force of life.

In July 1983 the BBC aired a *Ronald Blythe: Working at Home* profile narrated by the subject and directed by Tony Tyley. Around then, Ronnie spoke in vain for the Suffolk Preservation Society against the Sizewell B nuclear power station ('I stood before the tribunal, talking about poetry, music and botany, the Suffolk coast's influence on Britten's operas and the glories of this scrap of England, and felt eccentric and irrelevant').[9] Now a robust commentary ran from Sudbury to Bottengoms, via Thorpeness, Aldeburgh and Debach, and ended with an affirmation of life ongoing: 'When I think of Ben, or the Nashes, or James Turner, or a surprising number of these friends at the beginning, I recognise a strong absence of elegy in myself, for some of them are dead and yet at the same time living because I am living.'

Yet, he added as the camera followed him around a glittering oasis: 'I never feel that it is my garden. John used to say "I know where everything is" and of course he did. He used to tap on the window when I was weeding and call out "Mind your feet". And I can occasionally hear this call still.'

Ronnie's cut-glass enunciation was a residue of epic efforts to escape his history – for the necessary distance and disguise to put it lovingly into writing. But amid the privileges of privacy and security at Bottengoms, he found the speaking and writing voice of his late prime. His diction mellowed as smooth as seaglass while his prose style lightened and deepened. Within his circle he was open about physicality and sexuality; only the veil spread over the extremities of early poverty remained unlifted.

In August 1988, I (Ian Collins) walked down the track and entered the enchantment. The Ronnie met that day was classless, ageless: unique. That November, turning sixty-six, he wrote: 'It is eleven years now since John Nash died and it took a long time for this place to become "mine". Inheritance can be very inhibiting, I find. Bottengoms is beautiful, wonderfully inconvenient and no spot to get eighty in, but I close my eyes to its many impracticalities and enjoy its isolation.'[10]

Now Alan Cudmore, Ronnie's stalwart surveyor friend, was allowed to supervise major works, with a new wooden floor in the dry-rotted sitting room and an attached apple store opened up for a library. A retaining wall and dry moat were added to the side, and partly to the rear with its Georgian larder and lumber room, and a drain dug to keep at bay the natural desire of running water here to flow under the house. In the garden room old timbers were sandblasted and a new central oak post inserted to strengthen joists on the upper floor. A wood-burning stove was set on an open hearth next to a log store. Alan, fearful of bankrupting Ronnie with a £30,000 bill, was also aware that the work was really limited by a yen for writerly solitude.

Ronnie longed to be alone in a world of reflective magic – and a domestic sorcery recorded by Christine in her 1972 diary. Under the noses of the cats, mice had nibbled fruit on the sideboard and bitten off snowdrop flowers in vases. 'The next thing was even stranger. I had left the lid off a tin of salted almonds, & in the morning, in the tin were a pair of sunglasses, a box of matches, 2 velvet cloths from our spectacle cases, 2 pieces of string, a hank of blue cotton, some sweet papers & the head of a hellebore. It was a little frightening. I took them all out, but next morning back they all were again.'[11] Due to visitations like these, some house-sitters had thought the building haunted. Never unnerved, Ronnie was only intrigued.

The true ghostliness – ghastliness to many – lay in a cavernous roof space where tiny tomblike rooms, still white- and blue-washed, held the nocturnal resting places of farmworkers now permanently asleep in the churchyard. What caused latter-day handymen to flee, however, was torchlight on a hornets' nest. Guests below, aware of rodent scuffling in the night passed off by Ronnie as 'squirrels', could wake to find themselves in bed with drowsy hornets. No one was stung – the insects seemed to return the bard's love for them – but many were shocked. As Ronnie wrote: 'I put out some five hornets per morning, including one from my hair. But mostly the beautiful creatures beat against a sash window in the guest room, where one should have been able to boast about them as a gift, though apparently not. Releasing them from the glass, they zoom off like Spitfires, all go. Soon, the frosts will make them take cover, and the old room will not hear their organ music.'[12]

When builders had come and gone, he could write in contentment. The 'pleasantly gloomy' call of collared doves had changed their message. 'They used to say, "leave", "get out while you can", "travel". Now they say, "You won't find anywhere better than this".'[13] And: 'Old houses stay firmly isolated and islanded. My house listens impassively to distant amusements and crafts, cricket, remote dances, cries, none of them its business. It gapes wide to the landscape in hot late June, creaks with the heat and becomes a through-path for all kinds of creatures, not to mention a site for a particularly vigorous convolvulus which annually creeps through the brick floor of the kitchen and is not noticed until it begins to climb our cupboard.'[14]

Only that 'our' betrayed the wraith of an idea that Christine and John were still around.

44

Divine Landscape

FOR NEW YEAR 1964 Ronnie had made a rare stab at keeping a diary. On 17 February, as resolve was running out, he wrote: 'Vicar arrives 8.30 a.m. to say I have been elected to Parochial Church Council. Didn't wish this but accepted somewhat grumpily.'

Since rarely grumpy or complaining, his annoyance indicated how far he was being drafted into serving the Church of England. Already a Charsfield churchwarden, and due for the deanery synod, his preferred role came in 1974 when the bishop of St Edmundsbury and Ipswich licensed him as a lay reader for the 'united benefice' of Charsfield, Monewden and Hoo. Preaching, teaching and leading worship at non-sacramental services, the poetic wisdom of unpreachy sermons was noted from the outset. This lay reader gloried in reading aloud and sharing passing thoughts on the nature of awe.

Once at Bottengoms, he was relicensed by the bishop of Chelmsford to serve 800 disparate souls in Little Horkesley, Wormingford and Mount Bures. While locally rolling scenery was known to John Nash as the Suffolk–Essex Highlands, the mount of Mount Bures was a Norman earthwork seeming to Ronnie to raise its place of worship to special sanctity. Three distinctive parishes no longer had fine medieval churches in common: Little Horkesley's had been bombed to bits on St Matthew's Day 1940, hours after hosting an airman's wedding; he was killed six months later. An elegant 1958 replacement now covered an eerie interior. 'The strange thing was that so many old tombs survived,' Ronnie wrote.

'Splintered, fissured, charred and now patched up, their armorials continue to brag this side of the blast.'[1]

Ronnie would have to turn a blind or ironical eye rather often given a mixed bag of parsons in a benefice united only in name. He was contemplative and mystical, 'very much of the 1662 Prayer Book', whereas his first priest-in-charge was a robe-obsessed ritualist who carpeted him for brown shoes peeping out below his cassock.[2] His labours ran through the week and filled most Sabbaths. 'Choosing hymns for Sunday – carefully, of course, as our three churches have three different books. Three parish magazines as well. Three of everything. One of the vicar; one of myself. I consider our oneness.'[3]

'The three churches have varying degrees of churchmanship which only a born Anglican can understand, so best forget them and say one's prayers, sing, stare around, greet friends, listen to the ringers. They are kind enough to hear the same address, which is a combination of liturgy, natural and local history, poetry and diary . . . Often in my ear as I speak I catch the voice of someone on the Incumbents' Board, someone who spoke from where I am standing in 1350 or 1750, but alas I cannot hear what he is actually saying. Just a voice for his time.'[4]

The lay reader.

Each active church required a host of activists – councillors, wardens, organist, choristers, bell-ringers, Sunday school teacher, lesson readers, gravedigger and grass mower, cleaners and polishers, flower arrangers and candle tenders, door lockers and unlockers, hymnbook givers and collection takers, magazine makers, caterers and event organisers, accounts keepers, donors and fundraisers. Ronnie looked beyond practicalities, and the shrinking number of shoulders to bear the broad parochial burden, to muse on the mystery and beauty behind the ritual. 'I preach on the virtues of inattention, on the wandering eye. The old liturgy, which is part of the consciousness of England, allowed you to daydream. It washed over you, seeped in.'[5]

His mind would also wander among the assemblies with musings on a ninety-year-old Albert bell-ringing at Mount Bures 'as a line of Alberts had done since the Wars of the Roses'[6] or 'there go the last of the gleaners, and the last of those who rang for tea'.[7] Amid what might amount to derelictions of ritualistic duty, he was bent on channelling thoughts from another realm – charting the marvel and mystery in lapidary imagery.

'I'm moved by our small worshipping congregations, by the privacy of their public prayer, and by the impossibility of my ever knowing what is actually going on as they kneel, sit, stand, sing, say, dream. In service terms worship is that ultimate reverence which a community and an individual has to reactivate week after week. It must be familiar, even commonplace, and yet at the same time elevated and inspired . . . Wonder is unlikely to fill the entire act of worship, but I notice it creeping in here and there. Should it not, alas, alas.'[8]

If his fellow congregants were mysterious to him, he was even more of an enigma to them – a distinguished writer dressing in cassock, surplice and reader's scarf to ascend the pulpit to take matins, evensong, baptisms and funerals. During one interregnum, he considered living in the roomy vicarage with modern facilities and a stupendous view, then realised this would create more confusion. As his service to the benefice became inestimable, most parishioners saw him as their special vicar. His heavenly off-the-cuff addresses duly hallowed, his funerals to die for, his baptisms life-enhancing, he remained Ronnie to all. Funny Ronnie at times – as when his suggestion for the annual flower festival was to fill the church with cow parsley.

Walking the footpaths to and from the three churches, his robes in a small suitcase, was part of the experience of holiness – as was remaining reflectively at home. For all his love of the Anglican liturgy, he shared the Quaker reverence for silence. 'Frequently when we are quiet, maybe in church when there is nothing going on, perhaps when walking home, perhaps when lying wide awake in bed to listen to the wind rushing through the trees, we hear quite clearly being inwardly told what to do, where to go, when to speak. Or a voice which tells us: "Rest now, for I am with you always." The angel speaks.'[9]

He often walked through the valley and across the Stour to the little Norman church at Wiston to contemplate a mural of St Francis predating Giotto's Assisi frescoes tracing the saint's life. 'St Francis is preaching to the birds who are all turned to the east and paying attention. They say that this picture was painted only twenty years or so after his death, which proves how swiftly legends fly around the world.'[10] Ronnie's mystical spirit, borne of material sparcity and reverence for the natural world, was deeply Franciscan.

And Bottengoms, as he came to mould it beyond the everlasting monument to the Nashes, was half library and writer's retreat and half monastic cell. Behind the beauty of the mostly inherited objects and pictures, the grandeur of a rarely used drawing room with a piano never played, and the books cascading through the house, a successful man of letters continued to live as if he had taken a vow of poverty. So much was rickety, minimal or missing. His single bed, thinly blanketed and with sheets worn and darned, was scarcely wider or softer than a coffin. He had so little by prevailing standards yet wanted for nothing in an often visited anchorage on a nature reserve. Austerity bolstered a contemplative life; a cracked cup overflowed.

As his fame grew, he gave added Anglican service via local or national committees, conferences and causes. Alan Webster, dean of Norwich Cathedral and then St Paul's, made him patron of Cathedral Camps, to cheer on summer parties of young people assembled 'to dust, polish, record and mend, and also to enjoy themselves'.[11] Over twenty-five Augusts the non-driver navigated tricky journeys to praise the young cleaners. Ronnie was thrilled to have a friend at St Paul's who was a successor to the seventeenth-century poet John Donne. But Dr Webster and other senior clergy pressed in vain for ordination. Ronnie held fast to a lay ministry, noting that 'the laity means the people of God'. Also, although he did not mention it, too many books would have gone unwritten.

As it was, he reached an infinitely larger congregation in print. Broad meaning glinted in brief reflections. For instance: 'Nothing destroys worship as too much information.'[12] Or: 'Faith brings its own philosophy. It structures time.'[13] Or again: 'I actually delight when, in extremis, we sing unaccompanied.'[14] And wit was always at the ready, as in an account of the annual Readers' Day meeting in Cambridge: 'So here we all are once more at Selwyn College taking a yearly look at each other's faces and being surprised by what lies beyond us. The chaplaincy of Cambridge United Football Team for example. The largeness of the task silenced us.'[15]

The faithful philosophy of the gravedigger's son held that living and dying are eternally entwined. Introducing Tolstoy's *The Death of Ivan Ilyich*, Ronnie wrote: 'nature, art, religion, literature – all the great progenitors of our living awareness – tell us that death is a positive and quite individual occurrence, and that to refuse to look at it is the most certain way of shrinking our responses to everything else.' And: 'Acceptance of death when it arrives is one thing, but to allow it to upstage the joys of living is ingratitude.'[16]

As a governor of Wormingford's Church of England primary school, Ronnie walked through the fields to tell stories and take assemblies. 'All the children here are at the genius stage of painting,' he noted. He talked about books in many schools, but his mind went walkabout in meetings with grown-ups. 'What was the Diocesan Education Committee thinking about when it appointed me its representative?' he wondered while gazing out of the window. 'How I wish I was in the morning playground having a lesson on the rain gauge.'[17]

Ronnie spoke from pulpits and in church halls, opened fetes, judged competitions, put his hand continually in his pocket and never charged fees or claimed expenses. And then came appeals – as in: 'Quite a few years ago now the medieval tower of St Mary's Bildeston fell into the nave on – Ascension Day. Hidden below the neat plaster were the cracks caused, they reckoned, by wartime bombers from neighbouring airfields. The congregation had been singing: "And ever on our earthly path / A gleam of glory lies" when whoosh, what had been Perpendicular for centuries was a mountain of rubble. Everybody had gone home and only the brass couple were left looking up. What to do? Telephone John Betjeman. "I am laid low," he said, "ring Ronnie Blythe." Thus it was that I stood in for him on *The Week's Good Cause*, doing my best to wring hearts and wallets. I forget how much we raised, enough anyway to make order out of debris.'[18]

And finally the Society of Authors travel award was quietly put to good use in the logistics for nine purposeful walks. They led to a landmark 1976 book *Divine Landscapes: A Pilgrimage through Britain's Sacred Places*. The genesis of this tour for foot and head and heart was explained in a sermon at Great St Mary's, the University church in Cambridge. Ronnie had wanted to set out thoughts held since childhood 'to do with landscape, sanctity and my own imagination, holy people – and not the ones we usually think about – and a series of journeys'. Ideas were marshalled while tracing the paths of poets, mystics and martyrs – George Herbert in Wiltshire, John Bunyan in Bedfordshire, John Donne's London and Mother Julian to her anchorite cell in Norwich. One of the two Quaker pioneers named George Fox had been raised handily in Charsfield, so the marathon mission began in familiar fields. The more famous Fox was tracked in Lancashire.

That Cambridge event launched a particularly rewarding Anglican friendship. The vicar at Great St Mary's – talent-spotting Ronnie during a previous posting as head of BBC religious broadcasting – was Michael Mayne. The image of a medieval ascetic exuded the joy of being alive, with deep faith and humanity, and scholarship lightly worn. Naturally, he and Ronald Blythe bonded. Their grateful faith was founded in hardship: Michael had a rackety upbringing as an only child with a volatile mother after his vicar father jumped from a church tower. He wanted to be an actor while studying at Oxford, before finding a vocation in the priesthood in partnership with his wife, Alison, a bereavement councillor.

While friendship was fledging, Michael was felled by ME, which nearly cost him the deanship of Westminster Abbey. The post was deferred while he recovered and wrote an uplifting book, *A Year Lost and Found*. Ronnie joined the creative gatherings the Maynes hosted, wandering around the abbey after dinner deep in conversation, and staying the night in a 'haunted corridor'. Bringing in outsiders, Michael worked with asylum seekers and people with HIV/Aids, also instigating a memorial to 'All Innocent Victims of Oppression, Violence and War' alongside the Tomb of the Unknown Warrior. He opened Poets' Corner to the wayward likes of Oscar Wilde, A. E. Housman and Edward Lear.

The Maynes and Websters would have led Ronnie to John and Diana Collins, but the fiery canon of St Paul's Cathedral and his indomitable wife were busily 'retiring' to Mount Bures. So, Ronnie met the partners in protest – who had worked together against capital punishment, nuclear arms and apartheid – as neighbours. John died in 1982, but Diana remained a close friend for another twenty-one years until Ronnie took her funeral. She used natural authority and good connections to great purpose. When she and Ronnie discussed some new injustice, her parting shot might be 'I'll ring up the Prime Minister' (or the Archbishop of Canterbury). And she did.

Ronnie joined Diana at the University of Essex for Desmond Tutu's award of an honorary degree. Glimpsing Diana in the crowd, the South African bishop and Nobel Laureate ran from the academic assembly like a joyful child – catching her in an embrace and whirling them round in circles. The sight of two saints dancing was a novelty for Essex. Diana was a faithful Mount Bures lesson-reader, until skipping any cruel passage. Top of her refusals was the closing of the Red Sea on Egyptian charioteers ('Poor young men! Poor horses!').

Writing remained Ronnie's oxygen. He endorsed the Virginia Woolf line 'Life would split asunder without letters' even as his life threatened to be split asunder *by* them.[19] The delivery van bumped down the track daily – adding thousands of Royal Mail miles before a final insistence on a roadside collection box – and bringing an early bonus of a fling with a stand-in postman. It was the perfect physical relationship for Ronnie: friendly and fleeting.

Ronnie was priest-confessor for friends and acquaintances. As pastoral work increased via church activities, publications and personal appearances, his mailbag grew and *groaned*. Some wrote in selfless gratitude, barely giving names let alone addresses; many sent unburdenings: most hoped for replies. Light-filled Blythe letters generated more outpourings of gloom and anguish. A thankful missive starting 'Dear Ronald, I was happy to have your letter on a dark day' was blotted out by desperate bulletins along the lines of 'Dearest Ronnie, Horrible news, my dear; my other breast now has to be amputated . . .'

Like a surgeon, he became immune to bad news – with robust good health and a sunny outlook further protectives. He was the image of measured brilliance taking a village funeral: 'Thoughts run into each other: death, paradise, tea.'[20] Depression was alien to his nature, dismay rare and momentary. He weathered a blizzard of grumbles from novelist Penelope Mortimer – 'How do you write tears of rage and frustration?' – after April snow fell on her Cotswold garden. He would have found only beauty there. But when again citing Virginia Woolf – 'we live, all of us who feel and reflect, with recurring cataclysms of horror'[21] – he may have been thinking of his postbag.

Much as he loved friends and saw good in everyone, he adored bouts of solitude. This, too, had a spiritual foundation. 'For a Christian, solitude can be where he or she is least alone,' he wrote. 'The companionable Christ is often close at hand then. We daydream, we allow our thoughts to run free, we feel suddenly unpredictably happy, we have a realisation of the value of often-neglected things which reintroduce themselves to us. Money takes a step backward. Our bodies, even if they are not quite what they once were, feel good.'[22]

For Ronald Blythe, the faithful writer, a companionable Christ might seem indistinguishable from a compelling muse.

45

Vintage Journeys

IN 1978 RONNIE travelled to Stockholm to deliver the inaugural Nobel Symposium lecture. A talk entitled 'Feeling for Nature and the Landscape of Man' reflected on localist roots shared with John Clare, whose disintegration began with a move three miles from home.

Ronnie recalled aged village relations 'who sat fore-square in their lush gardens like monuments, as if growing out of the Suffolk clay itself, their bodies wooden and still, their eyes glittering and endlessly scanning leaves and birds and crops, their work done and their end near . . . These old country people were not so much figures in a landscape, as local men and women who, in their senescence, were browning and hardening back into its simple basic elements.'[1]

He himself had appeared to remain in his basic element. Until, in August 1987, amid all the criss-crossings of the country for a journeying writer in his prime, he crossed the planet for a first visit to siblings, nieces and nephews in their adopted land.

It was part duty call, part advance sixty-fifth birthday present to himself. 'I went to Australia last year to see my brothers, a half-dreaded, because left too long, trip which turned out enchanting,' he told Patricia Highsmith. 'It was very late winter. Sydney is a fine "water city" like Venice and San Francisco, very beautiful. And all the Australian relations and their houses were fascinating once I had got over my nervousness at finding myself closely connected with "strangers".'[2]

Staying with Harold and his wife in a spacious house, amid gum trees and a view to Gymea Bay, he came face to shoulder with medieval knight Sir Robert de Bures, via a rubbing of the larger-than-life brass memorial in Acton church. It was only the most outsized among many reminders of the old country for naturalised Australians who remained Far East Anglians.

He had waited until his mother's death, but now he could savour with his siblings the love of books and music she had instilled in them all. Given release from her overbearing religion, and needy burden of sadness, these traits provoked camaraderie and sympathy. From Covent Garden slum to Sydney suburb, the span of Tilly Blythe, née Elkin, now seemed a chilling life sentence of alienation warmed only by love for her children. Ronnie, ever respectful, could never return such visceral devotion.

There were trips to parks and landmarks, close encounters with wildlife and introductions to young clan members via that Australian institution of the barbecue. Proud and ever protective of his older brother, Harold, the business wizard of Oz, drove him to a suburban house sparkling in the sun: a fraternal gift if he would stay on for well-earned retirement. Ronnie felt a bolt of terror. Jumping the ancient Suffolk and Essex border was his migratory limit. Even now, when in Framlingham or Bury St Edmunds, he could dream of a

Ronnie and wallaby.

town house with a walled garden back in his native county. Most of all, he needed to advance in his work: life would wind down without a creative mainspring.

In 1989 Ronnie made a summer pilgrimage north to the Orkney archipelago. As he told Patricia Highsmith: 'For years and years I had been writing to and writing about the Orcadian poet George Mackay Brown, so one day, without telling him, I flew to Stromness. There are seventy islands and they are surrounded by drowned battleships from both world wars. Fearful winds and screaming birds. I loved it. It was so strange, a Norse country, harsh and brilliant.'3

In streets like paved canyons, the pilgrim saw houses built head-on to the sea to 'escape the brute force of the easterlies', and then the approaching figure of interest 'still far off, and surprisingly coatless'. After this, recognition, grins and clasping.

'I heard somebody had arrived.'

'Last night. Where is your coat?'

'There have been so many descriptions of his appearance, but to me he had the weathered tenderness of one of those vagrants whose face alters the day. A stranger, obviously myself, had been reading a book in the bar of the oilmen's pub the night before, "So I knew it must be you."'4

Ronnie explored Orkney via the writings of George Mackay Brown and a car driven by the organist of Kirkwall's St Magnus Cathedral. Then there was tea with the poet in his council flat above the ocean. 'He brings it in. "Mother's cups." He cuts cake from the corner shop. The coal fire blazes as it does every day, winter and summer. I sit facing the dining-writing table and George sits by the hearth where, famously every afternoon, he "interrogates silence". But he is all for talk now and I am struck by his facial resemblance to the poet James Turner, the concave features, the thick hair, the brilliant, drifting eyes. Tuberculosis marked both of them, separating them from the rest of us, making them fierce, determined – and delicate.'5

They talked about Hardy and Clare and collaborations with the composers Benjamin Britten and Peter Maxwell Davies. The northern adventure propelled Ronnie back to Aldeburgh and his backstory. 'It was nearly as cold as Orkney – and much freshened up with new paint since "our" day,' he wrote to Patricia Highsmith. 'I went to Ben and Peter's graves and remembered my early days there, and their kindness.'6

Then came long-awaited trips to America, for book events and lectures. *Akenfield* was a set text in schools and colleges. Ever since *The Age of Illusion*, Ronnie had held the attention of the *New York Times*. 'He is best known, of course, for the exquisite assemblage of village testimony called "Akenfield" (1969),' John Updike wrote now. 'As well as a good listener he is a keen reader, not so much a critic as a connoisseur, whose fresh enthusiasm would send us warmly back to the classics.'[7] Publishers and publicists packed his agenda in the hospitable city with private dinners and gallery visits between public appearances.

In Texas he was driven from Dallas to Waco through blinding heat, to lecture on war poetry and George Blythe's experiences at Gallipoli, in an air-conditioned car with tinted windows. The trip largest in his memory, for good and ill, was to North Carolina, to commemorate the first English settlement on American soil. ('It was one of those sad plantings that did not take. The first small group of men and women that Sir Walter Raleigh earthed on Roanoke Island returned to England; the next just vanished.')[8] Raised in a landscape depopulated by Puritan migration, he saw the other side now.

A fellow speaker at Duke University was Stephen Spender. Towering, overweight, crumpled, the doleful poet was rescued from a student cell and sent to a hotel after Ronnie's intercession, in sympathy for 'one of those writers who have condemned themselves to a Dante-esque circuit of lectures and readings which must continue until he hasn't the strength to climb aboard a plane'.[9] For all his activities, Ronnie knew that a writer must chiefly write.

And then a drive to a mystery destination – a white mansion in a park. 'The approach was like the opening of a novel, with the colonnaded house announcing itself in the half-dark amid box, willow oaks and apparition-like magnolias.'[10] What followed was even more like fiction, since the welcoming owner left him alone save for a cook coming in each evening. William Faulkner had written here, but the resident ghost was that of a Confederate soldier buried under the lawn when the Civil War was lost and the house newly built. Walking in surrounding Caswell County, Ronnie was haunted by how emancipation from slavery had led to bondage, racial segregation and lessons closer to home.

'It is impossible for an English writer to wander through the rural South and not become preoccupied with the evidence of slavery and racism . . . Britain made vast profits out of the "West India trade" and ploughed them into many of the ravishing country mansions that are now among its chief tourist attractions. What we didn't have were black people, or only such a scattering of them as to be a novelty. It is they of course who, since the 1770s, made Caswell's landscape, who dug and ditched its fields, planted its gardens, laid its roads and helped build its pretty houses and churches. (Ditto their anonymous village labouring men and women equivalents where I live . . .)'[11]

As usual, Ronnie retreated – or advanced – into a library, this one 'a dream, with more white pillars and proper mahogany library-steps for reaching the top shelves, and long runs of novels, plays and poetry'.[12] Here he found Evelyn Underhill's 1911 *Mysticism* – needed for a play he was writing for Chelmsford Cathedral. His drama conjured a meeting between Evelyn and the fourteenth-century Mother Julian of Norwich, whose *Revelations of Divine Love* was the first book written by a woman in English. He called his Julian Lecture, delivered in Norwich in 1995, 'All This Blessedness Is Ours'. The title said it all for both of them.

Reading and writing alone in the stately library with its sinister setting, Ronnie then sought habitual relief in painterly company. This time, Maud Gatewood ('a bluff, kind woman who paints not unlike David Hockney, only girls'). As Maud salted glasses for tequila and jollied the talk along, he found sensory refreshment. 'Iridescent humming-birds sip honeyed water from little vials on the window-sills, their wing motion so rapid that the green of their bodies becomes no more than a stain of air.'[13]

Lion-hearted loyalties kept him visiting Cathy Turner in Cornwall. To cut ties and bills, she had moved one last time, to a small flat in Wadebridge – too small, mercifully to both parties, for Ronnie to stay. He lodged nearby and took long walks alone. Cathy barely ventured outside. Conversation palled when Ronnie could no longer find something to say which would not be snubbed, so they sat on in silence. They had only a dead poet in common. When she died, the widow left him a stopped French baroque clock. It was beyond repair.

But Cornwall was always invigorating and talk-filled pub suppers continued with Charles Causley. The happiest time came one May at the 'Obby 'Oss festival with Richard Mabey – who remembered: 'On May Day morning we walked into Padstow, amazed at a village cleansed of cars, decked up with oak branches and cowslips, and with most of the citizens dressed in white. For the rest of the day we jigged and sang in the procession, ensnared by the hypnotic rhythms of the "Morning Song" and words that seemed like a remnant of some lost May fertility chant. Ale was drunk and Ronnie proved to be an adept communicant, whirling in slow motion like a very English dervish. He was deep in a pagan rite hundreds of miles from home, but never for a moment seeming to be "out of his knowledge".[14]

On trips to London, fame brought contact with the famous. There was a happy lunch with Ingrid Bergman, after she read one of his short stories; he sadly declined her invitation for a second – in Paris. One unsettling meal with actor-writer Dirk Bogarde, frosted in homosexual denial, was enough. A jolly dinner with T. S. Eliot's widow Valerie began when she shed her coat to reveal an array of sapphires. 'Mrs Eliot!' he exclaimed. '*Cats*, dear,' she answered, for a musical had made her rich. And Ronnie was prominent in the devising of a plan, finally realised in 2003, to return William Hazlitt's gravestone to St Anne's churchyard in Soho. It had been destroyed in 1870 for fear that the 216-word inscription against injustice might spark revolution. Michael Foot, Melvyn Bragg, Tom Paulin and a huge crowd joined him for the rededication.

Ronnie revisited his family in Australia in 1993 – Bernard going too so that all six Blythe siblings could be reunited. And then, in 2002, Harold bought business-class flights for Ronnie as an eightieth birthday treat. Hundreds of letters had flown back and forth across the world, with regular phone calls too, and now family bonds were reinforced in fondness. Ronnie was honoured as a brother, uncle and literary phenomenon. His success was a measure of how far they had all travelled.

He never saw Harold or Gerry again. Connie and Eileen came back to England for further visits; both were to outlive their beloved and last surviving brother, though only by weeks in Eileen's case. Gerry's economist son, Michael, called on his uncle whenever work brought him to England, and he carried on in retirement – finally representing the Australian clan at Ronnie's hundredth birthday party.

Ronnie never returned from anywhere without relief at coming home. Most journeys were in his own patch. He rejoiced, in 1996, over Richard Mabey's *Flora Britannica* encyclopaedia of flora and folklore. Citing Ronnie's comment that local plants were 'a form of permanent geography', Richard added that for many they were not only part of landscape but of autobiography.[15] The botanical walks the two authors took together were central to both their lives (though one close inspection of Stourside flowers with Roger Deakin also had nearly shortened Ronnie's when he fell in the river).[16] 'This was the one circumstance where I was the teacher,' Richard says. 'Ronnie knew the names of plants but not much more – though some of his insights into local terminology (like "grey parsons" for "grape hyacinths") found their way into *Flora Britannica*. Whether he retained anything I told him I doubt.'[17]

The closeness of their friendship did not erase difference: Richard, with his academically trained mind, was the consummate specialist; Ronnie the dragonfly-skimming generalist. Once, touring a church with a girlfriend, Richard overheard Ronnie telling her: 'Of course, Richard is architecturally illiterate.' He read into a specific truth a wider falsehood.[18] Ronnie was never known to be jealous or resentful, but there could be a certain tension when Richard visited with a new lover. We may be most critical of those we love most. But it remains a mystery as to why, when Richard's writing was so revered, Ronnie never dedicated a book to him. Then again, from their first meeting, he was present in every Blythe book.

While walking and botanising, they often talked about Gilbert White or Francis Kilvert, but mostly John Clare. And in the pub, they thought of him working as pot boy in the Blue Bell next to his family's Helpston cottage – or, better yet, chatting over mugs of ale.

46

John and George

FOR ALL THE far-flung journeys of Ronald Blythe in his vintage prime, one summer outing remained at the heart of his annual agenda. Every July for thirty-four years, Helpston beckoned around John Clare's birthday.

When the John Clare Society formed, in 1981, Charles Causley turned down the presidency. From that familiar address at 2 Cyprus Well, Launceston, the poet wrote: 'Presidents should be involved and prepared to join in the battle.' Cornwall lay too far, he felt, from the main fields of action. A keen driver proposed non-motoring Ronnie for the role.

Offered the Clare society presidency, Ronnie replied with that deceptive diffidence: 'I'd love to, if you think I can be of any help.'[1] Now he was spurred to set down thoughts about a writer with whom he shared a background of rural poverty and ecstasy. While he had secured perfect freedom, Clare followed his native landscape in woeful enclosure. Among lines Ronnie loved best, recited rather merrily while raking out the Bottengoms stream, were those in 'Remembrances', an early nineteenth-century manifesto for a modern right to roam and an appeal for rewilding:

> Inclosure like a Buonaparte let not a thing remain
> It levelled every bush and tree and levelled every hill
> And hung the moles for traitors – though the brook is running still
> It runs a naked brook cold and chill[2]

Ronnie let nature be, except in extreme circumstances. Arriving at a Bottengoms stripped of elms, he accepted twenty-five broad-leafed saplings from farmer neighbour Duncan Brown. A dead russet apple tree planted by John Nash in 1945 was draped with a Rambling Rector rose bringing a white-flowered luxuriance. While Great Storm ravages of October 1987 justified further replanting, vintage trees were heroic veterans.

'It suddenly struck me that the straight line of twelve oaks which lead to Bottengoms and which mark the parish boundary would have been planted when oaks were scarce due to the huge felling caused by Nelson's navy. Entire forests went to sea during the Napoleonic Wars. My c. 1800 trees shed their leaves with aggravating slowness so that there can be no complete rake-up before Christmas. And then, wonderfully beautiful and youthful though they are in full dress, stripped naked they reveal the pitiful lacerations of the great 1987 gale. Broken boughs, hang-limbs, wounds like those under the bright uniforms of naval officers, are bared for all to see. Every year I wait and hope for the winter winds to bring them down, but still they swing high up against the sky.'[3] His verdict on junk mail was 'poor trivialised trees to have ended like this',[4] and he honoured them enough to withhold medication and meddling. An ivy-cloaked ash in front of the house was storm-trimmed, with a saw for wind-fall boughs only.

John Clare was already a presence scattered through Blythe prose; now he took centre stage for presidential addresses in his home village and other talks too. When Ronnie lectured on Edmund Blunden in Long Melford church for his 1996 centenary, he spoke of their shared devotion to Clare. The sum of Blythe talks and thoughts would fill two books (*At Helpston* and *Talking about John Clare*) and spill into many more.

Ronnie loved Clare's 'The Peasant Poet' as a statement of religious belief and 'a perfect epigram' for Clare himself.[5] It was, in fact, a perfect epigram for them both.

> He loved the brook's soft sound,
> The swallow swimming by.
> He loved the daisy-covered ground,
> The cloud-bedappled sky.
> To him the dismal storm appeared

The very voice of God;
And when the evening rack was reared
Stood Moses with his rod.
And everything his eyes surveyed,
The insects in the brake –
Were creatures God Almighty made,
He loved them for His sake –
A silent man in life's affairs,
A thinker from a boy,
A peasant in his daily cares –
A poet in his joy.

Following his brother-poet through the seasons, Ronnie also wrote:

John Clare is the peerless reminder of what we have all forgotten, or believe we have replaced for the better – ordinary winter weather. He lived through one of those little ice ages . . . His life was part a winter journey in the madhouse and part the best and most accurate journey we have through the old rural experiences . . .

Withering and keen the winter comes
While comfort flies to close shut rooms
And sees the snow in feathers pass
Winnowing by the window glass[6]

Imagining the privations of John Clare's long confinement, Ronnie shivered over 'stingy' asylum fires. He himself had entered the twenty-first century still reliant on a stove burning garden wood with Christine's plug-in Aladdin heaters for back-up. But, as he approached his eightieth year, a show was held in Ipswich entitled 'The Nash Brothers and Their Circle' – prints and drawings from the plan chest in the study – and bumper sales transformed the climate of Bottengoms. A church contact having led to a fitter of industrial buildings, the longhouse was rigged with enormous lengths of copper pipe, running up walls, between ceiling beams and over the mantel-piece like a prized artwork. The centrally heated sitting room took the look of a ship's boiler room. From then on Ronnie liked his house piping.

When Ronnie became the John Clare Society president, Michael Mayne found his next cause at Westminster Abbey. Three petitioners

were needed for admission to Poets' Corner, so Ronnie chose Poet
Laureate Ted Hughes, Society of Authors president V. S. Pritchett
and Royal Society of Literature head Angus Wilson. That did the
trick. A memorial plaque for the enclosed poet of rural freedom
was unveiled in June 1989, with the inscription 'Fields were the
essence of the song'. Ted Hughes read 'The Nightingale's Nest' and
Ronnie spoke about the nature of belonging – for Clare and himself:

'To be a native once meant to be born thrall. Yet Clare's enthral-
ment by Helpston presents the indigenous eye at its purest. By his
thrilling ability to see furthest when the view is parochial he was
able to produce a range of perceptions which outstripped in their
accuracy and authority all the literary attitudes to the countryside
current in his day. His birthplace supplied his axis, and he recognised
early on that it was his only safe abiding place. Once, as a child, he
set out from Helpston to find "the world's end", only to find his
entire universe lurch and tilt:

'"so I eagerly wanderd on & rambled along the furze the whole
day till I got out of my knowledge when the very wild flowers and
birds seemed to forget me and I imagind they were the inhabitants
of new countrys the very sun seemd to be a new one and shining
on a different quarter of the sky."'[7]

Michael and Alison Mayne retired to Salisbury in 1996, where
Ronnie continued to visit them. When reduced to writing through
cancer of the jaw, the saintly Michael 'was able to give a language
to suffering which complemented that of medicine'[8] in a last hopeful
book, *The Enduring Melody*. He further enriched the Blythe life by
returning him to the home ground of George Herbert.

Ronnie had walked through Salisbury's water meadows to the
poet-priest's Bemerton for his book *Divine Landscapes*. Now he trod
and retrod this route when visiting the Maynes, then staying with
their friend Canon Judy Rees. Best of all, this procession of friendship led to a new walking companion when, in 2003, Bemerton
Rectory, Herbert's old house, was bought by the Indian novelist and
poet Vikram Seth.

Vikram's bestselling novel *An Equal Music* had taken its title from
the John Donne prayer he knew by heart and which Ronnie read
at village funerals: 'And into that gate they shall enter, and in that
house they shall dwell, where there shall be no cloud nor sun, no
darkness nor dazzling, but one equal light, no noise nor silence, but

one equal music, no fears nor hopes, but one equal possession, no foes nor friends, but one equal communion and identity, no ends nor beginnings, but one equal eternity.' Two roving writers held libraries in their heads and conversation converged, full of quotations, across beloved volumes. Ronnie felt kinship with mingled serious- ness and joyfulness in Vikram and George Herbert alike – reciting the latter's lines, from a prayer for 'Softnesse, and peace, and joy, and love and blisse' to the maxim: 'Living well is the best revenge.'

In 2003 Ronnie edited and introduced George Herbert's severe clerical rule *A Priest to the Temple* – becoming the poet's principal biographer since Izaak Walton in 1670. At a signing session, Judy took Herbert's communion cup from a glass case for Ronnie to use. 'It was one of those tall, Elizabethan vases in which the wine lies low.'[9] Then back to Bemerton with Judy and Vikram: 'We cross Herbert's garden and walk rather perilously – it is getting dark – over the unrailed bridge which spans the Nadder. The air is heavy with meadowsweet. We come to a second, safer bridge and pause, breathing in the night-time. I can hear nesting birds talking to each other. Vikram talks about the pike which lurk in the black water. He himself is full of light. Indoors he reads to us from Izaak Walton.'[10]

Faith in the writings of George Herbert also led Ronnie on regular devotional journeys to Cambridgeshire, one of which was remembered by the poet and priest Malcolm Guite. 'We were asked jointly to lead the annual pilgrimage . . . walking from Leighton Bromswold, the church which Herbert restored, five miles to Little Gidding, where Herbert's friend Nicholas Ferrar had formed a community, where the manuscript of *The Temple* was sent after Herbert's death, and, of course, the place that inspired the last of T. S. Eliot's *Four Quartets*.

'I was to preach at Leighton, and Blythe was to preach at Little Gidding. I was very much in awe of him, and glad that I was preaching first and didn't have to follow him; but I was delighted to meet him. He was charming, personable, a little shy, I think, and certainly carried no stand-offishness or any sense of his literary status. As we walked and talked together, on a dismally wet day, I sensed that he was walking in the company of visible and invisible pilgrims. He mentioned some of our contemporaries, and then, in the same breath, would quote Clare or Herbert, Robert Herrick or Gerard Manley Hopkins, with such natural familiarity that I would not have been surprised to turn around and find them walking at our side, or just ahead of us.'[11]

In July 1837 John Clare turned forty-three and entered an asylum. George Herbert had fewer than three years as a priest before a consumptive's death, at thirty-nine. Living no longer than the poet Thomas Traherne, cleric and naturist Francis Kilvert died at thirty-eight, days after his wedding. ('His coffin was carried beneath his bridal arch.')[12] As Ronnie sailed serenely towards his century, he revered poets who had died younger still – John Keats (twenty-five), Keith Douglas (twenty-four), Sidney Keyes (twenty) – magnifying a lifelong sympathy with martyred youth. Naturally, his *Desert Island Discs* selection included 'Winterreise' by Franz Schubert, dead at thirty-one.

But his own greatness as a writer was to come with great age.

47
Wormingford Words

HAILED AS A brilliant anthologist of other people's diaries, Ronnie had never found time to sustain a daily commentary of his own. He finally did so, from November 1993, thanks to a new mission for the Church of England – a gift, to the world, for his seventy-first birthday.

While the *Church Times* was being printed in Colchester, the editor, John Whale, often called at Bottengoms. As their Anglicanism corresponded across liturgy, poetry, history and landscape, Ronnie was invited to contribute a column on all these things for the back page. Gathered around a David Gentleman drawing of Bottengoms and its garden, the 'Word from Wormingford' essay came to comprise 400 words of essential reading for subscribers to the Church of England's house newspaper every Friday and to resonate with those of any faith or none.

Written in longhand on Monday, each column was typed on Tuesday and then walked, a two-mile round trek, to the post box. Every despatch represented the author's thoughts and feelings at a certain moment, perhaps after an outing, or musing on a season or festival, unravelling 'the muddle that is the writer's head, the criss-crossings of its existence, its beliefs and heresies, its strange convictions and sudden truths'.[1] A dragonfly mind darted from brick floor and garden flora to span a Heaven much like Mother Earth. All had a place, all connected.

Gems of observation, memory, meditation, quotation, appreciation

Bottengoms drawing by David Gentleman for the
'Word from Wormingford' column.

and acceptance illuminated lyrical prose zooming from personal to universal in a sentence and time-travelling in a short paragraph – pondering the past and what might pass for eternity, while always praising the present. 'And remember that the moth and rust must eventually reduce all that you physically possess to dust. A dancing dust, judging by the motes caught in the early March sun which streams through my room.'[2]

Dust was constant. 'I remember [Benjamin Britten] telling me about living in Snape mill, and how his piano was ebony black when he went to bed, and dusty white when he came down in the morning. Generations of flour had filtered down through the beams.'[3] At Bottengoms John's studio was recalled as 'a homily to dust. Tobacco dust, mortal dust from plants and insects, and to a degree, from the artist himself. It was never swept, and a single 40-watt bulb gave a discreet account of it.'[4] And in her bedroom 'Christine powdering her face by lamplight. Dead these thirty years, the simple make-up occasionally makes its presence known as I tread the wide floorboards from which not all the art of Dyson can draw the final dust.'[5] Dust to dazzling dust: the poignancy and merriment of earthly mortality.

Each palimpsestic text – light as air, fathomless in philosophy, with linguistic swoops from learned to lyrical and colloquial – laid out a magic carpet across time and space. Reading 'Word from Wormingford' is an exhilarating ride and a kind of benediction. 'Round and round we all go, the living, the departed, the abundance, the dearth, the planets, the prayers, the holiness of things, all our new toys and comforts notwithstanding.'[6]

Writing each morning and gardening each afternoon – with dashes indoors to jot down passing thoughts – Ronnie would pen 500,000 words from Wormingford in 1,200 essays over twenty-four years. Gathered into twelve selected volumes by the time of his centenary, their musings form the majority of life-revealing quotes in this book. They also contain much of his finest writing. Here, by way of entertaining and enlightening examples, are three quicksilver vignettes from the *Borderland* compilation.

Commotion below – the hunt is in the garden. A river of hounds is flowing through it, one of them having the impertinence to gollop up the cats' leavings en route. Three huntsmen appear behind the hedge, though hoping that it hides them. One of them does a little bugling but the dogs stream on, soft muzzle to whipping tail. Then they have gone, all of them, men and animals. The cats! I tear down to save them. One is sitting many feet up in an old willow doing her famous Lewis Carroll act, the other . . . Where is the other cat? I rush around calling, beseeching, composing in my head a letter to the Master of Foxhounds which will scare him stiff as I see pretty Kitty swallowed whole. The night comes and Bottengoms is in deep mourning for her. Look where she once laid, her favourite place, the imprint of her is there still. I put out, as usual, Whiskas for two and her sister eats the lot. Blinded with rage and grief, I fail to notice the sleeper in the piano. She stretches and makes a dissonance along the wires, a spangling of notes to accompany a greedy purr.[7]

The train stops by a nice wood but the woman on the mobile does not cease talking. She interviews a young man in her clear voice. She repeats everything he tells her, which is courteous of her. We trapped listeners might as well have both sides of her call. 'Your name is Raphael?' She writes it down on her pad. 'You are twenty-three, and you did say that you were a post-graduate?' She scribbles away. We hear that he will have a month's training and then be on his own. For four hours per evening. Soon, we realise, we will be picking up our telephones and hear, 'My name is Raphael and have you a minute while I tell you about our fitted kitchens?' We are told his full address and number, and so we could ring him up and tell him not to bother us . . . We travel on. Here is Manor Park cemetery, acres and acres of applicants for jobs. Miles of workers who applied 'in the first place' in handwriting on Basildon Bond, but who are now at rest. The phoning woman goes on, filling other vacancies, asking the same particulars, promising the same rewards.[8]

We baptise Garrow, that is Michael makes a watery cross on his brow and I read him a poem. The christening is wildly unpunctual due to there being Irish guests, including a Godfather who plays a tune on the flute. No, it is a tin whistle, and wildly musical it is. The church is cool and the churchyard is baking. Garrow is a year old and sports a rosary. He lolls on Michael's arm like a Florentine Christ-child, serene, forgiving, turning his full gaze on us as we applaud the tin-whistler. An uncle passes him to me to hold. I am astonished, having no idea that Christ-childs weigh a ton, well a stone. He stares past me, looks past all of us to see what only babies see.[9]

Weekly words were grounded in the house, garden, valley and three parishes, with a cast of passing friends, living and dead, and resident cats. Stripey had given way to Milo, then to the panther-like Max and then the famous white cat – who wasn't wholly white and who began the reign of felines as nameless as nature intended. ('The white cat, spread out on a radiator below the window, like a Roman at dinner, invites the winter sun to warm her.')[10]

Column after column took in the view, on which Ronnie meditated from every 6 a.m. over a mug of tea, watching the sun rise before picking up a book (the first of three or four in a normal day) to stir the creative juices. There were numerous references to Jean Brown's horses, their profiles on the brow of the hill an enduring attraction. Jean had taken in a retired racehorse before opening livery stables. That first arrival was ridden by Anglo-Nigerian teenager Helen Folasade Adu, who sang in Little Horkesley church choir. Ronnie the visionary had no idea that one of the girls galloping along and beyond his horizon became the soulful singer Sade.

Hospitals were glimpsed occasionally, following visits to friends. The one break in Blythe good health was covered over with pre-written columns and a swift return to fresh postings. In 1998, aged seventy-five, he collapsed giving a talk and suffered brief

The white cat.

delirium with acute urinary retention. Following a prostate operation and slow recovery from general anaesthetic, it took months before he felt like his old unmedicated self. Six years later the sun-worshipper was hospitalised again for the removal of a 'rodent ulcer' skin cancer from his face ('I keep wanting to call it a Rolex Oyster')[11] and a course of radiotherapy. With no pain, only a feeling of ugliness troubled him. No word of any of it appeared in his weekly column.

Words formed into an overarching architecture of biblical stories and the Anglican calendar. The soaring structure built up to a spirituality both omnipresent and hard to pin down. How to sum up religion for Ronald Blythe? Those who knew him well were still unclear. Christine Smith, directing the book publishing division of Hymns Ancient and Modern, worked with Ronnie from 1998 on fifteen new or reissued titles under the Canterbury Press imprint – including ten 'Word from Wormingford' selections. 'He rarely, if ever, spoke about his religious beliefs privately,' she says. 'Rather, he exuded enjoyment of their fruits – a quiet contentment, a sense of wonder and gratitude, an appreciation of beauty, a freedom from anxiety and endless nourishment from the wealth of stories and poetry, from the gifts of creation and from human and animal companionship.

'Although I never heard him preach, in a way I did hear his preaching voice as two of the books we published were collections of his sermons – reflections would be a better word. One volume was entitled *Talking to the Neighbours* which tells you everything about how he preached. Never at people, but gently sharing whatever delighted him. If the measure of faith is the ability not to be concerned to draw attention to oneself but to point to a greater reality, then Ronald's whole life was an expression of that.'[12]

Before they met, Christine had saved the Blythe column until last when reading the *Church Times* on homeward journeys from London to Winchester. 'I used to wish that I lived in Ronald's world until I realised the effect of his writing was to open my eyes to see my world as he saw his.'[13]

Ronnie's exact beliefs remained so much of a mystery that his Suffolk writer friend Julia Blackburn even wondered whether he really believed in God. His writing was a field flinted with half-hidden clues. As in: 'Our mistake has always been to have believed that our immortal life begins where our mortal life ends, when in fact these dual states of our being, the temporal and the eternal, run side by side from our birth.'[14] Eternity could sound much like living in the moment. When pressed, he declined to confirm a heavenly afterlife and even mused on whether immortality might be as brief as the period we are remembered. Artists last longest. But best to have faith in the regenerative powers of nature. The prayer like a pagan rite he recited to the end was taught to him by his mother:

> Let the blessed sunshine in.
> Let the blessed sunshine in.
> Open wide the window, Open wide the door,
> And let the blessed sunshine in.

In a 2013 interview Ronnie had seemed to compound a sense of ambivalence when he said: 'I take matins and evensong every week and sometimes preach at the cathedral, but I mustn't make it sound as though I'm immensely religious, which I'm not at all. They tried to get me ordained, but I should have been hopeless at running a parish. I love the atmosphere of churches. It's part of the poetry of life to me.'[15]

Ronnie became a close friend of the priest and theologian Frances Ward during her seven-year stint as dean of St Edmundsbury Cathedral – the 2013 'Word from Wormingford' compilation *Under a Broad Sky* was dedicated to her. Agreeing that he was not bound up with religious practice as an end in itself, Frances adds that he was 'deeply religious in the older sense of belonging, beholden to his faith as lived by the Church'. She places Ronald Blythe in a Christian tradition of natural theology stretching back to St Paul, St Augustine, Thomas Aquinas, Thomas Traherne and George Herbert – 'all his great loves'.

She continues: 'To understand the tradition of natural theology is to live within it: to perceive and respond to God as the ultimate reality in which all things "live and move and find their being". Again and again as you read Ronnie's words the natural world around reveals its participation in the life and love of God; he reads the reality of God in the sunshine and light, in the darkness of turned soil or the sludge of a pond, in the trumpet of a daffodil, in the song of the nightingale. All have their being from God and the stones cry aloud their participation in God . . . Ronnie's great contentment began and ended in his radical humility: the sense that he knew his skill as a writer was a gift, not a possession.'[16]

The Wormingford wordsmith became wedded more than ever to his readers – the postbag heavier with each weekly ray of light. But James Hamilton-Paterson, long irritated by a circularity of Blythe thinking which academic training could have scrambled into fresh enquiry, wrote in exasperation from Italy to a mutual friend: 'Unlike most of his readers I know his house intimately . . . many of the friends & villagers he names, all his historicky-painty-litty references and even a good few of his biblical ones.'[17]

James balked at being 'dragged back not just to Wormingford, which is an unremarkable hamlet in Essex, but to a world which scarcely allows itself to be seen unless within the hermetic bounds of famous dead people's eyes and ears. You can't see a spinney without being told that Constable used to date the corn chandler's daughter in it, or walk along a footpath undogged by the mystical, saintly, tubercular steps of George Herbert . . . I feel sad, sundered from a man by his prose, which says only too clearly that scorny old vandals like me will never enter that perfect little temple-on-the-hill of East Anglicanism.'[18] But loving Ronnie to the last, and though a self-styled 'professional absentee', James went back to the Bottengoms he had in part created. On a 2001 visit, when his host was momentarily absent while annoyances remained, he launched into a lampoon:

'Gilbert White used to say there is more wonder in a spoonful of horsepond than there are words in a scoffer's lexicon, and he was right. Doubters need only look around them to see how little has changed. Only the other day I was menaced by a pair of great bustards at Stoke-by-Nayland, descendants of the pair given by Lord Northcote to the poet Shelley for his Bar Mitzvah. This reminds me that I must go and set out some daily bread for the dodos nesting outside John Nash's gun room. The other day as I was tying back the Monk's Benison there I spied three great terracotta-coloured eggs in the nest. Pray the foxes don't get them! Yes this little prayer has a "hard meaning", as St Augustine would say, because foxes are on the increase hereabouts, perhaps as a result of the anti-hunting stance I took with that whiskery lady from Anglia Television. I told her it was intolerable having puce-faced hunters chivvying an exhausted and defenceless little animal across one's garden. Since then the foxes have proliferated and now hunt in packs, naughty things, and are quite fearless. These days one takes one's courage as well as a stout stick in both hands when slipping up the track to the village shop for one's weekly ounce of chocolate digestives.'[19]

Years later, he noted: 'I must have written this extravagant and not uncruel parody of poor Ronnie when I was feeling particularly fed up with his apparent refusal to admit to any sign of environmental change in the vicinity of Bottengoms, plus his unremitting *goodness* and a mind seemingly trapped in a hermetic circle of John Nash, George Herbert, John "Haywain" Constable, Maria Marten et al. . . . Perhaps worst of all, I'm quite sure he wouldn't be at all offended if he read it.'[20]

48

The Assassin

IN THE SUMMER of 1937, bicycling in the Suffolk–Essex borderland, Ronnie paused at a tiny village. An aged resident of Ovington, near Sudbury, pointed to an old house and said: 'A murderer lived there.' The killing, in 1628, haunted him ever after.

Half a century later, hurtling through Essex on a train to London, he glimpsed the chimneys of New Hall, near Chelmsford, and was returned to the deadly saga before the slaughter of the English Civil War. A prince and a courtier had ridden out from here to Madrid before their friendship took a fatally different direction. Now Ronnie began to plot in his head a book called *The Assassin*, ultimately his second and last novel.

One July excursion to Helpston brought a tour of Milton Hall, whose steward had been a friend of John Clare. The entrance hall held a gorgeous likeness of George Villiers, Duke of Buckingham – the courtier cantering with the prince to Spain, and the commander knifed in a Portsmouth pub. A word portrait then surged on paper.

Ronnie had co-judged the 1980 Booker Prize. A public tussle between two huge-hitting novels – William Golding's *Rites of Passage* and *Earthly Powers* by Anthony Burgess – hid the fact that the Blythe heart lay with the quietest and shortest contender, J. L. Carr's *A Month in the Country*. Jim Carr became a friend. But Ronnie readily conceded that Golding should win, and an author best known for *Lord of the Flies* was a Nobel Laureate three years later. The awarded book anyway had a big influence on the most generous of judges.

Rites of Passage follows a group of Britons on an 1812 voyage to Australia. Recounted via a caustic diary, tensions between officers, sailors and emigrants crammed below deck on a converted warship end with an unctuous cleric in a 'hell of self-degradation'. Ronnie was familiar with later passages to Australia and religious vocations descending into darkness. But what he really took on board from William Golding was the challenge of an epic historical novel. Meeting it claimed the best part of twenty years as draft after draft was fitted around other writing and doing.

The story of *The Assassin* begins in the Tower of London. Awaiting execution, Lieutenant John Felton pens a memoir of how he came to kill the bad, beautiful Duke of Buckingham – friend of his youth who rose to a king's favourite laying the kingdom low. The condemned man's life and times will be told via diaries and letters. He hails from the Essex–Suffolk border, a bookworm educated in libraries then drafted into armies. But drawing more on imagination than experience, a sweeping narrative embraces themes of war and peace, faith, art and science while exploring the workings of the seventeenth-century mind. It makes for a dense read with dazzling set pieces – as in a cameo portrait of James I, the duke's patron and lover first met on the hunting field:

'This King, it was broadcast, had no repose. He trotted and whirled his way through a Court which itself was never still, talking ten to the dozen. His vice was the hunt. So dedicated was he to the hunt that he shat in the saddle rather than miss a minute of it. Although he paid full respect to the royal hunt of the deer, his passion was the hare, and he would match its screams with his own at the killing. He had been in so much fright himself all his life that this creature-fright seemed to be a kind of understanding in the poor animal, for which he was grateful. The bloody body would be handed up to him to mouth and caress. There would be rheumy tears and thick Scotch pityings. The hounds themselves, they said, would weep. Then off the whole hunt would rush, for one hare could not fill a day, and those with state work to do would be leaping alongside his Majesty craving instructions.'[1]

Finally delivering the manuscript to Deborah Rogers, Ronnie then suffered in prolonged silence. His calls were fobbed off. And when eventually going to London to meet the doyenne of literary agents face to face, he spied, over her shoulder while she fussed over him, the manuscript shelved and seemingly untouched. James Hamilton-Paterson found a new agent in Andrew Hewson – by which point Ronnie had made a path for himself.

Norwich publisher Peter Tolhurst included Ronald Blythe in a selection of East Anglian short stories. Now Ronnie asked if he might take *The Assassin* too. 'I said yes immediately, before even reading it, as a way into publishing more of his non-fiction,' Peter says. 'For me it served a purpose.'² As a pre-internet outfit of one, Black Dog Books reached a limited audience, but gained from an established author's fan base. The enterprising soloist was to bring out six Blythe titles – including the excellent compilations *Aftermath*, *Field Work* and *Outsiders: A Book of Garden Friends* crafted from filed reviews and articles. *The Assassin* had the smallest sales: several hundred of a thousand printed copies were pulped.³

Peter recalls: 'It was always a pleasure to drive down to Bottengoms – especially that glorious last few yards down the rough track – and relay boxes of the latest title in a wheelbarrow along the garden path to the house where Ronnie would be waiting to sign them with fountain pen and blotting paper. We drew a crowd of the faithful wherever we went to launch his books, and people always talked so fondly of this kind and gentle man, a saint-like figure to some. The one time I stayed overnight, Ronnie told me I would be sleeping in the bed that Paul Nash had slept in on the only occasion when he visited his brother there. As a great admirer of Nash's work, I couldn't have been happier – not forgetting the inevitable question regarding the sheets. I woke the following morning to the buzzing of half a dozen hornets.'⁴

Ronnie wanted only to be in print and writing. Amid a surge of small-press editions, he was oblivious to shrinking sales. In 1999 *Akenfield* appeared as a Penguin Modern Classic, though subject and author seemed not to be modern at all. In the metropolitan world of contemporary literature around a new millennium, Ronald Blythe was dismissed as a rural, nature or regional writer. While still shining as anthologist and advocate, an original and universal author maturing into magnificence was eclipsed. When Viking Penguin gave way to Canterbury Press for 'Word from Wormingford' compilations, he was further marginalised as a Christian writer.

The Assassin was dedicated to Julia Blackburn. But, by the time of publication, intimacy had faltered due to the special Blythe candour saved for other writers. 'After the tragic death of my almost daughter, Tanya, I went to visit Ronnie,' Julia says. 'I did not expect that he would be able to offer much comfort, but I presumed he would wave to me on my sad island of grief. I was startled by him explaining with a sort of determined finality that he had never loved anyone enough to feel the pain of loss and therefore there was not much he could say. It broke a bond between us.'[5]

The triumph of art may come at the cost of life. 'You're only half there if you're a writer,' Muriel Spark said.[6] Graham Greene, recalling a youthful spell in hospital when a ten-year-old boy died in the next bed, wrote: 'There is a splinter of ice in the heart of a writer. I watched and listened.'[7]

Only later could Julia appreciate the key to Ronnie's nature. 'He was, in the very roots of his being, a solitary man,' she said at his memorial service. 'He loved everything and everyone with an equal passion.'[8] In that equality of love, empathy – a writerly feeling for the human condition – was stronger than sympathy. And as Angela Tilby put it in a posthumous tribute: 'There is no true contemplation without detachment.'[9]

Ironically, Ronnie was to be disconcerted by Julia's candid family memoir, *The Three of Us*, dissecting the tumultuous relationships between her painter mother, alcoholic poet father and herself. Ronnie shrank from a portrait of chaos. What he mourned in the saga were all the poems not being written and the paintings not being painted. It was more than a consolation that Julia had become a fine writer; but he loved her for every other book.

Richard Mabey perceived Ronnie's distance too. In 1999 Richard fell into acute depression. When unable to write, he became a patient in the old Northampton asylum. He would be saved by a move to Norfolk, and by his partner, Polly; when *The Assassin* was finally printing, he was writing up trauma in *Nature Cure*. It helped that Ronnie would be closer to hand for walks and talks, but Richard had already found the talking cure 'totally useless'. Tellingly, he never tested it on Ronnie. 'Maybe it was the meeting of two hard shells,' Richard says. 'He was warm and supportive but that was his usual self. The nearest I came to a confessional was speaking of the strangeness of being in the same mental hospital as John Clare, and that discussion led instantly in the direction of the poet.'[10]

As Ronnie said of himself when *The Assassin* was despatched: 'I

Richard Mabey.

feel as some people do when the guests have gone, released. I think of all the things I shall do with no book to cry "Write me!" as soon as I get up. I might read all the books that have been waiting for me to read this last year. Although I am not likely to be as deplorable as the late Jean Rhys and sit on the floor drinking gin at breakfast and browsing in old tales, smoking like a trooper and not giving a damn. But I might lie under the poplars to hear their summery clapping, one of the loveliest sounds in the world, and an immortal one I am sure.'[11]

The Assassin was lauded by fellow writers. James Hamilton-Paterson wrote: 'It seems to run together all the categories at which you excel: historical knowledge, feeling for place, gardening, religious & poetic sensibility and – a new one this – quite a campy pleasure in high drama . . . It has all the hallmarks of being deposited very slowly in tiny secretions over many years, like a pearl.'[12]

Acclaim from novelist Jane Gardam – for a 'fierce, sensuous, rich and agonising' story[13] – came early in a friendship played out in letters and at literary festivals. Jane had grown up in Cumberland and Yorkshire, the daughter of a schoolteacher with family roots in farming and religion. After studying English at Bedford College, London, she worked as a librarian while always seeing herself as a writer. The writing started on the day she took her youngest child to school.

Jane spent four warm months writing in North Yorkshire, from a farmhouse set in two rocky acres of Upper Swaledale. The rest of the Gardam year divided between Kent – a medieval former inn with a garden opened to the public – and Wimbledon. Tempting invitations were extended, but Ronnie ranged only as far as lunch in Wimbledon.

They shared the obsidian observation their hard-won art demanded, and that writerly distance for contemplation and compassion. Also, a firmness of faith. Jane, while blessed with loving family ties, found in Ronnie untrammelled integrity and a rock of support in an unflinching view of life and death. 'There is something satisfying about all things passing, even us,' he said.[14]

Books were swapped and Jane came to depend on Ronnie's letters. 'The envelope alone lifts my heart (but please don't send an empty one).'[15] She sent back difficult family news – her barrister husband David's slow decline with Alzheimer's; her daughter-in-law's death from cancer after a 'miraculous' two-year remission for which Ronnie was thanked for prayers. What really bolstered her spirits was Ronnie's joy in the present moment – an outgoing buoyancy however bad incoming news – and an openness to everyone.

Ronnie dedicated *The Circling Year* church addresses to Jane. When he sent her a paperback of the sequel, *Talking to the Neighbours*, she replied: 'I know this book very well, for it is my bedside book. Lately I've been turning into a serious insomniac . . . your vols. are the only things that make sense of death & sickness. You and the gospels, & the Book of Common Prayer. I read you most nights.'[16]

And again: 'Your letter came as I was most needing it: Please thank the rain & the cat for driving you indoors at that moment. I have been having sleepless nights of worry & fret & David's (now hopeless) vagueness makes for isolation. I shall have to learn serenity, as others have, but it is so tiring saying everything over & over again. For the week before your letter came I had been reading *Wormingford* – I keep all your books in the spare bedroom for guests & I now sleep in it myself – and they give me the best comfort about how to live.'[17]

49

Great Age

IN 2004, THE year of *The Assassin*, Jane Gardam wrote a concerned letter: 'You seem to be working very hard indeed? Three parishes, & that only the start of it. You were writing in the early, early morning & I saw a mountain of letters between you & the toast & marmalade. You must have such a formidable correspondence & I'm so lucky to be part of it.'[1]

Others feared that Ronnie might write his octogenarian self to a standstill. Delightful and dutiful letters ran across reams of foolscap like ants crossing a desert. Flattered by exhaustive replies, casual correspondents returned for more. Now I had cards printed with the Bottengoms address so that a few lines could replace a long epistle. This success prompted further interference.

The tiring nature of Ronnie's parish exertions had gone from plain to paining. He worked ever harder as vicars younger than himself prepared for retirement. One departee required Ronnie and a church-warden friend, veteran of the Western Desert, to clear a garage to ease the cost of removal men. Ronnie doubtless pictured the scene as novelised by Barbara Pym – while I decided to intervene.

Ronnie's friend Stephen Platten, then dean of Norwich Cathedral, was consulted. Stephen thought it high time for elevation from lay reader of three parishes to honorary lay canon of St Edmundsbury Cathedral. Meanwhile, Ronnie would be invited to lead Easter Week meditations in Norwich; he could stay in the deanery and recharge his spiritual batteries. Bury St Edmunds was a long bus ride from

Wormingford, so most weeks would surely be left free for venerated writing. I also set much store by that word 'honorary'.

In due course, arriving at Bottengoms, I found Ronnie gleeful. 'Read this,' he said, handing over the Bury invitation. 'What an honour!' I gushed. And, counting seconds for an afterthought: 'Now you can retire from the three parishes.' 'Oh no,' Ronnie said. 'I'll do the cathedral too.' I could have cried at the lovely installation service, but not for joy as I totted up the cost, in sacrificed books, of meddling.

But Ronnie was in bliss. He sat in his canon's stall when in Bury with a few minutes to spare, admiring his cushion embroidered with a quill pen rather than the computer he never used. And he was in his robes and place in July 2005 at the thanksgiving service for the completion of the cathedral's Gothic Revival tower. The lay canon had viewed the construction close up. 'We went up in baskets,' he said. 'It was like something from the Middle Ages with the masons chipping away with their mallets.'[2] He was most impressed with facings of Barnack stone – from the Hills and Holes quarry where John Clare played.

Between church duties, the creative regime continued at home: reading in the early mornings and evenings between days of writing and gardening. Given the late Renaissance of Ronald Blythe, twenty-one books – almost half the lifetime total – were published from his eightieth year onwards. Although some were compilations of earlier work, it was an astonishing achievement in quantity and quality and a beacon for the unretiring. With one leg glued back on, the work table went on and on. My old portable typewriter, brought to Bottengoms when replaced by a first computer, gave service for the next two decades.

The bard of Bottengoms, who used a landline sparingly 'with the result that it rings sparingly',[3] never wrote an email, sent a text or posted on social media. While morning arrivals heard an increasingly novel soundtrack of pattering type, broken by the ring of a line ending and the clatter of a carriage return, those in the know greeted any afternoon silence with loud coughing – to warn a gardener who might be as naked as Adam in Eden. If disturbed when sunbathing, he casually flipped a straw hat from head to middle. Then the visitor was invited to explore the garden while the host dressed and put the kettle on.

Now accolades rolled in, with honorary degrees and doctorates for a graduate of elementary education only – one from the University of East Anglia, where he was also a member of the history faculty. The year 2006 brought the Royal Society of Literature's Benson Medal, and 2007 the Diocese of Chelmsford's St Cedd medal to follow a master's degree from Lambeth Palace. His eyes shone with pride at awards ceremonies, and his talks to graduating students were masterclasses in encouragement. Cast away on *Desert Island Discs*, he was introduced thus: 'As *Akenfield* has become a classic, so its author has become this country's literary custodian of its rural values.' And as for his luxury in island exile: 'A nice lot of ruled foolscap – ever so much of it – and some pens. I can't keep writing with a stick in the sand.'[4]

Interviewers navigated their way down the track, and arrived to find their august host positively jaunty. He could only ever see the best in people and books. 'My pleasure in writing is so terrific, so enormous, that I become uncritical at times. Sometimes the pleasure of the reading overwhelms me.'[5]

Study of Ronald Blythe at Bottengoms
by Toby Wiggins.

When taken to model in casual writer's garb for a local amateur art group, Ronnie let on that he had posed naked for painter friends in the past. Now professional artists came to draw, paint, sculpt or photograph him in fully-dressed distinction. Toby Wiggins, making preparatory studies for an eighty-fifth birthday portrait, said: 'As great people do, he showed me a level of hospitality and attention that I didn't deserve. He made me feel as if I mattered.'[6] The artist Dan Llywelyn Hall found him 'enthralling company from the offing . . . straddling the ages effortlessly without nostalgia or sentimentality, unwavering and unapologetic about his place in the noise'.[7]

He inspired Craig Taylor's *Return to Akenfield* in 2006, though never read it, and, a decade later, was semi-fictionalised in Jill Dawson's novel *The Crime Writer*, where Patricia Highsmith's spell in Suffolk was recast for a murderous saga in the manner of the suspenseful writer herself. ('Ronnie had a great talent for both solitude and friendship, was capable of an unspectacular joy and endless wonder. That was why she felt easy around him; he was the perfect companion for a person of her character. Ronnie did not judge.')[8]

Nature writers – Mark Cocker, Roger Deakin, Robert Macfarlane – came to pay homage. Robert says: 'He existed largely as an angel in my life; hovering just out of vision, but with his glow always visible to me.'[9] A closer friendship ensued with Roger Deakin. In 2006 Ronnie read 'The Nightingale's Nest' at his deathbed and again at his funeral, and honoured him in print. ('He was somehow mature, although he had never quite grown up – a great achievement.')[10] Roger remained dearest to the Blythe heart for the gift of a lightweight scythe, which made swishing through orchard nettles an ongoing August joy. The donor, shirtless and in shorts, had wooed Ronnie with an artful demonstration.[11]

When Ronnie met the actor and gardener David Holt, who would become a good friend, he looked forward to manual assistance ('David is coming *with his chainsaw*!'). The helper learned the hard way about Ronnie's cavalier treatment of time, with the divine Claudius imagined in Colchester 'bowling along up the High Street in his chariot, past Woolworth's, past the George Hotel to the forum'.[12] Needing to fix the mower, David was directed to the fixer via a Roman city map. Amazingly, he made it.

In 2010, for the fiftieth anniversary of its publication, Ronnie's first novel, *A Treasonable Growth*, was reissued by Faber. And a

half-century of his selected writings appeared in an *Aftermath*
volume, prefaced with an appreciation by Richard Mabey. Ronnie
wrote in a letter of thanks: 'You overwhelm me . . . I hardly need
to tell you what your work means to me, and those long walks,
and those even longer talks over the years. What would I have
done without you?'[13]

Richard Mabey had gone to bed at Bottengoms when Ronnie
heard a nightingale singing in the ash tree in front of the house.
He shouted upstairs and the two old friends 'sat on the doorstep
and it sang there half the night and it was absolutely wonderful'.[14]
Animated song from a bluebell party at Tiger Hill, hosted by Dr
Grace's daughters Veronica and Rosemary each April, still rang in
their heads when a tyre of the car taking them home was loudly
punctured. 'It had been pierced by a beautifully worked flint tool
or weapon from the Stone Age village of Smallbridge,' Ronnie
reported. 'A great jagged hole. What a long time it had to wait
to do its work.'[15]

On trips by bus to Bury St Edmunds, Sudbury or Colchester, he
was inevitably caught up in the chain of current and historic affairs
locally and globally. 'On Monday I was shopping in Colchester when
the High Street was briefly closed for traffic to let a funeral pass. A
Union Jack coffin and a boy from Afghanistan inside. Soldiers
marching. A long procession. Girls crying on the pavement. The
sun beating down.'[16]

After Ronnie wrote about Bottengoms in *At the Yeoman's House*,
a book published in 2011, a document dated 1375 naming John
Bottengom was unearthed in the British Library. In early morning
silence he heard 'the old din of children, animals, machinery,
labourers, pumps' and always regretted the hushed invisibility of the
modern countryside. He longed to see 'country people in the fields
and meadows, though not as the serfs they were at the beginning
of the 20th century, but true inheritors of the land.

'It often saddens me that in all the rushing about to events and
theme-parks etc., and during all the brief travels to the shops or to
the school, no one any longer pauses to look at a field. In fact, a
growing field is likely to be the least visited part of a village. A huge
field, once six, lies the entire length of my farm-track and there are
not many days when I do not study its lines and swelling contours
in winter or its golden splendour in summer. When did you last

stop to look at a cornfield – or an onion field if it comes to that? Or just a stubble-field or a bare field with its flints pushing through?'[17]

Each June or September, Mary Beresford-Jones, Ronnie's Stour Valley neighbour, hosted a house party in an ancestral shooting box on a Perthshire moor. He adored the train journey, passing Durham Cathedral and St Cuthbert's, Lindisfarne, and the joy of evening arrival to pink and purple Grampian shadows on Loch Rannoch. 'Every morning the Highlands rearranges itself to create watercolour views. "Look!" we cry. "Did you ever see anything like it?" Yes, but only in Scotland. Each night, the harvest moon and Venus observe their images in the loch, and the sheep stop nibbling. But the Tay runs glitteringly every minute . . . Each teatime we close the high deer-gate. In bed, a tremendous quietness rules us. I find myself remembering my Scottish neighbour in Suffolk, Mr Anderson, who was judge at the sheep fairs, and who looked out at our table-land mournfully though uncomplainingly. Were he not in heaven, I would send him a postcard.'[18]

In the end, all markers pointed homeward. Mary Beresford-Jones, ensuring that Highland wanderings were botanical walks, urged a record of wildflowers on and around the Bottengoms two acres. The tally of 'desirable and undesirable' plants would run to 196 species. Ronnie came to see the list 'in small farm terms and not botanically . . . there was myself, a Suffolk boy and one of the last to weed fields for pennies. And there was John Clare in the Blue Bell with his pockets straggling with fritillaries or some such treasure. And, briefly, it was all of a piece, his weedy world and mine. Bent backs, not sprays. Clare saw glory in the ruts, his fellow labourers saw "the rubbish" . . . The bliss when poisons stopped the annual green tide!'[19]

In 1999 Edward Storey, celebrant of John Clare and Fenland, moved to the border of Herefordshire and Wales, to revive a shepherds' church near Presteigne with an annual arts festival in which Ronnie featured. As president of the Kilvert Society, honouring Victorian parson Francis Kilvert who recorded this landscape in his diaries, he had a ready subject. *Church Times* readers received regular reports: 'To Discoed – "the edge of the wood" – once more. Golden-grey October weather, the Radnor hills folding and unfolding ahead, the brief rains like curtains across the sun.

'A decade or so ago, the poet Edward Storey came here to find this church over the garden wall. Though not decrepit, it had the worn face of a building that needed more than the usual spring clean. Its history was patchy and indistinct. Poor shepherd folk had kept it going, and I loved them for it . . . Since I last arrived, the whitewash of ages had been brushed away to reveal fine stonework, and the very rafters seemed to sing in their freshness. Outside, a yew vying with Time itself, like the one at Fortingall in Perthshire, trees that were old before Christianity, darkened the nave wall.'[20]

When I partnered from 1991 with Joachim Jacobs, a German landscape architect and synagogue elder, there were many shared outings. One August our trio was transfixed by a cricket match. 'We come across this idyll unexpectedly and even hardened rustics such as Ian and myself are momentarily stunned by the perfection which stretches before us. We meant no more than to show Joachim the wall-paintings in Copford church but our way is blocked by the kind of unconsciously formed masterpiece which all comes together when a heatwave wills it. Living figures almost still in their whites on a living green, a long lime avenue coolly leading to a great house and in the churchyard the grave of Eric Ravilious, a fine artist killed in 1942.'[21]

Joachim and I came at Christmas, once pushing provisions in a wheelbarrow over tundra fields when the track was blocked by snow. Ronnie was captivated when the Nativity coincided with the Jewish Hanukkah festival of lights. But any Friday evening was holy: 'On Christmas Eve, Ian will arrive from the Barbican and Joachim from Berlin. Joachim will light the dinner-table candles, break a white roll in a snowy napkin, and say prayers for the evening of the Sabbath. Later, he will drive me to the midnight mass at Little Horkesley. Henry, our Vicar, will be assisted by James, the chaplain of Chelmsford Prison. I will administer the cup. Ancient hands, young hands, kneeling forms . . . Joachim is prayerful every day. He designs gardens near the Holocaust memorial in Berlin. When I hear him reciting the Shabbat psalm I think, "How could they?"

'I think of Joseph, Mary and Jesus reciting it, careful not to keep the expensive candles burning too long. Careful with the words. After the midnight mass, early on Christmas morning, we sit by the dwindling fire and have a whisky, three old friends who write books. It is our December rite from times long past. Habit, pattern, devoted repetition. Different sacraments . . . The main difference in an old farm-turned-house is the absence of creatures. A cat excepted. Pigs, horses and cows, chickens and ducks, would have been slumbering only a few yards from where we are still awake. Chomping and rustling, making their presence known. We would have gone around with the lantern to see that they were safe before we went upstairs. There would have been a nice smell of muck, and much breathing.'[22]

Note from Ronnie to Ian and Joachim.

Ronnie's gift was to make the specific universal and, typically, his festive meditation embraced all: 'Christmas, in spite of high spending and dense sociability, has moments of pure happiness and silence. Or a sublimity which must not be missed in the uproar. How to find it – that is the question. It is as likely to be as much in the High Street as in the old farmhouse, in a family-packed room as in a chancel. It comes and goes like firelight.'[23]

50

Sea of Memory

I N 2013, FOR Benjamin Britten's centenary, Faber brought out *The Time by the Sea: Aldeburgh 1955–1958*, a youthful memoir by Ronald Blythe. Nearing ninety-one, the author was returned to a major publisher with global distribution.

Rich in period atmosphere, an episodic and almost cinematic rite of passage seemed wrought in sea fret, with a romantic soundtrack of gull cries, waves on shingle and Britten music. It had great reviews and became the Blythe bestseller after *Akenfield*. Nobody spotted that the magical writing teetered on a brink quite separate from the North Sea.

Vicky Minet, Ronnie's friend and neighbour, had taken him back to Thorpeness and Aldeburgh and spurred the turning of ensuing memories into a book. He told Richard Mabey that, 'rather like a visit to the dentist', the experience was less painful than expected. 'It is like looking at one's profile in two mirrors.'[1] Vicky typed the manuscript, but deciphering Ronnie's now spidery script was not the sole challenge: the text rambled and repeated, straying far beyond the place name and dates in the title. She made a discreet edit, which Faber extended. Reworked magazine features and a short story were rejected. Near the end, the flagging author was unsure how to finish. What appeared in print was a magnificent fragment of the book which could have been produced a decade earlier.

With Ronnie's struggles in mind, a closing meditation is among his most poignant writings. It opens: 'The sea, and whatever sea it happens to be, is in a permanent state of cancellation as far as human activity is concerned, eventually wiping out our every mark.'[2] For sea, read memory. But a book which had again skirted the rocks of full confession rescued a telling, final image from oblivion: 'Fitting naked into the accommodating shingle on an August afternoon, I should have been writing, notebook and pencil being so near. But usually I did nothing. I listened. It was why I came here.'[3]

The book's rousing reception climaxed with Ronnie being named the *Oldie* magazine's 2014 Sage of the Year. He and Vicky went up to London for the awards lunch and the sage – deep in the erudite and eclectic commentary making him the best travelling companion – seemed unready to receive the honour. No scripted speech, nor barest notes. But the recipient rose to the occasion with superb spontaneity, waxing comical on the gifts of wisdom. He told of correspondence with a gloomy American lately terminated when she sent him a manual on how to commit suicide.

Full of life, his face uncannily unlined, Ronnie stayed astonishingly strong and agile – wellbeing in a life well walked and well worked. 'Lots of people take pills,' he said. 'They should go for long walks.' He never got used to the sight of inertia. Alighting from a bus while on a shopping expedition to Sudbury, he observed: 'Quite a few people are sitting about – sitting at ten in the morning! It would never have happened in my day. They cannot all have had a funny turn.'[4]

The afternoons of gardening still included heavier labour: clearing ponds, sawing logs, digging clay flower beds and vegetable patch. The heaviest job of raking out the watercourse was a yearly mudbath: 'I splosh my way upstream. For what water my house doesn't want runs on into the Stour. However, this time my way is barred. A big blackthorn, long dead, has crashed across the ditch, so back to collect gloves and the saw. The gaunt tree is oddly light. Were it not so torturously prickly I could have lifted it bodily with one hand and cleared the bank.

'Now I am at the source, the spring. It begins as a mere trembling of the earth but in six yards it is rushing over my feet on its tumultuous journey to the valley via the roof tank. I chop nettles and brambles and irritate nesting birds, and am ashamed of myself. Nature adores a muddle. So far so pleasant. The worst is yet to come, the bailing out of the brick sump which is the first stage of Bottengoms

Farm's last word in hydraulics. This is no job for the effete. It requires a brave descent into the kind of mud which beauticians would pay a ransom for, and it is invariably at this point in the ditch-cleaning that visitors arrive . . .'[5]

He did not share with his *Church Times* readers, though it had caused several visitors to be doubly startled, that this filthy – and silkily sensuous – task was best tackled naked. At the end of it: 'I touch bottom. The spring which has flowed since farmers settled here in Saxon days washes the bricks. I sit on the edge listening to its music as it presses across sand and stones, along pipes and a miniature aqueduct, and then impossibly up into the roof and down into the kettle.'[6]

While water quality was regularly inspected, the sole inhabitant never had a taste for it except in mugs of tea. Visitors offered a pot of refreshment when the plumbing had seized up were alarmed to find their host dipping a bucket in the stream – not quite realising that this was what came out of the taps at the best of times. Amid mounting health warnings about dehydration, Ronald Blythe thrived on the constitution of the Kalahari Desert. He loved the sight and sound of the trickling stream, but it was written in his DNA that water was not to be trusted.

Despite an inherited horror of waste, he wisely left the last bottle of home-made Vin Nash, from 1973, untouched. It lay in the larder like a Molotov cocktail, gifts of tinned or bottled delicacies remaining alongside for years or decades. Breakfast guests smiled when handed the marmalade with a breezy 'Give it a little scrape, dear'. But the back of the fridge could be a no-go area: twice a good plain cook contracted food poisoning from leftover meat left overlong.

Ronnie could never quite believe his good fortune. 'I feel very grateful for life,' he said. 'It has exceeded all my expectations.'[7] And he wrote: 'The man who came to mend something had been to Spain for a week. "But I expect for you, sir, it is all holiday." I had to agree.'[8] The ecstasy of it all. Once, in the garden, he read words in a hymnal through a dragonfly's wing – the ideal metaphor for his sensual and spiritual life.

Although sleeping soundly, to wake at dawn with no alarm, he could lie in bed listening. 'At midnight the valley is tremulous with summer movement, and yet at the same time profoundly still. The mill pool, if you listen hard, will, now and then, faintly splash with rising fish. And sometimes a wind that you cannot hear will disturb the dragging leaves at the water's edge, or make the corn talk dryly, or the sleeping birds settle more comfortably. A minute orchestra plays in order to create stillness. Nature's still, small voice precedes the fire of the dawn chorus and is worth lying awake for.'⁹ Or getting up for. He might still roam nocturnal paths to the churchyard. 'Gravestones are legible and there are dense scents. Young rabbits are dining off a wreath.'¹⁰

The word 'sploshing' recurred in Blythe prose approvingly. But friends planning winter visits enquired less anxiously about his health than that of the track. Deliverers ignoring signs of CARS TURN HERE and MUD waited for rescue vans. The last volume of original writing by the Church of England's poet, in 2015, was a book of nine short poems, *Decadal*. The longest – 'Down to the Dwelling House' – dwelt on the track as walkers and drivers saw it. A philosophical and historical sweep was summed up in three lines as he sensed

> The track thinking back to what farming feet
> Asked of it. Rough walkers on rough ground
> Who trod it without assurances.

Ronald Blythe's forty-eight years of active happiness after *Akenfield* might be summarised in A Tale of Two Shopping Lists. In that era his neighbours passed from hedgers and ditchers to hedge fund managers; his life altered too. The frugal 1969 tally was for stoking up in a cold climate. By 2017 a smaller basket of vital provisions confirmed that even the most self-denying and industrious cannot live on bread alone:

1969	2017
Butter	Whisky
Tea	Gin
Coffee	Sherry
Rice Krispies	Cinzano
Bananas	Bread
Cheese	Cake
Sprouts	
Firelighters	

'I don't really approve of alcohol,' Ronnie had declared. 'But I do like a little drink.' The sentiment held true even as he came to enjoy one little drink after another – sherry at lunchtime, gin-and-cin before dinner, whisky nightcaps and Guinness in a pub. Each drained glass invited a recap. This pouring of pleasure, and self-medication perhaps, helped in savouring the moment – the reflection, the conversation. Boozer Blythe, as he came to call himself, was always merry and never insensibly drunk. Life itself was intoxicating.

PART FIVE

The Clay Meadow

But now I only know I am – that's all.
John Clare, 'I Am'

Faith in His Fellows

FOR THE NINETIETH birthday – as *Akenfield* was being reissued in America by the *New York Review of Books* – Mark Cocker plotted an interview in Lincolnshire, to be recorded for Radio 3. When Mark's friend Adam arrived to drive Ronnie the agreed 119 miles, all was forgotten.

'He was busy in the garden, as almost always when I visited,' Mark reported. 'But he went inside to gather a few things and accompanied Adam, a complete stranger, without so much as asking where he would stay, who would look after him and what the event was in aid of . . .

'Ronnie appeared on stage and proceeded to hold forth, with audience in his palm, as if the whole thing was what he had planned to do that day. No hint of doubt, confusion, discomfort. Far from it. He was serene, kindly and filled with simple pleasure at talking to friends. I am not imbued with any kind of religious feeling but seeing Ronnie negotiate this small, albeit daily, adventure without a second glance, was to see a person with total faith in his fellows.'[1]

Ronnie was a house guest of the poet Kevin Crossley-Holland when missing his cue for the drive to a literary festival talk. He was discovered 'ensconsed in an armchair, rereading *Far from the Madding Crowd* – entirely transported, entirely trusting, guilty and innocent!' To his host, no man was ever so curious and generous, 'so grounded and yet well on his way to heaven'.[2]

Ronnie and sherry.

Extraordinary equanimity amounting to perfect poise was key to his longevity. Knocking ninety, he was the star turn at a formal dinner party. A candle-lit table was laid in a darkened garden. After the main course, the hostess asked the men to switch places. Ronnie pushed back his chair and fell with it into an unseen pond. Pulled spluttering from weedy shallows, a non-swimmer was dried off, kitted out in his host's spare dinner suit, and in his required position, with conversation duly sparkling, for the dessert.

He basked in love. Vicky says: 'Our trips to Waitrose in Sudbury were hilarious as Ronnie made a kind of stately progress round the store, being stopped in every other aisle by affectionate parishioners or admiring readers of the *Church Times*. He would speak to everyone, even when he mostly had no idea who they were, as the bottles clanked in the trolley.'[3]

Asked if he felt lonely at the end of the long track, Ronnie answered: 'Chance would be a fine thing.'[4] So many people, the invited and uninvited alike, beat a path to his door. His manners never fell short of impeccable. Genuinely interested in everyone, he had special rapport with young people. Village teenagers camped in the garden. Wild Writing students from the University of Essex came each November, bringing birthday cake and leaving with inimitable inspiration. Ronnie had enjoyed being part of a Writers in Schools programme, and now he mentored visiting children. They loved his appreciation of life and their individual potential. 'My world seems to be so enormous where it is,' he said. 'There is so much to work on where you are.'[5] His enthusiasm was infectious; he remained in extreme age perennially youthful.

But, past a ninety-fourth birthday, even the most remarkable resilience began to buckle under the burden of expectation. One afternoon in 2017, dropping in for the usual sherry and catch-up chat, I noticed muddle on the dining table. On unmet demands for payment, the cat was resting untaxed paws. Ronnie, normally so tidy and orderly, was not his old self. 'What a lot of bills,' I said. 'Leave them!' he almost snapped. 'They've had enough from me over the years.' Beyond soothing silence, I sensed bailiff wheels rumbling down the track.

Several years before, still with every methodical marble, Ronnie had given me financial power of attorney while sharing social care with Vicky too. So, bills were settled. It was the first step in a retreat from bad news – or maybe that had been a lifelong process. But for a man who had always done everything for himself, save only for the occasional assistance allowed from closest friends, it was a breakthrough when a stranger was permitted to cut the grass.

Writing fell away. A memoir of Christine and 'a kind of voyage book' based on his father and Rupert Brooke going to Gallipoli were pondered and abandoned. He had dearly loved Colm Tóibín's novelised life of Henry James in *The Master*, with its exquisite handling of stifled homosexuality. Having drawn back from the overt gay novel once planned for *The Assassin*, he thought the odyssey of Edward FitzGerald's love for a Lowestoft fisherman might carry some of his own feelings into print. But too late.

'Word from Wormingford' columns lasted longest. The 400-word meandering but broadly circular format best suited his mindset and could still encompass the harmony of the Blythe universe. Missed mailings prompted phoned dictations until these also ended in disarray. When the stream ran dry, the *Church Times* reran old columns – causing a flood of enquiries anxious for an esteemed writer's return. Repetition in Ronnie's church addresses had long been accepted affectionately, and no offence taken when two-minute silences reached three as the lay reader roamed in dreamland. A voice of gentle authority now whispered.

Then I opened a letter offering a CBE for services to literature. Like writers from Aldous Huxley to Philip Larkin and Evelyn Waugh, Ronnie had always repudiated state honours: they were embarrassing, compromising, or just redundant. Ronald Blythe, Commander of the Most Excellent Order of the British Empire *did* sound close to incredible. But on hearing the amiable offer, he asked: 'What should I do, dear?' 'Well,' I said, sensing a change of heart, 'if you don't hate the idea, it would make a lot of people happy.'

'All right. Tell them to send it.'

While London was clearly beyond him, even to see Prince Charles, known to be a Blythe fan, a homelier presentation was plotted in Wormingford church. The ceremony to be held on the eve of Ronnie's ninety-fifth birthday would also signal retirement from public life. The pink and turquoise enamelled medal was hung around his neck by a sword-bearing and chain-wearing Lord Petre, Lord Lieutenant of Essex. One of the most articulate speakers of the age, and a lay reader here for half a century, managed two short sentences of thanks before a party in a marquee. Fizz and sherry flowed as the heavens opened.

Much later, arm in arm with Ronnie, and bearing leftover bottles, Joachim and I steered the return to a vintage Rolls-Royce and a kindly neighbour at the churchyard gate. We settled back for the journey homeward into Ronnie's belated retirement. The Roller, only slightly younger than the commander, gave us an impression of sinking into a tilted leather sofa. The angle, the alcohol and the occasion had gone to three heads when the medal was found to be missing. Ronnie had trodden it underfoot.

Though several times dinked on the Bottengoms brick floor, so that the enamel was cracked and chipped for the final journey on the coffin, the gong had pride of place on a hook beside the mantelpiece. It was whipped off and worn at every opportunity, over a dressing gown or under a paper crown from a Christmas cracker; at birthday parties in final Novembers it looked resplendent alongside a remembrance poppy and a panic button never once pressed. The medal, as comforting as those of George Blythe in the 1920s toy box, was a solid sign of achievement as the books blurred into one. Ronnie said he was still writing, or about to write, and then: 'I can't just sit here doing nothing.' But he did. Or rather, stories continued spinning in his head and occasionally spilling onto his tongue.

One late Christmas Eve, after struggling to buy all the provisions I would cook and serve at Bottengoms, I heard Ronnie on the radio as the champion of evergreen tradition, relating how he was busy catering for two old friends as usual. Long after he had ceased tending the garden, visitors were told that he still did it all himself. ('John Nash got the credit, but I did all the work!') Time compacted in his writing; now it became comfortably and confidently elastic in his life. When I predicted an eventual Poets' Corner memorial his response – 'Well, I have written a lot of books' – was neither surprised nor falsely modest. He knew his worth.

And, with remarkable grace, he came to live out the words of one elderly monk reconciled to declining powers in *The View in Winter*: 'Be patient, be gentle, be nothing. Somebody said that the real vocation of old age was to give out love. So no more doing, but being.'[6]

Soon after the millennium, Ronnie had welcomed the Suffolk painter Mary Newcomb to Bottengoms, and two reticent people practically fell into one another's arms. Each knew the other intimately through kindred – odd, lyrical, visionary – art. Mary brought a basket of photos and drawings for book illustrations and her painting of a churchyard rookery provided the perfect cover picture for *Talking to the Neighbours*. They had barely met when a stroke left Mary mute and half paralysed in a nursing home for five last years. In a rich interior world, she carried on making pictures – tracing outlines with a finger in the air. Ronnie was in a similar place of calm contemplation as he waited with infinite patience for silence.

Fan letters continued, latterly unopened. When they were read to him, he said: 'How lovely. I must write back – tomorrow.' And that was that – another straw for the fragile 'Chippendale' side table which, long known to Ronnie as 'the groaning board', slumped under a growing weight of books; but its back never quite broke.

A few friends and more acquaintances refused to accept that he could no longer be his old obliging self. One bullied him into a long day's outing which left him exhausted and confused. That evening he was discovered, naked save for a dressing gown, in distress over his sexuality still not being accepted by James Turner, dead for more than forty years. One of the prayers Ronnie learned from his mother was 'Gentle Jesus, meek and mild / Look upon a little child; / Pity my simplicity, / Suffer me to come to Thee.' He recited the words throughout his life, latterly changing the last line to 'Suffer me to be.'

At the doctors' surgery there was bafflement on both sides. Why had so elderly a man almost never been medicated? they wondered. 'Why am I here now?' he asked. A prescription of paracetamol was binned. Less easily jettisoned was an instant diagnosis of dementia in the light of a failure to answer humdrum questions over which a darting brain would always have stumbled. It was the lack of recognition from childhood all over again, as well as the misrepresentation dogging the Blythes for centuries. He was just very old and finally winding down.

With lunches now provided by supporters in the three parishes, caring and nursing slowly followed. It was a milestone when Ronnie allowed his hair to be cut. He warmed to visits from the chiropodist during which they both admired his shapely feet. 'She is a good Christian woman,' he said cryptically. Church services and then visits from the vicar petered out unmissed. As ever, Ronnie lived his words. 'A friend in her nineties declines to come to church after eighty years' of attendance. She doesn't even feel any further need for the Sacraments. What her heart tells her is, "Be still". How valuable it is during the last years to alter one's attention.'[7]

The writer, alone with the companionable Christ-muse, had a deep but transient need of mortal company. He hailed 'some friends, the cat, some books, this landscape familiar to me since boyhood, and all in receipt of my inordinate affection. But if I am not covetous, it is because I have all I need.'[8] One departing friend was crushed after a cheery 'See you soon, Ronnie.' 'Not too soon!' came the reflex reply. Following a farewell at the door, perhaps with a fond embrace, Ronnie resumed a meditative, prayerful, grateful seclusion. Only once did I turn back to be surprised by my mentor still on the doorstep and apparently waving. He was, in fact, peeing.

Wallowing in an incoming flow of news, gossip and stories, Ronnie was moved beyond words when I related the modern Greek saga which followed the death of patriot, democrat and poet George Seferis in Athens in 1971 during a military junta. His widow, imperious as a statue, had commanded her daughters not to weep while they prepared to lead a huge funeral procession. Then, leaning into the coffin, she hacked off her long hair to give her husband a parting gift. Ronnie mused on this drama of marital devotion in dumbstruck admiration before returning to his senses. 'You wouldn't catch me cutting off my hair for anyone,' he said.

The shunning of medication covered cherished cats. When a feeble old feline tottered into the garden, Ronnie paused briefly from conversation with James Hamilton-Paterson to say: 'I believe Stripey is going off to die.' Later, they found the pet lifeless under a bush. Ronnie buried him with affection and swiftly sought a replacement. The lives of the successors were extended towards nine apiece by a vigilant neighbour. When the retired vet came to tea, pills were added to cat food unbeknown to Ronnie.

He returned from hospital in 2018, after a fall and a new hip, to more care. Friends brought in friends who fitted or flitted. It was somehow accepted that they just happened to be walking past, bearing meals. Subterfuge became deceit when a flu jab was rejected. On an approved meander around a pub lunch, the car passed the surgery at the allotted moment and a model of politeness stepped inside. Seeing fading sight as inevitable, he agreed to cataract removal to go along with what others wanted – and the result left him jubilant. When, during lockdown, he contracted Covid on his ninety-eighth birthday, two carers as fearless as he was got him through what could have been the darkest time. For all three it was enlightening, though lucky Ronnie was enabled to remain sublimely unaware that he was ever in danger.

In *The Assassin*, John Felton is under constant surveillance in the condemned cell. For the old Ronnie of diehard independence this spelt torture. Now came sweet surrender. He relished the cheerful coming and going, the serving of three square meals and a flow of little drinks daily. He marvelled at how his figure had never altered even as dear ones repositioned trouser buttons. Almost to the last he ate like a horse; but, while the horse could be led to water, none could make him drink. He was watered by tea and sherry, though latterly skipping the tea.

Since he never asked for anything, or admitted to any discomfort, it was hard to know what might be needed. Now banding themselves together as the Ronnettes, helpers arrived at the door, shaking off mud and rain, to be greeted with the words, 'Isn't it a lovely day!' As care increased, givers felt they gained. The philosophy of positivity did indeed make days lovely. A hospital bed was put in the garden room when it was thought that stairs could no longer be tackled. Getting him going took longer and longer. The walk with stick and helpful arm to armchair; the soaping, drying, shaving, combing; the buttoning and belting, pulling up socks, tucking in shirt; the jumper; the finishing touch of Old Spice. All slowly savoured. 'Thank you, dear. Couldn't be better.'

After one lunchtime, barely mobile it seemed, he was left in the armchair to snooze beneath a blanket and cat. When the carer returned in late afternoon, the ninety-nine-year-old was still sleeping – naked (save for a straw hat) on a fold-up chair in the garden. Creeping away to cut the grass, she came back to find him fully dressed in the armchair. She laughed and kissed his cheek, aware now that, while he could 'jump nimbly in and out of his clothes when the fancy took him', he had grown to love the helping hands.[9]

A daily high point came when Ronnie was washed, dressed, fed and seated, with a sherry glass and a helper reading aloud. 'It is almost my favourite thing – to be read to,' he had once written. 'When I lie dying, will somebody read to me? Shall I leave some suggestions? Poems by Hardy or Cavafy, Chekhov's short stories, the Book of Psalms? Make a note.'[10] In the event, the texts they all wanted were by Ronald Blythe. He listened dreamily until correcting pronunciation. One day, he cut in: 'Very good. Who wrote that?'

'You!'

'My word.' The writer settled back in fortified contentment.

52

Natural Causes

ON 19 SEPTEMBER 2022 Ronnie followed the funeral of Queen Elizabeth II on television. Philosophical to the last, he said as the ceremony ended: 'She was very, very old.' She was ninety-six. He was nearly a hundred and set fair for a final fling.

Publisher John Murray was plotting a centenary celebration with a pick of 'Word from Wormingford' columns. The book would appear as *Next to Nature: A Lifetime in the English Countryside* in October, with a Richard Mabey foreword and monthly selections introduced by different writers – fans and friends.

Ronnie nearly hadn't made it when found in the garden, bloodied and battered by a fall. Reporting a skull surely broken, ambulance paramedics forecast a one-way journey. During twenty-four hours of hospital upheaval – as Ronnie awaited admission to a ward he had opened – he insisted he was good to go, and X-rays agreed. Patched and stitched, he was returned to Bottengoms and a restorative glass of sherry. He had always maintained that the elderly are most resilient at home.

The publisher asked whether the author might sign some title pages to be sewn into books as they printed. No word had been written for four years, but no harm trying. A box arrived with 1,350 pages and, over weeks, Ronnie signed the lot. Then he returned with rolls of envelope labels, white trails corkscrewing under the table and around the room – to be batted by the cat. When a fan letter was read to him, he said: 'How lovely – I must answer it *now.*' Paper quickly provided, he composed a graceful and grateful paragraph.

Next to Nature was almost printed when Vikram Seth sent an acrostic poem 'For Ronald Blythe' from India. Recalling the time Ronnie guided him to a fine old elm, surviving alone on Gravel Hill above Nayland, it concluded the tribute.

> **R**ight hand and left make ten. Earth rings the sun.
> **O**n these two truths we mark your hundredth year.
> **N**ature performs its heartless, witless run.
> **A**rt presses us to see and smell and hear.
> **L**ucid and strange, your words transmit the sound,
> **D**iscordant and concordant, of Earth's round.
>
> **B**y fallow and by field, by rust and rose,
> **L**ittle or large, by whimsy or by worth,
> **Y**our transitory histories disclose
> **T**wo truths encrypted in the transient Earth.
> **H**earts that can sing educe the blackbird's song.
> **E**lms that stand far enough away live long.

Dedicated to dear ones who had brought him to his centenary, *Next to Nature* was a festive bestseller. Also formed into a cake for the hundredth birthday, it would be reprinted monthly until a spring paperback. 'All the charm, wonder, eccentricity and vigour of country life is here in these pages, and told with such engaging directness, detail and colour,' Stephen Fry wrote in an endorsement. 'To immerse yourself in this East Anglian year is to be reminded of why we love and value the rhythms and realities of rural life. Bliss.'

Ronnie set those who loved him most the challenge of thinking as he did. As he had written of life: 'Like grace, joy is there for the taking. We all deserve a bit of it, and if we miss it, it is mostly our fault.'[1] And of death: 'I feel little sorrow when the old die, more a sense of inconvenience when they can't come to supper as usual. But I am filled with sorrow for their last sickness and suffering, and pray for it to be over soon.'[2] Near the end, he was offered paracetamol or morphine. 'Paracetamol,' he said. 'Just one.' Ready to die, he did not want to lose a conscious moment. '"Neither look back nor forward", advised Jesus, "or you will miss today." Generally speaking, I would not miss today for anything.'[3]

He would still watch the lunchtime news on television when his meal was served, but the daily diet of global distress was overlain with philosophy. 'When you get very old you realise you can no longer worry about everything,' he said after his hundredth birthday. 'The world is what you can see and touch.'[4]

Now boundless curiosity was also turning to the business of dying. A last ambition was to die in his own bed, and the Ronnettes stepped up to deliver this wish, moving into the house in a rota for final weeks so that a stalwart of solitude was never alone. At a low ebb, he said only: 'No hospital.' George, his father, had made the same request in vain. Ronnie was altogether luckier.

Late in the evening of Saturday, 14 January 2023 he said 'Get up!' Bare feet were helped to touch the uneven floor for one last vertical minute. He had especially loved to scrub the bricks. Water gave a brief brightening in which an imprint of wild flowers was illuminated. As he wrote: 'the patterns created by moist clay set out to dry on Stuart and Georgian grass show up vividly after a dose of Flash.'[5] Now words of thanks as he sank back in bed from the clay meadow, to die peacefully – a century of life true to a last split second.

After the carers' night-long vigil, with a reading aloud of *The Time by the Sea*, a past vicar of plain Blythe-style holiness led a prayer. Gathered round the deathbed in the barnlike room, they seemed to merge with Christine's painting, *The Nativity*. When undertakers arrived for Ronnie's last journey up the track, dear ones lined the path in a ragged guard of honour – a teenager with shorts and muddied knees straight from the rugby field, his parents, the family of friends. A robin sang. There was a smell of leaf mould nurturing the next green growth.

Richard Mabey emailed: 'I hope that our dear dear friend – and hero – may at last be recognised as one of the great prose writers of the past century.'[6] A single false note came with a dud death certificate. It carried the wrong date and mistook the cause for dementia. Four months earlier, the Queen had been allowed to die of 'old age'. Ronald Blythe died as he had lived – simply and grandly – from natural causes.

Ronnie's favourite hymn, 'My Song Is Love Unknown', was sung at both a Wormingford funeral and St Edmundsbury Cathedral memorial service. Taking that line from George Herbert, Samuel Crossman penned the words in 1664 after ejection as parson at

Little Henny near Sudbury. Some 260 years later, John Ireland set them to music on the back of a menu over lunch. Ronnie's anthem is wrapped in enigma for a solitary man. As is his tombstone epitaph – 'Love bade me welcome', opening Herbert's best-loved poem. That first line ends 'yet my soul drew back'. Love made him write.

Frances Ward came down from Cumberland to take the funeral. Her empathetic and quote-laden address made for such a perfect fit that Vikram Seth thought Ronnie must have written it. 'He was a man of gifts,' she concluded. 'The greatest gift was his appreciation of gift. Not for him any sense of entitlement, or petty resentment, or grievance, or right. No – the opportunities that came his way, the friends, the service and care and kindness he gave and received – all were gifts . . . This was Ronnie's life. Enchanted. Full of grace. Bonny and blithe. Good and gay.'

Tombstone designed by Teucer Wilson.

The coffin was carried by dear ones. Another, walking behind, reported: 'His pallbearers were not chosen for the regularity of their height and so his wicker coffin went a bit this way and a bit that way, like the floors of his old house, not even, but with a story.'[7] He was laid to rest under an oak tree, a few feet from John and Christine. A straw hat, lifted from the coffin top by a yew bough, was skimmed into the grave.

In her cathedral tribute, Julia Blackburn spoke of the 'knowledge of poverty and loneliness of being' sparking kinship with John Clare. 'Ronnie always referred to him with such an easy intimacy, it was as if he was talking about his favourite brother, albeit one who did not have the same good fortune. Clare ended his troubled life in the Madhouse, whereas Ronnie found peace and contentment and a sense of belonging in the sanctuary that was Bottengoms . . . he was not afraid of dying and I think he would have understood his own death in the words of John Clare's poem "I Am". He read it to me at our first meeting':

> I long for scenes where man hath never trod
> A place where woman never smiled or wept
> There to abide with my Creator, God,
> And sleep as I in childhood sweetly slept,
> Untroubling and untroubled where I lie
> The grass below – above the vaulted sky.

Bishop Martin Seeley, also ending his homily with 'I Am', said: 'Like Clare, he wanted to preserve, but understood the delicacy of not interfering, and like Clare he found beauty and glory in the mundane, the extraordinary in the ordinary. A way of seeing, of being, of faith.' A tribute was read from Rowan Williams, poet and former archbishop of Canterbury: 'Ronnie took his stance as a watchman, quietly determined to share what he could see with a society both less wide awake and more feverishly hurried.'

As Ronnie had planned, Vicky read the lesson and David Holt 'The Nightingale's Nest'. Cellist Natasha Holmes played 'The Fall of the Leaf' by Imogen Holst and Clare, Countess of Euston, Suffolk's Lord Lieutenant, read 'My Little Owls', a roll call of Wormingford happiness, on behalf of King Charles:

Pear blossom. Six a.m. tea. Matins for a dozen in the chancel. Making my sweat pea wigwam. Seeing strangers pass. Listening to the director of the British Museum on the radio. Watching the manes of the horses on the hill being caught in the wind. Reading Psalm 96. Eating a miser's meal – pot d'jour, a curling crust, cheese ends, and a wizened apple. Loving my little cat. Not going to the party. Sploshing up the farm track. Remembering the Garretts in Cambridge. Listening to David Holt reading George Herbert. Seeing the boundary ditch full of water. A whisky at bedtime.

Silence. Oaks before ash promising a splash. Re-reading *Swann's Way*. Finding the nail scissors. Visiting the new bookshop in Stoke-by-Nayland. Watching the world greening. Remembering the Turners in Cornwall. Finishing a chapter. Choosing a page of Kilvert's Diary for a sermon. Hearing a climbing rose scratch against the window, like Catherine Earnshaw's escape-me-never hands.

Eating olives. The lawnmower starting at first pull. Feeding chaffinches. Watching Dan draw. The unbelievable scent of bluebells. The kindness of strangers at the hospital. Ash log fires. New jerseys. Giving Vicky plants. Hearing bumble bees . . . Touching the sun-warmed Roman bricks of the Saxon tower in Colchester and imagining the hands that formed them. Seeing beautiful girls lean on the thousand-year-old doorway. Myself seeing for the thousandth time the house of John Wilbye, the madrigalist, whose patron gave him a sheep farm for his services. Listening hard, what bliss to hear him singing among the shoppers.

Catching sight of my little owls in the blackthorn, where they have always been. The satisfaction when flowers and creatures know their places.[8]

Epilogue

RONNIE WILLED BOTTENGOMS to the Essex Wildlife Trust as a retreat for writers, artists and naturalists. Darren Tansley, an ecologist for the trust who camped in the garden while growing up in Wormingford, has hailed 'a place that filled me with wonder and inspiration; a house that had taken root in the landscape and was part of the natural world rather than an intrusion upon it.'[1] As Ronnie and his environmentalist friend Jules Pretty envisaged, Bottengoms will become a model, for the art of looking and living sustainably with nature. Spending next to nothing, he left a surprising fortune. After generous bequests to institutions and individuals, the wildlife trust also inherited £500,000.

Book royalties were left to the Royal Literary Fund in thanks for help to James Turner. Christine's two great paintings, never shown

Memorial plaques and the Gloire de Dijon rose.

in her lifetime, were accepted by the Tate Collection. Ronnie wished his papers to lodge in the British Library. The last cat, lustred in celebrity, was happily rehomed.

As Ronnie approached his centenary, an expanded Gainsborough's House in Sudbury and ongoing field studies courses at Flatford Mill, subject of Constable paintings and scene of John Nash art classes, were joined by a restoration plan for Cedric Morris's Benton End. Bottengoms could be the fourth corner of a conservationist and creative picture in and around the Stour Valley.

For all the natural losses, otters are back in the Stour and buzzards returned to nest in a willow below the garden from 2007. In his final summer, Ronnie heard chiffchaffs and cuckoo as he sunbathed amid dragonflies. He could no longer reach nightingales on Tiger Hill but was lulled to sleep as always by hooting tawny owls and snuffling badgers.

And in spring, as this book took shape in Ronnie's study, a hare crouched on the doorstep, leverets probably hidden in the garden. Each morning there were fresh deer tracks by the stream.

I sometimes hear God questioning us as we enter Paradise:
My beautiful Earth, why didn't you enjoy it more?
Next to Nature

Ronald Blythe, 1922–2023.

Acknowledgements

M Y FOREMOST DEBT is to Ronald Blythe for the pleasure of his company and the honour of writing this biography.

Without the dear ones, whose support enabled Ronnie to exceed his prediction of living to a century, and to remain happily at home, the story would have been shorter and poorer. All thanks to Flea and Rupert Tozer, Zoé, Colin, William, Amélie and Louis Brown, Vicky, Luke and Thea Minet, Linda Rice, Caroline Post, Amanda Cocksedge, Suzanne Albert, Natasha Holmes, Caroline Despret, Chris and Ruth Matthews, Kate Charlton-Jones and Emily White.

While any error remains my own, I am hugely grateful to readers and improvers of the draft text: Julia Blackburn, Nicholas Clark, Alan Cudmore and Hazel Thompson, Andy Friend, Maggi Hambling, James Hamilton-Paterson, David Holt, Joachim Jacobs, Richard Mabey, Vicky Minet, Peter Paul and Kate Nash, Jules Pretty, Hilary Spurling and Frances Ward. Zoé Brown and Keith Roberts have been invaluable at every stage.

Special thanks to my agent David Godwin and to Rachel Taylor and Philippa Sitters at David Godwin Associates. To all at John Murray – especially Nick Davies and editor Abigail Scruby, Juliet Brightmore, Howard Davies, Hilary Hammond, Amanda Jones, Sara Marafini, Tim Ryder, Caroline Westmore and Corinna Zifko. And to Clays printers of Bungay for keeping this book a Suffolk saga.

Further thanks to institutions and individuals – and to some friends in memoriam: Will Atkins, David Baker, Patrick Barkham, Paul Barnes, Wilhelmina Barns-Graham, Hugh Barrett, Terence Blacker, Mary, Christopher and Nicholas Beresford-Jones, Melissa and Michael Blythe, British Library, Britten-Pears Archive, David Burnett, Alison Cannard, James Canton, Ronnie Carless, Charles Causley, John Chandler, Christine Chaplin, Beth Chatto, John Clare Society, Susan Clifford, Mark Cocker, Trish Coe, Peggy Cole, Diana

Collins, Sarah Cook, Mike Crisp, Kevin Crossley-Holland, Andrew Dawson, Jill Dawson, Roger Deakin, James Dodds, Danae and Robin Duthey, Christopher Elliott, Elizabeth Esteve-Coll, Marianne Fry, Stephen Fry, Jane Gardam, Jane Garrett, Adrian Glew, Heather Godwin, Lawrence Goldman, Jeremy Greenwood, Malcolm Guite, Charles Hall, Jenny Hall, Nicki Hall, Keith Hay, Gill Hedley, Valerie Herbert, Andrew Hewson, Matthew Hodges, Bob Jellicoe, Simon Lawrence, David and Georgina Lewis, Griselda and John Lewis, Dan Llywelyn Hall, London Library, London Metropolitan Archives, London School of Economics, Angela King, Robert Macfarlane, Susan Marling, Dan Meek, Tim Miller, Glyn Morgan, Richard Morphet, Francie Mount, Twig O'Malley, Ruth Padel, Peter Parker, Andrew and Penelope Phillips, Stephen Platten, Neil Powell, Rex and Polly Pyke, Robin Ravilious, Judy Rees, Nicole Roberts, Sainsbury Centre for Visual Arts and the University of East Anglia, Norman Scarfe, Joan Schenkar, James Scott, Mary Scott, Ronald Searle, Martin Seeley, Vikram Seth, Garrow Shand, Andy Sheppard, Rick Shepperson, Slightly Foxed, Christine Smith, David Smith, Eileen Smith, Shirley Smith, Oliver Soden, Hugh St Clair, Stephen Stuart-Smith, John Spurling, Edward Storey, Rosamund Strode, Sudbury Heritage Centre and Museum, Sudbury Library, Suffolk Archives, Suffolk Libraries, Suffolk Regiment Museum, Alan Swerdlow, Tate Archive, Alan Taylor, Craig Taylor, Yorgos Tegos, Sue and Timothy Tibbetts, Angela Tilby, Peter Tolhurst, Roy Tracey, Anthony Tyley, Tony Venison, Caroline Walter, Claire Wallace, Ulrich Weber, Wellcome Library, Toby Wiggins, Connie Willis, John Whale, Colin Whyles, Rowan Williams, Andrew Wilson, Ed Wilson, Teucer Wilson and Christopher Woodward.

Picture Credits

Inset pages 1–8

1: © Zoé Brown. 2 above: © Ian Collins. 2 below, 3, 4: © Christopher Matthews. 5 above: The National Gallery, London/Alamy Stock Photo. 5 below: Courtesy of Sotheby's. 6 above and below: © Estate of Christine Kühlenthal. All rights reserved 2024. Photos Christopher Matthews. 7 above: © Estate of John Northcote Nash. All rights reserved 2024. Photo Tate Images. 7 below: © Estate of John Northcote Nash. All rights reserved 2024. Photo Royal Academy of Arts, London. 8: © Toby Wiggins.

Text illustrations

Ronald Blythe Archive: pp. 22, 27, 29, 31, 37, 53, 70, 77, 83, 94 drawing by G D Johnson, 98, 103, 108, 111 photographer unknown, 117, 121, 135, 146, 149, 165, 172, 189 illustration by John Nash, 203, 211 photographer unknown, 232, 238, 244, 274, 309, 325. © The Trustees of the British Museum, reproduced by permission of the artist: p. 222. © Zoé Brown: pp. 352, 367. Courtesy of Benton End House & Gardens: p. 126 photographer unknown. Courtesy of Britten Pears Arts: p. 177 photographer unknown. Ian Collins Archive: pp. 2, 225, 227, 342. Photogravure by P.H. Emerson, plate 3, from *Pictures of East Anglian Life*, 1890: p. 14. © David Gentleman: p. 322. Fay Godwin/British Library archive/Bridgeman Images: p. 301. © Estate of Ursula Hamilton-Paterson: p. 260. John Hedgecoe/ Popperfoto via Getty Images: p. 295. Kurt Hutton/Picture Post/ Getty Images: p. 170. © Kurt Hutton/Report IFL Archive/report-digital.co.uk: pp. 182, 197, 199, 206, 219. © Joachim Jacobs: p. 4. © Cedric Morris Estate, reproduced with permission: p. 128 photo Tate Images. © Estate of John Northcote Nash. All rights reserved 2024: pp. 7, 44, 55, 157, 239, 289, 349. Courtesy of Elizabeth Orcutt: p. 333. Courtesy of Rex Pyke: p. 266. Courtesy of the Estate of

Notes and Sources

The following books by Ronald Blythe
have been quoted in the notes:

Akenfield: Portrait of an English Village, Allen Lane, 1969
Aftermath: Selected Writings 1960–2010, Black Dog, 2010
The Assassin, Black Dog, 2004
At Helpston: Meetings with John Clare, Black Dog, 2011
At the Yeoman's House, Enitharmon Press, 2011
The Bookman's Tale, Canterbury Press, 2009
Borderland: A Country Diary, Black Dog, 2005
The Circling Year: Perspectives from a Country Parish, Canterbury Press, 2001
Divine Landscapes: A Pilgrimage through Britain's Sacred Places, Penguin Putnam, 1986
Field Work: Selected Essays, Black Dog, 2007
First Friends, Viking, 1999
Forever Wormingford, Canterbury Press, 2017
From the Headlands, Chatto & Windus, 1982
Going to Meet George and Other Outings, Long Barn, 1999
Immediate Possession and Other Stories, MacGibbon and Kee, 1961
In the Artist's Garden: A Wormingford Journal, Canterbury Press, 2015
Next to Nature: A Lifetime in the English Countryside, John Murray, 2022
Out of the Valley: Another Year at Wormingford, Viking, 2000
Outsiders: A Book of Garden Friends, Black Dog, 2008
Private Words: Letters and Diaries from the Second World War, Viking, 1991
River Diary, Canterbury Press, 2008
The Stories of Ronald Blythe, Chatto & Windus, 1985
Stour Seasons: A Wormingford Book of Days, Canterbury Press, 2016
Talking about John Clare, Trent Books, 1999
Talking to the Neighbours: Conversations from a Country Parish, Canterbury Press, 2002
The Time by the Sea: Aldeburgh 1955–1958, Faber, 2013
Under a Broad Sky, Canterbury Press, 2013
The View in Winter: Reflections on Old Age, Allen Lane, 1979
Village Hours, Canterbury Press, 2012
Word from Wormingford: A Parish Year, Viking, 1997
A Writer's Day-Book, Trent Editions, 2007
A Year at Bottengoms Farm, Canterbury Press, 2006

All essays and articles are by Ronald Blythe unless otherwise stated.

The papers of John Nash, and letters and diaries of Christine Nash, are in the
  Tate Archives, London (TGA 8910).
Letters of Charles Causley, University of Exeter.
Letters of Patricia Highsmith, Swiss Literary Archives, Bern. © 2003 Diogenes
  Verlag AG Zürich.
Letters of Roy Tracey, Tracey Family Archive.
Letters of Joan Warburton, Tate Archives, London (TGA 968/1/1).
Papers of Benjamin Britten, Britten-Pears Archive, Aldeburgh.
Peter Hall's diaries, private collection.

Quotations from Andrew Wilson © Andrew Wilson, 2003, *Beautiful Shadow: A
  Life of Patricia Highsmith*, Bloomsbury Publishing Plc.

Prologue

1. *Out of the Valley*, p. 126.

Chapter 1: Suffolk Stock

1. *Under a Broad Sky*, p. 52.
2. *Stour Seasons*, p. 4.
3. *Under a Broad Sky*, p. 52.
4. *River Diary*, p. 124.
5. *Village Hours*, p. 81.
6. 'The Shepherd Observed', *Going to Meet George and Other Outings*, pp. 67–8.
7. *Outsiders*, p. 173.
8. *Akenfield*, p. 48.

Chapter 2: Pack Up Your Troubles

1. Valerie Herbert and Shirley Smith, *No Glorious Dead: The Impact of War on
   Sudbury* (Foreword by Ronald Blythe) (Sudbury Museum Trust, 2009).
2. *Akenfield*, p. 39.
3. Ibid.
4. Ibid., pp. 40–1.
5. Ibid., p. 33.
6. *Talking to the Neighbours*, pp. 63–4.
7. *Stour Seasons*, p. 141.

Chapter 3: Tilly Elkin

1. *Report of the Medical Officer of Health for The Strand District, London*, 1895,
   Wellcome Library, London.
2. Notebook to *Maps Descriptive of London Poverty 1898–1899*, Charles Booth
   Archive, LSE Library.
3. J. L. Carr, *A Month in the Country* (Cornucopia Press, 1990), pp. 8–9.

Chapter 4: The Murder House

1. 'At Swan Gates', *Immediate Possession and Other Stories*, p. 179.
2. Patrick Barkham, *Badgerlands: The Twilight World of Britain's Most Enigmatic Animal* (Granta, 2014), p. 302.
3. *From the Headlands*, p. 13.
4. *River Diary*, p. 68.
5. 'Ronald Blythe in Conversation with Mark Cocker', *Twenty Minutes*, BBC Radio 3, 4 December 2012.
6. *Word from Wormingford*, p. 36.
7. *Borderland*, p. 115.
8. *Stour Seasons*, p. 81.
9. *Borderland*, p. 344.
10. *In the Artist's Garden*, p. 10.
11. *Outsiders*, p. 58.
12. *Borderland*, p. 51.

Chapter 5: The Satan Tree

1. 'The Shepherd Observed', *Going to Meet George and Other Outings*, p. 68.
2. 'Memories of Trees Past', *PULP!* (Common Ground, 1989).
3. *Word from Wormingford*, p. 96.
4. 'Particles from a Suffolk Parish', *The Countryman*, Spring 1987, p. 80.
5. Introduction to *My Favourite Village Stories*, ed. Ronald Blythe (Lutterworth Press, 1979), p. 14.
6. *Stour Seasons*, p. 123.
7. 'The Windfall', *Immediate Possession and Other Stories*, p. 121.

Chapter 6: The Coming Down Time

1. *A Writer's Day-Book*, p. 127.
2. Hugh Barrett, *Early to Rise: A Suffolk Morning* (Faber, 1967), pp. 93–4.
3. Ibid., pp. 97–8.
4. *Outsiders*, p. 48.
5. Ibid., p. 115.
6. *Borderland*, pp. 210–11.
7. *Out of the Valley*, p. 218.
8. *In the Artist's Garden*, pp. 112–13.
9. *Out of the Valley*, p. 10.

Chapter 7: Child of Nature

1. *Word from Wormingford*, p. 48.
2. *Outsiders*, p. 2.
3. Ibid., pp. 75–6.
4. *A Writer's Day-Book*, pp. 144–5.
5. *From the Headlands*, p. 8.
6. *Stour Seasons*, pp. 85–6.

7. 'Memories of Trees Past'.
8. *Out of the Valley*, p. 115.
9. *Ronald Blythe: Working at Home*, BBC 2, 24 July 1983.
10. *A Writer's Day-Book*, p. 3.
11. Roger Deakin, *Wildwood: A Journey through Trees* (Hamish Hamilton, 2007), p. 44.
12. *In the Artist's Garden*, p. 33.
13. *Stour Seasons*, pp. 105–6.
14. *Borderland*, p. 86.

Chapter 8: Creative Dreams

1. *Village Hours*, p. 81.
2. Jon Wyand, *Introduction to Village Schools: A Future for the Past?* (Foreword by Ronald Blythe) (Evans Brothers, 1980), p. 7.
3. Ibid., p. 6.
4. *Word from Wormingford*, p. 130.
5. Philip Thicknesse, *A Sketch of the Life and Paintings of Thomas Gainsborough Esq* (1788).
6. *Going to Meet George and Other Outings*, p. 36.

Chapter 9: Watchful Vigilance

1. Craig Taylor, *Return to Akenfield* (Granta, 2006), p. 4.
2. *Divine Landscapes*, p. 36.
3. *Borderland*, p. 346.
4. *Stour Seasons*, p. 3.
5. Letter to Patricia Highsmith, 24 October 1973.
6. 'Memories of Trees Past'.
7. *Borderland*, p. 206.
8. *A Writer's Day-Book*, p. 78.
9. 'The Packhorse Path', *Immediate Possession and Other Stories*, p. 108.
10. *In the Artist's Garden*, p. 62.

Chapter 10: A Pauper Palace

1. *Private Passions*, BBC Radio 3, 19 August 2000.
2. *Ronald Blythe: Working at Home.*
3. *Out of the Valley*, pp. 79–80.
4. *Borderland*, pp. 250–1.
5. Talk at Sudbury Quaker Meeting House, 14 March 2014.
6. *Village Hours*, p. 30.
7. *Stour Seasons*, p. 2.
8. Ibid., p. 116.
9. *Out of the Valley*, p. 33.
10. *The Circling Year*, pp. 199–200.
11. *The Bookman's Tale*, p. 111.
12. *Out of the Valley*, p. 154.

13. *The Countryman*, April 2001, p. 13.
14. *The Bookman's Tale*, p. 14.

Chapter 11: Writerly Company

1. Paul Bolton, 'Education: Historical Statistics', House of Commons Library, 28 November 2012, SN/SG/4252.
2. 'Bride Michael', *The Stories of Ronald Blythe*, pp. 14–15.
3. Interview with Harry Mount, *The Oldie*, April 2019.
4. *A Year at Bottengoms Farm*, p. 101.
5. *A Writer's Day-Book*, p. 105.
6. *Stour Seasons*, p. 117.
7. *A Writer's Day-Book*, p. 104.

Chapter 12: Great Explorations

1. Extract from 'The Parish Church', *Ronald Blythe: Working at Home*.
2. *A Writer's Day-Book*, p. 4.
3. 'Memories of Trees Past'.
4. *Out of the Valley*, p. 196.
5. *Stour Seasons*, p. 13.
6. *Village Hours*, p. 151.
7. *The Bookman's Tale*, p. 17.
8. *Borderland*, p. 171.
9. *Word from Wormingford*, p. 172.
10. Julian Tennyson, *Suffolk Scene: A Book of Description and Adventure* (Blackie & Son, 1939), pp. 129–30.
11. *Out of the Valley*, p. 254.

Chapter 13: Gunner Blythe

1. *Church Times*, 3 October 2014.
2. *In the Artist's Garden*, p. 79.
3. Letter to Christine Nash, 9 October 1955.
4. Sidney Keyes, *Poems*, selected and introduced by Ronald Blythe (Greville Press, 2011).
5. *Private Words*, p. 288.
6. Ibid., p. 219.
7. Ronald Searle obituary, *Independent*, 7 January 2012.

Chapter 14: To the Headland

1. *The Countryman*, Summer 1970, p. 221.
2. Ibid., p. 222.
3. *Borderland*, p. 181.
4. *The Countryman*, Summer 1970, pp. 221–3.
5. *Stour Seasons*, p. 142.

Chapter 15: War and Peace

1. *Borderland*, pp. 94–5.
2. Ibid., p. 95.

Chapter 16: Bloody Books

1. *Village Hours*, p. 38.
2. *In the Artist's Garden*, p. 116.
3. Ibid.
4. Ibid., p. 117.
5. *Borderland*, p. 218.
6. *Suffolk and Essex Free Press*, June 1946.
7. Alan Cudmore, *Glimpses of Ronnie: A Memoir of Ronald Blythe* (privately circulated, 2021).

Chapter 17: Sloth Incarnate

1. Richard Chopping obituary, *The Times*, 26 April 2008.
2. *Under a Broad Sky*, p. 31.

Chapter 18: The Pied Piper

1. James Turner, *Seven Gardens for Catherine: An Autobiography* (Cassell, 1968), p. 192.
2. James Turner, *Sometimes into England: A Second Volume of Autobiography* (Cassell, 1970), pp. 108–9.
3. Ibid., pp. 13–14.
4. Ibid., pp. 14, 15.
5. *Ronald Blythe: Working at Home*.

Chapter 19: Cedric and Lett

1. Turner, *Sometimes into England*, p. 18.
2. *Outsiders*, p. 166.
3. Ibid., p. 165.
4. Ibid., p. 156.
5. *Village Hours*, p. 152.
6. *Outsiders*, p. 157.
7. Letter to Joan Warburton, 5 April 1988.
8. *The Time by the Sea*, p. 208.
9. *Outsiders*, pp. 157–8.

Chapter 20: After the Whirlwind

1. Turner, *Sometimes into England*, pp. 27–8.
2. *The Time by the Sea*, p. 181.

3. Ibid., p. 182.
4. *In the Artist's Garden*, p. 54.
5. *Outsiders*, p. 95; Colette, *My Mother's House and Sido* (Secker & Warburg, 1955), p. 162.

Chapter 21: Personal Gods

1. *From the Headlands*, p. 70.
2. Ibid., p. 72.
3. Ibid., pp. 72–3.
4. Letter to Roy Tracey, 26 August 1954.
5. *A Year at Bottengoms Farm*, p. 21.
6. *Under a Broad Sky*, p. 78.
7. *Word from Wormingford*, pp. 105–7.
8. Turner, *Sometimes into England*, p. 35.

Chapter 22: Christine and John

1. *The Time by the Sea*, pp. 52–3.
2. Ibid., p. 54.
3. *Hortus 5*, Spring 1988.
4. *At the Yeoman's House*, p. 81.
5. *Outsiders*, pp. 168–9.
6. Ibid., p. 169.
7. Note from Christine Nash, n.d.
8. Note from John Nash, n.d.
9. *At the Yeoman's House*, pp. 82–3.

Chapter 23: Storm Tides

1. Christine Nash, diary, 13 February 1953.
2. Richard Huggett, *Binkie Beaumont: Eminence Grise of the West End Theatre, 1933–1973* (Hodder & Stoughton, 1989), p. 249.
3. Peter Parker (ed.), *Some Men in London: Queer Life, 1945–1959* (Penguin Classics, 2024), p. 169.
4. Ian Harvey, *To Fall Like Lucifer* (Sidgwick & Jackson, 1971), prologue.

Chapter 24: Times by the Sea

1. Letter to Christine Nash, July 1954.
2. Letter to Roy Tracey, 26 August 1954.
3. *Borderland*, p. 348.
4. *Ronald Blythe: Working at Home*.
5. Ibid.
6. *The Time by the Sea*, p. 4.
7. Evidence to the public inquiry into the Sizewell B nuclear power station, 1983.

8. *The Author*, Summer 1985.
9. Letter to Christine Nash, January 1955.
10. *The Time by the Sea*, p. 3.
11. Ibid.
12. *A Writer's Day-Book*, p. 50.
13. *The Time by the Sea*, p. 9.

Chapter 25: It Has Begun

1. Letter from E. M. Forster, January 1955.
2. *The Time by the Sea*, p. 20.
3. Ibid., pp. 21, 20–1, 118.
4. *Ronald Blythe: Working at Home*.
5. *The Time by the Sea*, pp. 13–14.
6. Letter to Christine Nash, n.d. (late 1955 or early 1956).
7. Ibid., 25 March 1955.

Chapter 26: Ben and Peter

1. *The Time by the Sea*, p. 79.
2. Letter to Christine Nash, n.d. (May 1955).
3. *The Time by the Sea*, pp. 80–1.
4. Ibid., pp. 81, 83.
5. 'Side by Side with Imogen Holst', *Guardian*, 30 May 1988.
6. Letter to Christine Nash, 31 August 1955.
7. Ibid., 12 September 1955.
8. Neil Powell, *Benjamin Britten: A Life for Music* (Henry Holt, 2013), p. 214.
9. Letter to Christine Nash, n.d. (summer 1955).
10. *The Time by the Sea*, p. 22.

Chapter 27: Along Crag Path

1. *Ronald Blythe: Working at Home*.
2. *The Time by the Sea*, p. 156.
3. David Sieveking, *Airborne: Scenes from the Life of Lance Sieveking, Pilot, Writer & Broadcasting Pioneer* (Strange Attractor Press, 2013), p. 46.
4. *Borderland*, p. 209.
5. Letter to Christine Nash, November 1956.
6. *Borderland*, p. 209.
7. Letter to Christine Nash, n.d. (late 1955 or early 1956).
8. Ibid., n.d. (late 1955 or early 1956).
9. 'Ronald Blythe in Conversation with Mark Cocker', *Twenty Minutes*.
10. 'Imogen Holst: Perfectionist', *The Lady*, 20 June 1957.
11. 'Side by Side with Imogen Holst', *Guardian*, 30 May 1988.
12. Jenni Wake-Walker, *Time and Concord: Aldeburgh Festival Recollections* (Autograph Books, 1997), pp. 45–6.
13. *The Time by the Sea*, pp. 109–14.
14. Letter to Christine Nash, 31 August 1955.

Chapter 28: Dappled Hemlock

1. *In the Artist's Garden*, p. 42.
2. *The Time by the Sea*, p. 120.
3. Letter to Christine Nash, 28 July 1955.
4. Ibid., 13 August 1955.
5. Ibid., 9 September 1956.
6. Ibid., 13 August 1955.
7. Ibid., 13 September 1956.
8. Ibid., November 1956.
9. Ibid., 17 February 1956.
10. Letter from Eugene Walter, n.d.

Chapter 29: A Country Estate

1. Letter to Christine Nash, 24 April 1956.
2. Ibid., 1 April 1956.
3. Ibid., n.d.
4. *The Time by the Sea*, pp. 151–2.
5. Letter to Christine Nash, n.d. (September 1956).
6. Ibid., 1 December 1956.
7. Christine Nash, diary, 20 February–1 August 1957.
8. Christine Nash, diary, 30 June 1959.
9. *Borderland*, p. 108.
10. *The Time by the Sea*, pp. 165–6.

Chapter 30: Family Matters

1. Gerald Blythe, diary, February 1952.
2. Letter to Christine Nash, 7 September 1957.
3. David Burnett, *Sudbury, Suffolk: The Unlisted Heritage* (Sudbury Society, 2002).
4. Letter from Christine Nash, 15 November 1957.
5. Letter to Christine Nash, 26 December 1957.

Chapter 31: Ronnie's Folly

1. Letter to Christine Nash, 9 October 1955.
2. Extract from 'The Prison Visitor', a chapter for *The Time by the Sea* dropped from the final book.
3. Letter from Christine Nash, 28 January 1959.
4. Letter to Christine Nash, 18 March 1959.
5. *The Author*, Summer 1985.
6. *Ronald Blythe: Working at Home*.

Chapter 32: Cornish Romance

1. Letter from James and Cathy Turner, 5 May 1959.
2. Ibid., 3 July 1959.
3. Ibid., 19 December 1959.
4. Ibid., 23 February 1964.
5. Letter to Christine Nash, 28 December 1959.
6. Ibid., 24 April 1956.
7. Turner, *Sometimes into England*, p. 123.
8. Ibid., p. 124.
9. 'Ronald Blythe in Conversation with Mark Cocker', *Twenty Minutes*.

Chapter 33: Little Bird

1. Turner, *Sometimes into England*, pp. 117–18.
2. Maggi Hambling, *The Spectator*, 15 June 2013.
3. Interview with Maggi Hambling, 5 August 2022.
4. *Outsiders*, p. 166.
5. *The Time by the Sea*, p. 203.
6. *Outsiders*, p. 155.
7. Ibid., p. 165.
8. Ibid., pp. 160, 154–5.
9. 'Ronald Blythe in Conversation with Mark Cocker', *Twenty Minutes*.

Chapter 34: Break in the Elms

1. *From the Headlands*, p. 164.
2. *Ronald Blythe: Working at Home.*
3. *Word from Wormingford*, p. 161.
4. *Ronald Blythe: Working at Home.*
5. *Out of the Valley*, p. 200.
6. *Desert Island Discs*, BBC Radio 4, 20 April 2001.
7. *Borderland*, p. 267.
8. *Word from Wormingford*, p. 127.
9. Letter to Christine Nash, 31 July 1962.
10. *Outsiders*, p. 100.
11. *Under a Broad Sky*, p. 82.
12. *Out of the Valley*, p. 37.
13. The author in conversation with Tim Miller, 14 December 2023.
14. *Outsiders*, p. 136.
15. *Borderland*, p. 186.

Chapter 35: Intensities of Love

1. 'Introduction' to *William Hazlitt: Selected Writings* (Penguin English Library, 1970), p. 10.
2. Richard Mabey, 'Introduction' to *Aftermath*, p. 11.
3. *Under a Broad Sky*, p. 72.

4. Letter from James Turner, 29 September 1966.
5. Ibid., 11 January 1968.
6. *Under a Broad Sky*, pp. 177–8.
7. *The Bookman's Tale*, p. 62.
8. Ibid., p. 61.

Chapter 36: First Friends

1. The author in conversation with Christopher Woodward, 29 August 2023.
2. *Matrix*, 21 April 1992.
3. Andy Friend, *John Nash: The Landscape of Love and Solace* (Thames & Hudson, 2020), pp. 93–4.
4. Christine Nash to John Nash, November 1916.
5. *First Friends*, p. 37.
6. Ibid., p. 112.
7. Christine Nash, diary, 19 November 1955.
8. Ibid., 31 December 1955.
9. The author in conversation with James Hamilton-Paterson, 14 July 2023.
10. Barbara Fell to John and Christine Nash, 21 November 1962.
11. Letter to Christine Nash, 5 December 1962.
12. Barbara Fell to John and Christine Nash, 21 November 1962.

Chapter 37: Ron and Pat

1. Letter to Christine Nash, 4 November 1958.
2. Letter from Patricia Highsmith, 30 January 1963.
3. Ibid., 26 November 1966.
4. Andrew Wilson, *Beautiful Shadow: A Life of Patricia Highsmith* (Bloomsbury, 2003), p. 251.
5. Quoted in the film *Loving Highsmith*, dir. Eva Vitija, 2022.
6. Wilson, *Beautiful Shadow*, pp. 254–5.
7. Ibid., p. 255.
8. Letter from Patricia Highsmith, 26 November 1966.
9. Quoted in the film *Loving Highsmith*, dir. Eva Vitija, 2022.
10. Wilson, *Beautiful Shadow*, p. 261.
11. Letter to Patricia Highsmith, 24 April 1970.
12. Letters from Patricia Highsmith, 25 August 1973, 20 November 1989, 5 June 1991.
13. Letter to Patricia Highsmith, 28 December 1967; letter from Patricia Highsmith, 22 May 1969.
14. Letter from Patricia Highsmith, 17 December 1968; letter to Patricia Highsmith, 7 August 1970; letter to Patricia Highsmith, 27 January 1973.
15. Letter from Joan Schenkar, 11 October 2004.

Chapter 38: Village Voices

1. Interview in the *Observer*, 30 November 1969.
2. Letter from James Turner, 23 February 1967.

3. *Akenfield*, p. 243.
4. Ariane Bankes and Jonathan Reekie (eds), *The New Aldeburgh Anthology* (Aldeburgh Music/Boydell Press, 2009), p 271.
5. *Listener*, 24 July 1969.
6. *Akenfield*, p. 69.
7. Ibid., p. 21.
8. *At Helpston*, p. 89.
9. The author in conversation with Andrew Phillips, 25 January 2023.
10. *Outsiders*, p. 98.
11. *Ronald Blythe: Working at Home*.
12. *Desert Island Discs*.
13. 'Ronald Blythe in Conversation with Mark Cocker', *Twenty Minutes*.
14. The author in email conversation with Jeremy Greenwood, 17 April 2023.
15. *Ronald Blythe: Working at Home*.
16. *The Studs Terkel Program*, 98.7 WFMT Chicago, 19 September 1968.
17. Letter to Patricia Highsmith, 19 January 1970.
18. Benjamin Britten to Julia Watson at Penguin Press, 25 March 1969.
19. Geoffrey Moorhouse, *Guardian*, 8 May 1969; Edward Candy, *The Times*, 10 May 1969.
20. Letter from Lord Stradbroke, 29 March 1973.
21. Adrian Bell, *Eastern Daily Press*, 8 May 1969.
22. Letter from Patricia Highsmith, 5 July 1969.
23. Letter from Charles Causley, 7 October 1969.
24. James Morris, *New York Times*, 21 September 1969.
25. Letter to Patricia Highsmith, 18 October 1969.
26. John Gale, *Observer*, 30 November 1969.
27. Angus Wilson, *Observer*, 11 May 1969.
28. *The Other Half: 4: Angus and Tony*, BBC 1, 29 February 1984.
29. Letter from Sylvia Townsend Warner, 18 October 1969.
30. Letters to Patricia Highsmith, 19 January and 23 July 1970.
31. Interview with Christian House, *Independent on Sunday*, 11 November 2012.

Chapter 39: Home Movie

1. *Evening Standard*, 17 October 1969.
2. *Observer Magazine*, 26 January 1975, p. 24.
3. Peter Hall, *Making an Exhibition of Myself: The Autobiography of Peter Hall* (Sinclair-Stevenson, 1993), p. 25.
4. The author in conversation with Jenny Hall, 8 July 2023.
5. Akenfield synopsis, 1970, Ronald Blythe archive.
6. Peter Hall, 'Footing It Back Home: An Akenfield Diary', October 1974, p. 5.
7. *The Time by the Sea*, pp. 93–4.
8. Letter to Patricia Highsmith, 10 October 1972.
9. Peter Hall, diary, 26 August 1972.
10. Interview with Paul Barnes, *Suffolk Magazine*, November 2014.
11. *Guardian*, 20 November 2004.
12. Hall, 'Footing It Back Home', 3 March 1973, p. 11.
13. Letter from Rex Pyke, 27 June 1973.
14. *28th Aldeburgh Festival of Music and the Arts: 6–23 June 1975*, p. 6.

15. Interview with Paul Barnes, *Suffolk Magazine*, November 2014.
16. Quoted on *Akenfield Now*, BBC Radio 4, 19 October 2019.
17. Letter to Patricia Highsmith, 24 October 1973.

Chapter 40: After *Akenfield*

1. Peter Hall, diary, 6 October 1974.
2. John Lahr (ed.), *The Diaries of Kenneth Tynan* (Bloomsbury, 2002), pp. 222–3.
3. *Peter Hall's Diaries: The Story of a Dramatic Battle*, ed. John Goodwin (Hamish Hamilton, 1983), p. 144.
4. Nancy Banks-Smith, *Guardian*, 27 January 1975; *Private Eye*, February 1975; George Ewart Evans, *Listener*, 13 February 1975; *Listener*, 20 February 1975.
5. Rex Pyke, 'About Akenfield the Film', n.p., 2012.
6. Letter to Patricia Highsmith, 24 October 1973.
7. Paul Barnes, *The Oldie*, August 2009.
8. Stephen Fay, *Power Play: The Life and Times of Peter Hall* (Coronet, 1996), pp. 291–2.
9. Peter Hall obituary, *The Times*, 13 September 2017; Peter Hall interview, National Film Theatre 2004; Oliver Soden, *Michael Tippett: The Biography* (Weidenfeld & Nicolson, 2019), p. 402.
10. The author in email conversation with Andrew Dawson, 23 June 2023.
11. Interview with Paul Barnes, *Suffolk Magazine*, November 2014.
12. Letter from Christine Nash, 17 July 1970.
13. Letter to Patricia Highsmith, 4 January 1971.

Chapter 41: Disciple to Mentor

1. *The Time by the Sea*, p. 228.
2. The author in conversation with James Hamilton-Paterson, 14 July 2023.
3. Letter to Patricia Highsmith, 28 December 1967.
4. James Hamilton-Paterson, *Seven-Tenths: The Sea and Its Thresholds* (Hutchinson, 1992), pp. 137–8.
5. The author in conversation with James Hamilton-Paterson, 14 July 2023.
6. Letter to Patricia Highsmith, 17 May 1969.
7. Ibid., 10 October 1972.
8. The author in conversation with Richard Mabey, 10 May 2023.
9. Richard Mabey, *Gilbert White: A Biography of the Author of 'The Natural History of Selborne'* (Century Hutchinson, 1986).
10. Turner, *Sometimes into England*, p. 117.
11. *Stour Seasons*, p. 40.

Chapter 42: View on Winter

1. Letter to Patricia Highsmith, 27 January 1973.
2. Carmen Callil obituary, *Guardian*, 18 October 2022.
3. Letter to Patricia Highsmith, 27 January 1973.
4. *Desert Island Discs*.
5. 'Ronald Blythe in Conversation with Mark Cocker', *Twenty Minutes*.

6. *The View in Winter*, pp. 202, 198, 190–1.
7. Ibid., p. 235.
8. Letter to Christine Nash, 2 January 1971.
9. Letter to Patricia Highsmith, 18 December 1973.
10. Letter to Christine Nash, 15 April 1974.
11. Ibid., 9 March 1974.
12. Ibid., 15 April 1974.
13. Christine Nash, diary, 20 August 1966.
14. Letter to Christine Nash, 12 July 1976.
15. Barbara Langston to John Nash, 16 November 1976.
16. John Lewis, *Such Things Happen: The Life of a Typographer* (Unicorn Press, 1994), p. 193.
17. Letter to Alan Cudmore, 18 November 1976.
18. Letter from Maurice Partridge, 24 September 1977.

Chapter 43: Postponed Possession

1. Letter from Barbara Langston, n.d.
2. Letter from Patricia Highsmith, 14 February 1978.
3. Letter from Fidelity Cranbrook, 18 January 1979.
4. *Places: An Anthology of Britain*, selected by Ronald Blythe (Oxford University Press, 1981), p. 38.
5. The author in email conversation with James Hamilton-Paterson, 15 August 2023.
6. The author in email conversation with James Hamilton-Paterson, 17 August 2023.
7. *Front Row*, BBC Radio 4, 21 November 2022.
8. *Next to Nature*, p. 309.
9. *Field Work*, p. 35.
10. Letter to Patricia Highsmith, 7 November 1988.
11. Christine Nash, diary, n.d. (1972).
12. *Next to Nature*, pp. 331–2.
13. *Hortus*, Summer 1989.
14. *Country Life*, 29 July 1989.

Chapter 44: Divine Landscape

1. *Out of the Valley*, p. 211.
2. The author in email conversation with Alan Cudmore, 20 August 2023.
3. *Stour Seasons*, p. 46.
4. *Talking to the Neighbours*, 'Preface', pp. ix–x.
5. Interview with Maureen Cleave, *Evening Standard*, 25 April 1997.
6. *Next to Nature*, p. 56.
7. *Word from Wormingford*, p. 54.
8. Ibid., p. 168.
9. *Talking to the Neighbours*, p. 189.
10. Ibid., p. 78.
11. *Word from Wormingford*, p. 74.

12. *Village Hours*, p. 139.
13. *Stour Seasons*, p. 99.
14. Ibid., p. 145.
15. *River Diary*, p. 28.
16. 'Introduction' to Leo Tolstoy, *The Death of Ivan Ilyich* (Bantam Classic, 1981), pp. 12–13.
17. *Word from Wormingford*, pp. 130, 46.
18. *A Year at Bottengoms Farm*, p. 73.
19. *A Writer's Day-Book*, p. 41.
20. *Under a Broad Sky*, p. 36.
21. *A Writer's Day-Book*, p. 43.
22. *Talking to the Neighbours*, p. 46.

Chapter 45: Vintage Journeys

1. 'An Inherited Perspective', *From the Headlands*, p. 8.
2. Letter to Patricia Highsmith, 7 November 1988.
3. Ibid., 28 November 1989.
4. *Going to Meet George and Other Outings*, pp. 82–3.
5. Ibid., p. 93.
6. Letter to Patricia Highsmith, 28 November 1989.
7. *New York Times*, 27 February 1984.
8. *A Writer's Day-Book*, p. 113.
9. *Going to Meet George and Other Outings,* p. 115.
10. *A Writer's Day-Book*, p. 113.
11. Ibid.
12. *Going to Meet George and Other Outings,* p. 119.
13. Ibid., p. 122.
14. Richard Mabey, *John Clare Society Journal*, July 2023.
15. Richard Mabey, *Flora Britannica* (Chatto & Windus, 1996), p. 10.
16. Patrick Barkham, *The Swimmer: The Wild Life of Roger Deakin* (Hamish Hamilton, 2023), p. 266.
17. The author in email conversation with Richard Mabey, 23 October 2023.
18. Ibid.

Chapter 46: John and George

1. Edward Storey, 'Foreword' to *At Helpston*, p. 12.
2. *At Helpston*, p. 115.
3. *Borderland*, p. 397.
4. *Out of the Valley*, p. 16.
5. 'Introduction' to John Clare, *The Morning Wind*, selected and illustrated by Nicholas Perry (Tern Press, 2006).
6. *Outsiders*, pp. 170–3.
7. *Talking about John Clare*, p. 49.
8. *River Diary*, p. 131.
9. *The Bookman's Tale*, p. 53.
10. *Next to Nature*, p. 264.

11. Malcolm Guite, *Church Times*, 27 January 2023.
12. *In the Artist's Garden*, p. 88.

Chapter 47: Wormingford Words

1. *A Year at Bottengoms Farm*, p. 64.
2. *Word from Wormingford*, p. 58.
3. *Stour Seasons*, p. 143.
4. *In the Artist's Garden*, p. 140.
5. *River Diary*, p. 45.
6. *Word from Wormingford*, p. 245.
7. *Borderland*, pp. 105–6.
8. Ibid., p. 136.
9. Ibid., p. 230.
10. *Forever Wormingford*, p. 11.
11. Letter to Richard Mabey, 29 April 2004.
12. The author in email conversation with Christine Smith, 29 August 2023.
13. Ibid.
14. *The Circling Year*, p. 92.
15. Interview with Peter Parker, *Daily Telegraph*, 6 July 2013.
16. The author in email conversation with Frances Ward, 15 December 2023.
17. James Hamilton-Paterson to Ann Wordsworth, 22 July 1997, New York Public Library.
18. Ibid.
19. James Hamilton-Paterson, 'Quiet Words', 2001.
20. The author in conversation with James Hamilton-Paterson, 14 July 2023.

Chapter 48: The Assassin

1. *The Assassin*, p. 80.
2. The author in email conversation with Peter Tolhurst, 25 October 2023.
3. Ibid., 5 November 2023.
4. Ibid., 25 October 2023.
5. The author in email conversation with Julia Blackburn, 16 October 2023.
6. Alan Taylor, 'The Vital Spark: Appointment in Arezzo', *Book of the Week*, BBC Radio 4, January 2018.
7. Graham Greene, *A Sort of Life* (Bodley Head, 1971), p. 185.
8. Julia Blackburn, St Edmundsbury Cathedral, 1 March 2023.
9. Angela Tilby, *Church Times*, 27 January 2023.
10. The author in email conversation with Richard Mabey, 17 October 2023.
11. *Word from Wormingford*, p. 149.
12. Letter from James Hamilton-Paterson, 24 March 2005.
13. Jane Gardam, *The Spectator*, 4 December 2004.
14. *Under a Broad Sky*, p. 144.
15. Letter from Jane Gardam, 28 August 2003.
16. Ibid., 18 February 2004.
17. Ibid., 2 July 2005.

Chapter 49: Great Age

1. Letter from Jane Gardam, 1 June 2004.
2. *Ipswich Mercury*, 29 June 2006.
3. *The Bookman's Tale*, p. 16.
4. *Desert Island Discs*.
5. *The Spectator*, 15 June 2013.
6. Toby Wiggins, *Church Times*, 9 June 2023.
7. Letter from Dan Llywelyn Hall, 20 May 2024.
8. Jill Dawson, *The Crime Writer* (Sceptre, 2016), pp. 50–1.
9. The author in email conversation with Robert Macfarlane, 10 December 2023.
10. *In the Artist's Garden*, p. 31.
11. Barkham, *The Swimmer*, p. 263.
12. *Word from Wormingford*, p. 239.
13. Letter to Richard Mabey, 1 August 2010.
14. *Desert Island Discs*.
15. Letter to Jules Pretty, 22 May 2006.
16. Letter to Richard Mabey, 2 July 2008.
17. *A Writer's Day-Book*, p. 144.
18. *Under a Broad Sky*, p. 120.
19. *At the Yeoman's House*, pp. 107–8.
20. *Church Times*, 5 November 2008.
21. *Out of the Valley*, p. 176.
22. *Under a Broad Sky*, pp. 187–8.
23. *Stour Seasons*, p. 152.

Chapter 50: Sea of Memory

1. Letter to Richard Mabey, 28 February 2012.
2. *The Time by the Sea*, p. 235.
3. Ibid., p. 240.
4. *Next to Nature*, p. 189.
5. Ibid., p. 207.
6. Ibid., pp. 207–8.
7. *Desert Island Discs*.
8. *Word from Wormingford*, p. 141.
9. *Under a Broad Sky*, p. 80.
10. *Next to Nature*, pp. 235–6.

Chapter 51: Faith in His Fellows

1. Mark Cocker, Facebook post, January 2023.
2. The author in email conversation with Kevin Crossley-Holland, 7 May 2024.
3. The author in email conversation with Vicky Minet, 3 December 2023.
4. The author in conversation with Terence Blacker, 30 August 2023.
5. *Desert Island Discs*.
6. *The View in Winter*, p. 235.

7. *River Diary*, p. 3.
8. *Word from Wormingford*, p. 198.
9. Zoé Brown, 'The Airing Cupboard', podcast, May 2023.
10. *Under a Broad Sky*, p. 150.

Chapter 52: Natural Causes

1. *Stour Seasons*, p. 7.
2. *River Diary*, p. 72.
3. *Under a Broad Sky*, p. 72.
4. The author in email conversation with Zoé Brown, 4 January 2023.
5. *Places: An Anthology of Britain*, p. 38.
6. The author in email conversation with Richard Mabey, 15 January 2023.
7. Brown, 'The Airing Cupboard', May 2023.
8. *Next to Nature*, pp. 122–3.

Epilogue

1. Darren Tansley, M. W. Bewick and Ella Johnston (eds), *Est: Collected Reports from East Anglia* (Dunlin Press, 2015).

Index

Page numbers in italic indicate illustrations.

St Ives, 98–9
St Juliot, 279
'Saint Nicolas' (cantata), 188
Saints, the (area of villages), 86–7
Salisbury, 318
Sandlings, the (coastal region), 162
Sargent, Malcolm, 186
Sassoon, Siegfried, 21–2, 245
Sauvan-Smith, Bob, 135–6
Sayers, Dorothy L., 138
Scarfe, Norman, 254
Scarlet Pimpernel, the, 77–8
Schenkar, Joan, 248–9
Scotland, 14, 94, 159–60, 163, 340
Scott, Paul, 191–2, 281
Searle, Ronald, 96
Second World War, 86, 89–92, 96, 100, 102–5
Seeley, Martin, 363
Seferis, George, 356–7
Seth, Vikram, 318–19, 360, 362
'Seven Sonnets for Michelangelo' (song cycle), 178
Seven-Tenths: The Sea and Its Thresholds (book), 275
Shand, Garrow, 262–3, 271
Sharp, Margery, 181
Shaw, George Bernard, 59, 115, 141, 281
Shaw, Harry, 60
Shaw, Martin, 133, 296
shepherds, 9–11
'Shepherd's Calendar, The' (poem), 317
short stories by Ronald Blythe, 150, 159, 164–5, 190, 192, 194, 196, 250, 331; 'Bride Michael', 78, 233; 'The Church Mouse', 232; 'The Common Soldiery', 193; 'Immediate Possession', 192; 'The Packhorse Path', 66–7; 'The Windfall', 39–40
Shute, Nevil, 201
Sickert, Walter, 144
Sieveking, Lance, 183
Sieveking, Maisie, 183, 209
Simon & Schuster, 256
Sitwell, Edith, 179, 189
Sitwell, Osbert, 138, 210

Sizewell, 221, 297
Sketches in the Life of John Clare by Himself (anthology), 139
Skye, 159–60
Smart, Elizabeth, 116
Smith, Christine, 325–6
Snape, 183, 275, 322
Snape Maltings, 171, 261–2
Society of Authors, 272, 305
Somerville, Peggy, 183–4
Songs of Praise (television programme), 65
Southwold, 2, 151, 162
Spark, Muriel, 332
Sparling, Rev., 132
Spender, Stephen, 311
Spring-Rice, Margery, 179
Sprott, W. J. H. (formerly 'Sebastian'), 168
Spurgeon, Mr (schoolmaster), 15
Spurling, Hilary, 192
Staverton Thicks, 152
Stevens, J. (choirmaster), 195
Stevenson, Robert Louis, 78
Stiff Pull, A (photograph), 14
'Still Falls the Rain' (Canticle III) (song), 179
Stockholm, 308
Stoke-by-Nayland, 51, 142
Stopes, Marie, 137–8
Storey, Edward, 340
Stour, River, 59, 72–3, 142, 144, 303, 314, 344, 366
Strachey, Lytton, 238, 296
Stradbroke, John Rous, 4th Earl of, 255
Strangers on a Train (film), 246
Strasburg, Ivan, 263, 269
Stromness, 310
Sudbury, 60, 71–5, 77, 79–80, 133, 339; cemetery, 47; churches, 38, 73–6, 79, 91, 117; Corn Exchange, 105; Cutmore's (bookshop), 79; flooding (1947), 116–17; Gainsborough's House, 366; general election (1945), 110; Jubilee Road, 68–70, 70, 77, 91, 103–4, 198, 202, 205; museum, 104–5; public houses, 66, 68, 89;